MARY DOUGLAS: AN INTELLECTUAL BIOGRAPHY

Mary Douglas's works span the second half of the twentieth century. A crucial figure within British social anthropology, her works have been widely read and her theories applied outside anthropology. In the first full-length appreciation of her life and ideas, Richard Fardon traces the influences of her family background, convent and Oxford education, and early researches in central Africa on her mature works of synthesis: the celebrated *Purity and Danger* (1966), and the controversial *Natural Symbols* (1970). The author then provides a detailed account of her forays into the fields of contemporary American and Old Testament religion, risk analysis and environmentalism, consumption and economics, which have excited debate across the humanities and social sciences.

In his assessment of Douglas's place in the history of British and European anthropology, and of her efforts to extend the discipline's methods to contemporary western societies, the author has provided an account that will be essential reading – not just for anthropologists – but within the many disciplines which Douglas's ideas have contested. As an aid to further research, the book provides both the first complete bibliography of Douglas's own writings, and a comprehensive listing of reviews of her books.

Richard Fardon is Professor of West African Anthropology at the School of Oriental and African Studies, University of London.

Mary Douglas 1976
Source: © Mayotte Magnus

MARY DOUGLAS: AN INTELLECTUAL BIOGRAPHY

Richard Fardon

London and New York

First published 1999
by Routledge
11 New Fetter Lane, London EC4P 4EE

Simultaneously published in the USA and Canada
by Routledge
29 West 35th Street, New York, NY 10001

Typeset in Baskerville by Routledge
Printed and bound in Great Britain by
Biddles Ltd, Guildford and King's Lynn

British Library Cataloguing in Publication Data
A catalogue record for this book is available from the British Library

Library of Congress Cataloging in Publication Data
Fardon, Richard.
Mary Douglas: an intellectual biography/Richard Fardon.
Includes bibliographical references and index
1. Douglas, Mary. 2. Ethnologists—Great Britain—Biography.
I. Title.
GN21.D68F37 1999
305.8′0092—dc21
[b]
98–25907
CIP

ISBN 0–415–04092–2 (hbk)
ISBN 0–415–04093–0 (pbk)

TO CATHERINE DAVIES

CONTENTS

ILLUSTRATIONS

ARTWORK

Cover illustration and chapter icons by Pat Novy

PHOTOGRAPHS

DIAGRAMS

PREFACE

Writing this book I have occasionally taken heart from comments Mary Douglas expressed when reviewing a biography of the anthropologist Margaret Mead, 'His book suffers the usual limitation of hagiography, strong in praise […] and weak in dealing with the enigmas and problems of a person living in a particular time and place' (1983h: 759). Noting that as a popularizer Mead failed to stick at problems or projects, adopting a 'hurry-hurry, single issue style of fieldwork', Mary wondered:

> How much did she choose to be an outsider, how much was the choice a response to the opportunity structure she found herself facing – it is impossible to say. Yet, a man who showed such an early brilliance would have been sought by major institutions which would have forced the conflict of ambition and independence to be played within supporting structures eminently able to bestow rewards on their favourites.
>
> (1983h: 759)

The phrase omitted in the first quotation is 'strong in praise [of the deceased]'; for that Mary Douglas assuredly is not; she has never been more productive. But in writing about a living author it has been comforting to return for a plot to her own expectations of a biographer.

Mary Douglas's five decades of writing as an anthropologist constitute one of the major bodies of work in twentieth-century British anthropology: an *oeuvre* in the full sense. It is also one of the best known to a non-anthropological readership, albeit in parts. Offering an account of the development of her work has posed a more formidable challenge than I imagined when Chris Rojek and Bryan Turner suggested the project at the end of the 1980s. My final title: *Mary Douglas: an Intellectual Biography* suggests the modest ambitions of this work.

This is not a biography of Mary Douglas as a private individual but a textually-based, developmental account of her writings. For the most part it is also descriptive – an explication rather than an evaluation. I have tried to show why she has written as she has, how her ideas have developed, and how she has attempted to surmount the problems her project has entailed. (I have not, by and large, tried to describe how others have taken up her ideas, although the interested reader would be able to trace their works from my bibliographies.) The development of Douglas's ideas over five decades is more important to this project than it would be to a synoptic evaluation of her project.

The book has a biographical plot in three parts. In Part I, I provide a slightly fanciful reconstruction of Mary Douglas's early life, which is followed by a chapter on her time in the brilliant environment of the Oxford Institute of Social Anthropology of the post-war years, and another on her ethnographic research and writing as an Africanist. These chapters roughly, and only roughly, correspond to decades of her life. Her training equipped Mary Douglas to remain a professional ethnographer and writer on Africa for the remainder of her career. Nothing in it determined the different course she took; but, given that course, it is apparent how much she draws upon this early formation. Over-broadly one might say that the contrast between her experiences in Africa and those of her convent education, understood with the means available from her Oxford anthropological training, are both the initial and enduring sources of much of her distinctive, cultural and sociological imagination.

Part II has a different character: consisting of close readings of *Purity and Danger*, unarguably Douglas's best known book, and its close successor *Natural Symbols*, arguably her most significant. In these two books, written in the 1960s, Douglas achieves a synthesis of ideas that will be both the basis for her subsequent excursions into disciplines neighbouring anthropology, and a recurrent point of return and fresh departure for her developing theoretical project.

Part III, *Excursions and adventures*, consists of four chapters which follow her forays into substantive fields – roughly, and with the proviso that Douglas does not withdraw readily from areas of other disciplines once colonized – in the order they engaged her intensive interest. Her concern with consumption theory and welfare economics was mediated by the investigation of food habits and thus ritual (Chapter 6). After economics came the most controversial of Douglas's collaborative ventures: an analysis of risk and ecological concerns in the contemporary USA (Chapter 7). Chapters 8 and 9 respectively examine Douglas's analyses of contemporary religion and, her latest project, a renewed and more intensive investigation of the Pentateuch.

Part III posed particular problems. As a social anthropologist and Africanist ethnographer with a first degree in economics (even if dated by a quarter century), I have been reasonably well equipped to follow Douglas's wide-ranging curiosities so far as Chapter 6. The discipline of risk analysis has relations to economics which have assisted my pursuit of her further footsteps. However, scholarly appreciation of the finer points of her revisionist account of the books of the Pentateuch lie well outside any pretence to competence on my part. Particularly in Part III, but in fact more generally, I have benefited from Chris Rojek's suggestion to trace the reviews of Douglas's work. Identifying and locating reviews in more than a hundred journals has been time-consuming but valuable: not just as a source of professional counsel but also as an indication of the reception of Douglas's work. The sheer numbers of reviews of Douglas's books in specialist, non-anthropological journals provide an indication of the attention her excursions have attracted.

The two concluding chapters of Part IV contextualize Douglas's work in relation to some aspects of philosophy, politics, religion and the development of anthropological theory. Chapter 10 is a detailed discussion of the ways Douglas has revised her own theoretical scheme in the course of applying it so widely. In Chapter 11, I suggest that this work represents a reconvergence of strands of French post-Reformation social thought that have been refracted and developed through both mid-twentieth-century British social anthropology (in its debt to Durkheim and his predecessors) and her Roman Catholic education and commitments. Her espousal of hierarchical organizations, her sociological conservatism, and her emphasis on the social foundations of collective thought can all be related to these sources.

Mary Douglas's writings have influenced many who cannot be considered ideological fellow-travellers. Leaving aside the certainty that some of her preferences went unrecognized by many of her readers, one needs to add that Douglas's sociological conservatism is allied to an extraordinarily liberal cultural imagination and expression. There is no finer exponent of the telling phrase or arresting sentence in British anthropology; no writer of the British modernist tradition before Douglas ranged so widely in her interests and sources. The sense of excitement and intellectual risk that she generates galvanizes others to share her interests and insights. Douglas is the undisputed master of the lateral connection, more often than not one between the seemingly exotic of ethnographic report, and the seemingly mundane of British middle-class existence: household dusting analogized to purification, shopping and dining as ritual events, a symbolic system distilled in a single, humble biscuit. As translator of custom she makes the homely bizarre and the bizarre homely. But these same talents can be frustrating for the devoted reader. The architecture of her extended arguments sometimes seems shifting and elusively analogical; the despair of professional philosophers. These are the conflicting strands assessed, as best I can, in the concluding chapters.

How to address the audience that Mary Douglas's writings command has been a constant concern. By extended quotation I have usually let her speak for herself. While I have primarily kept in mind a readership concerned with twentieth-century social anthropology, I have included more basic information on the discipline's history than that readership needs or wants. Non-anthropologists will find my translation of their specialist concerns to anthropologists naive. It has been a fine line to draw, but I hope that the biographical narrative thread has an interest of its own. Even this is not straightforward; Mary Douglas has been a consistent reinterpreter of her own earlier work, construing her project in a determinedly progressive fashion. Douglas on Douglas is always interesting but occasionally selective. While building on the 'loops' of Douglas's recollection, I have sometimes questioned the inevitability she attributes to her intellectual development.

It has been impossible to ignore Mary Douglas's sense of marginalization from the discipline that launched her career. This involves matters of personality as well as institutional context. In a broad sense, an English, middle-class, conventionally Roman Catholic woman of Mary Douglas's generation who harboured high ambitions was almost bound to feel some degree of marginalization from a discipline which – other than being definitionally middle-class – was none of these things. Her period 'in the ranks' at Oxford and during her first fifteen years at University College London were her best integrated, culminating in the publication of *Purity and Danger* (1966). *Natural Symbols* (1970), with its preliminary presentation of grid and group theory, and its thorough embeddedness in contemporary issues of student revolt and Roman Catholic reform, struck some commentators as severally scandalous. Whatever one thinks of her views, in retrospect the furore caused by her dragging social anthropology into engagement with contemporary issues seems ludicrous. Moreover, the estrangement continued on several fronts. To some commentators, Mary Douglas appeared to have abandoned what they considered to be anthropology in the interests of colonizing other fields of study on anthropological authority. The tide was swinging towards a deconstructive anthropology that may have been conducive to her liberal cultural imagination but was anathema to both Douglas's conservative sociological theorizing and her sense of commitment. Add to this a penchant for developing ideas oppositionally, an ambivalent mixture of self-confidence and insecurity that might culminate in anxious aggression, and a tendency for her closest supporters to adopt a somewhat sectarian outlook – with high entry costs and occasional expulsions – and you have some indication of the brew. *Risk and Culture* (1982), written outside a conventional institutional base in anthropology, created a greater rumpus than had *Natural Symbols*, and presumably introduced a reinforcing functional loop into the situation of the sort that Douglas has analysed so insightfully elsewhere. However, much less disciplinary ado has been made of intellectual differences, or capacities for awkwardness far exceeding Mary's own, on the part of her male contemporaries. Once the dust has settled, posterity will rightly acknowledge that Mary Douglas played a crucial role in normalizing the contemporary acceptance of the West as a legitimate field of anthropological investigation.

Finally, in introduction, where does the intellectual biographer come into the picture? From my Kentish Grammar School, I entered University College London in 1970 to read for a BSc in Economics and Social Anthropology. Having only the most general idea what anthropology was, I signed up for it in the hope of avoiding some of the narrowness, not to speak of the obligatory advanced mathematics, I thought an exclusive diet of economics might offer. During a fairly dutiful first two undergraduate years the subject failed to enthrall me. Then, in my final year in 1972–73, I sat agog through a year-long course when Mary Douglas lectured twice weekly on the subject of 'Religion, morals and symbolism'. Not all my contemporaries remember her as an inspiring lecturer; taste in instruction is idiosyncratic. Mary Douglas lectured with little recourse to notes but with a clear sense of where a lecture was supposed to go. She gave the impression of thinking on her feet, following a train of thought rather than guided by the need to present this or that from the past canon. If occasionally she lost the plot, this kept me on the edge of my seat wondering how she would pick up the thread that allowed her to culminate an initial problem posed by a final suggestion of its resolution. This, I realized, was how anthropologists think; the discipline could be about anything, what mattered was a way of addressing a subject. I returned in autumn 1973 to pick up an undeserved postgraduate award and resume a faltering postgraduate career under Mary Douglas's supervision. Projects, including an ethnography of oil rigs and a restudy of the Lele, foundered on practical difficulties and personal confusion; eventually I got back on track when I began fieldwork in Nigeria in mid-1976. I add this confessional note to record that despite Mary Douglas's alleged impatience with ineptness and incompetence, and my early postgraduate career was a triumph of both, she continued to take a supportive interest in my hopeless case. Although somewhat awed by her, I was disappointed to find she had left University College when I returned from fieldwork.

Between then and the proposal that I undertake this project a decade and a half later, I cannot recall us having any significant contact. Although I was not a member of her theoretical circle, Mary Douglas endorsed Routledge's suggestion that I undertake this account and has been unfailingly generous with her time and support: in the provision of published and unpublished texts and in discussion whenever I wished. Unless I sought her help, Mary left me to my own devices. The years of composition have required her patience. While Mary Douglas was relinquishing administrative and teaching concerns (the term 'retirement' would mislead), I assumed the burdens of mid-career within a university system subjected to unprecedented pressures and a dizzying decline in research environment and opportunities. During this time, Mary Douglas has produced more than a third of her extant published writings, leaving her pursuing scribe panting in her wake. A term of a sabbatical year has given me the chance to accelerate sufficiently at least to enter the trail of dust in that wake; however, as I write Mary Douglas has a further two books in press which this account does not cover. I have, then, certain advantages for this task: nationality and present class, personal acquaintance, co-residence on adjacent hills in North London, fellow experience of University College London, training in social anthropology, economics and African ethnography. And there are some differences: family origins, generation, gender, religious affiliation, and an ignorance of some of the fields of her endeavour there is not time to redress. But I hope that this account, and its bibliographic apparatus, will assist scholars with more specialist concerns, or anyone who may wish one day to write the biography this is not. Yet, having said that this is an intellectual biography rather than a biography, the long-seated hours spent on it have reminded me of Hans Keller's wise dictum, 'In this biography-obsessed age we like to think that the life explains the work, more often it's the work that explains the life.'

Without Mary Douglas's inspiration I would not have become an anthropologist; this book is an act of gratitude for a vocation I enjoy. I would know less about the life of a female professor, brought up in part by grandparents, with three children and a house in North London, if I did not share my life with Catherine Davies. Not just for these reasons, or because she has lived with it for so long, or even on account of her advice and support, this book is dedicated to her: while I have been writing it, the noun 'anorak' and adjective 'trainspotterish' have entered the English language to describe sadly obsessive individuals who spend their available time collecting arcane and fugitive details. See Appendices, enough said.

Richard Fardon
London
April 1998

ACKNOWLEDGEMENTS

With many extended interruptions, writing this book has occupied almost a decade. Frustrating at the time, finally my delay has been beneficial. Living with Mary Douglas's work so long has helped me to inhabit her concerns more thoroughly than would a rapidly despatched, summary volume. I have also benefited from a diffuse, but real, change in the atmosphere of social anthropology: specifically I think, and hope, renewed sympathy for sociologically based analyses following the normalization of some crucial insights from deconstructive, post-colonial and postmodern anthropologies. These have substantially affected the British anthropological tradition for the better, but not in my estimation provided grounds for the wholesale abandonment of what is distinctive about the long argument of that tradition. These are reasons to believe the end years of the 1990s to be a conducive moment to discuss that strand of British social anthropological modernism of which Douglas is the key late exponent.

I have also profited from my tardiness in more specific ways: Mary Douglas's return to studying the religion of the Old Testament has assisted my biographical plot by providing what she would recognize as a 'latch' rejoining and recasting her earliest interests. Crucial insights into Franz Steiner's importance to the post-war Institute of Social Anthropology at Oxford University followed from meeting Michael Mack and collaborating with Jeremy Adler (Professor of German at King's College London) on a contextualized re-edition of Steiner's anthropological papers. Over the years I have delivered chapters of this book to seminars at the LSE, University of St Andrews and University of Calgary and been generously advised.

My re-engagement with Mary Douglas's thought followed Jonathan Benthall's invitation to review *How Institutions Think* for *Anthropology Today* in 1987. Jonathan has been a bountiful source of references and ideas since then. Before he moved on to fresh challenges, Chris Rojek's counsel at Routledge was responsible for the transformation of the slim volume I had anticipated into this more exhaustively researched monograph. My close colleagues at SOAS, Lisa Croll, David Parkin and John Peel, have supported my work with judicious advice over a long period – uninterrupted in David's case since his assuming the Oxford chair.

Although I decided against wide-ranging interviews which would have changed the character of this work, I have spoken informally to a number of people who include: Paul Baxter, Basil Bernstein, Adrian Edwards, Adrian Hastings, Michael Herzfeld and Wendy James about various aspect of Mary Douglas's work. If Andrew Turton despaired of again seeing his annotated copy of the first edition of *Natural Symbols*, he was kind enough never to mention the fact to me; I am also grateful to Rijk van Dijk, Mark Hobart, Michael Twaddle and Simon Weightman for help with matters bibliographic. I am indebted for their advice to librarians at SOAS (especially San San May), St Andrews, Oxford and numerous specialist libraries of the University of London (particularly Heythrop College), as well as to Vivien Cook at OCLC Europe. The anonymous toilers of the on-line BIDS bibliographic service are one of the good things that happened to academics in the 1980s.

Aside from Mary herself, I have been assisted to locate and reproduce the photographs in this volume by Bernadette Porter (Principal of Digby Stuart College, Roehampton Institute), Sister Mary Coke (Provincial Archives, Society of the Sacred Heart, Roehampton), Garry Marvin (Roehampton Institute), Susanna van Langenberg (Syndication Manager, National Magazine Company), Chris Wright and Joanna Ostapkowicz (Photographic Archive, Royal Anthropological Institute), John Mack (Keeper of Ethnography of the British Museum) and Paul Fox (SOAS photographer). Mayotte Magnus gifted me not only fresh prints of her two portraits of Mary Douglas that appear here, but a complete set of her 1976 portraits of women anthropologists which are now in the Photographic Archive of the Royal Anthropological Institute. Mary Douglas allowed me access to the extant negatives and prints from her Lele fieldwork, which have now been donated to the Ethnography Department of the British Museum. Jane Whetnall (Queen Mary Westfield College) supplied inspiration for part of the artwork from her collection of illustrations of women readers and writers. A special word of thanks is reserved for Pat Novy for the chapter icons and cover artwork, which we enjoyed plotting as a visual counterpart to the text, and for the most recent photographic portrait of her sister, Mary Douglas.

The penultimate draft of the book was commented upon helpfully by Catherine Davies, Adam Kuper, David Parkin and an anonymous American reader. The first three made time to do so in busy lives, and I am sure that also goes for the fourth. Mari Shullaw at Routledge negotiated my authorial demands about the book with good humour and sense. Angie Doran and Mary Warren expended patient care on its production and editing. As acknowledged in the Preface, I owe a great debt to Mary Douglas and, I must add here, James Douglas too for their hospitality and many kindnesses in the face of my intrusions.

MARY DOUGLAS'S MONOGRAPHS AND COLLECTED ESSAYS

A note on referencing style

BOOKS

References are to the most recent British editions (in 1997) of Mary Douglas's monographs (full publication histories are to be found in the bibliography); reference is by acronym and page:

LK: 1963 *The Lele of Kasai*, London/Ibadan/Accra: Oxford University Press/International African Institute.

PD: 1966 *Purity and Danger. An Analysis of Concepts of Pollution and Taboo*, London: Routledge (1996).

NS1: 1970 *Natural Symbols. Explorations in Cosmology*, London: Barrie and Rockliff, Cresset Press.

NS2: 1973 *Natural Symbols. Explorations in Cosmology*, revised edition, London: Routledge (1996).

WG: 1978 (and Baron Isherwood) *The World of Goods. Towards an Anthropology of Consumption*, London: Routledge (1996).

EP: 1980 *Evans-Pritchard*, Glasgow: Fontana.

RC: 1982 (and Aaron Wildavsky) *Risk and Culture: an Essay on the Selection of Technological and Environmental Dangers*, Berkeley/Los Angeles/London: University of California Press (1983 paperback).

RA: 1986 *Risk Acceptability According to the Social Sciences*, London: Routledge and Kegan Paul.

HIT: 1987 *How Institutions Think*, London: Routledge and Kegan Paul.

IW: 1993 *In the Wilderness: the Doctrine of Defilement in the Book of Numbers*, Sheffield: *Journal for the Study of the Old Testament*, Supplement Series No. 158; Sheffield Academic Press.

ANTHOLOGIZED ARTICLES

First reference to an article subsequently anthologized in Mary Douglas's volumes of collected essays is by original date of publication and acronym of the essay volume; subsequent reference is by acronym and page:

IM: 1975 *Implicit Meanings. Essays in Anthropology*, London/Boston: Routledge and Kegan Paul.

ITAV: 1982 *In the Active Voice*, London/Boston: Routledge and Kegan Paul with Russell Sage Foundation.

RAB: 1992 *Risk and Blame: Essays in Cultural Theory*, London/New York: Routledge.

OAO: 1992 *Objects and Objections*, Monograph Series of Toronto Semiotic Circle No. 9, Toronto: Victoria College, University of Toronto.

TS: 1996 *Thought Styles, Critical Essays on Good Taste*, London/New York: Sage.

REVIEWS OF MARY DOUGLAS'S BOOKS

References to reviews of Mary Douglas's monographs are by acronym of the book title followed by acronym of the title of the journal in which the review appeared. Thus, (PD/AA) a review of *Purity and Danger* in *American Anthropologist*. A full listing of journal acronyms and reviews can be found in Appendix 2. Where relevant or necessary I have also cited authorship and page reference.

Part I

BEGINNINGS: 1920s–1950s

1 'MEMORIES OF A CATHOLIC GIRLHOOD': 1920s AND 1930s

It has been the most passionate affirmation of Mary Douglas's writings that the taken-for-granted beliefs, ideas and emotions of a period, place or person never be considered aside from the social circumstances which gave rise to them and then sustained them. This is not the weak notion that all ideas are born in social circumstances, but a stronger assertion that they continue to be part and parcel of the social world in which they are used. Beliefs are self-evident, or hotly contested, among people related to one another in specific ways. Among other people, differently related, the same ideas would need different interpretation. To break this rule of method at the outset would sever my account from the way its subject might want to see herself. Mary's social background is the context in which to locate the inception of many of her ideas; but an account of these ideas must also show how their significance to her changed with her circumstances.

FAMILY BACKGROUND

Margaret Mary Tew was born in San Remo on 25 March 1921, the first child of Phyllis Margaret Twomey (1900–33) and Gilbert Charles Tew (1884–1951). Her parents, who had married the previous year, were holidaying on the Italian Riviera *en route* for home leave from their colonial posting to Burma, where her father served in the Indian Civil Service as a District Commissioner for twenty-five years (1908–33). In one way or another both sides of the family were widely travelled; but in Mary's recollection the Twomey connection was the more romantic as well as the more formative.

The Twomeys were of Irish ancestry and, like so many nineteenth-century Irish familes, by the twentieth century were scattered over much of the English-speaking world. Reference books record O'Twomey to be a well-known west

Munster name predominantly associated with County Cork. In the mid-seventeenth century, O'Twomey was the most common name in the county after Murphy – one Sean O Tuama (1706–75), a publican of Croom, is said by MacLysarght (1972) to have been the most distinguished later bearer of the name. 'Great grandfather Twomey', Daniel Twomey (1830–1900), Mary's mother's grandfather and a picaresque character in family memory, raised seven children, most of whom went into the professions, and many of whom travelled and died abroad. They included a journalist who died in his twenties in Australia, and a doctor who died in his fifties in Nigeria, as well as emigrants to Canada and to the USA with land grant tickets. Great grandfather Twomey was able to educate his offspring from the proceeds of a chandlery called Bleak House, at Carrigh Touhil in Cork. On a small piece of land there, he kept animals awaiting slaughter to provision the ships that sailed to America. Until disabused of the idea by her American relatives, Mary long believed, on account of this land, that her great-grandfather had been a farmer. He married above himself and, on the collapse of his fortunes, his wife, a Ryan twelve years his junior, left him to take up residence on the Isle of Wight, at which he took to drink. Nonetheless, his efforts had seen his children into the professions and largely out of Ireland as middle-class emigrants.

Daniel Twomey's son – another Daniel Twomey and Mary's maternal grandfather (Sir Daniel Harold Ryan Twomey 1864–1935) – served in the Indian Civil Service (1882–1920), becoming Chief Judge in Rangoon for three years before his retirement in the year Mary's parents married. Roman Catholic by birth, Mary's grandfather had married May Ponsford, the daughter of a Protestant navy chaplain, who ran away from home to become a nurse at Guy's Hospital. This, apparently formidable, lady fulfilled her promise to bring up Phyllis Twomey, Mary's mother, as a Roman Catholic.

Tew, Mary's maiden name, is an old Celtic name.[1] Her father (Gilbert Charles Tew 1884–1951, Photograph 1), from Warwick, was of less remarkable antecedents than her mother, but clever. The working-class, grammar-school-educated, son of a gas works' manager, he won a scholarship to read classics at Emmanuel College, Cambridge and entered the colonial service, as a result of which her parents met. A passionate angler, he wrote numerous articles published both in Rangoon and Britain.[2] Mary attributes her own concern with literary style to her father's sensitivity as an Edwardian essayist. A decade and a half older than his wife, whom he outlived by almost two decades, long years of quinine use – and frequent bouts of malaria – took a toll on his health in later life. Portraits suggest a lean and dapper man; his younger wife, buxom and pretty. Family shots from Burma show the couple dressed up for charades or playing with their children on a typically colonial veranda. To Gilbert Tew's sufferings was added osteoporosis, which confined him to a wheelchair for the last four years of his life, when he was nursed by his younger daughter. He died, before seeing any of his grandchildren, in 1951: the year he attended the Douglases' marriage.

4

Photograph 1 Gilbert Tew, Mary Douglas's father, a passionate angler

Source: © Mary Douglas

Vignettes of early family life in Mary's later writings are of the women on her mother's side; her father's parents died before she knew them. There was an eccentric Great Aunt Ethel, her maternal grandmother's sister, 'a caravan-dweller, a painter, the bohemian artist in the family [who] raised angora rabbits and ran a troop of Wolf Cubs. She ate nuts and fruit, and wore bright hand-woven garments, wooden beads, brilliant embroidered waistcoats which set off her white hair' (1992hOAO: 49–50). Mary's sister Pat Novy, whose illustrations adorn many of Mary's books (and this one), seems to have inherited her artistic gifts. Then there is May Ponsford, Mary's doughty maternal grandmother, chided by her son-in-law for wishing to learn Spanish in her old age in order to read *Don Quixote* in the original (in press, 'Why I have to learn Hebrew'); and her mother's friend, daughter of another colonial servant, her godmother and 'London aunt', who did not mean offence but embarrassed her student nephews and nieces by enquiring after visitors' taste in tea with the politically incorrect, 'Chink or Ink?' (Douglas 1996h: 117). Strong and capable women, then, but women who belonged in a world now vanished.

From the age of five (in 1926) when she began school, Mary was left with her mother's retired parents in Totnes, Devon, while her mother and father were in Burma. She later saw this as a difficult circumstance – common to the families of the Indian Civil Service – in which everyone was doing their best, but at the time she felt abandoned. In 1933, the year her mother died in London after a struggle with cancer, her father retired in poor health, and Mary and Pat were taken back into his care. Mary was transferred from a local school to continue secondary education as a boarder at the Sacred Heart Convent in Roehampton. As a result of family ties to the school, which her mother had attended (Photograph 2), and the bereavement, Mary and her sister received bursaries; otherwise the school would have been beyond their family means. Mary's grandfather, with whom she and Pat had been living, died two years after his daughter. The years that Mary Tew spent at the Sacred Heart Convent were to be formative – even more than the years between twelve and seventeen are for most people – and are mentioned in every autobiographical summary of her life. Following separation from her parents, and the deaths of her mother and maternal grandfather, the young Mary seems to have found stability, and a sense of belonging, in this secure and secluded women's world. The idealized organization of the convent school, where she was an outstanding pupil, serves in her later work as an implicit exem-plar of her description of differentiated, hierarchical organizations as a focus of loyalty, commitment and order. Her education, and perhaps the relative absence of an adjacent generation in her upbringing, imparted a self-confidence little tested by conflict. But we must move cautiously in establishing the connections and backtrack a little.

Photograph 2 The Junior School (under ten years old) of the Sacred Heart Convent by the lake about 1906. Phyllis Twomey – Mary Douglas's mother – seated second from the left

THE SACRED HEART

The society of the Dames du Sacré Coeur was founded in Paris in 1800 by Saint Madeleine-Sophie Barat; she was canonized in 1925 (O'Leary 1992: 85). The statutes of the order, modelled on those of the Jesuits, had been drawn up by the Jesuit Père Varin. The order was to serve the double purpose of venerating the Sacred Heart and providing for girls' education. To find the immediate origins of devotion to the Sacred Heart of Jesus we must go back a further century and a quarter.

> Under the influence of her director, the Jesuit La Colombière, Marguerite Marie Alacoque (d. 1690), a nun in the Salesian convent at Paray-le-Monial in Burgundy, practised a fervent mystical devotion to Christ which resulted in ecstasy. According to her account, on June 16, 1675, when praying before the sacrament, she saw Jesus 'showing to her his heart on a flaming throne, surrounded by thorns and surmounted by a cross; and he told her that it was his will that a special devotion should be offered to his Sacred Heart in reparation for irreverences committed against him in the most holy sacrament, and that the Friday after the octave of Corpus Christi should be set apart for this devotion.'
>
> (Kolde 1911: 146–47)

Initially, the new devotion was not well received in Rome. However, the advocacy of the Jesuits, its popularity, and the miracles claimed of it, forced concessions to devotion to the Sacred Heart by stages. Marguerite Marie Alacoque was beatified in 1864, and during the final decades of the nineteenth century the standing of the devotion was ratified.

> At the Vatican Council of 1870, the majority of the bishops asked for the elevation of the feast [of the Sacred Heart] to the rank of a double (i.e., a feast at which the antiphon is said both before and after the psalm) of the first class (i.e., one which takes precedence in case two feasts fall on the same day) with octave (i.e., lasting through eight days, with special emphasis upon the celebration on the last day), but it was then granted only to the Jesuit order, in recognition of their services in spreading the devotion. The rank was extended to the whole Church, though without an octave, by Leo XIII in 1889.
>
> (Kolde 1911: 147)

Accounts claim earlier precedents for devotion to the Sacred Heart and elaborate upon its symbolism.

> Every form of cult rendered to Christ's humanity has for its ultimate or total object the Second Person of the Blessed Trinity, the God-Man

Christ in His concrete totality…each particular form of devotion [has its particular proximate or special object] composed of a psychological (or spiritual) element and a sensible element that has some intelligible connection with the psychological element. In the devotion to the Sacred Heart the special object is Jesus' physical heart of flesh as the true natural symbol of His threefold love: the human love, sensible and spiritual (infused supernatural charity), and the divine love of the Word Incarnate.

(Moell 1967: 818)

Precedents for this interpretation have been sought in the scriptural promise of living waters in the Old Testament which were fulfilled at Christ's death in the piercing of His side. 'From the first Pentecost on, the waters of salvation (the Spirit) have flowed from the pierced heart of the Messiah.' Over the years, a complex ritual has been created that 'springs from the character of this special object' (Moell 1967: 818).

Specific forms of the devotion are: celebration of the feast on the Friday following the second Sunday after Pentecost with the act of reparation prescribed by Pius XI; observance of the monthly First Friday with Holy Hour, votive Mass, and communion of Reparation; annual renewal of Leo XIII's act of consecration on the feast of Christ the King; the litany and other prayers; consecration of families, nocturnal adoration and enthronement of the Sacred Heart in the home.

(Moell 1967: 818)

The details of these accounts are less important to my immediate purpose than the complex nexus of symbolism, ritual practice and authoritative interpretation on which they rest. Incorporation into the convent school involved introduction to a richly constructed world, but not simply as a set of dogmas. The convent school was also a setting, an institution in the sense Mary Douglas was later to favour, within which beliefs, attitudes and ideas were given a practical life. This educational experience helps us understand what it might have meant to her later when she titled works as: *Purity and Danger*, *Natural Symbols*, *Rules and Meanings*, *Implicit Meanings*, and *How Institutions Think*. The eighteen-year-old Mary Tew, who went up to Oxford University, was already equipped with much of her intellectual mindset and many of her ethical precepts (Turney 1996: 84). Of course, she shared her educational background with thousands of young women who did not go on to become noted anthropologists. Nonetheless, the influences of her schooling are very specific and left distinct traces. Before exploring these in greater detail, it is necessary to fill in a little of their broad context.

ENGLISH CATHOLICISM IN THE EARLY TWENTIETH CENTURY

> Very probably the [Roman Catholic] Church in England had, in proportion to the number of Catholics, more convent schools than the Church in any other part of the world and the effect of this on the character of religious practice was not inconsiderable.
>
> (Hastings 1991: 144)

Growth in the number of convents had been helped by anti-clerical laws passed in Germany and France which brought many continental nuns to work in England, as many as 300 from France alone (Hastings 1991: 143; O'Leary 1992: 79). Their influence strengthened the existing overseas links of the English Catholic community. In the earlier part of the century, tensions between Anglicans and Roman Catholics still ran strongly. The composition of the Catholic community in England and Wales, numbering about two million in 1920, had been changed by large-scale Irish immigration – impelled by the famines and attracted by the jobs provided by industrialization – from the 1840s onwards. This predominantly working-class population had come to outnumber the 'old dissent' – the English recusants consisting of old gentry families and the nineteenth-century converts from the Oxford Movement. The class structure of the Catholic Church in England thus tended to be divided between the upper classes and manual labourers, a structure unlike that of the other main churches. The consequences of this difference for Catholic life in the earlier part of the century were considerable. Working-class religiosity was based on a mixture of

> ancient pieties and nineteenth-century continental devotional innovations…No one questioned that the mass should be in Latin, that lay participation in it should be almost entirely silent, that communion should be in one kind, that priests should be celibate and dressed in black cassocks…within the Church's normal circles any challenge to the whole hard, objective, apparently unchanging order of hierarchy, creed and sacrament was simply unthinkable.
>
> (Hastings 1991: 137)

International in outlook, distinct from its English setting, polarized in its class composition, the Roman Catholic Church was intensely aware of its social basis and had spent the previous decades institution building – notably in the provision of religious schooling: the convent school that was to evolve into the Sacred Heart, Roehampton, had been established in 1842 (O'Leary 1992). Theologically, the Church was becoming increasingly Romanized (ultramontane), and this influence was particularly strong in the convent schools:

[ultramontanism] had few more effective instruments than the convent school with its French nuns, absence of theology, but unquestioning commitment to the new Catholicism; an intense devotion to the Pope and to everything connected with Rome, novenas, indulgences, canonizations, eucharistic congresses, pilgrimages to Lourdes, all that was most characteristic of ultramontane spirituality – the absolute stress upon ecclesiastical obedience as the sum of all virtues, coupled with an often heroic self-immolation and other-worldliness, an apparent ruthlessness in the treatment of people.

(Hastings 1991: 149)

On one view, ultramontanism,[3] with its emphasis on all things Italian, provided a critique of Englishness, not only in relation to the Anglican Church and the anglicanizing of Catholicism in England, but as a more general critique of the British *status quo* from which Catholics were in 'internal exile'. But another view suggested that the Catholic tradition was the true English tradition, from which British society itself was in exile. The class composition of the Church further polarized matters for a thoughtful Catholic intellectual: elevated from non-Catholic intellectual circles by spiritual insight, yet not alienated in the manner of most intellectuals by virtue of belonging to 'a warm mass of people' of the working classes; of the 'warm mass' yet simultaneously superior to these faithful by virtue of cultural sophistication and education. Terry Eagleton suggested that the ability to 'transcend' and 'totalize' their host culture went part way to explaining the importance of exile and émigré writers in twentieth-century English literature (Eagleton 1970). As he acknowledges, this argument is foreshadowed in Perry Anderson's influential critique of the parochialism and empiricism of English national culture (Anderson 1968); a charge of intellectual torpor from which Anderson largely exempted British anthropology on the grounds of its infusion of ideas and personnel from abroad. The severally marginalized position of an English middle-class Catholic woman may contribute to explaining Mary Douglas's experience of 'metaphorical exile': in Eagleton's words, 'an enduring commitment to the "style" of one's social world coupled with an encroaching uneasiness [in this case, rather, self-consciousness] about the substantial values which that style embodies' (1970: 219, 220).

THE CONVENT SCHOOL

The exact impression that convent schooling might have made upon the young Mary Tew has to be guessed, although we have her own assurance that it was substantial and conducive (Hale 1977: 73). In 1850, Elm Grove, a country house in Roehampton village, then outside south London, was bought to rehouse the enclosed order of nuns and their convent school: 'An establishment for young ladies directed by the Religious of the Sacred Heart, Roehampton' (O'Leary

1992: chap. 2 and p. 36). The house and its extensions continued to accommodate the school until the Second World War, when it was firebombed after the students were evacuated. The house was entirely destroyed, but the site and some surviving buildings – the convent, small chapel and dormitory wing – now form part of the Roehampton Institute of the University of Surrey, one of the more rural parts of London's southward sprawl. The culture of school became more anglicized as the nineteenth century wore on, but long after French had ceased being the medium of instruction many French terms survived for games and other activities (O'Leary 1992: 39).

Two semi-fictional, autobiographical works – both favourites of Mary Douglas's – are particularly helpful to an outsider trying to appreciate the set-apart, value-laden, exclusively female space of the Catholic convent school.[4] I have borrowed the title of this chapter from the first of these works, *Memories of a Catholic Girlhood* (1963, originally 1957) by the American author Mary McCarthy, to signal both concern with how Mary remembers her girlhood and the indirect means available to me to suggest this recollection.

Mary McCarthy was born about a decade before Mary Tew. McCarthy was left an orphan with a younger brother; like Mary, she was for a time raised by her grandparents and later sent to study with the Mesdames of the Sacred Heart. Given these parallels, it is unsurprising that Mary counts McCarthy's memories among her favourite books. However, if there are pitfalls in a literal reading of the memories of an author concerning her own life, the sympathy of our author for the life of another has to be handled even more delicately. McCarthy warns us of these problems in the introductions and codas to her recollections, questioning the accuracy of her memory, and noting where she has altered facts of the past to portray truths that concern her recollections at the time of writing rather than the irrevocably lost experience of the life as then lived. The American literary critic, John Paul Eakin (1985), drew upon McCarthy's work to illustrate the self-consciously fictional character of autobiography in his study of the genre.

The nuns themselves impressed both Marys. As women counterparts of the learned Jesuits, a few of them seemed – I think the word is not misplaced – glamorous female intellectuals. The Dames du Sacré Coeur retained their original names after admission, prefixing the honorific 'Madame'. Their costume, like their order, reflected nineteenth-century France: a black dress, a cap with a white frill, and a black veil (Kolde 1911: 147; illustrated in O'Leary 1992). The Sacred Heart nuns were considered to be 'ladies' (see Boyle 1991; Hayes 1991); they seemed elegant and, in certain respects, worldly. 'The rumour in the convent was that our nuns had a special dispensation to read works on the Index [of works restricted by the Church], and that was how we liked to think of them, cool and learned, with their noses in heretical books' (McCarthy 1963: 10). A common curriculum, modified to fit the educational system of the countries in which the convent schools were founded, was biased towards humanities with a strong component of theology and history, particularly the history of the

Catholic Church and faith. McCarthy notes, 'If you are born and brought up a Catholic, you have absorbed a good deal of world history and the history of ideas before you are twelve, and it is like learning a language early; the effect is indelible' (1963: 25). She goes on,

> To care for the [religious] quarrels of the past, to identify oneself passionately with a cause that became, politically speaking, a losing cause with the birth of the modern world, is to experience a kind of straining against reality, a rebellious nonconformity that, again, is rare in America, where children are instructed in the virtues of the system they live under, as though history had achieved a happy ending in American civics.
>
> (1963: 25)

McCarthy, in common with Antonia White (see below), rebelled against her convent schooling. Mary Douglas, not a rebel to her upbringing, would not accept the notion of a losing cause; but the sense of being an outsider to the mainstream, a non-conformist, may be the more marked as a result. David Martin, a long-time commentator on her work, aptly called her 'radically conservative and conservatively radical' (WG/TLS), a stance one might anticipate of someone belonging nationally to a minority, but internationally to an older, wider and more powerful set of certainties. Although Douglas may have felt embattled, in a broader context she was far from alone. Let's return to the Mesdames,

> Like the Jesuits, to whom they stand as nieces, the Ladies of the Sacred Heart are a highly centralized order, versed in clockwork obedience to authority. Their institutions follow a pattern laid down for them in France in the early nineteenth century – clipped and pollarded as a garden and stately as a minuet. All Sacred Heart convent schools are the same – the same blue serge dresses, usually, with white collars and cuffs, the same blue and green and pink moiré ribbons awarded for good conduct, the same books given as prizes on Prize Day, the same recitation of 'Lepanto' by an English actor in a piped waistcoat, the same *congés*, or holidays, announced by the *Mère Supérieure*, the same game of *cache-cache*, or hide-and-seek, played on these traditional feast days, the same *goûter*, or tea, the same retreats and sermons, the same curtsies dipped in the hall, the same early-morning chapel with processions of girls, like widowed queens, in sad black-net veils, the same *prie-dieu*, the same French hymns ('*Oui, je le crois*'), the same glorious white-net veils and flowers and gold vessels on Easter and Holy Thursday and on feasts peculiar to the order.
>
> (McCarthy 1963: 89)

McCarthy attended the Sacred Heart Convent in Seattle in 1923; Mary Tew was a pupil of the Sacred Heart Convent in Roehampton about a decade later. But Sacred Heart schools seem to have been relatively changeless and extra-territorial organizations: 'If a "wrinkle in time" could have transported a girl from the late 1930s back to the school her mother knew, she would, with small details excepted, have no difficulty in finding her way round and fitting into the day to day routine' (O'Leary 1992: 63). 'Antonia White' (Eirene (Botting) Hopkinson) received two letters from 'old children' after the publication of *Frost in May*; one had left in 1883 and the other in 1927, both thought they must have been contemporaries of White who left in 1914 (White quoted by Forgan 1991: 1). The television personality Katie Boyle moved from the Sacred Heart Convent in Rome to find she was 'immediately speaking the same language' as girls at Sacred Heart convents in England (Boyle 1991: 44). Mary Douglas reacted well to the regimentation – the same regimentation that her mother, who attended the same school, had undergone. During her final year, 1937–38, Mary was head girl; a position her sister also held briefly (O'Leary 1992: 197–98). In sociological terms, the convent school was a total institution: a world apart, a literally enclosed, self-sufficient, coherent, and exhaustively comprehensive template for behaviour. For Mary Douglas, at least in retrospect, here was a home – run by women – demanding of her loyalty and identifica-tion, and offering in return stability and meaning. In disregard, even disdain, of the values of the world surrounding it, the convent school went about its busi-ness of creating young ladies. Minute regulation of the external features of the girls' lives was designed to work on their inner states: there was an hour for everything, a proper way to perform every action, a definite rhythm of chores and festivals, an encompassing hierarchy, and a clearly defined system of rewards and sanctions. Together these regulations encouraged the feeling that only within the rules could life have a full meaning. Insiders were uniquely privileged: 'I felt as though I stood on the outskirts and observed the ritual of a cult, a cult of fashion and elegance in the sphere of religion' (McCarthy 1963: 90). Adrian Hastings makes a similar comment of Antonia White's memoir,

> Antonia White's *Frost in May*…provides an extraordinarily vivid picture of the ultramontane convent world…[although] it is a partial, indeed a rather exterior picture of the nuns and their achievement…Such a school presented a model of Catholic life at its purest to the devout lay person and it impressed its ideals and spirituality upon the élite of Catholic womanhood in a way that had seldom been the case in earlier ages. The quintessential heart of the religious world was solemn Benediction of the blessed sacrament on a high feast in the convent chapel: the court of the great king, the girls all kneeling devoutly in their white veils and gloves before the golden monstrance, the many hundreds of candles lit around the altar, the clouds of incense, the

Latin hymns. Here was ultramontane Catholicism at its most appealing to many a convert, its most appalling to many a Protestant.

(Hastings 1991: 149)

The novelist and translator Antonia White was a school contemporary of Phyllis Twomey – Mary's mother. We join the heroine of her semi-autobiographical novel, whom she calls Nanda Gray, in 1908 when, at the age of nine, she is sent to the Convent of the 'Five Wounds' in 'Lippington' on the outskirts of London; when she was nine years old, also in 1908, Antonia White was sent to the Sacred Heart Convent in Roehampton; both the 'Sacred Heart' and the 'Five Wounds' are natural symbols of Christ's humanity. April O'Leary, in her account of Roehampton's history, described this account as one 'seen by a puzzled, sensitive and bitterly uncomprehending small daughter of a recent convert' (1992: 64). Although Antonia White was asked to leave the school for composing the early chapters of a novel considered unseemly (White 1934: 243–44), her recollections are also tinged with nostalgia.

Elizabeth Bowen perceptively remarks in her introduction to the Virago reprint of *Frost in May* (1978, originally published 1933) how the atmosphere of the convent school is international rather than English; she quotes one of the girls in the novel, 'Catholicism isn't a religion, it's a nationality' (1978: vii). In the next passage from Bowen I have transposed the fictional convent to which White sends Nanda Gray to that which she attended with Mary's mother,

A Roehampton girl is a Child of the Sacred Heart; she may by birth be French, German, Spanish or English, but that is secondary. Also the girls [at Roehampton] show a sort of family likeness; they are the daughters of old, great Catholic families, the frontierless aristocracy of Europe; they have in common breeding as well as faith.

(Bowen 1978: vii–viii)

Mary Tew's experience of education before the Second World War exactly resembled neither her mother's and Antonia White's before the First World War, nor Mary McCarthy's in Seattle between the wars, nor her own daughter's after the war (Photographs 3 and 4). But the social environment created within long-established schools does tend to change gradually. With caution about its details (some of which can be checked against April O'Leary's school history), what does a quasi-anthropological look at the world described in the novels describe to us? Following Mary Douglas's precepts, let's pay particular attention to the environment of rules within which any individual's experience can be appreciated to have meaning. What sort of world is modelled in the convent school?

Within the school building, spaces are imbued with religious values: each room is referred to by the name of a saint, and religious representations pack the walls of the schoolrooms, refectories and dormitories (White 1978: 26 *passim*).

Photograph 3 Mary Tew (second from right) at the Sacred Heart Convent, from a 1934 school photograph

Source: © Provincial Archives, Society of the Sacred Heart, Roehampton

Photograph 4 'Cricket XI, 1937, with Miss Hockley' (Mary Tew, seated, middle row, far right)

Source: Reproduced from April O'Leary (1922) *Living Tradition* by the Provincial Archives, Society of the Sacred Heart, Roehampton

The whole space of the school is enclosed by notices which restrict access to visitors and representatives of the 'secular' (White 1978: 38 *passim*). Everyday behaviour is minutely governed; strict rules govern the route girls will follow up and down to the laundry room (O'Leary 1992: 74). Food is taken at tables presided over by a president and sub-president (White 1978: 25–26). No matter how unpleasant the food may be, all must be eaten. One girl is shamed for her inability to eat a piece of liver with its 'pipes' showing by the Mistress General publicly sampling it herself (O'Leary 1992: 85). Apart from the school uniform described by McCarthy (and subject to gradual evolution within standards of extraordinary modesty, detailed by O'Leary), the girls put on veils and dark blue lisle gloves for evening prayers (White 1978: 31). At night they fold their clothes neatly on a chair at the end of the bed, which is not to be sat upon. Looking glasses are forbidden (White 1978: 33), and the girls undress inside screens around their beds which they leave to brush their hair. 'The [girls] that bite their nails have to wear white gloves…and Mildred has to wear *black* bags on her hands sometimes. She pinches, you see' (White 1978: 39).

Because of the mortification involved, cold water is preferred to hot for washing (White 1978: 44–45). Baths twice a week are taken wearing huge calico cloaks (O'Leary 1992: 66; White 1978: 44), that 'protected us from the scandalizing sight of our naked bodies' (White 1934: 231). Rewards and sanctions underpin adherence to the rules: pink ribbons are awarded 'for being almost unnaturally good for eight weeks' (White 1978: 23); exemption cards are issued by the mother at the end of the week: in blue marked very good, or dark blue with good, or in yellow with indifferent. The mother doesn't smile when issuing a yellow card, and a 'dirty green' coloured card, entitled bad, is not handed to the recipient who must pick it up herself. This card is a prelude to expulsion (White 1978: 40; O'Leary 1992: 89).

Deportment is regulated: girls learn to curtsey, and to emulate the gliding carriage of the nuns. A new girl volunteering to answer a question learns that 'we don't hold up our hands at Lippington' (White 1978: 23). Nanda Gray is taught to lie down to sleep fully extended, flat on her back with arms crossed, so that in the event of dying she would meet her maker in a seemly posture (White 1978: 34; cf. White 1934: 233).

Perhaps most fundamental to the framing of experience is the way that time is governed and divided. 'Whenever a bell rings, you have to stop doing whatever you are doing' (White 1978: 25).

> The whole day was punctuated by prayers. Besides the morning and evening devotions and the thrice-recurring Angelus, every lesson began with an invocation to the Holy Ghost and ended with a recommendation to Our Lady. Before supper, the whole school assembled to recite five decades of the rosary, and there was usually a novena in preparation for an important feast or a special intention to add some extra petitions to the list. The day ended with prayers in the chapel, and an

elaborate examination of conscience under the heading of sins against God, against one's neighbour and against oneself…On Saturdays every child in the school went to confession and, in the evening, after 'Exemptions', there were special devotions in the vestibule of Our Lady of Good Success…On Sundays all the children heard two masses and a sermon in the morning and went to Benediction in the afternoon.

(White 1978: 45)

The daily and weekly regulation of occasions was echoed in the splendour of the annual round punctuated by great days: like the Feast of the Immaculate Conception in December which was preceded by a fortnight during which the girls made strenuous efforts to gain good marks for outstanding examples of courtesy (White 1978: 63–64).

Overseeing the order of life was a strict authority: girls did not meet even their closest relatives without the presence of a *surveillante*. A system of small rewards, the most valuable of which were called permissions, was used to sanction the rules positively (White 1978: 63). These permissions 'written in an exquisite round hand on cream paper, twisted into a tiny scroll and tied with pink silk' might allow a girl to go to the farm to get eggs, to talk during lunch, to have a story book on a weekday, and so on.

The object of the regulation was the formation of a particular character. Both the autobiographical novels I have been considering feature episodes in which girls were deprived of coveted ambitions so that they might learn humility. Special relations with particular others were discouraged: close friendships were censured and the giving of presents thought appropriate only to close relatives (White 1978: 43). Yet, reward was earned as quickly as censure ('the rule was "small penances…quick rewards"' (White 1934: 255)), and the motherly devotion of many of the nuns to their young charges was complete (O'Leary 1992: 75).

Thanks to this regulation, life assumed a tight-knit symbolic coherence,

The donkey in the paddock reminded her that all donkeys have crosses on their backs since the day Our Lord rode into Jerusalem; the robin's breast was red because one of his ancestors had splashed his feathers with the Precious Blood trying to peck away the crown of thorns. The clover and the shamrock were a symbol of the Blessed Trinity, the sunflower was a saint turning always towards God, the speedwell had been white till Our Lady's blue mantle brushed it as she walked in the fields of Nazareth. When Nanda heard a cock crow, it cried: '*Christus natus est*'; the cows lowed '*Ubi? Ubi?*' and the lambs down at the community farm bleated 'Be-e-thlehem'.

(White 1978: 46; cf. White 1934: 235)

In describing the part that rules played in the creation of order in the first half of *Frost in May*, Antonia White deftly evokes the atmosphere of the convent school, and the impression it made upon pupils. Many years after her schooldays, Mary Douglas was to endorse enthusiastically the ideas of a sociologist of education, Basil Bernstein, who clearly distinguished the explicit from the implicit curricula of schools. The explicit curriculum is what concerns those who draw up lists of things that children should be taught. The implicit curriculum is implied by the way these things are taught, within what broader educational environment, and what relations are suggested between elements of the explicit curriculum by its context of transmission. The implicit curriculum provides the context of explicit pedagogy, and it is largely responsible for the significance attached to what is taught.

THE SOCIAL TEACHINGS OF THE CHURCH

From the explicit curriculum of her convent education, Mary Douglas recalls that she developed a broad background in the humanities. 'At my convent school we were taught Catholic social theory; and metaphysical logic was the everyday stuff of our lives. It was really exciting and I always wanted to do something that would combine these interests' (Douglas quoted by Hale 1977: 144). Although they did not allow the outside world to determine what they considered necessary for their girls, academic concerns and standards had been strengthened at the Sacred Heart Convent by the 1930s. In 1929, the Society of the Sacred Heart opened a small home for students, allowing nuns to study at Oxford University. This later developed into St Anne's College (of which Mary Tew was a member as a doctoral student) (O'Leary 1992: 91). Girls sat the national examinations that, at least in theory, allowed them to compete for university entrance.

One area of concern at the school was particularly to influence the way Mary Douglas pursued her interests when she left school. As part of the curriculum, the girls of the Sacred Heart studied the encyclicals that defined the social doctrine of the Catholic Church. In 1931 Pope Pius XI had issued his encyclical *Quadragesimo anno* to reconsider the church's social teaching 'in the fortieth year' after the first social encyclical – Leo XIII's *Rerum novarum* ('Of new things'). The first encyclical was a late attempt on the part of the Church to respond to industrialization and the deteriorating living conditions of workers during the nineteenth century. Its translation into English was undertaken by Cardinal Henry Edward Manning. The encyclical, with the descriptive title 'On the condition of workers', was partly designed as a response to socialist and Marxist analyses of the relation between labour and capital then current. The Church recognized, contrary to the socialists, a natural right to the ownership of private property justified by men's intelligent and independent use of their individual energies, and their responsibility to care for their families. The Church was to 'keep ever before men's minds the truths that certain inequalities are inevitable, that to suffer and endure is the lot of man, and that man's final end is not here but hereafter' (Newman 1967: 387). However, the Church was also concerned with the body: the promotion of justice and charity was recommended to alleviate poverty. The Pope rejected classical *laissez-faire* economics in arguing that the State, in addition to the protection of private property, ought also to encourage the wide distribution of property, ensure payment of a just wage and regulate working conditions. Finally, the encyclical defended the role of voluntary organizations, such as trade unions and Church bodies devoted to social action (Newman 1967). The rejection of *laissez-faire* economics was particularly important. Neoclassical analysis of microeconomic behaviour, based on the proposition that prices were fixed through the interplay of supply and demand in the market, had effectively severed links between ethics and economic behaviour that had been crucial to eighteenth-century thinkers (Gunneman 1986: 69). As well as responding to socialist ideas, 'Of new things' was also a riposte to extreme individualism.

This response to neoclassical economics was elaborated in the 1931 encyclical. In place of the paradigm of economic competition, *Quadragesimo anno* proposed an organic model of society. The producers (owners of capital and workers) and the consumers of each industrial product were to form functional groups based upon cooperation. These institutions would determine policies appropriate to each industry. A hierarchical organization of such functional bodies would furnish the charter for a reconstructed social order. Although neither of them was entirely clear, the principles of social justice and subsidiarity were both emphasized. According to the latter principle, more inclusive associations (including the State) should not abrogate from individuals, nor from intermediate organizations (families, trade unions etc.), any tasks or decisions they could accomplish by their own effort and initiative (Curran 1986: 432, 608). Organizations should be of the smallest scale appropriate to their tasks: 'It is an injustice, a grave evil and a disturbance of right order for a larger and higher association to arrogate to itself functions which can be performed efficiently by smaller and lower societies' (Pope Pius XI, 1931, quoted in the *Guardian* 'Leader' 7 July 1992). Subsidiarity remains an ambiguous principle – as the member states of the European Union have been discovering more recently. Who decides which level of the hierarchy most efficiently performs what functions? But as a guiding principle of hierarchy, subsidiarity remains a persuasive image of specialization, differentiation and organic coherence which reappears in Mary Douglas's mature typology of social forms.

Later (in Chapter 11), we shall note how the organic model of Roman Catholic teaching corresponds to some elements of French social thought, and how the Church's concern with the common good intersects with economists' ponderings about the provision of public goods, and with the relations between rich and poor nations (Gunneman 1986: 68). In her recollections, Mary Douglas credits her interest in social policy with a decision to study sociology at the London School of Economics, and then, persuaded by the Sisters that this step was too radical, to study the PPE (politics, philosophy and economics) tripos at Oxford. For all that her convent school was able to instil self-confidence and a lady-like bearing,[5] it was not really capable of adequately preparing girls for university entrance.[6] She left the Sacred Heart Convent School in 1938 and, on the suggestion of her godmother, spent six months in Paris. Placed with a rather quarrelsome family, and feeling her outsider status intensely, she attended the Sorbonne and nonetheless gained a 'Diplôme de civilisation française' with 'bien mention'.[7] To pass her Oxford entrance examinations, Mary returned to England and spent some months at a 'crammer' in the Cotswolds. 'The Association [of the Sacred Heart] Report records that she returned the following term to give the school a whole holiday in honour of her [being awarded] the "*Prix d'Excellence*", the most prestigious [school] prize there was' (personal communication, Sister Mary Coke, December 1997). A small bursary from her college, and low cost accommodation in the home for students established by the Order of the Sacred Heart in Oxford, allowed Mary to read for a degree, which would have been impossible had she been reliant on her father's pension.

The year was 1939, and Oxford academe was soon to lose many of its more exciting thinkers to war service. Mary recalls little about her first degree other than feeling badly out of her depth in the mathematical side of economics and achieving a second class honours degree. Her first year at university seems to have been an unhappy one as she thought through the crisis of belief that seems a common lot of cradle Catholics, and especially intellectually curious ones like herself. She divulges little about this, except that issues were settled with her faith. In 1942, she left university and spent the remainder of hostilities doing her war service in the Colonial Office from 1943 to 1947.

Mary Tew's background is, so far as I know, unique among the British anthropologists of her generation. But it does not seem remarkable that a woman of her background – an English Catholic of part-Irish descent, whose family served in the Indian Civil Service, who lost her mother young and was educated in straitened circumstances in an ultramontane convent school – should become particularly sensitive to social differences, to marginality, and to exclusion. Her commitments – among others to hierarchy, authority, structured organization, difference and its incorporation, and to ritual – all seem to stem from this early period, even if they became explicit as themes in her writing only in later years. The antithesis of Roman Catholicism, recalling that catholic means universal, is not Protestantism, but 'sectarianism…that holds that the church is a community of true believers, a precinct of righteousness within and over against the unredeemed world of sin, pronouncing judgement upon it and calling it to repentance but never entering into dialogue with it' (McBrien 1987: 430). In forming our predispositions we also absorb their antitheses: the contrast between hierarchy and sect (and a variety of contextually appropriate stand-ins for these terms) furnished the later Mary Douglas with one of the most fertile polarities in her mature thought.

Much was to change for the Sacred Heart Convent (O'Leary 1992: chap. 9): not just a new site, but the ending of the monastic way of life and enclosure for its teaching orders; habits became optional and largely disappeared; nuns could invite friends, relatives and colleagues into their previously inviolable living areas; as the numbers of secular teachers grew, so did the proportion of men among them. In 1985, the school was handed over to lay management by trustees and governors; the Convent of the Sacred Heart became Woldingham School; and, in 1990, the last members of the Order of the Sacred Heart left the teaching staff. In Chapter 5, we shall see Mary Douglas's reaction to the early stages of the disappearance of this way of life and the opportunity for pupils to participate in it.

Notes

1 Teowe in Anglo-Saxon and Tieu in French (Harrison 1918).
2 An anthology of these articles is among Mary Douglas's current projects.
3 'Beyond the mountains', i.e. Rome as seen from northern Europe. Ultramontanism includes strong emphasis on centralization in ecclesiastical government, papal infallibility, and freedom of the Church from interference by the State.
4 The lightly fictionalized character of Antonia White's account is confirmed by her autobiographical essay in the novelist Graham Greene's collection of essays on *The Old School*, which repeats passages from her book almost verbatim (see White 1934). Although Mary Tew and 'Antonia White' reacted in opposite ways to their immediate experience of convent education, I find it difficult to read Antonia White's account of young Eirene's travails as untinged by a nostalgic warmth Mary Douglas might share.
5 An ability to curtsey correctly was to lay dormant as a talent until the award of an honorary doctorate of the University of Uppsala.
6 In this respect, Mary's memory does not entirely accord with April O'Leary's (1992) account of the same period.
7 Her godmother arranged Mary's accommodation through a Paris-based friend, who was to become Mary's mother-in-law.

2 OXFORD YEARS: 1940s

BIOGRAPHICAL COUNTERPOINT

According to her own account, working at the Colonial Office during the war made Mary Tew an anthropologist.

> If I had joined the Board of Trade or the WAAF, my life might have taken a very different direction. But anthropologists tend to be people who have rejected something. Not being a socially well-adjusted person, I chose a dead backwater instead. It was there in the Colonial Office that I first began to meet anthropologists. They were the experts, while we civil servants were on the menial side, and I used to ask them, 'How do you get to be an adviser and not a servant?'
>
> (quoted by Hale 1977)

We may feel inclined to flesh out this disarming account, for not all the young women who happened to do their war service in the Colonial Office went on to become distinguished professors of anthropology (and not all of them would describe civil servants as servants 'on the menial side'). While war service may have been a proximate cause of her taking up anthropology, Mary's Indian civil service family background – which seems never to have been a consideration in her choice of research site – and her convent education prepared the soil in which her interest in social theories, and their applications to social action cross-culturally, grew.

Becoming an anthropologist in a Britain that was not yet 'multi-cultural' by self-definition, and remained a significant colonial power, was a different sort of decision from today, and many of the immediate post-war generation of anthropologists had striking if diverse personal motives for their choice; among them: that they were themselves from the English-writing world but not narrowly English, or that they had gained extensive 'colonial' experience, or because they had, broadly, romantic attractions to the non-industrialized world. Yet none of these seem quite to have applied in Mary Tew's case: her avowed motive was a fascination with problems of social theory.

Nearly fifty years ago I went to the Pitt Rivers Museum to be registered for the Oxford Diploma in Anthropology. The curator, the late Mr. Penniman, told me to read and reflect on Henry Balfour's 1937 Frazer Lecture and then return the next day to be questioned. The lecture, 'Spinners and weavers in anthropological research', was a parable on the philosophy of science: 'spinners' were the providers of information, 'weavers' were the theorists who took the spun yarn and turned it into theories. Clearly, the humble spinners were virtuous; the weavers, ambitious and sinister. The lecture was a strike for British empiricism against the complexities of German ethnology. When I was asked the next day whether I wanted to be a spinner or a weaver, clearly the right answer was to choose spinning. I failed the test, but the experience started me worrying about whether facts can exist without theory.

(Douglas 1995c: 262)

Study of the Catholic social encyclicals would have suggested to her that theoretical weaving was consequential for questions of social action and collective morality in a way that spinning was not. Relative to the standards of its time, social anthropology of the 1940s had an egalitarian and humanly inclusive view of the world. Perhaps such an impulse might on occasions amount to nothing more specific than the acceptance of common human worth, and therefore of uniform human mental processes. But, in Raymond Williams's suggestively vague phrase, this formed an important element in an overall 'structure of feeling' that became common currency of post-war anthropologists but was not generally shared by British people born in the 1920s. The most common way of accommodating this commitment theoretically in post-war British anthropology relied on strong appeals to the influence of social context upon human behaviour. Formally, and most simply, this move was not unlike its American anthropological counterpart which would weigh personality in the scales of culture. Both arguments shared a tactic – contextualizing the characteristics of a human individual in terms of those shared by the larger collectivity of which that individual was part – and allowed vigorous riposte to popular prejudices about either racially based essential differences among human beings, or else the differences that followed from some human beings being 'primitive' and others 'civilized'. Because they were so effective as ripostes, both cultural and social holism remained key ideas and provoked theoretical questions to which answers were sought in the ensuing quarter century of British and American anthropology. Here, I both simplify and run ahead of my argument, but whatever its source – and religious teaching seems as likely an influence as any – this temporally specific element of egalitarianism in post-war anthropology struck a chord in an already receptive student.

The business of the Colonial Office during wartime, as Mary Douglas later recalled it, consisted mainly of putting things on hold until the end of the war when there might be funds to do anything about them. But she was intrigued by the anthropologists, and especially impressed by two outstanding ethnographic descriptions of African peoples: Audrey Richards's *Land, Labour and Diet* (1939), for its methodological rigour in describing a system of agriculture, and E.E. Evans-Pritchard's *The Nuer* (1940), for the theoretical audacity of its analysis of political organization in an uncentralized society of the Sudan. Mary Tew was astonished on meeting Evans-Pritchard, to find him not the old man of her imagination (see Photograph 5 below); he was not quite twenty years her senior. Twenty years later, in the 'Acknowledgements' to *Purity and Danger*, she was to give pride of place to this volume.

> The place of [*The Nuer*] in anthropology is like the invention of the frameless chassis in the history of car-design…In the 1930s car designers found that they could eliminate the steel frame if they treated the whole car as a single unit…At about the same time Evans-Pritchard found that he could make a political analysis of a system in which there were no central organs of government and in which the weight of authority and the strains of political functioning were dispersed through the whole structure of the body politic.
>
> (PD: vii, viii)

In this account, Evans-Pritchard is credited with the development of structuralist thought in British anthropology independently of Lévi-Strauss.[1] Although not inconsistent with her later account of Evans-Pritchard's influence on her, to which I turn shortly, this comment reinforces a feeling that at different stages in the development of her own thought Mary Douglas was able to turn back to Evans-Pritchard to experience again the recognition that he had been there before her in important respects. This sense is very common; many of us turn recurrently to writers by whom we have been greatly influenced, in order to judge, from our changing relation to them, quite where we stand now.[2] Our readings necessarily change, and it becomes difficult to stand aside from our present interpretation to re-experience the original impact of that thinker upon the person we once were. Evans-Pritchard's influence on Mary Douglas's thought was – on her account – immense. But that is not to say it has always been the same, or quite the same as it was in the first instance. The influence is also controversial in a minor way, since Mary was to write a short intellectual biography of Evans-Pritchard that many other students and colleagues of the great man found provocative. The non-anthropological reader will need a little context to appreciate this.

EVANS-PRITCHARD AND THE POST-WAR INSTITUTE

Leaving aside the claims of the Pole Bronislaw Malinowski, who established modern 'British' social anthropology in the years after World War I, most

Photograph 5 E.E. Evans-Pritchard, RAI Presidential Portrait, 1949–51

Source: © Royal Anthropological Institute

contemporary British anthropologists would probably cite Sir Edward Evan Evans-Pritchard as the most influential British anthropologist of the twentieth century. His works have been widely read outside the boundaries of the discipline, and his pupils and colleagues went from Oxford to complete the institutional establishment of social anthropology in Britain after World War II.

Born in 1902 the second son of an Anglican vicar, Evans-Pritchard was educated at Winchester and at Exeter College, Oxford, from where he graduated with a degree in Modern History in 1924.[3] Developing an interest in anthropology, Evans-Pritchard moved in the same year to the London School of Economics to study under C.G. Seligman; Malinowski also arrived at LSE that year, and Evans-Pritchard joined his first seminar (Kuper 1996: 67). The two were to fall out in grand and enduring fashion. Under the sponsorship of Seligman, Evans-Pritchard completed a doctorate on the basis of Zande researches in 1927 and taught intermittently (and apparently despite Malinowski's opposition) until 1932 at LSE. Between 1932 and 1934, Evans-Pritchard occupied the Chair in either Philosophy or Sociology (he claimed to be uncertain which, Burton 1992: 20) at the Fuad I (now Egyptian) University of Cairo. When sociology was reduced from a full degree to a subsidiary subject, and Evans-Pritchard's query about this to the ministry elicited the response that sociology might have a 'subversive effect' on the 'young men of Egypt', he resigned (Reid 1990: 124). It was during these Cairo years, while in his early thirties, that Evans-Pritchard composed three papers delineating his own position by critique of a number of earlier, and in his view pejorative, sociological thinkers on non-Western societies. During his remaining pre-war years (1935–40), Evans-Pritchard was a research lecturer in African Sociology at the University of Oxford, where his undergraduate 'moral' tutor, R.R. Marrett, had secured his appointment. Together with A.R. Radcliffe-Brown and Meyer Fortes, he created what Adam Kuper has described as a new paradigm in British social anthropology (Kuper 1996: 80). As Burton notes, the majority of Evans-Pritchard's fieldwork was carried out between 1926 and 1936 in southern Sudan (Burton 1992: 37) and, thus, before the war. Evans-Pritchard's eventful war service, which was spent in the Sudan, Ethiopia and Libya, included stints as the commander of Anuak irregulars and two years as liaison officer with the Bedouin. 'Toward the end of World War II Evans-Pritchard was received into the Catholic Church at the cathedral in Benghazi, in Libya, an experience that was ultimately preceded by a long camel journey through the desert, and finally encouraged by some Catholic friends' (Burton 1992: 21). Having spent 1945 as Reader in Anthropology at Cambridge, Evans-Pritchard then succeeded A.R. Radcliffe-Brown as Professor of Anthropology at Oxford University and became a fellow of All Souls College, remaining in this position until his retirement in 1970.

In 1946, as Evans-Pritchard assumed the Oxford chair, Mary Tew, just 'demobbed' from the Colonial Office, set about resuming the education that war had interrupted. With a place to read for a BSc in Anthropology (the old title of the degree under Radcliffe-Brown) assured for the following October, she left with her younger sister Pat, who was about to return to art school after a spell as a cartographer in the Royal Engineers, to carry out a week's fieldwork-cum-holiday at the circus in a south-coast English town (amusingly recalled in 1991c).

> I had imagined from [E-P's] books that he would be old, because the lines of his thought were hard and clear, like late Rembrandt. But he was still only in his forties, and this was his first year at Oxford, which meant he could make new friends in a way that wouldn't have been possible later. Everything about that post-war year was fresh and exciting: it is still famous.
>
> (quoted by Hale 1977)

Mary and Evans-Pritchard remained close friends until his death in 1973. She was not alone in choosing Oxford at the time. There were few places to read anthropology in Britain in the immediate aftermath of World War II. The main competition to Oxford was from the London School of Economics under the leadership of Raymond (later, Sir Raymond) Firth, whom Mary had also known at the Colonial Office. Other places were either somewhat in the doldrums or yet to be established in their post-war incarnations. So the majority of anthropologists who were to be influential within the British branch of the subject in the next twenty years happened to be at Oxford just after the war – even if passing through only briefly.

Radcliffe-Brown had returned to Oxford from São Paulo and resumed lecturing at the beginning of 1945; Daryll Forde, whom Mary was later to join at University College London, had been temporary custodian of the Institute in his absence. During the 1945–46 academic year, Radcliffe-Brown was rejoined on return from West Africa by Meyer Fortes, a close friend of Evans-Pritchard who moreover shared his antipathy to Malinowski (Goody 1995: 62). Evans-Pritchard, Fortes and Radcliffe-Brown had briefly enjoyed a productive collegiality at Oxford before the outbreak of war (Goody 1995: 78–79), and after Evans-Pritchard assumed the professorship in 1946–47, '[f]or a few years Oxford was a power-house of academic activity' (Goody 1995: 80). At the beginning of the academic year 1947–48, Max Gluckman joined the department and he taught in tandem with Evans-Pritchard and Fortes for that year and the next, before Gluckman took the Manchester chair. The following year, 1948–49, also saw the recruitment of Godfrey Lienhardt – ' "a brilliant man", even if he had done no research; indeed he was still completing his undergraduate degree at Cambridge at the time' in F.R. Leavis's Department of English (Goody 1995: 81, internal quote from Evans-Pritchard's letter to Fortes) – and of the Indian anthropologist, M.N. Srinivas, who had completed his doctorate on the Coorgs of Southern India under Radcliffe-Brown's supervision (Srinivas 1973). Gluckman's departure to the Manchester chair made space for the Greek Cypriot anthropologist, J.G. Peristiany, another specialist in Nilo-Hamites; while Meyer Fortes was replaced, when he took the Cambridge chair in 1950–51, by the Czech Jewish refugee Franz Steiner, who had been Radcliffe-Brown's doctoral student (Adler and Fardon 1999): at the same time Mary Tew also became a member of staff. This, then, was the staffing of the Institute at the time when Mary was a student there: a mixture of those professionally seasoned before the war and the brightest of the Oxford products.

As Evans-Pritchard outlined to a meeting of the Association of Social Anthropologists in 1958, the Oxford syllabus for the single-year diploma and two-year BLitt or BSc consisted predominantly of social anthropology in the first year, although elements of 'ethnology, comparative technology, archaeology and physical anthropology' (largely provided by the Pitt-Rivers Museum staff) were also mandatory (Evans-Pritchard 1959: 122). Avowedly somewhat haphazard in planning, the social anthropology course was supposed to cover basics in the first term, followed by regional ethnographic coverage in the second term and a narrower focus on specific ethnographic problems in the final term. A second year, for BLitt or BSc students, was devoted to a thesis. Published lecture lists for the years of Mary Tew's studentship roughly fit the prescribed pattern, so we find the specialist courses largely reflecting the lecturer's current writing and research interests: Evans-Pritchard lecturing on the Sanusiya, he and Lienhardt presenting Nilotic societies, Srinivas lecturing on the Coorgs, Gluckman on Bantu peoples and on social change in Zululand, Fortes on West Africa generally and Tallensi in particular.[4] The same authors' publications around those years give a fair indication of the content of their lectures. In the single year of her own Oxford lectureship, 1950–51, Mary Tew contributed to collectively run courses on 'Problems of social change in the colonies', classes on 'Advanced fieldwork – land tenure' and 'The study of kinship', and offered as her specialist courses 'Lele village organization' and 'Lele kinship and marriage'. The synergy between teaching and research in this postgraduate institute was close; Mary Tew had registered for her DPhil in October 1949, officially under the supervision of M.N. Srinivas but under Evans-Pritchard's guidance, and was currently writing up the dissertation for which she would 'supplicate' in Trinity (third) term 1952. Aside from the usual courses on Nilotic and Nilo-Hamitic societies and the Dinka, Nandi and Nuer, Indian villages and the Coorgs – with an accent on religion in both cases – 1950–51 was also the first year in which Franz Steiner (Photograph 6) presented an extended series of twelve lectures on 'Taboo' which were to have considerable impact on Mary Douglas's later work (see Chapter 4).

Initially, Mary Douglas found herself in a relatively small group of students, but these were soon augmented by a majority of those of the immediate post-war generation of British-trained anthropologists: Laura and Paul Bohannan (close friends of Franz Steiner – Paul Bohannan was to replace Mary Douglas when she left), Louis Dumont (Srinivas's replacement), Jack Goody (to succeed Fortes in the Cambridge chair), John Barnes, Emrys Peters, Paul Stirling, John Beattie, John Middleton, Paul Baxter, David Brokensha, Ian Cunnison, Rodney Needham, Julian Pitt-Rivers, David Pocock, Kenelm Burridge, William Newell and numerous others. By virtue of being the centre of a British anthropology

Photograph 6 Franz Baermann Steiner

Source: © Estate of Franz Baermann Steiner (courtesy of Jeremy Adler)

which was enjoying a particularly prominent position in the discipline internationally, it is no exaggeration to claim that the Institute of Social Anthropology in Oxford was briefly the most significant anthropological institution in the world. In 1970 Evans-Pritchard wrote with pride:

> I believe we are the best, and best-known, postgraduate school in the world and I think we can be happy if we remain so…[S]ince I have taught at Oxford no student who has endured the full course of his academic career has failed to obtain a good post in a department in a University, were he so minded. During the past 20 years 179 students have been awarded post-graduate degrees in Social Anthropology. Of these, over 20 now hold appointments at full professorial level and well over a 100 hold Readerships or Lectureships.
>
> (Evans-Pritchard 1970: 106, 109; see also 1951, 1959)

While his judgement cannot reasonably be disputed for the immediate post-war period, it was thanks to Oxford's successful export of scholars that by 1970 his confidence was more debatable.

Evans-Pritchard's personality appears to have dominated the Institute, but despite (and also because of) this an enquirer not of the period faces considerable difficulty discovering quite what that personality was. Many reporters of Evans-Pritchard's period seem to discover themselves in their accounts of him, making each the carrier of a uniquely accurate picture. He confided in many people, but did so differently with what his close friend Godfrey Lienhardt was to describe as a 'well-judged intimacy' (Lienhardt 1974: 299). No one seems to have doubted his brilliance, even when he was doing little to demonstrate it. A tendency to intemperate expression in speech and letters, remarkably absent from his academic writings, became more pronounced in his later life. Reporters differently construe his provocations as dogma or guying. Recollections of the later Evans-Pritchard dwell on hours of yarning in Oxford pubs, and on his eccentricities. Yet the post-war Evans-Pritchard, for all that his teaching was so influential, had already committed the greater part of his monumental importance to British anthropology to paper. The greatest books on the Azande and Nuer were written, the field researches completed, and he was entering a different phase of life: centred on Oxford and the Institute, and to bringing up five children, after 1959 as a single parent. Ill-health exacerbated by drink and deafness began to dog his later years. So, part of the Evans-Pritchard myth in British anthropology seems to have been bred by the fact that those who knew him in his later life also knew who and what he had been in earlier life. And, in different ways, this reaching back to an earlier Evans-Pritchard is a theme of both the short book-length accounts of his work that have been published. This is hardly helped by the observation that

> He thought it a duty to adorn a tale before handing it on, and even if one knew better it was usually as well to accept the story as he told it. I

believed for some years on his authority that Franz Steiner had been in such straits when he first came to Britain that he had been forced to earn a living as a table-tennis player in Scotland.

(Lienhardt 1974: 300)

Evans-Pritchard's seminal works, which together had such immense impact on British anthropology, were written by a man in his thirties and early forties, and not by the older Evans-Pritchard of contemporary memory who was already creating his own memorial in anecdote. As Michael Kenny wrote, '[Evans-Pritchard] is still the centre of a rich folklore that helps bind those who perceive themselves to be in some way anthropologists of the Oxford persuasion' (1987: 9). But Evans-Pritchard, like Godfrey Lienhardt, denied there was any such a persuasion, 'we who taught in [the Institute] are always surprised when something called the "Oxford School" of social anthropology is claimed to exist or to have existed' (Lienhardt 1974: 302).[5] To outsiders, particularly those benefiting from hindsight, it is not just clear that such a persuasion did exist, but that denial of its existence was an integral part of the style that presented Oxford self-evidence as reasonable common sense.

If, as Kenny suggests, Evans-Pritchard's students have inclined to finding aspects of themselves reflected in their image of him, this is less of a drawback for my purposes than it would be for a biographer of Evans-Pritchard. As my guide to what Mary Douglas later thought that she had learned from Evans-Pritchard and her time in that brilliant Oxford circle, I shall take her own brief 'Modern Masters' volume on Evans-Pritchard.

MARY DOUGLAS ON EVANS-PRITCHARD

Because this volume was published in 1980, we cannot read it other than as an account of how Mary Douglas (some thirty years later) interpreted in the light of her own development what Mary Tew had previously learnt from Evans-Pritchard. As this tortuous way of putting things suggests, an account which attempted to describe the, as it were, linear progression of Douglas's developing ideas would have to be researched differently from the present one, which incorporates many of the temporal 'loops' of our subject's published recollections. Douglas's account was to be widely criticized by others of Evans-Pritchard's students and colleagues for presenting her own ideas in the guise of his; T.O. Beidelman was the most forthright: 'the figure that here appears is nearly unrecognizable as this reviewer's teacher: instead he turns out to resemble Mary Douglas' (EP/TLS). Mary Douglas's frankness about the status of her account cannot entirely disarm criticism. She forewarns her reader that

this is not a straight summary, and something different from a synthesis. I have made a personal reconstruction upon the writings, forcing them into closer confrontation with problems that were evidently present to Evans-Pritchard but which have become more public and explicit since…While I was pondering how to focus, I realized that a name for his method was missing. A name is a powerful concentrator of ideas. By naming a theory of social accountability, I can show more cogently the methodological advances that can only be built upon his work…The reader will have no difficulty, I hope, in distinguishing the master's original work from the pupil's presentation.

(EP: 11)

John Burton's textually based sequential account of Evans-Pritchard's thought carries the following two epigraphs, from early and late Evans-Pritchard, to its longest chapter 'Ethnography and interpretation': 'My interpretations are contained in the facts themselves, for I have described the facts in such a way that the interpretations emerge as part of the description' (Evans-Pritchard 1937: 5); 'explanation is no more than exact description which bears its own interpretation' (Evans-Pritchard 1973: 764). Explicit theorizing is hardly evident in Evans-Pritchard's ethnographic works (as Douglas also notes), while his later pronouncements, meant for students and the general public, do not directly address the overall programme of research which Douglas identifies as distinctively his. However, if Burton finds the Evans-Pritchard of Douglas's description unconvincingly single-minded over the duration of a long career (1992: 15), he still commends her 'insights and personal knowledge of Evans-Pritchard' (ibid.: 10). Douglas's account, like Burton's, dwells on the period before she knew him in order to foreground Evans-Pritchard's 'solitary confronting, in the 1930s, of intellectual dilemmas' (EP: 11).[6]

Controversially, Douglas begins her book with a discussion of Evans-Pritchard's knowledge by the 1920s of writings in psychology, memory and the selectivity of human attention. By establishing that Evans-Pritchard knew about, or referred to, some of the contemporary literature, Douglas wants to secure, on the one hand, his early commitment to a unified view of human cognition, with no distinction in principle between 'primitive' and 'civilized' varieties of human thought and, on the other hand, his equally strong commitment to demonstrating that apparent differences in human reasoning, memory and attention are to be considered as no more than the effects that differing social institutions have upon the human subjects for whom they furnish both a social background and some of the resources for social interaction. This brief excursus on 'human mental faculties' leads Douglas to the most crucial, and contested, chapter of her account entitled 'The continuity of Evans-Pritchard's programme'. Here she supports her argument that the major works were part of a preconceived plan of research by reference to those three major essays – published in the first three volumes of the *Bulletin of the Faculty of Arts* of the Fuad I University during and after Evans-Pritchard's tenure of a professorship there (1933, 1934, 1936 – largely republished as Evans-Pritchard 1965).[7] Given that Douglas's account emphasizes the importance of Evans-Pritchard's first monographs on both Zande and Nuer, written and partly researched during the same decade (and that she is far more circumspect in dealing with the last major monograph: *Nuer Religion* 1956), the claim of an Evans-Pritchard 'programme', at least during that period, is not as sweeping as it may seem. Through her description of the 'Cairo essays', Mary Douglas outlines how, in her own way, she incorporated many of the most typical features of British anthropology of her time. In what follows, I epitomize Douglas summarizing Evans-Pritchard, leaving arguments about what Evans-Pritchard might have meant to commentators better placed than myself to dispute it.

In his three essays, Evans-Pritchard subjected late nineteenth-century and early twentieth-century anthropological theories of knowledge to rigorous critique. Resolutely rejecting evolutionary models and invidious distinctions between the thought proper to supposedly civilized and primitive peoples, he argued that a general sociology of knowledge would not begin by contrasting civilized science with primitive magic, which were phenomena of different types, but would instead compare the everyday thought common to all societies. In both cases, he argued, following Durkheim and his *Année sociologique* school, that thought is dominated by representations which are collective within society. The anthropologist's task is to investigate the coherence of these collective ideas and their relation to the institutions of the societies in which they occur. The institutional organization of the society, rather than the mentality of any individual, maintains the plausibility of shared ideas. Seen in this light, ideas of the illogical, pre-logical and non-logical have no place in the discussion of primitive mentality. However, this does not mean that the 'mystical' – meaning 'those experiences which the scientific culture cannot include within objective reality' (EP: 35) – are not to be taken as real for those who believe in them, and therefore treated as seriously as non-scientific ideas occurring elsewhere. 'His method of research implicitly anchored each local version of reality to the local system of accountability' (EP: 35). The value of knowledge is not to be found by postulating that it refers to some fixed notion of reality, but rather by seeing how meanings are generated in human interactions by serving particular human ends. People's theoretical curiosity is, therefore, typically related to their social interests in one another (EP: 37).

Although Evans-Pritchard's magisterial study of *Witchcraft, Oracles and Magic among the Azande* (1937) has generated a copious secondary literature, largely dealing with issues of interpretation and rationality, compared with his equally influential *The Nuer* (1940) there is at least a broad consensus about what he argued: discussion has revolved around what later philosophers and anthropologists should quite make of it. *The Nuer*, to which I turn shortly, is a different case because much of its secondary literature argues over what Evans-Pritchard meant to say in the first place. *Witchcraft, Oracles and Magic among the Azande* dealt, as its title suggested, with three subjects that Europeans might associate with fear and irrationality, or superstition. Evans-Pritchard noted that the Zande appeared, so far as he could judge, one of the happiest people of the Sudan, and he set about demonstrating that, granted its basic suppositions, the systematic fashion in which Zande related their ideas of the operations of witchcraft and magic to their ideas about the efficacy of poison oracles, offered a coherent and practically adequate manner of coping with life and the questions it posed. If the researcher conceded (not believed) that witchcraft and magic existed, that they were phenomena of some regularity, and that the poison oracle offered a normally reliable way of finding out about them, then in terms of these concessions he would be able to run his life perfectly adequately *as if* he believed in the presuppositions of Azande thought. However, because the investigator conceded the bases of the system rather than accepted them, he would also note differences between Zande and Western notions. For instance, he would find that Zande tried to explain some things (for instance, why an accident happened to a particular person at a particular time) that Europeans would be liable to dismiss as unlucky coincidence. And in pursuing causality further than Europeans typically did, Zande would be looking for someone to hold responsible for things turning out as they had. This was not irrationality but derived from pursuing a causal sequence that bit further than most Westerners would. Taken in sum, Zande ideas could be led into paradox and contradiction (for instance, holding that the same person necessarily was and was not a witch, depending on the chain of reasoning pursued); but slippage in the overall logic of everyday ideas is not peculiar to African systems of thought. Everyday reasoning goes on in mundane circumstances to address urgent problems; nowhere, as they try to solve immediate issues, do people routinely interrogate the logic of their general conceptions, as if they were detached philosophers. This is so because they are not, anywhere, detached from the social interests of their own everyday lives.

Zande conceded certain questions to specialists, although they also recognized some specialists to be charlatans (some witch doctors faked their procedures), but nowhere – in Africa or Europe – could people reasonably be expected to conclude that the shortcomings of one practitioner undermined the supposition that there was such a thing as professional expertise (analogously the entire medical profession would have to be disestablished in the light of one malpractice suit). When the findings of poison oracles, for instance, were inconsistent, Zande tended to protect the premises of their way of thinking by appeal to what Evans-Pritchard borrowed a term from psychoanalysis to label 'secondary elaborations'. These 'secondary elaborations' explained why well-tried practices occasionally delivered unconvincing results. In the case of the poison oracle, Zande recognized that the poison might become ineffective under some circumstances and that the entire procedure of consultation might be tampered with intentionally. Again, the recognition that one consultation had gone awry encouraged them to exercise particular vigilance over their technical procedures and to ascertain the causes of error in the particular case, but it did not persuade them to abandon belief in poison oracles. Indeed, it would have been no more rational for them to have done so than for a scientist to abandon well-tested procedures in the light of a single aberrant experiment. Over several hundred pages, Evans-Pritchard argued – in ways only suggested here – that it was not human rationality that varied across cultures but the presuppositions for thinking rationally, and the institutional contexts within which such thinking occurred.

Douglas generalized from this that the presuppositions and social contexts of shared ideas become visible to outside observers when people are held responsible for misfortune happening to themselves or someone else. Different types of social accountability typically occur, and reliably characterize, different social systems and allow them to be compared:

> the essential point for comparison is that at which people meet misfortune. They may accuse others, they may accept responsibility. They count different kinds of misfortune as needing explanation. As they work their ideas of blame and compensation into their social institutions, they invoke existences and powers that are adapted to each particular accounting system.
>
> (EP: 12)

For Mary Douglas, the revolutionary impact of Evans-Pritchard's first book on the Azande lay in its demonstration that Zande could behave rationally while never sustainedly questioning the nexus of misfortune and culpability articulated in their acceptance that witchcraft and magic were abroad in the world. The Cairo essays, and the Azande book with its explicitly theorized argument, so obviously belong to a single period of Evans-Pritchard's writing when he addressed a clearly specified set of problems, that – while Douglas may have drawn from his argument conclusions about comparison not to be found in the original, or allowed Evans-Pritchard undue originality – it is unreasonable to argue a gross difference of spirit between the two.

Turning to Evans-Pritchard's major writings on the Nuer, it is much easier to argue that Douglas's recension has a selective and somewhat reinterpreting relation to the original. In terms of her thesis about the 'continuity' of Evans-Pritchard's programme of research, Mary Douglas needs to read the Nuer corpus as an elaboration of themes in the work published during the 1930s. However, commentators who believe Evans-Pritchard to have pursued a gradually changing set of interests would argue instead that the Nuer books address issues somewhat different from the Azande works and that, in particular, *Witchcraft, Oracles and Magic among the Azande* (1937) and *Nuer Religion* (1956) are books written by rather different men. To support this, they might point to the enormous impact Evans-Pritchard acknowledges his Nuer experiences had upon his own life, and to the fact that – however much his conversion to Roman Catholicism might have been more process than event – *Nuer Religion* is recognizably a more theologically inspired work than its predecessor by almost two decades on the 'mystical' side of Zande life. At base, one also senses different reactions to these two Sudanese peoples – who have furnished anthropology with such strongly contrasted exemplars – on the part of the teacher and his pupil. Mary Douglas is extremely sensitive to the impact that an egalitarian, proud and self-reliant people made upon the anthropologist whom she has admired above all others, but one cannot but feel that, for her part, she would have been far more at home as a fieldworker among the hierarchy, courts, intrigues and authority of the Zandeland Evans-Pritchard describes.

Evans-Pritchard's book on *Nuer Religion*, for which the author 'refreshed his knowledge of Greek philosophy, returned to the divinity books of his parsonage home, re-read the Bible, consulted Hebrew scholars, and generally ransacked the resources of his own culture to the best of his ability' (EP: 89), poses Mary Douglas problems of interpretation with which she deals gently. For instance, the chapter of her book immediately following that devoted to 'Nuer Religion' – in what is, after all, a brief account of Evans-Pritchard's work – devotes several pages to a description of the neighbouring Dinka written by Evans-Pritchard's colleague and confidant Godfrey Lienhardt. In effect, Douglas seems to be saying that what Evans-Pritchard set out to do in *Nuer Religion* was better realized by Lienhardt in *Divinity and Experience: the Religion of the Dinka* (1961). This plotting of Douglas's account reinforces her endorsement of early Evans-Pritchard in his entirety and of later Evans-Pritchard with a more selective eye. Commentators seeking to characterize a unitary Oxford Catholic style of anthropology might find this surprising, since *Nuer Religion* is usually taken to be the most theological, and least sociological, of Evans-Pritchard's monographs. I return to this issue in the concluding chapter, but for now note both that many distinctively Oxford anthropologists were not Catholics (recognizably, Oxford anthropology could be called a 'polythetic category', to borrow a term from one of its distinguished non-religious exponents, Needham (1975)), and that the relationship between an author's Catholicism and his or her writings is quite variable: especially between cradle Catholics (like Douglas) and converts (like Evans-Pritchard and a majority of the Catholic Oxford anthropologists). There is really no contradiction that the work generally thought to be Evans-Pritchard's most 'Catholic' causes Mary Douglas most misgivings.

'Equivalent to the Azande theory of witchcraft, the Nuer theory of sin is the touchstone of reality to which all their legal fictions relate' (EP: 71). In this single deft move, Mary Douglas sets about contextualizing those elements of Evans-Pritchard's Nuer trilogy which can be seen to continue his 1930s 'programme'. With scant justice to Mary's subtlety in this respect, I shall characterize her discussion under two headings: 'contrasts' and 'developments'. To take the contrasts first: Nuer could be typified in terms of their different biases in social accountability. If, for Zande, blame typically attached itself to others, the Nuer seemed to look to themselves for blame, and they were sure to find fault with themselves because of the complexity of the circumstances, many unavoidable, under which they could fall into a state that Evans-Pritchard translated as 'sin'. By contrast to the Zande, the egalitarian Nuer recognized that 'God' was singular in some fundamental respect, but also known to them through a multiplicity of refractions. Nuer individualism, self-reliance and absence of deference correlated with the fact that each of them was responsible for a personal relationship with God. Nuer seemed somehow 'more abstract' than Azande (EP: 62). Their social institutions and political system, theories of sin and of God, and their personal qualities could thus be represented interdependently, just as the same representation could be made of the very different Azande.

Most of the 'developments' in Evans-Pritchard's 'programme' are outlined in a chapter devoted to 'Reasoning and memory' which draws upon the Nuer trilogy as a whole. The subject of the chapter is, in short, the structuring of social consciousness and of social oblivion. Nuer are well known to anthropologists for the 'bovine' idiom of their social relationships. Evans-Pritchard's witticism was intended to summarize the sense in which all important relationships between people, which might be described in terms of kinship and affinity, could also be described in terms of the exchanges of cattle they necessitated. Cattle were not just one important source of Nuer livelihood, and a major determinant of how they lived (for instance in their enforced seasonal transhumance), but a crucial cultural value – a source of pride, joy, poetry, violence and much else. The result of the centrality of cattle – their care and their exchange – was that it made scant difference if an analysis of Nuer society started from the people or the beasts, because the changing relations and physical movement of one correlated relatively exactly with actual movement, or the promise of movement, of the other. Relations between cattle and people functioned as mnemonics: whatever could be remembered about one could be applied to the other. Thus, more complexly than I have indicated, the structuring of consciousness about relations between people was inseparable from its bovine idiom of expression; and the equation could be turned around to envisage relations between cattle in a human idiom.

Moving from memory to forgetfulness as aspects of a single issue, Mary Douglas dwells upon the central chapter of *The Nuer*, which is a celebrated teaching text in anthropology (and for many commentators the textual pivot of the monograph), because of its demonstration of the way the larger categories of time and space for Nuer are intimately related to classification of their social relationships with one another. Again, to understate the complexity of the relations involved, imagine people living in local groups which tend to be described as if they were made up of the descendants of a common ancestor in the patriliny or agnatically (that is, in terms exclusively of descent through men). Evidently if places are associated with agnatically defined groupings, then space and people are susceptible to description in terms of one another. Spatial distribution can be seen as a reflex of social categorization and vice versa. Thus, in important respects the complexity of spatial discrimination corresponds to the complexity of social distinctions relevant to a particular situation. Imagine further, in order to get the gist of how time can be fitted into this scheme, that we know that the depth of the patrilineal genealogies people use – when reckoning descent or territory – remains much the same. Given that people have continued to be born and die, there must be ways of forgetting about some of them so that the genealogy does not grow in depth. Why should this occur? It is not just a function of memory, because we know that societies without literacy vary greatly in the extent of genealogical recall that sometimes most people, sometimes just people with recognized ability in this respect, reveal to ethnographers. Instead, the extent of genealogical memory has to be accounted for in terms of the uses of this kind of social memory. If one of these uses is to provide an adequate description of the territory in which people live, then the genealogy requires only sufficient steps to discriminate the territorial divisions relevant to the categories of people who live in them. Social categorizations, spatial discriminations and ideas of time (or some aspects of all these) find their logic only in mutual relation. No ethnographer could hope to explain one of the three without recourse to the other two.

Now to anticipate a problem: what this analysis demonstrates (and I have simplified the ethnography and made the connections more functional than Evans-Pritchard did in order to get to this underlying point rapidly) is that there is coherence between spatial, temporal and social conceptions (or some aspects of these that we have chosen to highlight); we have not yet learnt anything about causal relations between our terms of reference. Specifically, we do not know how the correspondences came to be as they seem, and we do not know about causal relations among elements in correspondence once their relations are established (i.e. what is the effect of changing social composition, or new ideas of territoriality or of time?). Perhaps most damagingly for any theory of, say, sociological determination, we have not sorted out whether there is any sense in which it is useful to characterize these hypotheses about conceptual interrelatedness *as* causal. I introduce this caveat now, because there was a recurrent tendency in post-war British anthropology of, broadly, Durkheimian inspiration to slip from relatively weak statements (about the mutual implications of concepts) to much stronger positions (often phrased as sociological determinism or social constructivism) without addressing all the questions that were begged in doing so – questions about the status and explanatory role of social context. Returning from intellectual forays outside conventional anthropology, Mary Douglas's later work returned time and again to formulations of how such a move might be made (Chapter 10). I mention this now not just to flag a future concern but also to emphasize that there is nothing incidental about the recurrence of these linked problems; they are intrinsic to the elements she chose to draw from Evans-Pritchard and Durkheim when making the connections between forms of social life, cognition and morality the concerns of her life's work. We can plausibly motivate her choice of this cluster of concerns in Mary Tew's background – at least so far as this is ever plausible – but translated into an academic agenda it has intrinsic difficulties (not exceptionally knotty ones, of course, but nonetheless different from the problems another programme would have posed).

Mary Douglas adopted from Evans-Pritchard some of the characteristics quintessential of British social anthropology in Africa during the two decades after World War II – its concern with social structure, and with social structure especially insofar as it concerned the formation of groups, and with groups insofar as they took the form of lineages, etc. But she might as easily have absorbed these concerns from Evans-Pritchard's predecessor Radcliffe-Brown, or from the Africanist Meyer Fortes who taught at Oxford while she was a student there. There was a strong elective affinity between the concern for corporate groups in the British anthropology of Africa (easily the most important ethnographic region of the period) and some of the ways in which African peoples conceptualize their membership of groups – as if such groups were realizations of descent through their fathers or mothers, or both. Without this overriding focus, later ethnographers of Africa would not have devoted such attention to unpacking some of the different elements of the idea of the descent group in order to distinguish, for instance, between notions of procreation, gender and descent, patterns of recruitment and residence, and activities actually pursued jointly. Nor would they have realized by doing this quite how complicated such relations are.

General concern with social structure, and with problems of social solidarity, was a crucial feature of one reading that British anthropologists, especially those influenced by Radcliffe-Brown, made of Durkheim's sociology. Questions about groups – their boundaries, solidarity and definition – might have been particularly conducive to Mary given her school experience of an enclosed and minutely regulated world at the Sacred Heart. Twenty years later, a dimension called 'group' was to feature as one of two axes of her sociological theory. The second dimension, or axis, of the theory which she called grid was to be redefined frequently, but 'group' would remain recognizably tied to an original conception indebted to the general climate of ideas in post-war social anthropology. The other reading of Durkheim that informs her work (a reading that sees Durkheimian sociology as a sociology of knowledge) was less widely shared and more definitely attributable to Evans-Pritchard than to his predecessor. Much of her later work concerns how to make a Durkheimian sociology of 'groupiness' and a Durkheimian sociology of knowledge, as it were, speak to one another.

THE OXFORD INSTITUTE OF SOCIAL ANTHROPOLOGY

Listening to senior members of the profession who were at Oxford after World War II, one senses that the worst handicap in that brilliant circle was to have been ordinary. An older friend, who would not I think be offended by a description as an ordinary person – liberal, agnostic, intelligent, middle-class in an unmarked way – confesses to wondering quite what he was doing among so many brilliant and eccentric people and mostly listening in the hope of understanding what was going on around him. Thanks to the interruptions of war service, the postgraduate students and new staff were both older and more widely experienced and tested, physically and emotionally, than would be found in Britain, and probably most other places, today. As noted earlier, their origins and backgrounds were diverse: there were representatives, in its final moments, from the English-speaking Empire and Dominions (India, South Africa, Australia), from North America, from the European mainland displaced by war, returned prisoners of war; and there was Evans-Pritchard himself, fresh from his war service and already the author of seminal works of twentieth-century anthropology. The members of the department shared the war experience; many had campaigned, commanded and taken life and death decisions. Several of them also shared membership of the Roman Catholic Church. The presence of other Catholics at Oxford was one of many factors that persuaded Mary to pursue postgraduate studies with her war veteran's grant there. But unlike the many members of the Institute who were Catholic converts (Evans-Pritchard himself, Godfrey and Peter Lienhardt, David Pocock among others), Mary was born into the Catholic Church. Contemporary witnesses insist that there was no Catholic clique at Oxford, nor does it make sense to talk of a particular Catholic brand of anthropology. Other members of the Institute were Jews, though not all religious Jews (Fortes and Gluckman were not religious, Steiner was intensely so); Srinivas was a Brahman. Catholicism was not irrelevant, but it was an aspect of a broader outlook which rejected the straitjacketing of interests to a canon of self-consciously anthropological books and ideas. Evans-Pritchard introduced students to the anthropology of religion through the work of Robertson Smith and did much to enhance the reputation of the Scottish student of religions (Steiner 1956; Beidelman 1974; Evans-Pritchard 1981; cf. Douglas 1995g, 1996g). The Old Testament was considered a good source of examples for anthropologists, and one Mary Douglas was to use frequently. I suspect Mary Douglas had such as Evans-Pritchard and Godfrey Lienhardt in mind when she wrote in *Natural Symbols* about the members of the Oxford Movement in the nineteenth century who left the Church of England to embrace an ultramontane form of Catholicism and the saving experience of a 'real Holy Communion', and for whom:

> Conversion was not submission to an intellectual yoke, but a bid for autonomy…characteristic of intelligentsia and academics who in no way intend to give up their intellectual discourse. Where[as]…unritual-istic forms of revivalism tend to carry rejection of discriminating form and categories into intellectual life, to foreshorten their interest in history, to restrict their reading to the sacred book, and to limit the organization of their thought to correspond to the limited organization of their groups.

(NS1: 146)

John Burton quotes Godfrey Lienhardt's recollection of a conversation with Evans-Pritchard to remarkably similar effect:

> he [E-P] had mentioned that 'only in the Catholic Church could one find freedom of thought, since only those who knew what it was to affirm belief in so much knew what scepticism really could be'.
>
> (Burton 1992: 21; internal quote from Lienhardt 1974: 403)

And Evans-Pritchard culminated his 1959 Aquinas Lecture:

> The majority of anthropologists are indifferent, if not hostile to religion…and a minority are Christians…of the Christians, a considerable proportion are Catholics…it would seem to be a general tendency of our times…that Protestantism shades into Deism and Deism into agnosticism, and that the choice is between all or nothing, a choice which allows of no compromise between a Church which has stood its ground and made no concessions, and no religion at all.
>
> (Evans-Pritchard 1962: 45)

The Catholicism of Evelyn Waugh, Graham Greene, or of their, roughly speaking, contemporaries both in the Oxford Institute and elsewhere in British anthropology (notably, one thinks of Victor Turner) was – among much else – an aesthetic choice, a refinement of the person and judgement. Thus, the argument that for anthropologists to write sympathetically of religion, or as importantly of doubt and scepticism, it helped for them to know the state of belief at first hand. But in this company, for all the echoes of Evans-Pritchard's intransigence in *Natural Symbols*, Mary's cradle Catholicism was different. Converts often tend to disparage the religiosity of Catholics born in the faith; she devoted a chapter of *Natural Symbols* to the defence of the London 'Bog Irish', and the whole book indicted the gulf between intellectually motivated Catholic reformers and the beliefs of their flock. Mary's Catholicism may be aesthetic but it was also supported by loyalty to the institutions which had brought her up as a Catholic, that it is to say by a deeper sense of commitment to a group than to her personal or biographical development. The difference is clear when she prefers to relate religious belief to the experience of action within an institutional order (like Robertson Smith or Durkheim), rather than to the coherence of ideals. The diversity of Catholics is a cogent reason to be sceptical of the idea of a specifically Catholic anthropology; but it is not a reason to ignore the coherence between particular authors' anthropological writings and religious experience.

The religious experience of the members of the Oxford Institute, and their common experience of war, go some way to explaining a shared antipathy to the conceptions of human nature typical of some functionalist anthropology. There seems to be hubris – I think the word is appropriate – in claiming too much of

43

anthropology, or of social science more generally. There is so much one person cannot know about another, as Evans-Pritchard insists in *Nuer Religion*. The sentiment is not Evans-Pritchard's only:

> I have always been very conscious of the fact that modern academic anthropology is only one variant of the many anthropologies and that the very word, as a complement to theology, has a much older history and invites a much wider field of speculation than most of our colleagues seem to know.

(Jonathan Benthall 1990, quoting from a letter to him from David Pocock in October 1990)

Yet, again, Mary Douglas seems to be different. To take up the terms of my last chapter, although her cultural imagination might have been attuned to the humanist concerns developing in the post-war Institute of Anthropology, her sociological imagination was furnished by a much harder-edged Durkheimianism than was to flourish there.

Of all the Oxford anthropologists, Mary Douglas has most explicitly contributed both to anthropology and to theology – not questioning the division of labour between the two but stressing the contribution that an anthropological method might make towards reformulating the problems of theology in comparative terms, and showing how anthropologists can contribute to reading Biblical sources as cultural texts. This, of course, was how Robertson Smith scandalized the authorities of the church in Scotland. However, of all the Oxford anthropologists she eventually writes least about the mystery each of us remains to all others, or of the proper humility anthropologists ought to feel before the ultimate inscrutability of people's desires or the societies they create in the hope of realizing some of them. Mary Douglas has consistently been a constructor rather than deconstructor, a system-builder and not a systematic sceptic, a consistent believer in the ability of the social sciences to make progress and tackle problems that had once seemed unresolvable – how often does her writing include passages to the effect of 'if only Durkheim and Quine (or other favoured thinkers) could have enjoyed a few hours' discussion, then surely they would have put their heads together and unblocked one another's thinking in important respects'? (cf. Sperber TLS/IM). Such faith in progress may seem naive in circles where irony, detachment, and maybe even world-weariness, are the signs of intellectual sophistication. There is little enough satisfaction seeing the ironically detached overreach themselves and come to grief; and it is unlikely they would put themselves in such a position, or that we would be able to recognize the pratfall when it happened. Mary Douglas prefers to – probably cannot do other than – take huge intellectual risks (on occasions with no evidence of doing so consciously), trample disciplinary boundaries as if she hadn't noticed them, remain stubbornly optimistic about the prospects for grand theory building, and generally set about the business of explaining the world in which we live to anyone who cares to listen with an energy and commitment that age has only reinforced; I doubt that Geertz's characterization of her as a 'lapel-grabber' would distress her (NR/HIT): if you have something to say then by all means demand attention for it.

The older Mary Douglas probably idealizes Mary Tew's years at Oxford. This amounts to rather more than a common human tendency to look back fondly on times when we were younger; it involves a sense, perhaps for the last time in her long career, of really feeling that she belonged among fellow anthropologists. I doubt whether staying at Oxford would have made a difference. In terms of her own rather rosy picture of how a hierarchy should work, if you are young, content to be on a bottom rung, well treated by superiors whom you acknowledge as such with respect, and reasonably confident in your ability to mount the rungs as time goes by, then it's not so bad to feel yourself a small cog in a grand machine. This is not to say that the same feeling would have survived the passing years. For all that Mary enjoyed excellent personal relations with many of the scholars who were prominent in Oxford during the decades of the 1960s and 1970s, it is not easy to imagine how her system-building anthropology would have fitted with an Oxford style that was, in short, deconstructive *avant la lettre*. In her assessment, Oxford became increasingly 'idealist' after Evans-Pritchard's retirement; and 'idealist' is a sharply barbed term in the Douglas vocabulary.

In the next chapter, I shall explore Mary's ethnographic writings on the Lele, after which I follow her to University College in London where, after a relatively quiet decade intellectually speaking, when academic life had to compete with domestic obligations, she was to find herself among other system-builders – albeit builders of systems with different design specifications from her own.

Notes

1 A line consistent with that of Louis Dumont in the preface to the French translation of *The Nuer*, an essay Mary and James Douglas were later to translate into English (1975d).

2 Beidelman describes his similar relation to Evans-Pritchard, which may explain in some part the proprietorial quality of his reaction to Douglas's account (Beidelman 1974b).

3 Here and hereafter I draw for the main upon Burton (1992) and Beidelman (1974a, 1974b).

4 Details can be found in the *University Gazette* for the relevant years.

5 In a hitherto unpublished address on 'Superstition', Franz Steiner used the phrase 'the Oxford School' of Radcliffe-Brown's Institute as early as 1944 (forthcoming in Steiner 1999, vol. 1).

6 Most reviewers recognized Douglas's account as a formalization of Evans-Pritchard's years prior to his taking the Oxford chair (EP/Anth; EP/JHBS). Concern with omission of extended reference to Malinowski and Radcliffe-Brown, in comparison with others who influenced Evans-Pritchard's work in that earlier period (EP/AA; EP/NS), was matched by criticism of her account of tendencies in the later work. Douglas exercises judicious discretion about the breakdown in relations between

Evans-Pritchard and Radcliffe-Brown over the scientific or humanist character of anthropology (EP/NS; see also Goody 1995; Kuper 1996: 124–26), which Adler and Fardon argue is a crucial context of Franz Steiner's concern, in his Oxford lectures, with the status of comparison in anthropology (forthcoming, 1999). And she has little to say about Evans-Pritchard's related, but it must be admitted scarcely incisive, promotion of the similarities between history and anthropology (EP/IJAHS).

7 E.R. Leach devoted close attention to the dates and intellectual origins of the 'Cairo essays', noting that their agenda corresponds closely to a course outline composed by Malinowski to which Evans-Pritchard lectured at the LSE in 1931–32, and which in turn appears to have been related to the lecture series Evans-Pritchard delivered in Cairo in the following academic year – these being the basis of his published essays. Furthermore, Leach contends – on the evidence of the literature cited – that the essays were likely to have been published later than their dates suggest. '[I]n 1973 E-P, while reiterating his almost paranoid dislike of Malinowski, nevertheless declared that "I learnt more from him than from anyone else" ' (EP/LRB).

3 THE AFRICANIST: 1950s

BIOGRAPHICAL COUNTERPOINT

Evans-Pritchard scotched Mary Tew's ambition to continue her 'European' education – interrupted by her undergraduate PPE degree and war service – through ethnographic fieldwork in Italy or Greece. Africa was the place to go. She did not regret his insistence: as she later saw it, Africa required theoretical rigour, but an anthropology of the Mediterranean did not yet exist, and fieldwork there, she feels, would probably have led her to become a journalist. Why Africa?

The tendency of each period of social anthropology to locate its most pressing problems in particular areas of the world derives from a convergence of factors: theoretical agenda, accessibility, critical mass of scholarship, fundability, academic patronage, and institutional entrenchment among them. Mid-century British anthropology was overwhelmingly Africa-centred: colonized Africa was accessible and relatively safe; a majority of the senior British anthropologists had interests there (including Malinowski in his later career); the Rockefeller Foundation, and a government occasionally convinced that anthropology might usefully be applied, supplied funding (Kuklick 1991; Goody 1995); moreover, the Oxford Institute was institutional base to several of the most successful of Africanist fieldworkers. Their body of research and writing had established an agenda of research topics and a set of precedents for examining them. By the end of the 1940s these topics included kinship and marriage, residence patterns, political organization and economic life. Religion and symbolism were upcoming subjects in Britain. At Oxford, Mary heard Evans-Pritchard and Fortes on kinship and marriage among the Nuer and Tallensi (her own BSc library dissertation was written on marriage); Evans-Pritchard had embarked on the series of papers that would become *Nuer Religion* (1956), and he lectured on Nuer sacrifice; Fortes was working on Tallensi ancestral cults (IM: 204). It was relatively clear what fieldwork in Africa would involve; precedents for a Mediterranean anthropology were, as yet, wanting.[1]

The major breakthroughs in understanding patrilineal systems, at least so it seemed to Mary Tew, had recently been made by Evans-Pritchard's and Fortes' works on the Nuer and Tallensi, and in their pre-war collaborative editing of *African Political Systems* (1940). The unanswered questions concerned matrilineal systems, on which considerable research was under-way in central Africa by scholars predominantly affiliated to the Rhodes–Livingstone Institute in Northern Rhodesia, which Gluckman had lately left to come to Oxford (Werbner 1990). Mary Douglas rejects the notion that an even proto-feminist position underlay her decision to research among a matrilineal people (this position was hardly thinkable by the late 1940s); her choice was theoretically motivated within the developing terms of an Africanist anthropological agenda. Having rejected possible fieldwork among two patrilineal peoples, she looked for a fundable research opportunity in a matrilineal society. Selling her mother's fur coat to raise the fare, in 1948 she attended the International Congress of Anthropological and Ethnological Sciences in Brussels where she met Georges Brausch, a Belgian colonial officer (on whom, see Vansina 1987: 439).[2] Hearing she was looking for a 'romantic' and 'untouched' people, preferably matrilineal, and bearing in mind Evans-Pritchard's warning that she had better not get sick lest she prevent other women from gaining permission to do fieldwork,[3] Brausch suggested the Lele: they lived on deforested, rolling hills, a thousand metres up, between the rivers Loange and Kasai of the Belgian Congo in central Africa; the climate was healthy, the communications relatively good, the people 'properly pacified', and they were matrilineal, painted themselves red with camwood and used bows and arrows. Given what she was looking for, the Lele sounded ideal. The International African Institute was able to supply a fellowship to defray the costs of research. So with some linguistic training from Belgian experts and an Oxford BSc in anthropology under her belt, Mary was ready for fieldwork, which she carried out between 1949–50 and again, after submitting her doctorate, in 1953.

With the benefit of hindsight, Mary Douglas's writings between 1950–65 can be seen to foreshadow interests that were to dominate her later years. But, had she ceased to write in 1965, the profile of her published works would have been indistinguishable from that of a professional Africanist ethnographer (of whom there were many at the time) doing what was expected of her: turning out a couple of well-honed ethnographic articles a year and reviewing the literature on her region for specialist journals, completing her monograph, then moving on to comparative regional studies. This pattern was established in 1951, the year she moved to University College London from Oxford University, where she had occupied a lectureship for only a year under the Committee for Colonial Studies. Evans-Pritchard was displeased and tersely recorded that 'in 1951…Miss Tew also left (to get married)' (1970: 105). Her marriage was to James A.T. Douglas (b. 1919), a civil servant between 1940–50, who had just joined the Conservative Party Research Department as an economist. The first of their children (Janet) was born in 1951, and their sons (James and Philip) in 1954 and 1956. These were years of relative stability. In 1956, they moved to the family house where they still live, in a private estate on the slopes of Highgate Hill, an upper middle-

Photograph 7 Centre: the ethnographer in front of her hut; quadrants: fieldwork among
  the Lele

class area of north London that is topped by the imposing cupola of St Joseph's Catholic church. James's background was similar to Mary's in many respects: like her, his Englishness came from his father and his Catholicism from his mother; and the families belonged to the same Anglo-Indian world. James Douglas's father had been in the Indian Army before serving in France during the First World War, where he married a French woman, Marie-Louise Gorisse-Dollez.[4] Generations of Douglases had been educated at major public schools, followed by Oxbridge, and went on to become military officers or Church of England clerics. James was born in India and brought up, after his father retired in 1922, in Paris. His knowledge of economics, immersion in issues of policy, bilingualism and wide curiosity outside academia complemented Mary's more academic leanings and constantly provoked her to look beyond the limitations of the conventional anthropology of her period.

Mary Douglas recalls being happiest at University College during the almost twenty years when Daryll Forde was head of department.[5] As her first publication, she had already contributed a volume to the east–central survey of the project of comparative colonial ethnography in Africa that Forde was editing (1950a). Director of the International African Institute, he encouraged her to publish and review in the Institute's journal *Africa*, which carried the majority of her ethnographic articles[6] or in the even more specialized journal *Zaire*.[7] She contributed a chapter on Lele religion (1954b) to *African Worlds*, a collection of articles on African cosmologies edited by Forde (one of several influential collections on aspects of African life co-authored by Africanist anthropologists in the quarter century after 1940),[8] and they shared an interest in economics (e.g. Douglas and Forde 1956a). With another long-time colleague, Phyllis Kaberry, Mary was to co-edit *Man in Africa* (1969a), the collection of essays that honoured Daryll Forde's retirement from the University College professorship. Civil war in the Belgian Congo (on which she co-authored a pamphlet with Daniel Biebuyck (1961a)) broke out in 1959 and prevented further return trips after 1953 and before completion of her corpus of Lele writings a decade later. She was not to visit independent Zaire until 1987 when she was well into her sixties (1989a).

At the beginning of the 1960s, a fellowship from the Leverhulme Research Awards Committee, and a year-long leave of absence from University College, allowed Mary time to pull together the numerous essays she had written on the Lele during the preceding decade and complete *The Lele of Kasai* (LK 1963a). Publication of her major monograph, the disciplinary rite of passage into professional majority, proved to be a turning point in her interests that I describe in the next chapter. After *The Lele of Kasai* was published, she ceased to be a conventional British Africanist of her time, a fact reflected not just in her essays but also in her book reviews.

Unlike some senior anthropologists, Mary Douglas has felt it a professional duty throughout her career to find time to review the books of fellow scholars. She has always reviewed selectively, concentrating on works germane to her current interests, but these interests became increasingly inclusive over the years.

Douglas's reviews are usually a good indication of the current intensity and future direction of her writing. In the run-up to writing *The Lele of Kasai*, she reviewed a clutch of books on the Belgian Congo (1956b, 1960c, 1962c,d, 1963d,e,f,g,h,i,j), and assiduously followed works on central and southern Africa which at this time were dominated by the writings of Max Gluckman's 'Manchester School' – consisting both of scholars working in that university's Department of Anthropology and the 'old boys' (and girls) of the Rhodes–Livingstone Institute and Manchester University.[9] Her relations with the Manchester School were intellectually cordial but not uninterruptedly happy in personal terms. She was impressed by their use of statistical methods and detailed extended case studies – methods she incorporated, as she was able, into her own work – and excited by the cyclical character of witchcraft accusations which they were able to demonstrate corresponded to stages in the growth and break-up of central African villages. However, one of her reviews occasioned an acrimonious exchange of opinion in print with Max Gluckman whom she found an unattractive and domineering personality – a view he seems to have reciprocated. Although her reviews of their work were usually generous, and she particularly admired Clyde Mitchell's writings on the Yao, when her Lele monograph was published it went unreviewed by any member of the Manchester School. Whether pointed or not, this oversight could hardly fail to seem so when she had absorbed their methods to the point of virtually addressing her book to them.

A third cluster of reviews, somewhat overlapping the first, positioned her handily to comment on relations between English and French anthropological traditions when the somewhat belated impact of structuralism broke on British shores in the 1960s. At the time when Mary Tew carried out fieldwork, it was unusual for Africanist ethnographers of the British or French schools not to carry out research in their national colonies. If *The Lele of Kasai* never quite became the ethnographic 'standard' or 'classic' some reviewers anticipated it might (Kuper LK/AS: 135; Vansina LK/JAH: 142) this may be because, at least in Britain, it fitted ill into courses designed to teach areas of Africa extensively documented in English. Douglas's closest 'neighbours' as ethnographers were the Belgian scholars Luc de Heusch and Jan Vansina, both of whom reviewed her book favourably (de Heusch (1981) [1964] in the form of a reanalysis of her materials I discuss later). In addition to repaying their courtesy,[10] Douglas extensively reviewed the French language tradition of ethnography (of which de Heusch rather than Vansina was representative). She became fascinated by the contrast between the 'sociological', British approach to African ethnography and, what she saw as, the 'idealistic' methodology typical of Marcel Griaule's African ethnography (1958b) and expressed in his team's Dogon researches in West Africa (1967b,h, 1968c,d). Her early, intransigent criticism – later moderated – of Lévi-Strauss's structuralism stemmed from seeing it as a culmination of the least desirable features in this French tradition (1967d, 1970d). Douglas's familiarity with French theoretical works extended beyond structuralism to the dynamic functionalism of Georges Balandier (1965a) and the neo-Marxism of Claude Meillassoux (1970j) and, critical or not, this interest in mediating Anglo-French traditions made her an important representative of British anthropology whose later marginalization in Britain struck continental observers forcibly (de Heusch 1996).

That the publication of *The Lele* went relatively unnoticed in British anthropology reinforced feelings of marginality and undervaluation Douglas felt on various grounds. Ignored by British central Africanists because she wrote on a francophone area of Africa, she imagined she was not widely read by the French because her writings were in English. Although Catholics had been numerous at Oxford, Daryll Forde, himself an atheist, found the idea of a Catholic anthropologist distinctly odd. Her commitments to home and family severely curtailed the time she could devote to the university, and she felt marginal to the department. The University College department was small in those days – taking about twelve undergraduates a year, and a couple of postgraduates who would be supervised by Daryll Forde. Her colleagues were predominantly Africanists: initially including Phyllis Kaberry, Peter Morton-Williams and Ray Bradbury, later Robin Horton and John Middleton. So it was after Forde's retirement, and with expansion of the department, that her sense of marginality troubled her more.

THE LELE BOOK

Ethnographic conventions

The Lele of Kasai was neither unusual for being published a decade after Mary Douglas finished her fieldwork nor for its method of composition by compilation. Ethnographers frequently wrote up their material first in the form of a doctorate, then by publishing accounts of its particular aspects as journal articles addressing theoretical problems, and finally by compiling and integrating their previous writings into a standard monograph. Evans-Pritchard himself endorsed the piecemeal publication of essays prior to their collection in monograph form. In the less successful outcomes, the 'cracks' between the chapters clearly betrayed their origin as distinct essays. The most successful, including Douglas's Lele book, integrated previously published materials around an argument sustained throughout the volume so that the monograph benefited both from its coherence as a whole and from the intensively worked-up character of its parts. I can deal only with the overall argument of Douglas's monograph here. However, this will still involve us in a careful reading of the volume to allow the non-anthropologist reader to sense how complex an achievement an ethnographic monograph is, and why ethnographic resolution to a decade and a half of the most vigorous years of a life exercises such profound effect on an anthropologist's subsequent sense of sociological problem-solving.

Ethnographies of the period attracted broad anthropological readership (outside the narrow range of area specialists who felt obliged to read everything on their region) by seeming exemplary and imitable in some general way. As Jan Vansina has noted, modern ethnographies distinguished themselves from earlier ethnographic accounts and travelogues because their selection of facts was governed by the need to make a more or less explicit theoretical argument (Vansina 1987: 434). The volumes of Daryll Forde's monumental project, the International African Institute's *Ethnographic Survey of Africa* (to which, as I noted, Douglas contributed), never achieved wide use as teaching materials in anthropology because, in some respects, their conventions were already anachronistic. The survey volumes drew upon uneven existing reports to supply ethnographic detail to accompany a map of the peoples each volume covered. The map showed relatively bounded peoples, while the text explained what was known about them and what remained to be discovered. As much as a compendium of knowledge, the survey volumes were a catalogue of absences and a wish-list for future research. Modern ethnographies shared the convention of presenting people as bounded, but did so from a presumption of cultural intimacy on the part of the ethnographer. One effect of this concatenation of generic features (cultural intimacy, facts selected to present an anthropological argument, and a convention of tribal boundedness) was that the ethnographic description of a people and the anthropological argument they exemplified tended to merge, even to the point of slight caricature. Evans-Pritchard's depictions of haughty egalitarian Nuer and the problems of understanding their uncentralized political organization and relations before God, or of the wily Azande, and the rationality of their manipulation of poison oracles, are examples that would have been familiar to Douglas, and their influence is evident. Wittingly or not, the strategy is reproduced in many Oxford-inspired monographs to provide the reader anthropological problems with a human face. Douglas's opening introduces us to the Lele in a well-honed example of the style:

> This is primarily a study of authority – or rather of its failure. Those who have had anything to do with Lele must have noticed the absence of anyone who could give orders with a reasonable hope of being obeyed. They are not aggressive individualists refusing the right of others to command [like Nuer, RF]. On the contrary, Lele manners are humorously modest rather than self-assertive. Authority is supposed to reside with the senior person present in any situation. In practice, the senior receives deference, but not power. The lack of authority goes a long way to explain their poverty. By their own standards the Lele are poorer than their neighbours. Their soil is admittedly less fertile, but a lack of enthusiasm for cultivating it is also evident. Other projects engross them more than the creation of wealth. Second, therefore, this is a study in economic backwardness.
>
> (LK: 1)

This passage opens an eight-page thumbnail sketch of the people prefacing the book. The approach is explicitly comparative: the failure of authority is apparent relative to the small Lunda-ized chiefdoms of the neighbouring Chokwe and Ndembu, among whom chiefship is more highly valued. Lele failure to develop their agriculture to an economic optimum – an important limitation on their ability to influence the new colonial state – relates not to narrow economic factors, but to the overall relation between authority and the capacity to induce work.

> The principle of seniority applied throughout their social system made it in one sense an old man's world…[I]f any one desire seemed paramount, it would be to secure dignity and well-being for old age…[I]n a primitive economy everything is weighted against the old. To try to invest the weakest section of the community with authority smacks of the quixotic…[T]heir society was without real authority, *ridden with devious, hidden controls* and vulnerable to external pressures for change.
>
> (LK: 2, my emphasis)

The absence of well-defined and workable relations of authority among the Lele is the key both to the plot of the book and to the role that Lele will play as an instance of Douglas's broader, subsequent analysis of authority in societies marked by the presence or absence of hierarchy.

Unlike the majority of ethnographic treatises of the time, Douglas's account was written in the past tense. Rather than a principled objection to writing in the 'ethnographic present' (discussed later in this chapter), this was in reaction to the civil war raging in the ex-Belgian Congo, partly triggered by the attempted secession of the Kasai region in which Lele lived, that made the contemporary pertinence of Douglas's work a matter of great uncertainty. As she expressed it in her introduction, Lele society could be envisaged to have had an older form that had been 'interrupted for only one generation – between 1933 and 1959' (LK: 8). This older form had been overthrown by the combined efforts of Belgian administration, missionaries and Lele youth – quite what would take its place once the war ended was difficult to envisage. Thus, the book has a second overlaying chronological plot – not just to chart the quixotic and under-achieving nature of traditional, gerontocratic Lele society, but also to explain why that form of society had been so vulnerable to pressures for change and how processes of change had highlighted the nature of the older form of society for the ethnographer.[11]

Economy

The way that Douglas sets about this neatly articulates themes that were either present in the work of those close to her or more generally in the air at the time.

After putting the Lele 'on the map' – describing how these 30,000 or so individuals lived in villages averaging about 200 souls (but varying between fewer than thirty and more than 400), and how the seasons are dominated by nine months of rain, with a brief pause in February and a dry season from mid-May to mid-August – Douglas turns to a description of Lele economy. Giving economy so prominent a place in her description might owe something to Daryll Forde at University College, but the precedent of Evans-Pritchard's *The Nuer* is striking. Some years later, Mary and James Douglas were to translate the preface to the French edition of *The Nuer*, written by the sometime Oxford French anthropologist Louis Dumont, for inclusion in a festschrift for Evans-Pritchard (1975d). Dumont's reading of *The Nuer* concentrated on its division into three parts: first and last came descriptions of livelihood and political institutions; the passage between the two was supplied by a brilliant discussion of time and space. Evans-Pritchard began by describing ecologically embedded notions of time and space, largely dictated by the annual rains; then, little by little, he revealed how larger segments of time or space begged the social structure of the Nuer (see Chapter 2). Events, then genealogies, both revised for contemporary pertinence, provided markers of time longer than the annual or life-time cycles. Spatial notions were similarly inflected by the identities of those who lived in particular places. Douglas supplies a similar contextualization of the difference between Lele and their Bushong neighbours, the dominant people among the Kuba from whom in many ways – for instance language – Lele differed little: 'Everything that the Lele have or do, the Bushong have more and can do better….[I]n hunting, fishing and house-building the Bushong use more specialized equipment, in cultivation they spend more energy and time over a greater part of the year, and in craftsmanship they have more skilled specialists' (LK: 42).[12] When hunting, Lele did not invest time and labour in making pits and nets; fishing was the preserve of women whose techniques were limited to draining fish ponds or scattering poison. Both huts and furnishings were markedly inferior among Lele; although some Lele ornamentation of utensils was fine, they rarely bothered with it. Bushong planted five crops in a two-year rotational cycle, but Lele reaped a single annual maize harvest and practised no crop rotation. While the Bushong worked the year round, the Lele's single burst of activity coincided with the six-week peak of the dry season. Wet and dry season differed little in temperature, although to European and Bushong alike the low humidity of dry season made it cold, and welcome for that. 'But the Lele, enduring the sun beating down on them from a cloudless sky, while they were trying to cram in all their agricultural work for the year' dreaded the dry season (LK: 45–46). Thus, even the relative heat of annual seasons is keyed to people's social lives. She concludes, 'On the Lele side of the Kasai there was the anarchy of warring villages to contrast with the orderly devolution of control on the Bushong side' (LK: 270). Hierarchy and high production contrasts with anarchy and under-achievement.

Lele economy was geared to a low level of investment, lower employment of labour and a shorter cycle than its Bushong counterpart. But Lele nonetheless suffered from labour shortage. While Bushong strove for wealth and positions at court as incentives for the successful, Lele outlook was gerontocratic; they 'talked as if the most satisfying roles fell into an individual's lap in the ripeness of time, provided that he was normally virile' (LK: 49). These roles derived from marriage and parenthood. Lele society was polygynous (and polyandrous in some respects); Bushong society was monogamous. Lele elders had difficulty controlling the productive labour of their juniors, but they retained control over the one thing that Lele made more robustly than their Bushong neighbours – raffia cloth. And raffia, as Douglas goes on to explain, acted rather like a system of rationing (still a familiar analogy for British readers in 1963, see 1967e) for the most desired things in life – especially women for whom payment in raffia had to be made. Lele men remained bachelors until middle age (35–40 years), and in the old days raided for women against neighbouring villages. The older men monopolized access to women – Douglas likens this superficially to an 'old-age pensions scheme costing more than the society reckoned' (LK: 50).[13] Among the things not reckoned, apart from the loss of young men's labour, was the inability of Lele society to achieve an organizational extent wider than the village, which in earlier times had been a stockaded settlement virtually enclaved against most of its neighbours. Again the Bushong had outdone the Lele by organizing a chiefdom which exerted some control over 70,000 people.

Exchange

Lele villages were largely self-sufficient. Food and drink and other small items were given to kin and neighbours who reciprocated in kind or in some other measure as part of everyday life. A few goods (iron bars, tools, weapons, camwood for making red paste) were bartered from outside the village, and these might be exchanged against raffia cloth within the Lele economy. Raffia was also used to pay certain specialist craftsmen for, say, a new drum. Reciprocity and barter constituted two distinguishable spheres of exchange (see 1962a for this usage); a third sphere of exchange consisted of what, following Mauss, Douglas calls formal prestations (1990f). 'For entrance fees, fines and compensations, marriage dues and fees for ritual services, only certain standard goods were accepted in payment. These were raffia cloths, camwood, axes, in the old days copper wire or slaves, and in 1950 goats or Belgian Congo francs' (LK: 55–56). Later she sub-divides this third sphere to suggest a fourth: rights in persons (LK: 65). A strong young man, she tells us, might weave five cloths in a day working uninterruptedly at his loom. But to do so he would have needed a dried and combed supply of raffia at hand, and this was unlikely. Instead, when lumpy prestations were necessary, people had to rely upon stores of cloth or borrow or beg from kin and friends. In this relation between people and raffia cloth, we hear another echo of Evans-Pritchard's *The Nuer*: for whom cattle and people may signify one another. Control over supplies of raffia cloth provides Douglas with the solution to her conundrum: how older men were able to exert any direction within Lele society when their economic productivity was so low.

All dues were fixed in terms of raffia cloth, but could also be paid according to conventional equivalences: for instance, 100 raffia cloths were equal in worth to a copper bar, three large bars of camwood, or a slave. Small numbers of raffia cloths were given as gifts, for instance by a husband to his wife; larger numbers of cloths were sewn together into dancing skirts, which eventually formed part of a person's grave goods; overall there were innumerable occasions on which cloths were used to oil the wheels of sociality. Payments for wives, initiation into cult groups, settlement of offences ranging from adultery to fighting, all these required transference of raffia cloths. Whoever controlled raffia cloth was able to meet his or her social obligations. Heaviest charges fell on a young man:

> By the time he had entered an age-set, married, entered the Begetters' Cult [see below] and become a diviner, he would have disbursed a minimum of 300 cloths, and certainly have spent as much again in maintaining good relations with his wife, his in-laws, his own father and mother and settling adultery damages, to say nothing of medical fees for his wife's confinements.
>
> (LK: 58)

Older men received cloths while younger men needed them, and had to borrow from their elders. Although there was a cash economy by 1950, it remained unseemly to buy raffia cloth. To do so, says Douglas, would have been like being forced to buy Christmas cards to adorn one's own mantelshelf. Raffia was demanded of kin, or borrowed against the prospect of repaying with cloths received in the future. Transition to a market economy was strongly constrained by this existing system of exchange. Europeans could enter the barter system only if they had raffia cloth; items in the subsistence sphere had begun to be traded for cash, but only one item in the prestation sphere could be bought with money: camwood. In 1949, people earned money only to pay taxes; but when Douglas returned in 1953 Belgian Congo francs were more actively sought for such purchases as guns, bicycles and lamps. Yet owners of raffia cloth remained unwilling to part with it for cash; had they done so, Douglas explains, francs would have seeped into the systems of traditional payments undermining the older men's ability to control rationing and benefiting young cash-earners. Instead a more circuitous exchange of raffia for francs via goats had developed.

Raffia cloths functioned not as a medium of exchange, like money, but as a means of rationing: one that maintained inequality rather than ensuring equal access. In the final analysis, the scarcest good was the supply of marriageable girls: 'Their great value and relative scarcity were axioms from which the rest of Lele culture flowed' (LK: 66). Lele reluctance to commoditize raffia cloth reflected the prestige ranking of different spheres of exchange: no one would sensibly give up something of greater for something of lesser value.

Social organization and conflict

Here, Douglas leaves her initial formulation of the social embeddedness of Lele economy and, in keeping with the ethnographic conventions of the time, moves to consider how lineages and locality interact as organizational resources. Lele villages were autonomous units with 'corporate personalities' possessing 'communal wives, communal children, communal sons-in-law and a communal treasury' (LK: 3). The village was overwhelmingly the most significant unit of a person's affiliation, far outweighing clans, which were important only for allo-cating wives and widows, and organizing blood compensation. Each village had its head, who was simply the oldest man of one of the clans eligible to provide the headship, and a village was internally organized by criteria of age. Age-sets were founded roughly every fifteen years, so a village usually had six of them. However, the oldest set in the course of dying out typically merged with that below it. Age-sets were residential units. A village with four sets might be orga-nized such that one pair of alternate sets (1 and 3) occupied one side of the village and the other pair (2 and 4) the opposite side. The relation between age-mates was as close as any recognized in Lele society,

> Lele idealized many of the relations between men. They rhapsodized about what a man should do for his father, what a father should do for his son, the devotion of brothers. The love of true age-mates for one another was even more a favourite theme. Age-mates should have no secrets or reserves. They should share their goods and bear one another's hardships. No sacrifice was too great for an age-mate.
>
> (LK: 73–74)

When half a dozen boys reached about eighteen years of age they were recog-nized as a named age group and would club together to buy (or steal), or receive from their co-residential older age-set, a joint wife to live in their part of the village. This offered them some consolation for the greatly delayed age of marriage. These bachelor sets, which Lele explained were formed to allay the hardship of being wifeless, existed in an ethos of 'youth culture', involving mild revolt against their elders. A father could be assured the respect due from his son only if he never approached him in the company of his age-mates.

Age-sets outweighed the importance of descent among Lele. Lele traced kinship through both parents, but the important descent line was reckoned through women. Thus, a boy inherited not from his father but from his male matrikin. All Lele belonged to matriclans, the broadest recognized unit of common matrilineal descent, but these units were rather amorphous. Local concentrations of matriclan members occurred in villages which owed their foundation to that matriclan, but the privileges of belonging to the founding clan were few compared to the Lele's neighbours.

Anthropologists had become fascinated by matriliny, and by what Audrey

Richards had dubbed the 'matrilineal puzzle' in a celebrated article (1950). The puzzle took the following form among the Lele: men exercised authority over women; post-marital residence for women tended to be with their husbands; yet, thanks to matrilineality, children belonged to the matriclan of their mother's village (where their maternal grandparents lived). The puzzle involved the tussle likely to occur over the residence decisions of women and of their children. In most societies of pre-colonial Africa, supporters were worth more than material goods. And, in the game of attracting followers, men would try to play the rules to their best advantage: wanting both their wives and their sisters and sisters' husbands, both their sons and their sisters' sons, to live with them. There were, as Douglas neatly put it elsewhere, 'two standards of behaviour, one which applies in the first person, one which applies in the third' (1964e). Quite how this conundrum is practically resolved differs between central African matrilineal peoples (see Douglas 1957d on Yao, 1959d on Ndembu): Lele downplayed descent in order to welcome all young males. Although there was a slight preference for residence where one's clan was a village founder, this could be outweighed by other factors, and descent tended to be subordinated to criteria of age in village organization. Old men offered younger men both wives and protection from sorcery in order to attract them, but their only sanction on the young men's subsequent conduct was to threaten to withhold the same incentives they had first offered. Because clans were widely distributed, young men could move in the expectation of reattaching themselves to a local section of their clan. Usually men would stay in the vicinity of their father until he died (but given the late age of marriage this could occur while they were relatively young), subsequently they might stay where they were, move once to a conducive locality, or try a few different places. Between two-thirds and three-quarters of men censused were living away from their place of birth (LK: 89). In general, younger rather than older men changed residence,

> The result was a group of adult men, committed to living together permanently and yet avoiding the most obvious way of regulating their possible conflicts – discrimination between descent lines. To this I attribute the great anxiety which was expressed whenever disputes threatened to flare up.
>
> (LK: 4)

Later in her book Douglas defines the problem of authority as one of 'men trying to live together, expecting so much devotion and self-control while doing so little to define their relations' (LK: 96). Young men, as we have seen, worked little, enjoying the consolations of a village wife and the excitement of war between villages as compensations for the long wait to become elders and wield what little authority the society had to offer: 'Boys would be boys, until their mid-thirties' (LK: 49). Once married, as a son-in-law, a man was explicitly subordinate to his father-in-law, 'the one role of authority which was precisely defined without reference to age' (LK: 5). Lacking solidary matrilineages, and with marriage institutions that pitted adjacent generations of men against one another, the Lele were riven by ill-concealed dispute. Scant wonder that their level of economic achievement fell far short of their better organized neighbours.

> They were committed to hostility between generations in a village and hostility between villages, to ill-will and insecurity, enemies of sustained collaboration....[T]he special bias of their sorcery beliefs actually promoted the unity of the village by deepening suspicion of outsiders and provoking action against members who were unamenable to moral pressures. The general image of a sorcerer was an old man who was a skilled diviner. Consequently, diviners had a keen personal interest in diverting or checking indiscriminate accusations. They tended to cite the dead, or unnamed enemies from other villages, thus boosting village solidarity at the expense of friendly external relations.
>
> (LK: 6–7)

As Godfrey Lienhardt noted in review, 'Most anthropologists end by being strongly biased in favour of the people they have studied. Dr. Douglas, though showing some sympathy with some of the difficulties of the Lele…carefully avoids any such commitment' (LK/AfA: 298). One of her earliest articles in a non-anthropological journal had drawn attention to the very real consequences of hatreds and rivalries concentrated by the small scale of life when, in criticism of the 'functional approach', she noted that African villages were characterized both by 'merry insouciance' and by '[m]eanness, jealousy and desperate egoism....[L]ethal ordeals, which appear to rid the society of malefactors,…only confirm the fear of their presence, and establish more certainly the cycle of ignorance, superstition and terror' (1955c).

Women in marriage

Because every village consisted of an older generation of men who had to stay and a younger generation of men who would probably move away (the Lele variant of the matrilineal puzzle, LK: 94–95), and because new members were recruited to the village by playing on their fears of illness or by offering them wives (LK: 98), and no maximum was recognized for desirable village size, older men were persuaded to go easy on youngsters with an option of leaving. Young men potentially brought labour-power, but older men brought potential demands with fewer potential benefits. Inheritance was by close matrikin, whether resident or not, and by resident matrikin who might be more distantly related, and consisted not only of goods (like raffia and camwood) but also of widows and the various claims over people which belonged to the deceased. Rights in people formed part of a complex system of debts between other people (typically older men) and between the residential and descent groups to which they belonged. Women were crucial pawns in this male competition, and the subject of ambivalent male attitudes.

> Men spoke of women in several distinct styles. When they discussed a woman's looks, they spoke lyrically about regular proportions, slinky leopard's movements, a face like the rising sun. When there was prospect of a sexual adventure they spoke in a cajoling, teasing voice, as if to a child. But compared with men women were beasts, ignorant, unmannerly, worse than dogs. Capricious, weak and lazy, they could not be trusted, they did not understand clan affairs, they behaved badly on formal occasions…The notion that a woman's role was to be completely plastic in the hands of men suited the way in which men defined their relationship with one another, but it was difficult to make women accept that role. When the mission fathers taught the story of the Garden of Eden, and of Eve's responsibility for the introduction of sin, they assented, pagans and Christians alike, with deep conviction. But in all, men behaved as if women, in spite of their shortcomings, were the most precious, desirable *objects* in their lives.
>
> (LK: 113–14, my emphasis)

That the age of marriage was delayed for men but relatively young for women, who married around fifteen, had a curious effect for outside observers accustomed to closer age equality between spouses. A woman might be on the point of becoming a grandmother while her brother, of roughly the same age, still played the footloose bachelor among his age-mates. Lele tended to naturalize these differences between men and women, arguing that women grew up more quickly but that men remained sexually active longer and might often die younger than women. In this, as in the argumentativeness they also attributed themselves, and the antagonism between brothers they saw as part of their nature, Douglas argues that what is at work is the form of society they have created for themselves: it is their way of living together which leads them to view human nature as they do (LK: 117). This argument recurs throughout Douglas's later work. The fact that generations, which seen from a male point of view succeed one another rather slowly, from a female point of view come round in half the time, allowed Lele to maintain a rate of polygyny of two or three wives per married man. Their preferred forms of marriage recognized the debt incurred by a matriclan to the son-in-law who fathered their members. After his daughter married, a man was entitled to reclaim her daughters (his own daughter's daughters) whom he could marry himself, or give to one of his brothers (who belonged to the same matriclan as himself and was, like himself, a classificatory 'mother's father' to the girl), or give to a more junior clansman (his sister's daughter's son). He was not supposed to give wives to his own heir, his sister's son. 'When a man of one clan gave a female member to another in

marriage, in a sense it was giving the husband's clan a permanent right to inter-
fere in the marriages of women descended from himself' (LK: 115). If women
married at fifteen and men at thirty-five, which is close to the average, by the
time a man reached sixty he might have seen his twin sister, her daughter, grand-
daughter and great-grand-daughter married while his son remained single.
Because older men sought in the past to marry their grand-daughters to men of
their own generation, their relations with younger men were necessarily fraught.

Relations between husband and wives were, at least normatively, very close.
They ought to care for one another in ill-health, and the husband had special
responsibility to treat his wives with absolute equality. Co-wives were also
supposed to support one another, but their households had a high degree of independence from one another and attachment to their own female matrikin.
Responsibilities between members of the polygynous household were strongly
sanctioned by the belief that illness of co-spouses or their children automatically
followed the introduction of sexual pollution to the home, especially through adultery. Despite the absence of a feminist agenda behind Douglas's account, her
monograph is sensitive to the positions of women. This stems partly from the fact
that 'so many of Lele institutions hinged on men's control over women' (LK: 124),
and partly from Douglas having spent so much of her time in the company of Lele
women. While women could never command men, and a woman avoided her
sons, sons-in-law and – to some degree – her own father, Douglas suggests that
something more complex than complete subordination was involved:

> Notions of seniority and minority, while they hardly entered into the
> relations of women with women, were equally irrelevant in another way
> to the relations of women with men – *the two sexes were estimated on separate
> and incommensurable scales. In one sense, each sex belonged to a separate world,
> which only impinged on the other here and there.*
>
> Women spent most of their time with other women, and developed
> their strong emotional ties with their mothers, sisters and daughters. It
> was obvious that their interests did not coincide with those of their
> menfolk. A woman's confidants were her own mother and sisters, and if
> she was obliged to live far from them she suffered loneliness to say
> nothing of the hardship of doing without their help.
>
> (LK: 124, my emphasis)

Lele society consisted of the relatively separate social worlds, interests, loyal-
ties and desires of men and women which their system of marriage – itself an
insecure means of male gerontocratic control – took a major part in both
creating and mediating. Moreover the division of productive, as well as repro-
ductive, labour meant the two sexes needed one another. Women were largely
responsible for the solidarity of their clan sections, not least because it served
their interests to attend diligently to their obligations towards kin, which partly
tugged against those they owed their spouses.

Douglas's discussion of the 'private wife and private family' is followed in the next chapter by consideration of the 'communal village-wife and communal family'. The institution of the village-wife – the collective wife of younger age-sets – is introduced mischievously by quotation from a Belgian missionary describing how a little 'unfortunate' (*une malheureuse*), eleven or twelve year old, would spontaneously accept the 'shameful situation' (*situation honteuse*) of becoming a collective wife. Or, if no girl could be found who was sufficiently depraved to comply with the needs of these 'satyrs', the men might resort to violence, kidnapping, or threats of death by poisoning (LK: 128). The advocacy of the missionaries had led to the suppression of polyandry in 1947, and the threat of imprisonment had been 'energetically applied between 1947 and 1949…so much so that the institution was to some extent moribund and distinctly delicate to investigate' (LK: 128–29). A colonial government occupying moral high ground to the detriment of local custom is meat and drink to the anthropologist:

> To be a village-wife was a great honour. Her prestige figures in ritual. She would be compared to a chief, and if she died, the whole village mourned, not in silence, as for a commoner, but by dancing with special music, as for aristocrats [… noting that the chest of the stately bush-buck was reserved for consumption by the village wives]: in a spirit of gallantry, 'sweets to the sweet', they said that the most beautiful animal was the proper privilege of the most beautiful women and no man was allowed to eat its chest.

> (LK: 129)

Reference to the possibility that the bush-buck was avoided by men on account of being a sorcerer's familiar is tucked away in a footnote to the same page. In stark contrast to the missionary's image of depravity, Douglas sets out to show that a village-wife, more so than his private wife, is the object of romantic love for Lele men. Age-sets gained their wives either under the same rule as private wives (by marrying the daughter's daughter of a previous village-wife), or by abducting a girl from a neighbouring rival village. Her installation was by seduction in a broad sense: in the evenings she was escorted around to drink palm wine, given raffia cloths (and might help herself to others simply by assisting in their production in the slightest way or making a small charcoal mark on cloths during the process of their weaving), she was relieved of all the normal chores of a housewife and fed from her husbands' allowance of food. Plied with morsels of choice food, she would accept each husband into her hut for two nights 'scrupulously' attending to their seniority from oldest to youngest (LK: 131). This period came to an end after two to six months, before the birth of the first child. A girl might hold out to be allowed to become a private wife but, if she persisted in resistance to accepting her husbands, they might resort to the whip.

However, it transpires that all the raffia cloths given to the girl were not hers to keep, but only in her custody until given as marriage payment to her kin. A canny village-wife would then set about reducing the number of her house-husbands, although she was permitted to have discreet sexual relations with any man of the village in the 'privacy of the forest' (LK: 133). Ideas about sexual pollution were adjusted for the village-wives. Once pregnant they could sleep only with husbands who had previously enjoyed their favours. However, any of these husbands whose private wife was pregnant had to cease relations with the village-wife. The honourable position of the village-wife comes to seem compromised, even in terms of the Lele's own notions, since some parents feared that their daughter's husbands would be less careful of avoiding pollution than in the case of their own wives. Moreover, husbands whose attentions were unwelcome to the girl might resort to attacking her with sorcery (LK: 135). A couple of pages later, we learn that

> women did not normally envy the lot of a polyandrous wife…The institution of village-wife was a kind of safety valve which relieved excessive strains of the marital system, for the women as well as for the men. It was an alternative, but for most women not a very attractive alternative to an unhappy marriage with one man.
>
> (LK: 137)

Sons of village-wives were in potentially favourable positions. The men of the village as a whole, or rather the village as corporate personality, took responsibility for them and might achieve 'the ideal of fatherhood, lavish and indulgent…By acting the good son, he forced the village into its most pleasing role' (LK: 138). But a poor son would cause the village to lose interest in him.

Pawns and minimal hierarchy

Discussion of the distribution of rights in the persons of wives and offspring leads seamlessly into a chapter on 'blood debts'; marriage relations are simply one type of right in persons Lele recognized. Blood debts were paid as compensation for deaths caused by overt violence or, more commonly, as a result of sexual pollution or sorcery. The most common cases involved women who died in childbirth after confessing to adultery – and whose adulterous partners thus became responsible for their deaths. These lethal effects of adultery served to bring it into the open through confession, which in turn served to regulate relations within the village. Blood debts could be settled by the transference of pawns. Pawnship was not the extreme kinlessness of slavery. A pawn was a woman who has been transferred, along with the right to dispose of her matrilineal descendants either as wives or pawns, to a lord representing his clan or village. Lele might both be pawns themselves and have rights over pawns. The rules of the game were inordinately complex (LK: 144) and further compounded by a convention allowing clans to transfer cases involving pawns to villages.[14]

This brings Douglas to the problem of the 'aristocratic clan' recognized by the Lele. The subject may have been left towards the end of the book in order to accentuate the contrast between the gerontocratic Lele and the courtly Bushong.

> The precedence of the founding clan in the village was an intangible thing, giving subtle satisfaction to it members, but, politically speaking, null. The pre-eminence of the aristocratic clan might be seen as a larger scale model of the same kind. The aristocrats certainly enjoyed prestige, but they had to manipulate (not dominate) the existing political structure in order to maintain their prestige.
>
> (LK: 202–203)

Regional specialists have found these traces of aristocracy among the Lele more significant than Douglas acknowledged (e.g. Vansina LK/JAH, but apparently not followed by Vansina 1978). For Douglas, however, it is clear that it is the system of heritable rights and debts in people, rather than any hereditary principle *per se*, that characterizes pre-colonial Lele politics.[15]

Cults and sorcery

Douglas's final three chapters devoted to traditional Lele society turn successively to village cults, and to sorcery and its control. Lele, like many African peoples, acknowledged a distant God, but were more immediately concerned with the ancestors, ghosts and spirits important to the dominant values of healing individuals and the village. Lele concern for the frailty of women focused particularly on child-bearing. For men, there corresponded an emphasis on hunting in the forest. The special preserve of men, the forest, was automatically 'spoiled' by disputes and dissension within the village; women's infidelities threatened the sphere of childbirth. With a single exception, all Lele cults were concerned with averting the effects of human transgressions on fertility and hunting, or with the defeat of sorcery.

This exception was the cult of the Begetters, which functioned to honour fatherhood and to 'accentuate the social gulf between married men and bachelors' (LK: 209). Men might be initiated as Begetters once they had a child in wedlock; this not only allowed them to eat the chest of animals and their young without dying from coughing, but also gave them power to cancel the effects of others breaching this rule. The cult of the pangolin (scaly anteater) was reserved for men who had produced both a male and female child by the same wife; eligibility being further restricted to cases in which the man, his father and his wife all belonged to the founding clans of their villages. The pangolin cult was powerful in enabling conception and good hunting, and it controlled the special ritual of removal of the village to a new site. This anomalous little creature was to become almost iconically attached to Mary Douglas's most famous work, *Purity and Danger* (1966), and so we shall return to it in the next chapter.

Unlike those of the Begetters or the pangolin, other Lele cults were not voluntary. Lele diviners were chosen in dreams and possession, elected by the birth of twins, or said to have been summoned by God. Diviners were responsible for fathoming the causes of misfortune and detecting sorcery. Sorcerers used techniques similar to those of healers, but with malice, to attack their fellows; they paid their mutual debts with the lives of their own matrikin. Lele distinguished between occasional sorcerers and 'sorcerers for lust', whom they feared most. The victims of a sorcerer for lust were withdrawn from the cycle of reincarnation and turned into animal familiars. His presence was poisonous in the village, and since he acted irrationally, no motive could be sought for his behaviour (LK: 221). Old and neglected diviners – self-regarding, hot-tempered types – were the most credible suspects. This believed incidence of sorcery, Douglas noted, must relate, however indirectly, to the massive and precarious advantages enjoyed by the elderly. 'Accusations of sorcery must inevitably reflect the real distribution of power' (LK: 223). In reaction to sorcery, young men might threaten to, or actually, leave the village.

Usually Lele did not try to identify sorcerers since this might invite retaliation. Through their various types of oracle, diviners tended to place responsibility for deaths where it could not be disputed – on the dead (through justified posthumous vengeance sorcery), on breaches of rules governing sexual pollution, or else outside the village (LK: 226). Because the poison oracle administered to accused sorcerers in the final resort had been outlawed, the phenomenon of 'sorcery loomed larger and nearer' (LK: 243). Pawnship had been integral to this system, because compensation was paid to wrongly accused survivors of the oracle, as well as to relatives of a victim by the kin of those proven guilty by their death from the poison oracles. Douglas documents the series of anti-sorcery movements which were adopted by Lele even before it became impossible for them to turn to the final arbiter of the poison oracle. In 1953, missionaries, government officials and Christians were all opposed to the new Kabenga-benga cult which entered Lele country by purchase from the Bushong with the promise of cleansing entire villages of sorcery in perpetuity by virtue of entraining the automatic death of any who attempted to practise sorcery (see Douglas 1970f).

European impact

Only a brief final chapter of Douglas's monograph is explicitly devoted to 'European impact on Lele society', but that impact is one of its principal subjects. I noted in introduction that Douglas does not use the present tense in her account to report her fieldwork a decade earlier because she realized her experiences had been rendered historical by the civil war raging in the Kasai. The implication is that had she written up the materials sooner, they might have been described in the present tense. But the 'ethnographic present' is a temporally more complex construction than simple elision with writing in the present tense suggests. Most generally, it means writing as if the societies being described were timeless. But even this overstates the case, since no writers of the colonial period entirely failed to report indications of change in the societies they described. What changes they found noteworthy depended upon the manner in which they reconstructed a version of the society without those changes. Most Africanist ethnographies attempted, in one way or another, to factor out some of the influences of colonialism in order to discern an enduring structure of relations within the society and to put some life into this structure by imagining how it could have been reproduced over time without major change. How they did this makes the 'ethnographic present' a complex generic convention: despite a family likeness in many of its versions, it differed subtly in its case-by-case applications in ways that can be decided only by close reading of criteria internal to the text.

To itemize a few of the major changes Douglas tells us about: although Basongo, on the River Kasai in northern Leleland, had been a military post since 1917, it was the construction of a road system by forced labour in the first half of the 1930s that opened Lele country to the forces of administration, missions and industry and commerce. From this time, no armed force was used against Lele. Tribunals were also imposed, along with decrees which made illegal: warfare between villages, the use of the poison oracle by decree in 1924 (LK: 236), polyandry by decree in 1947 (LK: 128), various anti-sorcery cults, and so forth.

Despite repeated references to them in the main text, the Christians play a somewhat muted role in the Lele book. After uncertain beginnings, by 1949, when Mary Tew undertook her first fieldwork, the mission at Brabanta was thriving – with primary, secondary and technical schools, and vast congregations. Lele were sincere Christians of whom their pastors were proud (LK: 264). The nuns were famed as midwives and devoted themselves to their charges who numbered over 500 in 1951. Of the mission fathers Douglas writes:

> In ten years they had succeeded in smashing the framework of the pagan society, age-sets, polyandry, ordeals and the rest, so well that the ethnographer's task was already one of reconstruction rather than of straight observation. The young men and women under thirty were largely Christian, and the children, all enrolled in village catechist's schools, were fully expected to proceed to baptism.
>
> (LK: 265)

What then attracted Lele? Not the violence-prone fathers themselves, nor the lure of involvement in the cash economy – but the doctrine of monogamy. Missionaries targeted the younger generation: of girls about to enter the elaborate game of pawnships and marriage rights, and boys whose maturity would be delayed. Christians could pay off previous betrothals through use of cash in order to set up Christian households with Lele girls of their own age. The result was a society 'split between a rising generation of Christians and a declining generation of pagans [which] took place too suddenly not to leave a trail of bitterness' (LK: 268). 'I have described a society which was in the process of liquidation, which could not be understood at all without the interpolation of what must have been the scene a dozen years before' (ibid.: 268–69). But a dozen years earlier there was already another point of transition: pawnship was not being reproduced by the poison oracle, village raiding was already outlawed and initiation of warriors had ceased.

The civil war in the Congo had destabilized the situation again by Douglas's time of writing, leading her to wonder whether some of the older values might not be restored, especially since the new society introduced by the missionaries gave Lele men scant resources to protect their rights in a wife, should she run off with another man (LK: 270). Perhaps, the older system described also contained seeds of the future. The complex temporality of the monograph is something more than an attempt to reach back to a timeless, pre-colonial past. Indeed, it is moot whether it is about a particular chronologically specific time at all.

Case studies, diary notes, observations and most things statistical apply directly to the period 1949–53. Some passages appear to refer us to a time just before completion of the road network opened Lele country to routine outside influences during the 1930s. But other passages can be read to apply even earlier: to a period when villages warred and moved, when poison oracles were used routinely and polyandrous marriage was common. Aside from these specific temporalities, there is the time internal to the model of the Lele: the recurrent time in which elders dominate juniors and in which women are transacted as wives and pawns.

A STRUCTURALIST REANALYSIS

This last, processual, time is the dimension in which Luc de Heusch's structural reanalysis of Douglas's monograph is situated. A year after the book's publication, de Heusch's detailed re-examination began by hailing *The Lele* as 'the most important monograph ever devoted to a Bantu society', and one which 'cries out irresistibly for a structuralist reading' (1981 [1964]: 82). Since I shall have cause to refer to structural analysis in later chapters, de Heusch's reanalysis allows me to show what one highly relevant structuralist reading looks like. However, I shall refer only to elements of his analysis concerned to discover an implicit Lele ideology (rather than with Lele practice), and even within these confines can note only a few major points.

De Heusch radically simplifies Douglas's account in order to discern a structural logic implicit in Lele representations of their society. The first of a series of homologous 'general dualisms' involves the very clear way in which Lele separate the sexes and their duties as distinct and interdependent in all contexts. A second dualism revolves around age, such that adjacent generations are distinguished and alternate generations identified: this is made visible in the residential grouping of alternate age-sets in sections of the village. The same principle can also be found in the kinship system, since a man may receive a wife from his maternal great uncle (mother's mother's brother) and may be tempted to reside with him on account of this. Age-sets, as we have seen, are characterized as egalitarian groupings, quite unlike the relations among brothers, between whom there is rivalry and obligatory formality since they are distinguished by their relative age. Thus, another dualism is established between age organization and kinship organization. Age organization is fundamental to the village, while kinship organization relates to matriclans, and clans are dispersed rather than localized. From this de Heusch deduces yet a further dualism: the village exists in space and the clan in time. The two are also opposed in terms of their marital regimes: the village-wife is married polyandrously to several members of an age-set whose relations are egalitarian, but the domestic wife is married to only one man who is probably married to other women polygynously.

In keeping with structuralist orthodoxy in the analysis of kinship systems, de Heusch looks for clues to the functioning of these general dualisms in the ways in which women circulate between men. Lele recognize two preferred forms of marriage: a man's first daughter's marriage is decided by his wife's father. This discharges the debt between the two clans, because the clan which received a wife has returned a daughter. Although the girl's grandfather can marry her himself, he is as likely to give her to a younger clan member, one who cannot be his inheritor but is likely to be his sister's daughter's son (that is a member of the alternating rather than adjacent generation). Since this young man incurs a debt when he marries his wife, he will return a daughter to his wife's father, balancing the reciprocity over two generations. The second form of preferential marriage involves returning a daughter to her father's father. Thus, each clan is involved in relations of delayed reciprocity with two other clans. But because these transactions occur in alternate generations, theoretically each clan must be involved in giving and receiving wives with at least four other clans. The exchange between clans thus assures that at least some women always marry within a close circle of intermarrying villages.

Following Douglas, de Heusch notices that the term *mbai* for men who belong to the same age-group (or to alternate age-groups) and are equals (and thus strongly contrasted with brothers) is also extended to some men related by ties of kinship. In all cases, the men so designated belong to alternate generations and are potentially also brothers-in-law, since the older may give a wife to the younger man. *Mbai* also transpires to be a term commonly used between brothers-in-law. If *mbai* applies to the givers and receivers of women, then it becomes quite comprehensible, de Heusch argues, that the same term is also used of commercial partners. In these ways (and also through the system of pawnship which I cannot explore here), the village and the clan '[a]lthough irreducible on a structural level, are obliged to come to terms with one another' (de Heusch 1981: 100).

De Heusch is able to reduce Lele social organization to a series of dualisms mediated by the circulation of women. And, although this kind of analysis can be made to yield a transformational logic for which temporal referents can be specified, it is fair to say that de Heusch's analysis is informed by a more atemporal conception of Lele society than is Douglas's.

CONCLUSION

The Lele book shared the assumptions of its period; this means the period it was researched as much as the time it was written. Critical attention to history in Africanist anthropology, to the problems of reifying tribes in ethnographic writing, and to reflexivity in writing about 'participant observation' had only just begun to seem pressing. The current state of the art required the writer of a monograph on an African people to merge two of their readers' horizons of expectation by presenting an ethnographic description in terms of a social anthropological plot.

Aside from being an incisive analysis of a complex and, for Europeans, unfamiliar organizational form, what clues does *The Lele of Kasai* offer to Douglas's later writings? Her belief that Africa would require theoretical rigour was clearly justified, and we shall see how the intellectual tools and examples she gained from Africanist ethnography have continued to serve her explorations of European and American society, as well as her more general theorizing. The anomalous status of the pangolin was to lead to a general study of mediators; the multiple taboos automatically triggered when breached by Lele men or women led to her general thesis that dangers in the environment correlate with social concerns.

Douglas's Lele book was already unusual in being a single-volume account of aspects of social organization that were increasingly coming to be the subject of a series of works (politics, economy, religion, kinship and marriage). She was able to do this because she envisaged, as she has continued to envisage, social forms synoptically and functionally. Lele economic under-performance correlated with the absence of hierarchy and failure of authority. Religion and marriage could also be portrayed as elements of the same overall form of tenuously based gerontocracy. Lacking, as we have seen, an explicitly feminist agenda, the monograph is nonetheless a sensitive portrayal of women's lot among the Lele; even if, in her portrayal of the village-wife, we may detect some over-romanticizing in Mary Douglas's desire to overturn the opprobrium of her appalled priestly commentator. I have also noted a morally evaluative quality in her work; or to put it differently, a refusal to suspend a humanist stance (1955c). It was not enough to argue that witchcraft, for instance, can be analysed as a factor in social organization – albeit she endorsed this argument. When people actualize the consequences of their belief in the 'fantastically depraved level of existence' of neighbours and kin (such as an elderly woman accused of defecating in the crown of a palm tree) urgent questions are raised about the nature and direction of human violence (1969d).

Apart from these substantive concerns, there are also glimpses of the style Douglas was later to favour – comparisons between the exotic and the mundane. I have noted a few in passing during this chapter: Lele gerontocracy likened to an unanticipatedly expensive pension scheme, raffia cloth likened to ration coupons, and the need to buy your own raffia cloth analogized with the sad plight of the individual forced to display Christmas cards he had bought for himself. These are early indications of Douglas's cultural imagination and written expression that were to make her works accessible and relevant to a Western readership of non-anthropologists.

Notes

1 Mary recalls that Julian Pitt-Rivers had to use his private means to research in Spain for the doctorate that became *The People of the Sierra* (1954). This was the foundational text of British social anthropology of the Mediterranean. By the 1960s, the hegemony of Africanist interests among British anthropologists was definitely on the wane.
2 Her acquaintance with Brausch, and his wife, was renewed during fieldwork, and she later reviewed his account of administration in the Congo (1963d).
3 Goody cites Evans-Pritchard's letter to Fortes in 1937 that 'Women ought not be allowed to do fieldwork. I have always considered their intrusion undesirable' (1995: 70, and fn.10). Perhaps Evans-Pritchard's attitudes mellowed, or maybe this is another instance of his tendency to provocation (here, in the context of antipathy to Audrey Richards), but his insistence that Mary Tew carry out African fieldwork, albeit safely, seems to tell a different story of his practice.
4 James's mother was the friend of Mary's godmother who arranged accommodation for her studies in Paris on leaving the Sacred Heart Convent (see p. 23, n. 7).
5 Hazel Holt, Barbara Pym's biographer and fellow worker at the International African Institute, provides a striking portrayal of Forde at the Institute: four-square, brash, energetic, incisive, impatient and entirely single-minded (1990: 139–43). On taking up her post in 1946, Barbara Pym had written to a friend, 'I work for dear Professor Daryll Forde, who is brilliant, has great charm but no manners, and is altogether the kind of person I ought to work for!' (1994 [1984]: 180). Pym's recollections tend to portray herself in the role of the recalcitrant, in some awe of her Director; however, a close relation developed over the years. Forde continued to run the International African Institute following his retirement from University College until he died in May 1973: 'at work one day and dead that same evening' as Barbara Pym wrote to the poet Philip Larkin (1994: 274).
6 On the Lele 1951a, b, 1952a, 1957a, 1958a, and on central Africa comparatively 1964b, 1967a.
7 On the Lele 1955a, b, 1957b, 1959a.
8 Among the volumes in the line of succession to Evans-Pritchard and Fortes 1940 *African Political Systems* were: Radcliffe-Brown and Forde 1950 *African Systems of Kinship and Marriage*, Middleton and Tait 1958 *Tribes without Rulers*, Fortes and Dieterlain 1965 *African Systems of Thought*, Forde and Kaberry 1967 *West African Kingdoms in the Nineteenth Century*.
9 See Douglas 1952b, 1954c, 1963k on Gluckman; 1957d on Mitchell; 1959c on Watson; 1952b, 1960d on Colson; 1959d, 1970g, 1984e on Turner; 1962b on Cunnison; in related vein see also, 1952c on Wilson; 1960b on Richards; 1961c, 1966f on Marshall Thomas.
10 Douglas 1966e, 1993l on Vansina; 1960e, 1973i on de Heusch.

11 Douglas's monograph also shares the contemporary convention of occluding her fieldwork experience to a marked degree; this is a pity, since her later prose style suggests she would have made telling use of a more first-person and anecdotal ethnographic style. Initially, she established her fieldwork site in the village of Ngoie, just south of the Kasai River and relatively close to the mission, commercial and administrative centres of the region (LK: Map VI). She found her gender strongly circumscribed her access to men's affairs there and so, at the suggestion of Makum Elias, her assistant, moved eighty miles south to his village Yenga Yenga (identified as such in some of her articles, but called South Homba in her monograph). She pitched her tent in Yenga Yenga until she was found a house. Douglas's field photographs (now in the British Museum), augmented by those taken by Bill Fagg on a brief visit to Yenga Yenga, contain numerous portraits of Lele, particularly Lele women, with whom she spent her time, and document a wide range of Lele handicrafts, farming, fishing, hunting, ritual events, etc.

12 Douglas presents the Lele as an 'independent and unruly' outpost of Kuba culture, just as Emile Torday had roughly a half century earlier (LK: 9). For re-evaluation of Torday's representations, see Mack 1997.

13 A trailer for the Lele monograph appeared as Douglas's first contribution to the periodical *New Society* and drew out the analogy between pension provision in the West and Lele gerontocracy. Her effort to find a larger readership for anthropology is discussed in the next chapter.

14 Having completed her Lele monograph, Mary Douglas wrote a number of essays in comparative central African ethnography. One of these, on pawnship in central Africa – contrary to the alleged indifference of colonial ethnographers to history – pointed to the fundamental relationship between matriliny and heritable rights in pawns in a swathe of societies from coast to coast before colonial suppression of the institution (Douglas 1964b).

15 The importance to pre-colonial African political systems of partible, transferable rights in people had been recognized by Douglas's Oxford colleagues. Laura Bohannan's seminal article, 1949, had formalized this insight in relation to marriage systems, and Franz Steiner acknowledged his debt to her in applying similar reasoning to African slavery in his unpublished doctoral dissertation. Douglas herself extended the argument to pawnship among the Lele and in central Africa more generally (1964b).

Part II

SYNTHESIS: 1960s

4 *PURITY AND DANGER*
REVISITED

In 1980, the *Times Literary Supplement* published the text of a lecture entitled *'Purity and Danger* revisited' which Mary Douglas had delivered that May at London University's Institute of Education during a trip from the USA, where she then worked. In the lecture, she drew out some of the implications for debates over the environment of her most famous book, which had appeared fourteen years earlier. Detailed consideration of her analysis of the ecological movement belongs later (in Chapter 7); but three excerpts from the article illustrate a change in style, tone and address which characterizes Douglas's writings from the mid-1960s onwards.

> The earth's girdling waters and envelope of atmosphere are no longer the source of divine vengeance, visiting thunderbolts on liars, and floods and flames on godlessness. Without moral agency of their own, they are becoming the passive, vulnerable condition for life on this planet.
> …it will be an act of cultural bigotry, of intellectual blindness of the most inexcusable kind, with disastrous consequences for the world to brush aside as irrelevant to our unique condition the experience the human race has already had with perversion and impurity.
> With us, no more than with our forebears, nature and purity are not technical terms: when the border uses them, the centre is being arraigned for causing pollution. When the centre uses them, a contagious border is being cordoned off.
>
> (1980c: 1045)

The opening quotation employs the resonant imagery of the Old Testament to describe a cosmos that was once alert and responsive to human morality but has now become the passive environment of human activity. The reversal has been total, where once a vigorous environment cajoled cowed humanity, now overweening humanity threatens the conditions of its own survival. The second quotation by implication puts into question the first: challenging the uniqueness of our experience by thorough condemnation of the hubris that might convince us of the irrelevance of past human experience. In the third quotation, the first is refuted, we discover that we are not at all different, our uses of the ideas of nature and purity are just as interested as those to which our forebears put them.

What are the characteristics of the style, tone and address our author employs? The quotations are heavily rhetorical and their effect is cumulative. Any single quotation taken out of context risks missing the reversal or rethinking of a subsequent statement. The technique is to establish a starkly delineated position which is then taken as the subject of the next position in which it is modified. This modification then becomes the subject of the next move in the argument. The technique is unsettling; it is difficult to know when our author has finished her chain of thought, quite what we should consider to be the conclusion. Each move is open-ended, promising a further intellectual response. But this is not to say that the address is self-effacing; here is an author asking to be heard. Her tone is committed and urgent. We are addressed inclusively – as an 'us': an invitation is extended to the reader to identify with the writer and to make common cause with an intellectual position that has wide ramifications. Quite who 'we' are is not always the same. In *Purity and Danger*, where the device occurs often, 'we' may be Anglo-Saxons, moderns, Christians or humans; but always there is a 'we' with whom to identify and a commitment to the view this 'we' might share. Any 'we' by necessity predicates its 'they'. The relation between the 'we' and 'they' of the writer is subject to the device of shifting rebuttal I have noted above. The identities of these 'we' and 'they' are the subject of Douglas's most engaged arguments. These are arguments, in short, about the identity of the moral community to be carried along with the writing. The passionate concerns of the writer constantly demand loyalty from the reader; controversy and schism attend Douglas's later writings, and this is both because of what she says and because of the way in which she says it. If all this seems a far cry from the style of the Mary Douglas who finally published her Lele monograph in 1963, when she was in her early forties, then it may be worth spending a few paragraphs describing the transition.

BIOGRAPHICAL COUNTERPOINT

Despite the fact that her academic duties at University College during the 1950s were relatively light – at least by current standards – the decade had passed busily.[1] The youngest of Mary's three children, born in 1956, started primary school during the year she was given a sabbatical to complete the Lele monograph. Up to this point she had been, in her own terms, 'chugging along'. With her obligations to Africanist scholarship and her children's early infancy discharged, Mary Douglas began to channel her always startling energy into postponed projects; the delays occasioned by the war and family responsibilities must have made her intellectual ambitions more urgent. There is no mystery about the timing of her career changing gear, what of the form this took?

During the 1960s, Mary's husband James, who had joined the research department of the Conservative Party in 1950, rose to become Head of the Economics Section, Research Organiser and, finally, Director of the Research Department in 1970. He was identified with a 'progressive approach' within the department which was later to be marginalized, following Edward Heath's election failures, on the rise to power of Margaret Thatcher (Ramsden 1980). These events concern us later; the 1960s must have been years when the application of social theory to policy issues was a topic of concern to the Douglas household and its frequent visitors. Mary recalls often being asked by her husband whether social anthropology had something to say about contemporary Western society or was concerned only with the exotic. The foundation of a new magazine in autumn 1962 gave her a platform from which to experiment with a wider dissemination of anthropological ideas.

New Society (originally sub-titled 'The social science weekly') apparently arose following a suggestion over lunch by the sociologist Michael (later, Lord) Young (first chairman of the Social Science Research Council founded in 1965, see Douglas 1995i) to Timothy Raison. Raison had already established *New Scientist* (in 1956) to which *New Society* was to be a social science counterpart. As an article published in its final issue recalled, 'Unashamedly rationalist, the magazine was established in the confident belief that the study of the social sciences would contribute greatly to the improvement of the human condition' (Platt 1988: 19). Its first issue announced the intention of the magazine to link the experience of practitioners with the research of the academic (ibid.: 19); and this occurred during a period of rapid expansion of the social sciences, and particularly sociology, in British universities. Mary Douglas first published in the magazine in 1963, following a meeting with Raison – who was himself to become a Conservative Member of Parliament[2] – at a party, and she continued to provide an article, book review or both to its pages most years for a decade afterwards.[3] Her first article, entitled 'Tribal policies for the old', briefly summarized the analysis in her monograph of the quixotic policy by which the Lele invested authority in their elders. The nod towards broader relevance was fairly peremptory, consisting of a brief sentence exploring the fact that, 'In England an ageing population has made us familiar with the social problems of retirement' (1963b: 13). But she was soon to get into the swing of a more generalizing style, of which the appeal to an 'us' – as in the previous sentence – became a recurrent feature. An article on 'Taboo' (for a regular feature called 'Concepts') published the following year (1964c) moved from a recent suicide in Durham Cathedral to a consideration of classification that was to be expanded in *Purity and Danger*. If taboo was really an example of a broader issue, that of classification and boundaries, then better to start with 'us' rather than 'they', with our attitudes to dirt rather than with rules of avoidance in exotic societies. A four-part article (1967c1–4) published three years later provided anthropological counterpoint to a psychologist's observations on the family in contemporary Britain. The review of Godfrey Lienhardt's *Divinity and Experience* under the title 'The contempt of ritual' (also the title of Douglas's Aquinas Lectures) began to broach the subject matter of *Natural Symbols*, arguing that 'Public rituals, by establishing visible external forms, bring out of all the might-have-beens a firm social reality' (1966b: 23). Both articles shared a theme germane to the conclusion to *Purity and Danger* – that only ritual which unified experience offered the chance for people to celebrate what was rendered anomalous by the classifications on which those rituals rested. Later articles included her inaugural lecture as Professor of Anthropology at University College London, as well as her work on food classification. For a period, most of Douglas's published academic concerns had a more popular counterpart. Rather than cultivating two distinct written styles, she seems to have settled on slight modification to a high demotic tone that was a bit academic for a journalist, but mildly populist when read in the context of academic writings.

The editors of *New Society* repaid her interest with serious consideration of her books (*Purity and Danger* was reviewed in their pages by Alasdair MacIntyre, and *Natural Symbols* by James Littlejohn) in a serious but popular medium that achieved a circulation of 40,000 copies by the mid-1970s (Platt 1988: 20). The *New Society* essays were quickly followed by broadcast essays for the BBC – reprinted in the BBC's magazine *The Listener*, another vehicle of serious, popular journalism until its demise. On occasions between 1968 and 1977, the *Listener* allowed her to air what might seem arcane subjects before a general audience. Under the title, 'Smothering the differences – Mary Douglas in a savage mind about Lévi-Strauss', she decided that 'Somewhere between phrenology and the Piltdown man is where history will probably rank *The Raw and the Cooked*' (1970d: 313).[4] More personally revealing is a 1968 popular recension of her views on the ethnography of the Dogon according to the French ethnographer Marcel Griaule (1968d). This was a subject she treated academically on several occasions (basically contrasting British empiricism with French idealism, see also 1967b/h, 1968c, and lately 1995e). Her 1968 essay – a transcript of a broadcast for the BBC Third Programme – is a fluent and engaging meditation on the subject of inspiration, and more specifically on the problem of deciding to be creative. Early on she notes a sort of 'helplessness in the attitude to creativity' (1968d: 328). 'Inspiration', she observes, 'is treated like a horse which gallops off when you try too hard to catch it, but may come and nuzzle your face when you decide to give up in despair.' One trick may be to attempt to stand back from a question in order to see it in its most general terms, and specifically to see it in terms of one's general commitments in life:

I am convinced that a scientist solves his theoretical puzzles when he suddenly sees them relating to his own inner life. I believe that he gets blocked because (for whatever reason) the technical problem has become separated from his deepest concerns...there is nothing random about the inspired idea's choice of a moment to arrive…it comes when the thinker's other experiences in some abstract way dramatise the problem at issue… In some vivid experience the thinker has recognised a simplified abstract patterning of the theoretical problem.

(1968d: 328, 329, 330)

The extracts I have conflated here arise in the course of Douglas describing how the Dogon in Mali put their problems before the pale fox, brother to their creator God, in the form of a grid of lines outlined in the sand, each square representing some element of life, within which are placed pebbles, twigs and so forth representing a person's preoccupations about those areas of his life. The nocturnal creature disturbs the grid that the enquirer has prepared for it, leaving behind traces that may be read as a solution to the problem posed. The enquirer has been forced to codify an initial problem in its broadest context and then to reflect upon the disorganization of the pattern the fox brings about. Leaving aside the masculine pronouns Douglas employs, 1968 was the mid-year between publication of her two most famous works, so it is plausible to suppose close autobiographical reference (perhaps even to the grid/group diagrams, see Chapters 5 and 10), and that the decade or so in which these two works were composed was the time she achieved just such a mutual charge between personally pressing concerns and theoretical practice.

Mary Douglas did not continue to publish in either *New Society* or the *Listener* once she left London for the USA. But her reviews and essays began to appear in the *Times Literary Supplement* and the *Times Higher Education Supplement* from the 1970s onwards, and during the 1980s her writings were also published in the *New York Review of Books* and the *London Review of Books*. These journals tended to publish reviews of the work of those who wrote and reviewed for them, so publication of Douglas's later books became intellectual events of the sort noted in general reviews – as my listing of reviews confirms (Appendix 2).

Having jumped a little ahead of my subject, let me return to the early 1960s. In some ways, so far as the United Kingdom was concerned, the 1960s did not begin with the turn of the decade but a few years later. Thirteen years of Conservative government came to an end with the election of Harold Wilson's Labour government in 1964, and even the 'swinging sixties' of the Liverpool sound and a mini-skirted Carnaby Street were not much evident more than a year before that. So the early 1960s were the tail-end of a rather sleepy seeming awakening from post-war austerity – already punctuated by crises in Egypt, Kenya and elsewhere. Mary Douglas's turn to Western society for subject matter coincided with some of the cultural shocks of the 1960s, which provided her subject matter (Chapter 5). Perhaps because of her journalistic writings, her interests in 'Western society' became highly contemporary while her Africanist examples continued to be drawn in large part from the 'traditional' representations which scholars of the 1940s to 1960s had made of pre-colonial Africa. Although it is to *Natural Symbols* that we need to look for an engagement with

fully contemporary events, *Purity and Danger* gives us many clues why the commitments of that book turn out the way they do.

PURITY AND DANGER

Reception and inspirations

If readers know of, or have read, only one book by Mary Douglas that book is
likely to be *Purity and Danger*. Since publication in 1966, it has not been out of
print in English and has been translated into a dozen other languages (see
Appendix 1); it has sold steadily in a number of paperback editions thanks both
to wide use as an introductory text in anthropology and to its general appeal to a
non-anthropological audience wishing to know something about the subject.
Sections of the book have gained even wider readership thanks to reprinting in
popular course readers in the anthropology and sociology of religion (of which I
give only a couple of examples in the bibliography). The book is widely cited in
non-anthropological works and has given rise to a body of application, rebuttal
or development within anthropology.[5] Ten years after its publication, Dan
Sperber could refer uncontroversially to *Purity and Danger* as a seminal work
(IM/TLS). By any standards, this is an acknowledged modern masterpiece of
anthropology. But its influence has been wider: the book has recently been
included among the hundred most influential non-fiction works since the Second
World War, and its thirtieth anniversary occasioned further tribute.[6]

   Being so well known, I had thought that *Purity and Danger* would yield to
succinct summary; but rereading it several times, two decades after I last read it
cover to cover, I realized how selective my memory of it had become. This
would not be worth mentioning, except that other accounts of how to read *Purity
and Danger* (including some by Mary Douglas herself) also dwell upon elements of
the book's argument to the detriment of the book as a whole. None of the
accounts stressed the order in which the argument of *Purity and Danger* is
presented; yet, if my analysis of the self-correcting tendency in Mary Douglas's
argument – on the basis of her article cited at the beginning of this chapter –
has any validity, this would seem to be an author whom we must follow sequen-
tially in order to grasp her intent. This persuaded me that Douglas's two works
of synthesis and transition (*Purity and Danger* and *Natural Symbols*) would repay
close presentation.

   Just how committed a book was *Purity and Danger* may not have been apparent
to many of its readers; it certainly went unremarked by contemporary reviewers.
Three reviews by Oxford anthropologists concurred that the book was lively,
'modern', provocative and thought-provoking, but not original.

   The approach is not in a strict sense novel…but this is an essentially
   modern book. It carries forward much that is implicit in recent thinking

and applies it with admirable skill to the resolution of some old problems.

(Ardener PD/Man: 139)

The issues she raises touch upon problems of the utmost theoretical
importance. She fails to resolve these but she formulates them in a
provocative and highly readable manner and consequently may help to
deseminate [*sic*] the argument of a small but growing school of modern
social anthropologists who see 'structural analysis' as an important
recrudescence of the profound sociological insights first presented by
Durkheim, Mauss, van Gennep, Hertz and others of their distinguished
tradition.

(Beidelman PD/Anth: 908)

She writes in a distinguished scholarly tradition that may be traced from
the *Année sociologique* school to the late Dr. Franz Steiner, and those who
have absorbed the ideas of Durkheim, Mauss, Hubert, Van Gennep
and their congeners will feel that they are in a familiar intellectual
ambience. The average social anthropologist will feel at home also with
most of the sources used, and will probably gain little in the way of
substantive knowledge.

(Needham PD/TLS: 131)

All three Oxford reviewers saw *Purity and Danger* as a talented recension of the
Oxford interpretation of French ideas in anthropological theory. The book was
to be recommended as a summary of a patented brand of enquiry, but it was not
hailed as a breakthrough. Quite what this common approach consisted of we
shall see shortly. One American reviewer also recognized the school to which the
work belonged, but took the opportunity to lambaste the book as a catalogue of
unsupported assertions (Spiro PD/AA).

  From the safety of a quarter century of hindsight, it is remarkable how
similar were the readings of the book. All concentrated on the role of boundaries and hence anomalies in the classification of experience; all particularly
applauded the example of the Jewish dietary regulations specified in Leviticus.[7]
The reviewers generally noted that the book contained a critical account of the
development of anthropological theories of religion in Britain, but they paid
little attention to the author's concern with the similarities and differences
between primitive and modern societies, or to the arguments about the ethical
and intellectual insights of different cultures that the author advanced. None
noted that, in parallel with an argument concerning classification that relied on
structural and functional types of argument, the author also developed a broadly
evolutionary theory of culture and religion, and that much of the complexity of
the book resulted from the attempt to correlate these two arguments built on
rather different foundations. Because reviewers read pretty much the book they

expected *Purity and Danger* to be, there grew up the general impression that there was a hiatus between certain ideas expressed in that book and in its immediate sequel *Natural Symbols*. This was my impression too, so I take this opportunity to scrape away some of the patina of past readings in order to highlight the continuities.

From a biographical perspective, *Purity and Danger* synthesizes almost all the preceding influences on Mary's thought but stops short of making the selection among them that becomes apparent from *Natural Symbols* onwards. Some of the themes important to *Purity and Danger* are hardly developed later, while some of its minor themes dominate her later work. By the middle 1960s Mary Douglas had absorbed most of the influences that were to define the main lines of her later enquiries. Let me recap what I think these influences were.

From her Catholic upbringing, Mary was familiar with a world of rich symbols and hierarchically articulated, authoritatively organized community. She felt intense loyalty to this world and sought to defend its values against what she construed as a hostile social and intellectual environment. This stance relates closely to what I have called her sociological conservatism. From her convent education she brought a humanist bias to her anthropological writings, so that she did not hesitate to mix poetry, novels and literary criticism with ethnography in a way that was less current in the two post-war decades than it is now. Her first degree in Politics, Philosophy and Economics at Oxford gave her familiarity with – and, more importantly, enormous curiosity about – the curricula of the social sciences outside anthropology. Evans-Pritchard's championship – at Oxford – of the French tradition in the sociology of knowledge was the most important element of her anthropological training. But this went along with other British anthropological interests in corporate organization (especially stressed in Meyer Fortes' teaching) and with interpersonal relations and their manipulation (especially in the Manchester tradition). Oxford anthropology in the immediate post-war years had additionally been concerned with theological issues (only in the sense specified earlier); and this interest is reflected in *Purity and Danger* in a form that was not to be a lasting element in her work. Her acknowledgements in *Purity and Danger* to Professor Srinivas and Franz Steiner (friend and teacher at Oxford) who 'as Brahmin and Jew, tried in their daily lives to handle problems of ritual cleanness' (PD: vii) show how Mary was, and continued to be, interested in the lives of people who were religious, regardless of creed or sect.

I deferred consideration of the impact of the Jewish Czech scholar, Franz Steiner, on Mary Douglas from Chapter 2, where it chronologically belonged, until now in order to highlight the impact of his lectures on taboo to her project. Steiner did not live to complete the third year of his Oxford lectureship; but contemporary recollections suggest his intellectual influence there was substantial.[8] His posthumously published *Taboo* (1956) is the crucial point of departure for *Purity and Danger* for which three misconceptions had to be cleared away. Franz Steiner in his lectures on taboo first showed how misleading, lazy-minded and even fatal to comparative religion it is to subscribe in any sense to a two-compartment theory of religion. We must break down the division between the alien, exotic compartment in which magic and irrational taboo run riot and the other civilized, enlightened and ethical compartment of advanced religion. No one would now wish to defend a 'we'/'they' position in this subject. Second, he reinstated religion as total cosmology, concerned with active principles of all kinds. Ethics belong within the religious view but do not circumscribe it. Third, he reduced the sacred to the status of a relationship, often a matter of a hedge or boundary-making around the idea of divine power. At least the Hebrew *qodesh*, and Polynesian *taboo* and Latin *sacer* appropriately modified can be handled in these terms, and they enable our own word sacred to articulate better with consecrate, desecrate, sacrilege and sacrifice when this side of its meaning is to the fore. Once Steiner had done this we were back where we might have started from, with taboos as rules of avoidance which express danger attitudes.

(1964c: 25)

This lengthy quotation from Douglas's recension of the argument of *Purity and Danger* for *New Society*, under the title 'Taboo', fully acknowledges the debt and runs immediately to introduce one of the celebrated themes of her later book: the tidying of dirt, conceived as 'matter out of place', as a mundane example of action in the service of classification.[9] We shall find that much of Douglas's critical apparatus in *Purity and Danger* is close to Steiner's, particularly his attention to the 'Protestant bias' in previous anthropological theorizing. More generally, and perhaps more enduringly, Steiner's thought allied the most subtle of sociological insight with intense loyalty to the beliefs of his religious community, suggesting not just that there was no necessary antinomy between the two, but that sociological insight might be used in the defence of religious orthodoxy.

The final consideration we need to bear in mind in reading *Purity and Danger* is Douglas's commitment, noted repeatedly, to demonstrate the relevance of anthropological enquiries to an audience outside her narrow academic circle. The philosopher, Alasdair MacIntyre's conclusion – 'she continually makes points which illuminate the philosophy of religion and the philosophy of science and help to show the rest of us just why and how anthropology has become a fundamental intellectual discipline' (PD/NS: 27) – must have been particularly gratifying.

A rereading

With these indications in place, we can start with the most conventional of readings: *Purity and Danger* is justly recalled as a plea for a holistic approach to classification. Its most celebrated examples are drawn from the Jewish dietary prohibitions and behavioural norms specified in Leviticus, and from the Lele cult of the pangolin. In both cases, Mary Douglas shows how the treatment of anomalous creatures (the despised pig for the Jews, the revered pangolin for the Lele) is explained by the special ways that the characteristics of these creatures challenge the integrity of indigenous principles of classification. Most references to and quotations from *Purity and Danger* highlight these analyses – which became exemplars of a particular style of enquiry in subsequent anthropology. In the limited sense of furnishing exemplary instances, these analyses can be said to have become anthropological paradigms. But, for what plots (or intellectual storylines) were these stylish demonstrations the triumphant dénouements? The full analysis of Leviticus occurs in an early chapter of the book; the exploration of the cult of the pangolin is part of the book's conclusion. In fact, the two famous examples are used differently.

Read as a whole, *Purity and Danger* contains a potentially bewildering richness of both constructive and critical arguments. The criticism is embedded in a variety of historical plots with diverse connotations. The complexity of the book derives from the way in which the plots are interrelated. Fortunately, the breaks in the argument coincide to a marked extent with the organization of the chapters. In a highly formal fashion, the ten chapters of the book can be broken down in the following way.[10] The first, middle and last chapters (Chapters 1, 5 and 10) are concerned with two historical plots that hinge around the question of the differences between 'them' (primitives) and 'us' (moderns). Chapter 1 catalogues erroneous attempts to oppose an 'us' to a 'them'. When these oppositions have been shown to be poorly founded, largely thanks to mistakes in our understanding of ourselves, then Chapters 2, 3 and 4 can demonstrate how 'we' and 'they' are basically the same. In Chapter 5, this procedure is reversed and an extended argument is made about the differences between 'us' and 'them' – but, of course, these differences are not those which have been deconstructed in Chapter 1; they are differences understood in the light of the similarities that have just been established. The chapters of the second part of the book (Chapters 6, 7, 8 and 9) are concerned to analyse some of the precise features of the differences among the newly defined 'them'. So far, the text has moved from an erroneous account of difference, through an account of sameness, to a new and more detailed account of difference. The joker in the pack is the final chapter which is ambiguous but can plausibly be interpreted, in some respects, as a further corrective to the account of difference that tends to lead us back to a concluding account of human similarity. In formal terms, this is the reading I shall be pursuing in the remainder of this chapter. Nowhere in *Purity and Danger* does Mary Douglas offer the reader a set of instructions from which my route through the text might be verified. In its defence, my reading addresses the whole book, weighs its parts equally, and tends to solve problems that otherwise occur in relating *Purity and Danger* to *Natural Symbols* – works that were written end-to-end.

The history of unfounded differences (Introduction and Chapter 1)

The beliefs of 'primitive' peoples have been systematically mangled in Western attempts to understand them. These attempts have been pejorative and prevented 'we moderns' from appreciating the profundity of the metaphysical problems that 'primitive' religions address. Moreover, the way that moderns have failed to appreciate primitives exactly mirrors ways in which moderns have misunderstood certain of their contemporaries. We need to flesh out this rudimentary version of part of the plot.

The Introduction to *Purity and Danger* begins with a nineteenth-century misapprehension to which the author will return in her concluding chapter:

> The nineteenth century saw in primitive religions two particularities which separated them as a block from the great religions of the world. One was that they were inspired by fear, the other that they were inextricably confused with defilement and hygiene.
>
> (PD: 1)

The opening sentences establish an initial opposition between 'them' (believers in primitive religion) and 'us' (members of great religions) that Mary Douglas immediately sets about deconstructing: modern ethnographies do not portray members of primitive societies to be dominated by fear. This attitude does not distinguish 'them' from 'us'. Furthermore, pollution beliefs are not specific to primitive societies. Attempts to control disorder, to clean or avoid dirt, are positive gestures found in all societies. Why are pollution beliefs universal? Because they serve two ends: they offer a strong language of mutual coercion that people may use to cajole one another into line, and at 'a more interesting level…some pollutions are used as analogies for expressing a general view of the social order' (PD: 3). Here is a striking instance of the style of argument I remarked earlier. Apparent antinomy between types of people is undercut empirically and then analytically by recourse to a functional argument. Not only is difference replaced by similarity, the apparent difference is shown to result from an insufficient self-knowledge. The first chapter (titled 'Ritual uncleanness') sets about the deconstructive task in greater detail.

> For us sacred things and places are to be protected from defilement. Holiness and impurity are at opposite poles.…Yet it is supposed to be a mark of primitive religion to make no clear distinction between sanctity and uncleanness. If this is true it reveals a great gulf between ourselves and our forefathers, between us and contemporary primitives.
>
> (PD: 7–8)

The greatest debt of the ensuing analysis is to Mary's teacher, Evans-Pritchard, and especially to the account of the development of scholarship in comparative religion outlined in his early Cairo essays (and largely reiterated in his 1965 book, *Theories of Primitive Religion*, which is almost contemporary with *Purity and Danger*). Previous writers set up numerous binary distinctions, usually of an 'us' and 'them' variety, which are wrongly founded, practically unhelpful, and ought to be banished. Some previous writers are almost without redeeming quality – for instance James Frazer, in his conviction that primitive magic posed an intellectual problem of mistaken belief in instrumental efficacy – 'No doubt about it, the savage was a credulous fool' (PD: 24). Other writers are more interesting because their basic insights were sound even if the solutions to the problems they set themselves were flawed. The heroes and villains of the account are largely as they were for Evans-Pritchard or Steiner. The claim of Robertson Smith to have been the founder of anthropological studies of religious practice is strongly supported (as it is by Beidelman 1974c). Robertson Smith emphasized the stages by which religion became an increasingly exhaustive ethical outlook. He therefore separated religion, a community affair, from magic (a class of automatically effective ritual). Magic was a residue of his interest to isolate religion as an ethical system; but in the emphasis upon the 'common elements in modern and primitive experience', Robertson Smith not only founded the social anthropology of religion, but founded it with a particular bias. Note how Mary Douglas editorializes this move:

> In a sense magic was to the Hebrews what Catholicism was to the Protestants, mumbo-jumbo, meaningless ritual, irrationally held to be sufficient in itself to produce results without an interior experience of God.
>
> (PD: 18)

> Whatever the Scot's motives the historical fact remains that comparative religion has inherited an ancient sectarian quarrel about the value of formal ritual.
>
> (PD: 19)

The relational reference to Catholicism, and the glance towards the 'contempt of ritual', are indicators of an argument to become crucial in *Natural Symbols*; however, the theme is already present in *Purity and Danger*. In the next but one chapter (Chapter 4 'Magic and miracle') Douglas returns to a variant of the same idea. The problem, she is arguing, is to understand why Europeans believe there is such a thing as primitive magic (not the primitive belief itself which is highly questionable); her argument is similar to Lévi-Strauss's who similarly dismissed the phenomenon of totemism, or Steiner's who distinguished the Polynesian *tabu* from the, largely, Victorian taboo (Steiner 1956; Lévi-Strauss 1963 [1962]).

86

A contrast between interior will and exterior enactment goes deep into the history of Judaism and Christianity.

(PD: 61)

In wave upon wave the Reformation has continued to thunder against the empty encrustation of ritual. So long as Christianity has any life, it will never be time to stop echoing the parable of the Pharisee and the Publican, to stop saying that external forms can become empty and mock the truths they stand for. With every new century we become heirs to a longer and more vigorous anti-ritualist tradition.

(PD: 62)

A series of homologous binary distinctions that have organized debate between Western traditions of Christianity have also structured relations between the 'great religions' and the 'primitive'. Thus the relation Protestant/Catholic is analogous to the relations: Hebrew/pagan, religion/magic, interior will/external enactment, belief/ritual, and so forth.

Robertson Smith's intellectual successors drew upon different parts of his work. In Britain, Frazer drove anthropology up a long blind alley studying the savage as an Aladdin rubbing the lamp who believed in principles of magical efficacy achieved through properties of sympathy and contagion (in symbolic terms: metaphor or metonymy). Durkheim was successor to Robertson Smith's sociological project, but restricted its pertinence to pre-modern societies and retained the distinction between magic and religion – thus accepting the distinction between 'us' and 'them'. 'The more intractable puzzles in comparative religion arise because human experience has…been wrongly divided' (PD: 29).

Similarity reinstated (Chapters 2–4)

With difference apparently deconstructed, Chapter 2 sets out the elements of a better approach. The psychology of perception suggests that we (regardless of who 'we' are) experience the world on the basis of already held categories.

Perceiving is not a matter of passively allowing an organ – say of sight or hearing – to receive a ready-made impression from without, like a palette receiving a spot of paint. Recognising and remembering are not matters of stirring up old images of past impressions. It is generally agreed that all our impressions are schematically determined from the start. As perceivers we select from all the stimuli falling on our senses only those which interest us, and our interests are governed by a pattern-making tendency, sometimes called *schema* (see Bartlett 1932) [*Remembering: a Study in Experimental and Social Psychology*]….As time goes on and experiences pile up, we make a greater and greater investment in our system of labels. So a conservative bias is built in. It gives us confidence.…We share with other animals a kind of filtering mechanism which at first only lets in sensations we know how to use.

(PD: 37–38)

The individual's capacity to order knowledge and experience is logically required for that individual to be able to have experience or knowledge. This is the position that Durkheim also accepted from Kant. Durkheim moved immediately from this to note the generality of categorical schemes within a society: if the categories are shared they cannot be individual in origin. If not individual then they must be social in origin (since individual–society is a basic dualism in Durkheim's thought). And if social in origin, then Durkheim argued, society must be the model from which other classificatory schemes are derived. Thus, other schemata are analogies of social classification (the classification, that is, of other people). This notion – that classifications of other people are isomorphic with classifications of things – is a train of argument that Douglas occasionally follows also. But her main argument is more nuanced. Leaving the tracks established by Durkheim, she takes what might seem a branch line from the main argument: a clear system of schema must make sense of an inherently untidy world. What happens to all those things that do not fit in: either because they are anomalous (in terms of the schema) or because they are ambiguous (difficult to allocate definitively)? Culture, used in this context (PD: 39–40) to mean the standardized values of a community, has to make provision for the elements that do not fit into shared classificatory schemes. At the end of Chapter 2, she lists five options found in 'any culture worthy of the name' – a favourite and recurrent phrase (see 1964c: 25) – for dealing with ambiguous or anomalous events.

1   Anomalies can be settled by definitive reclassification (often confirmed by a ritual): 'So the Nuer treat monstrous births as baby hippopotamuses, accidentally born to humans and, with this labelling, the appropriate action is clear. They gently lay them in the river where they belong.'

2   The existence of anomalies can be controlled physically: 'Thus in some West African tribes the rule that twins should be killed at birth eliminates a social anomaly, if it is held that two humans could not be born from the same womb at the same time.'

3   'A rule of avoiding anomalous things affirms and strengthens the definitions to which they do not conform': thus the dietary avoidances of Jews.

4   'Anomalous events may be labelled dangerous…Attributing danger is one way of putting a subject above dispute.'

5   'Ambiguous symbols can be used in ritual for the same ends as they are used in poetry and mythology, to enrich meaning or call attention to other levels of existence' (PD: 40–41).

By this point, the rejected dichotomies of nineteenth-century thought have been replaced by the antinomies that are the hallmarks of *Purity and Danger*. The most basic of these is the contrast differently phrased as that between form and formlessness, or order and disorder, or structure and its absence. These antinomies are often presented as the outcome of a process: both the natural world and human experience are treated as potentially anarchic and threatening. The imposition of order is the prerequisite of comprehensible human experience or predictable human sociality. But in the imposition of order, a residue of disorder is created (from diverse sources ranging from the unruliness of the original materials to the arbitrariness of the rules themselves). Cultures may be classified according to the way in which they handle ambiguity and anomaly in different areas of classification. 'We', whether we are primitives or moderns, are subject to the same rules about the schematic ordering of experience; the rules apply equally to sacred and to secular matters (PD: 41). It follows that any study of classification needs to be holistic – that is to say, capable of grasping the design of the overall patterning that produces anomaly and ambiguity. It is in illustration of the general thesis about classification, that the celebrated third chapter on 'The abominations of Leviticus' is introduced:

> Defilement is never an isolated event. It cannot occur except in view of a systematic ordering of ideas. Hence any piecemeal interpretation of pollution rules of another culture is bound to fail. For the only way in which pollution ideas make sense is in reference to a total structure of thought whose key-stone, boundaries, margins and internal lines are held in relation by rituals of separation.
>
> (PD: 42)

There is not space to reproduce all the details of the dense analysis Douglas carries out on Leviticus, but we can review its technique and conclusions (see also Chapter 9). Two classes of alternative explanation are ruled out: those that rely upon arguments about the functions of particular avoidances (in terms of 'medical materialism' – i.e. the avoidance of unhealthy foods – or in terms of self-discipline, or allegorization) are ruled out because they beg results of which the Israelites could not have been aware, or because they beg a disparity of means and ends – why have such an elaborate set of rules to reach such limited goals? Alternatively, these explanations fall foul of the injunction to holistic explanation. Even if we accept that the Israelites avoided pork because it was dangerous in hot climates, this does not help us to explain why they did not eat the rock badger, camel or hare. We are faced by a multiplication of arguments in order to account for each of the enormous variety of injunctions. Better that we 'start with the texts', and with the fact that every injunction is 'prefaced by the command to be holy, so they must be explained by that command' (PD: 50).

Holiness in Hebrew means set apart, blessing, also wholeness and completeness. 'Holiness is exemplified by completeness' (PD: 54). 'Holiness means keeping distinct the categories of creation', and creation was itself achieved through naming. Holiness is completion and perfection: religious officiants and sacrifices should be perfect; types of animals should not be mixed (but nor should types of fabric, nor sexual roles). Genesis describes the separation of realms of earth, waters and firmament, and Leviticus specifies the characteristics of edible animals in each: two-legged fowl that fly in the sky, fishes with fins and scales that swim in the sea, and for the pastoralist Israelites, edible animals that walk upon the earth with cloven hooves and chew the cud. Thus, things that swarm upon the ground or crawl (but not hop), things in the water without scales and fins (crustaceans), and several types of bird are unclean. Since the pig uniquely is cloven-footed but does not chew the cud it evokes an intense reaction; the rock badger and camel are cud-chewing but not cloven-footed; however, they are not uniquely anomalous, nor are they kept only for food. The reaction to them is less intense.

The analysis of the Jewish sumptuary laws, which has justifiably achieved a paradigmatic status in anthropological teaching, is not an end in itself. The observance of dietary rules directly enables an extension of the argument of the book in Chapter 4:

> it is a mistake to suppose that there can be religion which is all interior, with no rules, no liturgy, no external signs of inward states. As with society so with religion, external form is the condition of its existence…*As a social animal, man is a ritual animal*. If ritual is suppressed in one form it crops up in others, more strongly the more intense the social interaction…Social rituals create a reality which would be nothing without them. It is not too much to say that ritual is more to society than words are to thought.
>
> (PD: 63, my emphasis)

Quite how strong an argument this is depends upon the sense that is being given to ritual, which here seems to stand for an enormous range of relatively formalized behaviour that is recognizable across the different contexts in which it occurs. If this is the case, then, to say with Durkheim that ritual belongs with a social theory of knowledge may risk generalizing from especially marked forms of behaviour to all formalized behaviour. Douglas argues that just as speech can create thoughts, so ritual can create perception. Ritual is a frame of experience and therefore increases the experiences to which the individual has been prepared to be receptive. Ritual, she argues, has real effects. Ndembu healers in central Africa bring about the reordering of social relations – rather like social workers (PD: 71–72). Cuna shamans dramatize the difficulties of a woman in childbirth through a mythical journey to conquer the obstructions to successful delivery – in the effects they achieve they might be compared to psychotherapists (PD: 72–73). In these two examples of similarity, the movement towards effacement of the differences between 'them' and 'us' reaches its climax. Note that this movement has involved two types of argument: structural argument, about the universal design of cognitive systems, and functional arguments, about the effects of acting in terms of – and upon – shared social classifications.

Difference reinstated (Chapter 5)

The chapter, 'Primitive worlds', takes up the case for a difference of degree between 'them' and 'us'. Like her teacher Evans-Pritchard, Douglas – at least in the mid-1960s – is concerned to retain a distinction between primitive and modern societies. The theme of the difference has been stated in the previous chapter with reference to the Nilotic Dinka:

> Dinka culture is unified. Since all their major contexts of experience overlap and interpenetrate…But our experiences take place in separate compartments…we do not bring forward from one context to the next the same set of ever more powerful symbols: our experience is fragmented.

> (PD: 69, 70)

Generalizing the case, 'Progress means differentiation. Thus primitive means undifferentiated; modern means differentiated' (PD: 78).

If the first four chapters of the book can be traced to the intellectual influence of Durkheim and Mauss's essay on *Primitive Classification* (1903), this argument looks like a straightforward reiteration of Durkheim's distinction between mechanical and organic solidarity, or any of the other evolutionary schemes that correlated modernity with an increasing division of labour. Societies held together by similarity gradually transform into societies based on difference. But why should social differentiation and intellectual differentiation be related? Douglas's argument about the differences between 'them' (primitives) and 'us' (moderns) begins by pointing to the self-evidence of increasing differentiation driven by technological factors. But this does not automatically entail intellectual differentiation: many African and Australian cosmologies are extraordinarily complex, albeit their division of labour is low. Douglas adds a more specialized sense of intellectual differentiation: the Kantian principle that thought can only advance by becoming aware of the conditions of its own subjectivity. Reflexivity is the difference, she argues, between primitive and modern worlds. Primitives live in a pre-Copernican world, which is why in the introductory chapter of the book she refers to the primitive society as an energized structure: or later claims that, 'the universe is man-centred in the sense that it must be interpreted by reference to humans…it is expected to behave as if it was intelligent…[and do so with] discernment' (PD: 86, 87, 88).

Technological problems have been long solved in primitive societies; the pressing problems concern dealing with one another: 'to serve…practical social ends all kinds of beliefs in the omniscience and omnipotence of the environment are called into play' (PD: 92). The entire cosmos is called upon to play a role in supporting social relations. Sanctions of a cosmic nature are especially necessary in situations when political institutions are unable to maintain order. In an account with resonances of Foucault's delineation of man's self-knowledge, the history of our increasing self-awareness – or at least our impression of having attained such knowledge – transpires also to be a history of political and economic practices of taxation and monetary incentive, law enforcement by police, regimentation into armies and the other agencies of social control. And the historical expansion of these agencies (at least in European history) has been accompanied by the retreat of religious authorities into contemplation of a restricted and strictly 'religious' set of problems. Lévy-Bruhl noted that 'primitives' appeared to make leaps in their reasoning and sought the reasons for this in terms of mental difference; according to Mary Douglas, he ought to have looked at the differences between primitive and modern social institutions. 'One inevitable by-product of social differentiation is social awareness, self-consciousness about the processes of communal life' (PD: 93).

This historical scenario suggests – albeit with some ambiguity – that 'progress' from the primitive to the modern may be liberating intellectually. For the time being, we are presented with an evolutionary vision of societies ranked in terms of their progress towards self-awareness. But the possibility of revision of this scheme is already envisaged in a loose end in the argument. *Purity and Danger*'s first chapter, the reader may recall, presented a fallacious argument for difference in terms of primitive and great religious traditions. This difference has been replaced by another difference between primitive and modern societies. What then is the status of great religious traditions, the missing term in this new account? The answer we are given is unsatisfactory and involves changing the sense of the past that has organized the chapter thus far: from a global evolutionary account to a particular historical account.

> Christian believers, Moslems and Jews are not to be classed as primitive on account of their beliefs. Nor necessarily Hindus, Buddhists or Mormons, for that matter. It is true that their beliefs are developed to answer the questions 'Why did it happen to me: Why now?' and the rest. It is true that their universe is man-centred and personal. Perhaps in entertaining metaphysical questions at all these religions may be counted anomalous institutions in the modern world. For unbelievers may leave such problems aside. But this in itself does not make of believers promontories of primitive culture sticking out strangely in a modern world. For their beliefs have been phrased and rephrased with each century and their intermeshing with social life cut loose.
>
> (PD: 93)

This is an uncomfortable piece of special pleading. Members of the great religions are exempted from all the foregoing analyses: both evolutionary and sociological. Believers are justified by their beliefs having been cut loose from the very social life in which metaphysical problems arise. Moreover, unbelievers are treated as if they were unconcerned by questions about the misfortunes that befall them. Neither of these arguments survives into Douglas's later work; however, the argument of *Purity and Danger*, so far as modern societies are concerned, is left at that for the time being in order to develop a comparative account of the relations between systems of classification and the diverse social structures of primitive societies.

The social dimensions of difference in primitive societies (Chapters 6–9)

Chapters 6 to 9 add a social dimension to the discussion of classification and ritual; a task which had been put to one side during Chapter 5 in order to re-establish primitive society as a legitimate subject of investigation. However, Chapter 6 also begins with a re-establishment of the widest common 'we',

> Granted that disorder spoils pattern; it also provides the materials of pattern. Order implies restriction; from all possible materials, a limited selection has been made and from all possible relations a limited set has been used. So disorder by implication is unlimited, no pattern has been realised in it, but its potential for patterning is indefinite. This is why, though *we* seek to create order, *we* do not simply condemn disorder. *We* recognise that it is destructive to existing patterns; also that it has potentiality. It symbolises both danger and power.
>
> (PD: 95, my emphases)

Society also has a formal structure. Like the classificatory system, the social system has its well-defined areas and its ill-defined interstices. Social anomalies and ambiguities are both dangerous and powerful, like their counterparts in other structured areas of experience. Unborn children among the Lele may be credited with capricious ill-will, but the mentally sick and prisoners in our own societies are in the same structural position; as, for instance, are young people undergoing initiation rituals in Africa. Both the choice of 'we' and the choice of examples to illustrate our common condition show that the argument has returned to the canvas of a shared human predicament. The chapter continues by developing an analogy between the formal structure of society and the formal allocation of powers and dangers. In a way we have noted previously, the argument sets out from a bold hypothesis which is then subjected to modification and reformulation.

Many ideas of power, we are told, 'are based on an idea of society as a series of forms contrasted with surrounding non-form' (PD: 99). Explicit powers are attached to well-articulated parts of the authority system; where social structure is ill articulated, and people are forced to occupy ambiguous roles, we should expect them to be credited with uncontrolled powers (PD: 100). Internalized, unformed psychic powers are attributed to people who disorder society. This initial hypothesis predicts direct analogy between social structure and the types of power available to those who occupy positions in it. However, the formulation runs into immediate problems. First, if social structure is defined from the local viewpoint then it is only another element of the system of classification. The formulation becomes tautologous, or at best no more than an expectation of consistency in social classification. Douglas avers to the differences actors may entertain about relevant social structure in different contexts, and adds that the sociologist's view of social structure may not coincide with that of local actors. But the exact status of the concept 'social structure' is not a problem she faces squarely in *Purity and Danger*. Is disorder a residue of the formal system or an intrinsic aspect of that system? Quotations could be found to show both assumptions at work. Consideration of this problem is forestalled by one that is more urgent. Pursuing the analogy between social structure and power, Douglas arrives at a threefold classification: those in authority wield defined and formal powers, those in interstitial positions are credited with inchoate powers, and pollution powers are not credited to anyone but represent an automatic response to infraction of formal structure. However, in many parts of the world people in interstitial positions are credited with the use of sorcery (a consciously controlled power), 'So the correlation I have tried to draw does not hold' (PD: 106). Anyway, she concludes, both social structure and mystic power are highly complex, and so the two are difficult to correlate.

Rather than ditching an argument that has run aground, a new direction is proposed which will involve distinguishing powers biased towards failure from those biased towards success. Suppose that those in authority fail to discharge the obligations of their offices, then it is predictable that they should be subject to the accusation of using illegitimate powers. Where authority is weakly defined, then sorcery may be part of the means to compete for power. Both witchcraft and sorcery are beliefs biased towards failure and may be contrasted with success-based beliefs such as *mana* (in Polynesia) and *baraka* (in North Africa). The hypothesis of correlation between belief and social structure is now so far weakened as to suggest only that beliefs in spiritual power are not independent of the formal system, or that if they are this is because the system is so weak as not to be a system at all. Pollution is then introduced at the very end of the chapter as a power not inhering in the psyche but in the structure of ideas. 'A power by which the structure is expected to protect itself' (PD: 114). Where this argument might lead is not explored further until *Natural Symbols*, when the idea of distinguishing different social forms allows a reformulation.

Chapters 7, 8 and 9 deal respectively with different aspects of classificatory systems: their handling of external boundaries, of internal distinctions and of contradictions generated by classification. My summary must be brief. Chapter 7 begins with the idea of society; an image with clear boundaries and internal divisions, which even by itself can 'stir men to action' (PD: 115). Although any human experience of structure can symbolize society, the structure of living forms is especially well suited to reflect complex social forms. As part of the 'common fund of human experience', the body especially is used as an analogue of society. From this weak position – that the body may be used to symbolize society – Douglas moves immediately to the strong notion that it must do so.

> We cannot possibly interpret rituals concerning excreta, breast milk, saliva and the rest unless we are prepared to see in the body a symbol of society, and to see the powers and dangers credited to social structure reproduced in small on the human body.
>
> (PD: 116)

After a detailed refutation of some psychoanalytic approaches to bodily symbolism in primitive societies, Douglas offers her own interpretation of the preoccupation with body margins and discharges in the pollution beliefs of the Coorgs in India, like Israelites a minority set apart.[11] 'Ritual protection of bodily orifices', she concludes, '[is] a symbol of social preoccupations about exits and entrances' (PD: 127). In other words, we are to expect direct analogy between the pressures on the social boundaries of groupings and their preoccupation with the boundaries of the bodies of their members. 'The rituals enact the form of social relations and in giving these relations visible expression enable people to know their own society' (PD: 129). The cursory analysis of this chapter is once again to be resumed at length in *Natural Symbols*.

Chapter 8 moves from consideration of the external boundary of society to analysis of the distinctions that must be maintained within it. Again the analysis is avowedly provisional. Our author cannot show that pollution rules coincide with moral rules. Only 'here and there' do we find that what is polluting is also judged wrong (PD: 130). Nonetheless, it is possible to fulfil the more modest ambition of showing that pollution rules have 'some connection' with moral rules. The argument of the chapter is wholly functionalist. Pollution rules support morality in society by determining what are to count as infractions where morality is ill defined, by reducing conflict between rules, by mobilizing public outrage, and by providing sanction where otherwise there is none (PD: 134). When breaches of pollution rules rebound not upon the guilty party but upon a closely related innocent victim, for instance the child of an adulterous woman, this serves to increase the pressure on the guilty party to undergo rituals of purification. However, the efficiency of purification rituals may also take on a cultural life of its own, allowing frequent breaches of the codes the pollution rules are supposed to uphold because cancellation of the effects of transgression is anticipated.[12] Such honouring of rules in the breach cannot be taken as evidence of breakdown in the system's functioning, unless 'other forces of disintegration are at work' (PD: 139). Again the chapter ends with the apologetic note that a 'cursory sketch is as far as I can go on the relation between pollution and morals' (PD: 139).

Finally, in this section of the book, Chapter 9 considers the problem of contradiction between the rules of social life. The examples are instances of contradictory expectations in relations between the sexes. Where male dominance is directly enforced, pollution rules are absent (as among the Australian Walbiri). Pollution beliefs are also absent where male rights in children are stringently upheld (among Sudanese Nuer). But where men marry the daughters of their enemies (New Guinea Enga), or where men simultaneously attempt to treat women both as people and as a transactable commodity (central African Lele), or where men must simultaneously aspire to control both their wives and sisters (Bemba), then contradictory principles are at work and pollution rules express this contradiction. The four exploratory and avowedly provisional chapters of the fourth section of *Purity and Danger* thus appeal to different and not wholly compatible analytic assumptions: Chapter 6 presents a complex argument about political process and notions of power; Chapter 7 argues for a simple correspondence between bodily and social boundaries; Chapter 8 presents a functional account of the way pollution beliefs uphold social structure; Chapter 9 seems to rely upon a structural argument in which pollution beliefs reflect contradictions between social norms. But each chapter, in its way, is supposed to suggest the particularity of primitive universes responding as energized entities to human conduct.

Similarity reinstated (Chapter 10)

The final chapter of *Purity and Danger*, entitled 'The system shattered and renewed', breaks with the preceding section and returns to the historical sub-plots of the book (that I have argued also dominate the opening and central chapters). We are promised an answer to the question with which the book began, 'Can there be any people who confound sacredness with uncleanness?' (PD: 160). The answer we are given partly subverts the conclusion of Chapter 5, in which we had been told that as societies increase in social differentiation so they increase in social awareness; and, thus, 'we' (moderns) are more self-conscious than 'they' (primitives); again the position of the world religions is awkward:

> In a given culture it seems that some kinds of behaviour or natural phenomena are recognised as utterly wrong by all the principles which govern the universe. There are different kinds of impossibilities, anomalies, bad mixings and abominations. Most of the items receive varying degrees of condemnation and avoidance. Then suddenly we find one of the most abominable or impossible is singled out and put into a very special kind of ritual frame that marks it off from other experience. The frame ensures that the categories which the normal avoidances sustain are not threatened or affected in any way. Within the ritual frame the abomination is then handled as a source of tremendous power.
>
> (PD: 166)

This insight opens, but only for a moment, a project identified by William James: 'The completest religions would therefore seem to be those in which the pessimistic elements are best developed' (quote from *Varieties of Religious Experience*, p.161). But this prospect is immediately ruled out as being 'utterly beyond the scope of objective scholarship....All live religions are many things' (PD: 166). Public or private rituals may be inconsistent among themselves, and the two categories may not carry the same message, some beliefs may be unritualized, people may not even listen to their preachers. Reaching for a conclusion to *Purity and Danger*, Douglas returns to the pangolin, 'a mystery of mediation' between the human and animal realms of the Lele:

> In their descriptions of the pangolin's behaviour and in their attitude to its cult, Lele say things which uncannily recall passages of the Old Testament, interpreted in the Christian tradition. Like Abraham's ram in the thicket and like Christ, the pangolin is spoken of as the voluntary victim. It is not caught, but rather it comes to the village. It is a kingly victim: the village treats its corpse as a living chief and requires the behaviour of respect for a chief on pain of future disaster. If its rituals are faithfully performed the women will conceive and animals will enter hunters' traps and fall to their arrows. The mysteries of the pangolin are sorrowful mysteries: 'Now I will enter the house of affliction', they sing as initiates carry its corpse round the village. No more of its cult songs were told to me, except this tantalising line.
>
> (PD: 170)

The search for explanation is truncated in the 'sorrowful mysteries' of this line, and the developmental argument of the book turned dramatically around:[13]

> the subject of this chapter [the system shattered and renewed] is impossible to discuss except in the light of men's common urge to make a unity of all their experience and to overcome distinctions and separations in acts of atonement.
>
> (PD: 170)

For Lele men who have produced both male and female children, eating the pangolin (or scaly anteater) is the vehicle of this dramatic self-discovery:

> By the mystery of that rite they recognise something of the fortuitous and conventional nature of the categories in whose mould they have their experience. If they consistently shunned ambiguity they would commit themselves to division between ideal and reality. But they confront ambiguity in an extreme and concentrated form. They dare to grasp the pangolin and put it to ritual use, proclaiming that this has more power than any other rites. So the pangolin cult is capable of

> inspiring a profound meditation on the nature of purity and impurity
> and on the limitation on human contemplation of existence.
>
> (PD: 171)

It is not germane to our present task to ask in whom the profound meditation is inspired,[14] and what our evidence is for its character among the Lele. Douglas herself tells us that the evidence for her reading comes from her apprehension of pattern: 'It may well seem that I have made too much of the Lele pangolin cult' (PD: 174). Anyway, this inspiration is only a part of Lele belief, for in confronting any particular death their attitude is quite different. Particular deaths of those who do not reach old age are deemed due to sorcery, and sorcery is an evil in the world to be expunged both routinely by seeking those responsible for it and periodically through the adoption of millennial cults that promise to introduce a world free from such evil. Only the rites of the pangolin give the analyst 'a glimpse of another level of religious insight', for most of the time Lele diviners 'seem no better than a lot of Aladdins rubbing their magic lamps and expecting marvels to take shape' (PD: 173). And so the routine activity of Lele diviners is finally described in the terms earlier applied to Frazer's characterization of savage credulity.

Such belief in the instrumental efficacy of ritual can be protected from disbelief in the face of the inevitability of death only by secondary elaborations. By admitting the power of an enemy without or within, people may confess to the weakness of their religion. Or they may demand moral requirements of the people, as did the prophets of Israel, in order for ritual performed on their behalf to be effective. Or religions may change their tack so that 'all this pious effort is disparaged, contempt is thrown on right behaviour, materialistic objectives are suddenly despised' (PD: 176):

> a narrow focus on material health and happiness makes a religion
> vulnerable to disbelief. And so we can suppose that the very logic of
> promises discreditably unfulfilled may lead cult officials to meditate on
> wider, profounder themes, such as the mystery of evil and of death. If
> this is true we would expect the most materialistic-seeming cults to stage
> at some central point in the ritual cycle a cult of the paradox of the ulti-
> mate unity of life and death. At such a point the pollution of death,
> treated in a positive creative role, can help to close the metaphysical
> gap.
>
> (PD: 177)

And so the book closes with a series of descriptions from African ethnographies of willing human or human-like victims from the Lele pangolin, mediator between the realms of the human and animal, to the Ndembu white spirit, an ancestor mediating between living and dead, to the Dinka master of the fishing spear choosing the time of his living interment in order to transmit his spirit to his successor. Primitive existentialists escape the chain of necessity by choosing the moment and method of death.

> When someone embraces freely the symbols of death, or death itself, then it is consistent with everything we have seen so far, that a great release of power for good should be expected to follow.
>
> (PD: 179)

The dance of similarity and difference is finally ended, at least textually – and at least in this text – on the side of similarity. And the similarity derives from a shared need to transcend the everyday limits of cognition by closing the metaphysical gaps in our classificatory systems. But perhaps it would be as just to say that the book stops rather than ends. The curious movement of internal rebuttal and reformulation invites us to believe that another twenty pages on our author would have turned around this argument also. *Purity and Danger* is indubitably a profound book, and its profundity is partly due to what Needham, in review, called the 'rare and exciting spectacle of a mind at work' (PD/TLS). The work involves conjecture, adventure, reformulation, doubt and frequent apology for questions partly or wholly unanswered. The arguments of the book unfold in parallel, proceed recursively, are far from logically consistent and at points are mutually contradictory. But that is part of the complexity of the effort at synthesis that *Purity and Danger* represents. A lesser effort might have produced a more elegant, but not a more honest – or more interesting – book.

In the light of *Natural Symbols*, *Purity and Danger* is particularly instructive for where and how it stops. Religious celebration of the violation of the most fundamental boundaries of mundane classification, the self-sacrifice of the form of being which most fundamentally transgresses, permits the system to renew itself in the moment of its complete negation. The conclusion is metaphysical as much as sociological, and its effect is to align primitive and contemporary believers. The final antinomy is, therefore, not between a 'them' and 'us' defined as primitive or modern, but between a 'them' and 'us' who do or do not subscribe to the possibility of transcending mundane life.[15]

Notes

1 There is a brief portrait of Mary Douglas during the academic year 1951–52 in Jan Vansina's memoir of his interlude as a student at University College (1994: 10–12).

2 Timothy (later, Sir Timothy) Raison was Conservative Member of Parliament for Aylesbury (1970–92) and held a succession of government posts, eventually becoming Minister for Overseas Development (1983–86). Issues of health, welfare, development, education and environment loomed larger in his concerns than among Thatcherite Tories.

3 Essays: 1963b, 1964c, 1967c1–4, 1970c, 1971b, 1974a (with Michael Nicod); reviews: 1966b, 1969d, 1970c; letter: 1972f.

4 This was a less temperate version of criticisms phrased in more academic terms in (1967d); and her review of Luc de Heusch's comparative study of Bantu mythology

on structuralist lines is positively generous about the results achieved (1973i), suggesting some softening of her line on structuralism.

5 For a celebrated psychoanalytic reworking, see Kristeva 1982. Literary recensions have been numerous, e.g. Spearing 1980; Hinnant 1987; Labanyi 1996 – with thanks to Nic Argenti and Catherine Davies for the two latter references.

6 The list of a hundred works emerged from deliberations of a distinguished panel set up to foster a 'common market of the mind' while the 'Iron curtain' still divided Europe (Timothy Garton Ash (ed.) 1995 *Freedom for Publishing, Publishing for Freedom: the Central and East Asian Publishing Project*, Budapest: Central European University Press, reported in the *Times Literary Supplement*, 6 October 1995, p. 39). Douglas was one of only four women writers on a list which included, among anthropologists, Claude Lévi-Strauss, Clifford Geertz and Ernest Gellner. Silvia Rodgers wrote a piece for the *Sunday Times* the following year on *Purity and Danger* as the book that 'shattered my assumptions about just about everything…[T]his dazzling book concentrates on what has always fascinated me: the dangers and joys of being out of place' (Rodgers 1996). The book also laid the foundation for Douglas's inclusion in the *Sunday Times* '1000 Makers of the Twentieth Century', serialized in autumn 1991; unfortunately, the author of her entry mistakes the African country in which she researched as well as the date of her move to the USA.

7 Frustrated by her textual analysis of Leviticus being read out of sociological context, Mary Douglas was later to embargo anthologization of this chapter.

8 His epistemological insights are acknowledged by Douglas (1995h: 24). Jeremy Adler and I have undertaken a re-edition of Steiner's lectures and papers for which several Oxford contemporaries generously provided testimonies we have cited in two essays (see Adler and Fardon 'Introductions' to Steiner 1999, 2 vols; and also Adler 1992, 1994b, 1994c, 1995; on Steiner as poet see Steiner 1992 and Adler 1994a).

9 Numerous writers have noted that the formulation is not reversible: all matter out of place is not dirt.

10 Readers who make it to Chapter 9 of this book will find the inspiration for my approach to *Purity and Danger* in Douglas's account of the Book of Numbers.

11 Her use of Indian and Jewish sources to argue a general point about 'primitive rituals' reinforces our earlier concern about her equivocation over the relation between the dichotomies primitive religion/great religion and primitive society/modern society.

12 This argument presumably relates to Douglas's sense that the suspension of rules, and bestowal of forgiveness, are qualities intrinsic only where the rules are otherwise firmly upheld – as in institutions such as the convent school.

13 In his account of the British Catholic novel, Thomas Woodman notes the evocation of 'the miseries of our fallen condition' in the phrase 'sorrowful mysteries': he continues, 'It is death…the greatest natural evil, above all that puts secular and temporal goods to the question and inevitably raises metaphysical issues that seem to touch on the fringes of the supernatural' (1991: 128).

14 Ioan Lewis (1991; see also Douglas 1993o; de Heusch 1991) has noted this is a relevant ethnographic question.

15 These implications were seen most clearly by a young Terry Eagleton attempting to reconcile Roman Catholicism and Marxism; he agreed both that 'articulated human structures', including the Church, are the enabling environment of humanity, and that 'the ambivalence in the concept of the sacred lies in the fact that…weak and inarticulated points in the structure are felt to have a potent and dangerous dynamic which is oddly similar to that power which sustains the structure' (1967: 404). He went on to draw a social lesson which, its Marxist language apart, would be conducive to Douglas: 'For the Christian, the presence of the sacred in the world

takes two major forms. Christ is present in that articulated structure of signs we call the church. He is also present, more fundamentally, in the oppressed and exploited. These men…are the "dirt" which falls outside the carefully wrought political structures, those whom society cannot accommodate' (1967: 405), and see Chapter 6.

5 *NATURAL SYMBOLS* DEFENDED

MAN IS A RITUAL ANIMAL

In the same year [1966] that Masters and Johnson published the results of their sex research, England won the World Cup at football, which millions saw as the bestowal of a special grace on the nation; John Lennon boasted that the Beatles were more popular than Jesus Christ and, to the disappointment of many, was not struck dead by a thunderbolt; Evelyn Waugh died, shortly after attending a Latin mass celebrated in private by an old Jesuit friend; Friday abstinence was officially abolished in the Roman Catholic Church, and the American Sisters of Loretto at the Foot of the Cross became the first order of nuns to abandon the habit completely…at Duquesne University, Pennsylvania, and a little later at Notre Dame University, Indiana, small groups of Catholics began to experiment with 'Pentecostal' prayer meetings, praying for each other that they might be filled with the gifts of the Holy Ghost as described in the New Testament – the gift of faith, the gift of tongues, the gifts of prophecy, healing, discernment of spirits, interpretation and exorcism…Public interest in the Catholic Church was still focused on the cliff-hanging saga of contraception.

(David Lodge 1980: 102)

And, also in 1966, with *Purity and Danger* published, Mary Douglas turned her attention to *Natural Symbols* which she completed, in its first edition, in July 1969. The years of composition saw the student struggles of 1968 on the streets of Paris and in the universities of Britain and America, as well as the general flouting of convention that was part of 1960s youth culture. A Labour government had come to power in Britain in 1964 after thirteen years of Conservative rule which had seen the independence of a majority of Britain's erstwhile colonies. The trend of legislation was 'liberal' on issues of race, gender, capital punishment and hereditary privilege, though not as radical as the rhetoric it was sometimes dressed in. *Natural Symbols* has to be read against this local background, some of which Mary Douglas found unconducive. It is a passionate, even angry, book which addresses diverse audiences in polemical tones. Reviewers were disconcerted: some expressed bafflement, others a variety of opinion, from E.R. Leach's intemperate outburst:

> [Dr Mary Douglas's] recent work gives the impression that she is no longer much concerned with the attainment of empirical truth; the object of the exercise is to adapt her learning to the service of Roman Catholic propaganda.
>
> (NS1/NYRB: 44)

to the more ironic conclusion of David Martin:

> one cannot help but admire an argument which manages to dish the Reformation, liberalism, capitalism, *and* the revolting students all at one blow.
>
> (NS1/BJS: 344)

As an anthropology book, *Natural Symbols* was eccentric. Although it was not meant solely to be an anthropology book – but rather a 'bridge between anthropology and other disciplines' – *Natural Symbols* was meant also to be an anthropology book – of which 'anthropologists must be [the] most important critics' – and a hugely ambitious one at that (NS1: xvi). The anthropologists were generally less welcoming than the non-specialists (NS1/NYRB/Man; NS2/Soc). Nothing in Mary Douglas's career was to be quite the same, the polemic never again so strident. A reader coming directly to her later writings, say on risk or consumption, might even be unaware of the extent to which the theory used there had been forged in the heat of controversy about the meaning of events in the 1960s. Yet the materials Mary Douglas attempted to synthesize were, in the main, the same as those in *Purity and Danger*, and *Purity and Danger* had not been a controversial book in the eyes of the Oxonian reviewers whose views I quoted at the beginning of the last chapter. An anonymous reviewer in the *Times Literary Supplement*, possibly a theologian and presumably known to her given a reference to her home on the lower slopes of Highgate Hill, perceptively noted an element of spiritual autobiography in *Natural Symbols* (NS1/TLS).

Natural Symbols is a very personal book and, in terms of her intellectual career, undoubtedly Douglas's most important book: 'the mine of ideas I have been quarrying for practically everything that I have written since' (1996b: xi). But *Natural Symbols* was written hurriedly, even excitedly, and it shows. As a critic noted:

> this book tries to say too many things at once…The book has rightly been judged confusing. It treats of different elements of symbolism in the same sentence without making needful distinctions…[in relating authority, beliefs and morals] it treated, as if they were single manifestations, elements which needed to be separated by different levels of analysis…The diagrams…were encrusted with unacknowledged importations from hidden dimensions, such as power, or density or commitment.
>
> (1982d: ix, xx, xxiii)

The author of these criticisms, as the reader may have guessed, was Mary Douglas herself in her Introduction to an American re-edition of the first edition of *Natural Symbols*. Unpacking, refining and defending the arguments jammed together in this relatively slim volume was to take her twenty years. The task began immediately when the 1970 edition of *Natural Symbols* was hotly followed in 1973 by a revised edition in which sections were reordered, definitions of concepts changed, a few passages suppressed and new ones added. So far as I know, it is the only one of her books to have had a heavily revised re-edition. Never a writer to dwell over her work, Douglas's tendency to think aloud on paper is more marked in *Natural Symbols* than elsewhere, and the revised second edition stood little chance of taming the unruly profusion of ideas committed to paper at the outset. From the perspective of someone tracking the development of her thought, this rush into print has the advantage that most of her first thoughts (and second, third, …) are in the public domain. The untidiness of *Natural Symbols* derives from its ambition: four long books might have begun to explain clearly what she was trying to do; a single short one could only put down markers against arguments to be developed later.

Natural Symbols is a defence, both passionate and reasoned, of the importance of ritual to social life. It is also an explanation of what Douglas took to be the pronounced antipathy to ritual typical of the 1960s, and an attack on those who supported this antipathy by reference to what was 'natural'. Contrary to the impression an inattentive reader might derive from its title, the book argued – not that symbols were natural – but that naturalizing symbols was social. In order both to defend ritual and explain why others held it in contempt, she was moved to propose a new methodology for comparative anthropology. Properly applied, this method, dubbed 'grid and group' analysis, would account for comparative variation between cognate societies and cultures. Moreover, the utility of the method was to be demonstrated not just by reference to ritual but by a wide-ranging exploration of the symbolism of the body in different types of society. As if this were not ambition enough for one book, Mary Douglas not only sets about developing these arguments simultaneously in the text but cannot resist pursuing lateral connections as they occur to her. While Douglas's capacity to spot the more unlikely byways of an argument is one of the delights of her insight as a social commentator, it does occasionally muddy waters that are already murky.

Photograph 8 Mary Douglas in her office, University College London (1976); on the
pinboard are illustrations of the cassowary, pangolin, Lele fishing basket and
animal hooves drawn by her artist sister, Pat Novy, to illustrate *Implicit
Meanings*

Source: © Mayotte Magnus
Note: Originally published, cropped, in *Harper's Bazaar and Queen*, January 1977, in an article by Sheila
Hale

Part social theory, part spiritual autobiography, part polemic, prelude to what
one reviewer dismisses as an 'anthropological astrology' (Urry ESP &
ITAV/Mank), the controversial *Natural Symbols* is also the uncontroversial *Purity
and Danger* rewritten. Most of the substantive elements juggled in *Natural Symbols*
– the Oxford recension of Durkheim, Sudanese and central African ethnography, the dietary codes of the Israelites – also appear in the previous book.
However, there is a major difference in plot. In the last chapter, I argued that
Purity and Danger ran two plots in parallel: a functional and structural account of
cognition and classification, and an evolutionary, or occasionally historical,
account of the differences between primitive religions and societies, great religions and modern societies. The second of the arguments contained numerous
hiatuses, shifted its terms, and occasionally ran out of steam entirely. The first
argument, about classification, reappears in *Natural Symbols* with developments
and revisions; the second argument disappears other than in an important sub-
plot to do with our contemporary capacity to understand the social conditions of

our lives. Other than this, it is replaced by a non-evolutionary, ahistorical plot, the inspiration for which Douglas attributes to her discovery of the work of Basil Bernstein, who was exploring the significance of language and curriculum design on education. Bernstein's ideas allowed Mary Douglas to place the current events that affected her keenly in theoretical terms. Of these the impact of the Second Vatican Council, and its ambition to develop Roman Catholic ritual in a vernacular comprehensible to the congregation, most powerfully motivates the text. But the Second Vatican Council also functions as an icon of liberal reformism more generally; what goes for Vatican II also goes for much else that occurs during the same period.

The Second Vatican Council (the first had been in 1870), a general council of the Roman Catholic Church as well as non-Catholic observers, which sat between 1962 and 1965, followed on the heels of ecumenical overtures within the Church. The Archbishop of Canterbury of the Church of England had met the Pope for the first time in five centuries in 1960. Adrian Hastings, who took an opposing view of the outcome of the Vatican Council to Mary Douglas, claims – and here, at least, I suspect she would agree with him in fact and in phrasing – that:

> There can be no question that the Vatican Council was the most important ecclesiastical event of this century, not just for Roman Catholics but for all Christians. It so greatly changed the character of by far the largest communion of Christendom (and, by and large, in a direction which we may describe not too unfairly as one of 'Protestantization'), that no one has been left unaffected.
>
> (1991: 525)

Apart from revision of the Mass (finally authorized in its entirety in 1967), the Vatican Council modified the Church's teachings on authority, especially elevating the importance of revelation over tradition, and generally weakened the distinction between Roman Catholics and other Christians. Michael Hornsby-Smith's detailed investigations endorse Douglas's sense of the dissolution in England of a distinctive Catholic subculture in the post-war decades (1987: 210; 1991: 7). 'No longer was being a Catholic a part of one's intrinsic identity, an indication of ancestry and membership of an identifiably distinct religio-ethnic community, something normally ascribed' (Hornsby-Smith 1991: 9). Ensuing debates, including that following *Humanae Vitae*'s reaffirmation of opposition to artificial contraception, provoked fear in the traditionalists either of the disintegration of the Church, or of its transformation into something quite unrecognizable and hardly distinct from other Christian denominations. Mary Douglas felt that the reforms failed to appreciate the power of symbols that social anthropology was demonstrating.[1] This was where she found Bernstein's ideas helpful.

Basil Bernstein had delivered a paper on 'Ritual in education' to a conference on education at the University of London's Institute of Education (across the road from University College). Mary Douglas was attending the same meeting.

> She came up to me after the paper, delivered the following and disappeared: 'It's the Convent of the Sacred Heart all over again! See you in September.' It was then late June. What could one do, except read her work. I was well equipped when we met in September…Over the years we drew upon each other's work whilst retaining our individual focus and growth.
>
> (Bernstein 1975: 6)

For her part, Mary Douglas wrote a generous appreciation of Bernstein's work for *New Society* (1972e/IM) and was stimulated to adapt some of his ideas to her own ends in *Natural Symbols*. The relation between their works is not simple to summarize, though I try to do so below, and Douglas remarks throughout her text how pale a reflection of Bernstein's original she believes her borrowing to be. Bernstein's work offered her indications of how an array of complex and varied materials might be reduced to a single schema and thus made comparable. Her ideas were analogies of his rather than copies, and the link between them rested in their shared intuition that concern with form was crucial to their respective interests in the structuring of knowledge via educational curricula, and in ritual. But why was it 'the Convent of the Sacred Heart all over again'?

The immediate textual precursor of *Natural Symbols* can be found in lectures given at two invitations: the St Thomas Day lecture at Blackfriars, Oxford, and the Munro lectures at the University of Edinburgh. The second are apparently not extant, but the Aquinas lectures were published in 1968 under the title 'The contempt of ritual' and constitute an early version of the argument of the book (1968e). 'The contempt of ritual' had been used previously as the title for a review in *New Society* of Godfrey Lienhardt's 1961 monograph on the religion of the Nilotic Dinka published the same year as *Purity and Danger* (1966b/ITAV). Some of the 'message' of *Natural Symbols* is clearly present in the review published four years earlier,

> Without rituals moulding his [the Dinka but also the 'primitive' more generally] experience from infancy there could be no belief, and without belief not only no [Aladdin's] treasure cave, but no self, no world, no human destiny.
>
> If this has any moral for us today, we must start by recognising the poverty of our rituals, their unconnectedness with each other and with our social purposes and the impossibility of our having again a system of public rituals relating our experiences into some kind of cosmic unity.

> Ritual has so far only been denigrated. It is time for it too to be grasped and its creative potential to be understood.
>
> (1966b: 24)

The 'contempt' shown to ritual spotlighted in the St Thomas Day lecture is specifically the challenge to Catholic tradition represented by the Second Vatican Council. This challenge is personified in the opening paragraph by an anonymous 'religious reformer' who fails to ask how free religious lay-people are to follow the proposals for reform he is making (his place is taken in the text of *Natural Symbols* by the anonymous sociologist who uses ritual as a term for meaningless outward form). The reformers of the Second Vatican Council who want to replace merely magical behaviour with an ethical commitment are the Protestants of the twentieth century (they promote another version of that schism between inner convictions and outer signs of the Western Judaeo-Christian tradition which Douglas claimed, in *Purity and Danger*, to have pervaded anthropological theories). They accept:

> a Teilhardist evolutionism which assumes that a rational, verbally explicit, personal commitment to God is self-evidently better than its alleged contrary, formal, ritualistic conformity...As an anthropologist descended from the Bog Irish, I would like to challenge all of this.
>
> (1968e: 476)

The terms which describe the difference between ritualism and its contrary echo Bernstein's early distinction between elaborated and restricted codes of communication. A child learning to communicate absorbs speech codes which themselves carry dispositions to recognize particular types of relevance and relation. The child also learns social structure and reinforces this learning in the very business of talking. Two types of code are distinguished: restricted and elaborated. The first is learned in the positional family, and correlates with its explicit social structure: much remains implicit because communication is closely tied to the position of the communicator: 'Do this because I am your mother'. The second type of code, the elaborated, values internal states and feelings, and is learned in the personal family: 'Do this because Dad will be upset if you do not'. Where code and social structure coincide we have two possibilities: personal control plus elaborated code, and positional control plus a restricted code. Both Bernstein and Douglas subsequently built considerably greater sophistication into this schema as they tackled the very different problems they posed for themselves. Their applications of the initial hypothesis are almost diametrically opposite – Douglas effectively stands Bernstein on his head. Whereas Douglas is concerned to defend ritual as a version (or versions) of restricted code, Bernstein is interested to explain the consistent under-performance of working-class children in formal education. His early formulation of this problem notes that formal education is carried on in the elaborated code. Thus, middle-class chil-

108

dren are educated in the code to which family life has already accustomed them; working-class children are not and so must master not only the curriculum but also the manner in which it is conveyed.

To the figure of the, probably middle-class, Teilhardist reformer Douglas opposes the, presumably working-class, Bog Irish of the London parishes:

> Friday abstinence [from eating meat] is the core of their religion: it is a taboo whose breach will bring automatic misfortune. It is the only sin they think worth mentioning in confession and they evidently believe that it will count against them more heavily on the day of judgement than breach of any of the ten commandments.
>
> (1968e: 476)

As a set-piece, suitable for a public lecture, this is splendidly provocative. The Bog Irish should seem abjectly magical to her cultivated audience, but what distinguishes this belief from the idea that the Christian who approaches the sacrament must be in a special ritual condition? And where is the line between belief in the sacraments, as specially instituted channels of grace, and belief in the resurrection itself? The slope is slippery. Magic and ritual, as she had argued in *Purity and Danger*, share a concern with symbolic boundaries and the belief that 'specified symbolic acts can be efficacious to change events' (1968e: 477). The antinomy between the Kantian view of progress, in which thought becomes liberated by reflection on its own conditions of possibility, and the possibilities for transcendence implied by the acceptance of strong classification is given a fresh twist: 'people who have become unritualistic in every other way…will eventually lose their capacity for responding to condensed symbols such as that of the Blessed Sacrament' (1968e: 482). Why should people believe?

> the most important determinant of religious behaviour is the experi-ence of closed social groups. The man who has that experience associates boundaries with power and danger. The better defined and more significant the social boundaries, the more the bias I would expect in favour of ritualism…Half the thesis, of course, is Durkheim's.
>
> (1968e: 479–80)

The other side of the same thesis is that with weak social boundaries there will be weak ritual and 'doctrinal emphases on internal, emotional states' (1968e: 480). Taken together, the two halves of the thesis entirely revise the distinctions between primitive religion, great religion and modern society that became so tortuous in *Purity and Danger*. A radically sociological hypothesis predicts that not all primitive religions are equally magical, 'interest in magical efficacy varies with strength of the social group' (1968e: 482). Differentiation, the stressed variable in the account of social evolution proposed in *Purity and Danger*, is now to be mediated by its effects on the immediate social environment as the setting for experience of sociality.

The remainder of the lecture begins a tentative exploration of correlations between social environment and belief I prefer to follow in detail with reference to *Natural Symbols*. However, the underlying argument, and especially its positive statement that strong groups correlate with ritualism that was delivered in this polemic against the reforms of the Second Vatican Council delivered to an audience gathered to recall St Thomas Aquinas, is faithfully reproduced in the book.

NATURAL SYMBOLS

A comparative anthropology

Douglas's willingness to amend, defend and apply her schema of grid and group, and later 'cultural theory' (see Chapter 10), suggests that she has been concerned less with the details of any particular formulation than with the aims she set her analysis. I suggested, with reference to the shifting uses of 'us' and 'them' in *Purity and Danger*, that, among other things, this project has been preoccupied with the way that anthropologists unite and differentiate human experiences in different contexts. Only a contextual account of similarity and difference can tell us when, and what, previous human experience can help us understand ourselves. From *Purity and Danger* onwards, Douglas increasingly presents herself as an anthropologist of Western societies. Although she ceases to be an active Africa specialist, her Africanist knowledge continues to be a resource on which she draws when confronted with a new problem. The juxtaposition of contemporary and exotic materials, often but not always African, has become a hallmark of her work on Western society. This is not a matter of apt illustration, nor is it an attempt to provoke intellectual frisson in the reader; rather, Douglas's juxtapositions derive from her desire to create a genuinely catholic, in the sense of universal, comparative social anthropology. Her frequent complaints against those who have the hubris to believe contemporary societies so different from those that preceded them have to be understood in the light of this ambition.

The two editions of *Natural Symbols* flesh out the argument of 'The contempt of ritual' in ways that are readily traced back to the stock of ideas in *Purity and Danger*. Take, for instance, the idea from which the book takes its title, and which opens the first edition of *Natural Symbols* by addressing the condition of a common, human, 'we',

> Most symbolic behaviour must work through the human body…The human body is common to us all. Only our social condition varies. The symbols based on the human body are used to express different social experiences.
>
> (NS1: vii)

This is a clear restatement of the chapter on 'External boundaries' in *Purity and*

Danger. Novelty lies in the emphasis given to social experiences, and the way in which they are to be calibrated. We are told to ignore political structure, ecological variation, industrial complexity – initially as a point of methodology, and later because they are irrelevant to social experience. Rather than these, we are encouraged to look towards foundational social experiences which transcend any politico-economic context. This experience is of those close to us to whom we can be related in a limited number of ways. The social environment is other people.

Social experience is amenable to classification in two dimensions. The first of these, 'group' – the experience of a bounded social unit – will remain relatively unproblematic in the development of the theory, although it is later subjected to some redefinition. Group is prerequisite to the classic instance of the Durkheimian hypothesis in which society is expressed through ritual; group formation was also a major focus of Africanist research during the colonial period (Chapter 3). In the first edition of *Natural Symbols*, group is independent of the second variable, which Douglas calls 'grid'.

Grid continues to be the more problematic dimension of the analysis, or its salvation, depending how you look at the frequent revision this concept undergoes. On this first definition, grid consists of 'rules which relate one person to others on an ego-centred basis' (NS1: viii). Grid and group are both sociological dimensions: group is the creature of British corporation theory, while grid is initially related to the social network theory of the Manchester School, with its focus upon the individual. Or, this might be one way to read the distinction were it not for the fact that the contrast drawn is between 'experience' (of social groups) and 'rules' (of ego-centred relations): two ideational constructs.

Douglas's use of diagrams to develop her analysis (see Chapter 10) is of a piece with the way she writes about – presumably thinks about – the formal or abstract properties of human relations. It may help to note here, in anticipation of later discussion, that the images are very persistent. Ideas, if not presented erroneously as if they 'float free', must be grounded in the social dimension. Group evokes boundary, an enclosing circle; grid may either picture the individual as a nodal point from which relations radiate, or else place the individual within a 'cross-hatching' of rules, distinctions and regulations. The thought of individuals grounded in these social dimensions is channelled into the 'grooves' worn by the thoughts of previous residents of the same institutional space. The formal characteristics of both the 'thought-style' and the institutional space within which it arises are similar. Much of the revision to the methodology of grid and group, and of her 'cultural theory', can be seen as an ongoing effort to give these persistent images convincing textual and diagrammatic form.

Leaving aside these considerations for the moment, and accepting the two dimensions, then experience of the body is supposed to reflect social experience rather directly; and we have three possibilities for social experience: group plus grid, group without grid, and grid without group. With both grid and group well defined, the external boundary of the community and its internal regulation are fully specified. By analogy, the body is experienced as both bounded and internally organized. With strong group, but no grid rules, the external boundedness and confused internal organization of social experience are replicated in knowledge of the body: also felt as bounded but vulnerable to internal disorder. Those who have this type of social experience are likely to have a witch-fearing cosmology, to tend to political negativism, despise gluttony, generally treat sex with caution, and view unregulated sex with horror. There is a uniquely elaborated set of bodily attitudes for this type of social unit (NS1: viii–ix). The last type of social experience is less bothered by bodily symbolism. Bodily boundaries make poor analogies for the type of society, without group but with grid, based predominantly on ego-centred networks. Such societies tend to be secular in outlook and practical minded. This outlook is claimed to be common to the competitive societies of New Guinea, the nomadic Basseri of Iran, and the modern city. This is a correspondence theory of symbolism, justified by the drive to achieve coherence in human experience.

The gross tendency in the movement to modernity, crucial to *Purity and Danger*, is now restated as a decline in group-centred experience and a movement towards ego-centred networks. This would be conventional, except that Douglas neither superimposes this distinction directly on to the historical distinction between modern and pre-modern societies, nor does she claim that the movement to ego-centred organization is true in a wholesale sense of all historically modern societies. This marks a considerable advance over the formulation of *Purity and Danger* which left present day believers, for all the pleading to the contrary, looking very much like promontories of the primitive sticking out into the oceans of modern life. Pre-modern societies, she now claims, include all the varieties of grid and group, group without grid, and grid without group. Modern societies have their enclaves of strong group, like the Bog Irish. The terms 'them' and 'us' have, thus, been modified. An 'us' consisting of individuals whose social experience involves ego-centred networks shares that experience with New Guinea entrepreneurs; while any 'us' who belong to strong groups can recognize the social experience of members of lineages in Africa as similar. If this is accepted, then it follows that attention to the relation between social experience and bodily experience will 'discover implicit forms of the great theological controversies' (NS1: xiii) that have preoccupied Western Christianity in the beliefs of primitive societies. Which is the note on which *Purity and Danger* ended.

This simplified formulation in the Preface to the first edition of *Natural Symbols* is immediately replaced by a more complex account of grid and group in the second edition. The features that survive the different versions accord with Douglas's deep-seated preferences and aversions. The form of argument should neither be idealistic, assuming that ideas float free of their social moorings (a reproach she levels repeatedly at French anthropology, e.g. 1967b,d,h, 1968c,d, 1970d), nor should it be utilitarian, assuming people's ideas can be explained entirely by reference to individual advantage. Rather, the theory should be sociological in the *Année sociologique* tradition; it should relate socially shared knowledge (including religion, morals and symbolism) to social organization. How these are to be separated, and how once distinguished they can be related, is open to reformulation; the basic design consideration is not. The theory should also be capable of handling wide-ranging comparison. How wide-ranging is again open to further testing. But the range required must encompass the types of society that feature as exemplary in her work and, furthermore, order these examples in such a way that their relation one to another becomes comprehensible. If we enumerated the societies that feed her sociological imagination, they would include the witch-dominated, small-scale societies of central Africa in which she had worked or about which she read, as well as the lineage-based societies of the Nilotes of Sudan, among whom her associates at Oxford had worked – Evans-Pritchard (Nuer), Lienhardt (Dinka) and Jean Buxton (Mandari); but additionally they would include the closed, hierarchic, highly ritualized convent school in which she had been educated, and the more amorphous, middle-class world of intellectuals, politicians and businessmen of her professional and married life (occasionally the social recluse makes her appearance too). It is as if these different elements of her life needed somehow to be made to speak to one another. Some later writings put grid and group to one side in order to present societies as exemplary types. Even where this approach is not explicit, passages from her writings avowedly framed by continuous variation within the two dimensions of grid and group can be read in terms of a more restricted concern with three, four or five exemplary or ideal types of society, each of which is drawn by exaggerating the features of a type of society with which she felt familiar.

These predilections left room for a variety of uncertainties: it was not clear quite what should go under the name of grid, and this was true to a lesser degree of group. Nor was it self-evident what was supposed to be determined with reference to the two variables. If economists name two dimensions price and quantity and plot the demand and supply curves for a product, their intersection establishes the price that will prevail in the market. Is there an analogous outcome to plotting grid and group? There are points in the argument of *Natural Symbols* when something like this seems to be envisaged. If group is the strength of group boundedness and grid the strength of ego-centred networks, then establishing these two sociological dimensions might yield a prediction about the symbolism and ritual of the society in question. Why might such a relation hold? There are a number of possible arguments to fill the gap and to which we must revert (Chapters 10 and 11):

1   Following Durkheim and Mauss (in *Primitive Classification* 1903) it might be argued that social categories are logically prior and that other classifications mirror these (NS2: 11–12). But as Rodney Needham observed in his preface to the English edition of that work (1963), this argument introduces a dubious temporalization so that social categories have to be considered prior to, and logically distinct from, other types of classification.

2   Alternatively, an argument for consistency could be made by reference to cognitive style and people's need to achieve consonance between different elements of their experience. But this would involve making cognitive style the ghost in the theoretical machine and thus run directly contrary to Douglas's general injunction to herself to avoid 'idealism'.

3   A third tactic might be to emphasize individual strategy and transaction: to ask how people bring one another into line and hold each other to account under different forms of social organization. It could be argued that in a particular type of society only some explanations of fortune and misfortune will be credible. Such an account would make relations of power crucial, since carriers of different accounts would try to impose their versions of the world on one another. This argument becomes more prominent between the two editions of *Natural Symbols* – for instance, Douglas writes about theories of 'justification' in a passage added to the second edition (NS2: 145) – and will assume an increasing burden in later developments of the theory.

4   Finally, it might be possible to revert to a functionalist argument in which beliefs corresponded to the systemic needs of different types of society, and mechanisms could be identified to explain why such beliefs did indeed occur – for instance, on the lines of the association between accusations of witchcraft and the routine splitting of villages noted in central Africa (see Chapter 3).

Natural Symbols actually employs a shifting combination of all these arguments. And, given that the book is only a staging post on a journey of theoretical development to last another twenty years, it may be more to the immediate point to note the slightly inchoate state in which the argument emerges. Our difficulty in pinning the author down to a specific line of argument is compounded in the second edition of the book, when the definitions of grid and group are changed, but sections of text remain which employ these key terms under their original definitions. The textual amendments of the second edition are less substantial than they appear at first sight (see my brief concordance in Appendix 3). While sections of text are swapped around, the redefinition of grid and group has little effect on the early chapters of the book or on its ending; major revision occurs in Chapters 6 to 9. The overall pattern of textual tinkering reinforces the impression that Mary Douglas knew with certainty where her argument began, and where it was going to lead, but she was less sure of the most economical course to argue her way between these two points.

The first edition of *Natural Symbols*, in drawing on Bernstein's ideas about elaborated and restricted speech codes, portrayed ritual as a type (or types) of restricted code. In the restricted code, social structure is directly replicated in notions of body; however, there is equivocation whether the elaborated code is to be related to its local social structure, or whether somehow it manages to escape social structural determination (NS1: xiv). The second edition explicitly moves beyond the distinction between elaborated and restricted codes to take account of Bernstein's ideas about the organization of the curriculum as a way of connecting pieces of knowledge together.

The senses of grid and group also change markedly between the two editions. In the second edition, group has retained its original sense but has much of the old grid dimension shifted on to it. Group now indicates the pressures of collective organization on the individual. Grid has taken over the sense of the value that was previously determined: the coherence of the classificatory scheme (NS2: ix). In the chapter of the second edition retitled 'Group and grid' (previously Chapter 4 'A rule of method'), grid is defined as 'order, classification, the symbolic system'; group is 'pressure, the experience of having no option but to consent to the overwhelming demands of other people' (NS2: 58).

Rather than being confined to one of the quadrants (as she puts it – Chapter 10 examines the evolution of these diagrams) societies are now envisaged as scatters over the diagram. The problem then becomes, what does the scatter represent? Are the features of the societies in fact derived from grid and group characteristics or from exemplars of the four types?

Following Leach, Douglas notes four views of the body:

1   Where group and grid are both strong (though she occasionally still refers to grid as high) then the body should replicate the boundary and internal coordination of the well-ordered social group.
2   Where group is strong, but grid is weak, we again find the small group menaced by its failure to resolve internal problems. The bounded but threatened body mirrors this social predicament.
3   Where group and grid are both weak, we should anticipate highly pragmatic attitudes on the part of those who manipulate others and exercise power.
4   Where group is weak but grid is strong, we find those who are oppressed by the manipulators in type 3. For them the body represents all that is organized and thus threatening to them. By analogy with their social experience they value extra-bodily experience.

The quadrants are clearly based on four exemplars: 1. the hierarchy of the convent school, a conducive setting for Christian doctrines; 2. the fractious, small group, villages of central Africa; 3. the competitive societies of both Western capitalism and big-man New Guinea societies; 4. the weak of the societies of type 3 who are prone to millennialism or withdrawal from the competitive world in which they are worsted. The same correlations can be drawn whether we reason from the parameters of grid and group or from the exemplary types of society. Douglas appears to think in terms of the bold characteristics of the ideal types and only subsequently attempts to integrate these as examples of continuous variation in terms of grid and group.

Methodological caution is stated in both editions but placed more prominently in the second. Comparison is more fruitful when the *ceteris paribus* condition can be met best: ideally, comparisons should be drawn from societies that differ only in some respects while being culturally or temporally close. Variations in grid and group can then be calibrated relatively (that is to say, by claiming grid to be stronger in society A than in society B; for this understanding applied, see Chapter 6, 'Test cases' in NS2; or Gerald Mars 1982). In principle, it is difficult (perhaps methodologically impossible) to make isolated judgements about the strength of grid and group when no close comparison is to hand. This is not, however, a rule that Douglas invariably respects.

The argument developed

The attempt to achieve greater methodological rigour in its second edition leaves the polemical side of *Natural Symbols* untouched. This is because the polemic is grounded somewhat differently. *Purity and Danger* had been organized around the opposition of form versus formless, and introduced a strong (if qualified) argument to the effect that ritual is on the side of form. *Natural Symbols*, as we have seen, derives one of its inspirations from explicit concern with Catholic ritual, so that its initial problem is posed in terms of the ritualized versus the non-ritualized. Catholic reformers are lined up with a vaguely identified New Left, with the Protestant Reformation, with young radicals and revolting students as the enemies of form and ritual. To cope with the variety of the unritualized, a further distinction is made between the unritualized, or secular, and those who are definitely antipathetic to ritual, the anti-ritualists. This leaves us with three positions to explain: ritualist, secular and anti-ritualist.

Anti-ritualists see ritual as worthless external form that is devoid of inner conviction. Their case is explored in the first two chapters, 'Away from ritual' and 'To inner experience', which largely reiterate the argument of 'The contempt of ritual'. Church reformers who value the inner sense of conviction and devalue outward show do not realize that it is the outer show that brings about the inner state. But this is understandable, since they are ill-equipped to respond to condensed symbols having been brought up and moved as professional people in the elaborated code with its emphasis on individual feelings and its stress on verbal articulateness. 'Alas for the child from the personal home who longs for non-verbal forms of relationship. By rejecting ritualized speech he…thwarts his faculty for receiving immediate, condensed messages given obliquely along non-verbal channels' (NS1: 53). These reformers, and most of her readers, are assumed to be in a relatively low grid and low group position. Particular scorn is reserved for Dutch bishops who play down transubstantiation:

> They can't take it, the Dutch bishops who issued this catechism and the open-minded English teachers who seize on it as a watered-down expression of a faith that has practically lost meaning for them. The mystery of the Eucharist is too dazzlingly magical for their impoverished symbolic perception. Like the pygmies (I say it again, since they seem often to pride themselves on having reached some high peak of

intellectual development) they cannot conceive of the deity as located in any one thing or place.

(NS2: 49)

The Bog Irish, and 'vast unlettered flocks scattered over the globe do not share this disability' (NS2: 49). An analogous reasoning locates a similar gulf between students and their teachers. Students are in a situation of strong grid, but they are weakly grouped. Order seems intrusive to them (she refers to the destruction of library card catalogues at the University of Illinois, and problems at the LSE provoked her to write a letter to *The Times* (1967i)). Staff are in a small group competitive situation: relatively down grid but strongly bounded. This means that the staff of university teaching departments share their social predicament with other small groups – including the witchcraft-fearing inhabitants of central African villages (which may give an indication of how she was beginning to feel about her professional life at University College). However, the point of the analogy is to show that it is predictable that the students and staff should find themselves at cross purposes, since their social experiences predispose them to find different cosmologies self-evident.

While none of the ensuing chapters is strictly limited to a single theme, in brief, here is how the argument is developed. Chapter 5, 'The two bodies', returns to the theme of the body as a natural symbol; this, as she has clarified in the second edition, is not to say that the physical body (the same everywhere in terms of its boundedness) is experienced as the same in different cultures, but that the social and physical bodies are 'naturally' experienced analogously (NS2: xxi, 69). Thus, highly formal social roles usually demand formality in bodily presentation and, because organic eruptions are screened during social intercourse, they are available as a means of disrupting or subverting such occasions. From this Douglas begins to develop an argument relating informality, and then bodily abandonment, to social context. The more loosely structured a social environment, she claims, the more likely that states of dissociation, such as trance, will be seen positively. Speaking in tongues, for instance, is not a compensation for social deprivation but a representation of a marginalized social condition. This theme is pursued further in Chapter 6, 'Test cases'. A close comparison between Nilotic peoples studied by Oxford anthropologists (Nuer, Dinka and Mandari) seeks to demonstrate that bodily control is weakest where social control is also weak.

The next two chapters look at different quadrants of the grid and group diagram. Although Chapter 7 is entitled 'The problem of evil', and a new passage appears in the second edition discussing the ways evil is explained in different societies, it is really about the prevalence of witchcraft in small bounded communities, especially those of central Africa. The strong external boundary and weak internal organization of the social body is mirrored in fears about physical boundaries. Evil cannot be controlled and so must be expelled. What goes for central African villages also applies to sects – she cites the Plymouth

Brethren and West Indian Pentecostalists – and is analogous to Strindberg's description of mid-nineteenth-century Sweden, and even to the effects of the Reformation in Europe as described by Jung. The absence of coherent, publicly recognized symbolic structures is argued to be disastrous for the development of the individual.

Chapter 8, called 'Impersonal rules', is specifically about the experience of living in societies marked by weak grid and group. The big-man societies of New Guinea and the historic Teutons, as well as contemporary business entrepreneurs, live in competitive social environments which value success and deride failure. But only the successful prosper while the majority find their paths to advancement blocked until 'one day their luck or demons may become more effective' (NS2: 137). The unsuccessful find themselves in a position of weak group but strongly coercive grid. Periodically, the disadvantaged lose faith in the competitive egalitarian principle that effectively benefits only a few. In Melanesia their revolt takes the form of a cargo-cult promising them immediate material rewards. In the second edition, passages on student revolt (and specifically the destruction of library catalogues) have been moved from the preface into direct comparison with other millennial movements (NS2: 140–41):

> [T]he destruction of categories of any kind is a symbolic act which replicates social life over-structured by grid, the experience which has always driven people to value unstructured personal experiences and to place their faith in a catastrophic event which will sweep away all existing forms of structure.
>
> (NS2: 141)

The overtly polemical message of the book peaks in the penultimate chapter, 'Control of symbols', one of the most heavily revised in the second edition of the book. The burden of the chapter can be stated like this: if the reader accepts the demonstration that symbolic acts reflect the social experience of those who carry them out then, first, what does this tell us about contemporary events? And, second, does this imply that we are without choice whether we simply replicate our social experience in our symbolic acts? The seriousness of this question is conveyed by the tone of its opening passage, certainly unlike any routine anthropological text I know of, and closer to a sermon:

> According to the Book of Genesis our ancestor fell from a state of natural innocence when he ate the ambiguous fruit. To attain knowledge of good and evil is still the god-defying and distinctive goal of human beings. And always we find ourselves unable to bear the knowledge, and always erecting filters to protect the idea of our own interior innocence. One such filter is the strong resistance made by many scholars to the very notion of social determinants of belief. They would rather think of beliefs floating free in an autonomous vacuum, devel-

oping according to their own internal logic, bumping into other ideas by the chance of historical contact and being modified by new insights. This is an inverted materialism. In the name of primacy of mind over matter, its adherents evade their own responsibility for choosing the circumstances for their intellectual freedom. To ensure autonomy of mind we should first recognize the restrictions imposed by material existence.

(NS2: 145)

Who are the 'we' who cannot bear the knowledge that we are not autonomous? To what congregation is the reminder that we are all socially determined addressed? Apparently to a readership of middle-class individualists. What seems most to jar for Mary Douglas is the belief of some reformers that they are less determined than those they seek to reform when, instead, 'the apparent anti-ritualism of today is the adoption of one set of natural symbols in place of another. It is like a switch between restricted speech codes' (NS2: 170). How are they to recognize the restrictions of their existence? By attention to Mary Douglas's sociological analysis which itself changes the conditions in which we choose.

A following page and a half, added to the second edition, summarizes that method. To each social environment corresponds a theory of justification. Within each theory are certain unstated, implied or presupposed assumptions about the ultimate nature of reality. 'Such shared assumptions underlie any discourse, even the elaborated speech code which is developed to examine them' (NS2: 145). Moreover these assumptions 'betray how the social bond is constituted in the secret consciousness of individuals' (NS2: 146). The four types of environment are outlined again with their particular weak points: for all the security he normally enjoys, the rule-bound individual of the hierarchical society is like matter of place when in transfer between statuses; then there is the competitive society of weak grid and weak group, 'charming though its world view is, and rosy its concept of human nature, it is a temporary resting place which turns barren for the long-term resident…Intellectually it is as null as it is ineffective in organization' (NS2: 146). With grid strong but group weak we find the society of mass alienation produced by elite competition, prone to millennial movements. Where group is strong and grid weak we find the small group scenario: the witch-hunt within mirrored in bodily imagery of boundedness and threat.

Complex societies pose the added problem of reaction between these different worldviews and their bearers. To go back to the question which opened the book: what are the origins of the contempt of ritual? One source is rapid change that makes ritual corresponding to a previous social environment appear otiose. More insidiously, processes of gradual change are constantly bringing about slippage in the relation between social environment and cosmology. Periodically, ritual must be brought into line with society, and this may involve a revulsion against old ritual. However, the move is not necessarily out of ritual –

St Augustine embraced Manichaeism in the sixth century. Moreover, the Oxford Movement of the mid-nineteenth century embraced Roman Catholicism as a form of freedom from proximate Anglicanism (quoted in Chapter 2). A third type of anti-ritualism is expressed in the limited code of the alienation of the oppressed who are treated as objects. Anti-ritualism is the idiom of revolt. Unfortunately, in accordance with the social determination argument, the mass adopt behaviour expressive of their social position, experiencing control by objects they 'rush to adopt symbols of non-differentiation and so accentuate the condition from which they suffer. This is the dangerous backlash in symbolic experience of which *we* should beware' (NS2: 153, my emphasis). Instead:

> They should get organized. This would involve them in hierarchical discriminations. But expressive action is easier, more satisfying and may possibly have some instrumental value. So they use marches and mass protests as expressions of revolt…The drive to achieve consonance between social and physical and emotional experience envelops the mind also in its sweep. Hence the failure of revolutionary millennialists to write a programme that in any way matches the strength of their case. Hence the apparent flippancy or unserious abandon with which they pronounce their diagnosis and their remedies. It is as if the symbolic mode has overwhelmed the freedom of the mind to grapple with reality.
>
> (NS2: 154)

The denunciation continues in a passage removed from the second edition:

> This argument relates to religious ecumenism and demythologizing psychologists and literary critics as also to the new radicals and student revolt. This is the sector of the society which we expect to be weak in its perception of condensed symbols, preferring diffuse, emotive symbols of mass effect. The religious style is spontaneity, enthusiasm and effervescence. Bodily dissociation in trance, induced by dance or drugs, is valued along with other symbols of non-differentiation. Distinguishing social categories are devalued, but the individual is exalted. The self is presented without inhibition or shyness. There is little or no self-consciousness about sexual or other bodily orifices and functions. As to intellectual style, there is little concern with differentiated units of time, respect for past, or programme for the future. The dead are forgotten. Intellectual discriminations are not useful or valued. The general tone of this cosmological style is to express the current social experience. In the latter, there is minimum differentiation and organization; symbolic behaviour reflects this lack. In the field of the intellect it is disastrous.
>
> (NS1: 149)

Both editions conclude, 'The cosmology which goes with the experience of mass, undifferentiated human solidarity has a fatal attraction for those who most vehemently wish to remedy its failures' (NS1: 149; NS2: 154).

In contradistinction to this apocalyptic and disgusted vision of non-differentiation and anti-ritualism, of millennial movements that create more misery and oppression than the ills they seek to cure, Douglas argues:

> The solutions to the problems which provoke [millennialism] is not to join the stampede. To throw overboard differentiating doctrines and differentiating rituals is to reach for the poison that symbolizes the ill. Anti-ritualists around us who feel this excitement in the air, rather than yield, should feel more practical compassion for the rootlessness and helplessness that inspire it. Then, instead of sweeping away little rituals, such as Friday abstinence, which shore up a sense of belonging and of roots, and instead of belittling the magic of priesthood and sacraments, they would turn their attention to repairing the defences of grid and group.
>
> How to humanize the machine is the problem, not how to symbolize its dehumanizing effects. When bureaucrats hear the catchword 'equality' (a symbol of non-differentiation) they should beware. The way to humanize the system is to reject equality and cherish the individual case. The institution which runs by strict adherence to general rules gives up its own autonomy. If it tries to adopt equality or seniority or alphabetic order or any other hard and fast principle for promotion and admission, it is bound to override the hard case. Furthermore, it is bound to abandon its traditions and so its identity and its original special purposes. For these humanizing influences depend upon a continuity with the past, benevolent forms of nepotism, irregular charity, extraordinary promotions, freedom to pioneer in the tradition of the founders, whoever they were. Instead of anti-ritualism it would be more practical to experiment with more flexible institutional forms and to seek to develop their ritual expression.
>
> (NS1: 155; slightly revised in NS2: 158–59)

This might be the end of the book. Indeed, the original overall conclusion of the final chapter (Chapter 10, 'Out of the cave') is moved to cap the penultimate chapter of the revised edition. Addressing reforming theologians in particular, but other reformers more generally, Douglas suggests that by demolishing meaningless rituals they are simply going 'where the tide sweeps them [which] cannot be their proper calling' (NS2: 159).

The final chapter, 'Out of the cave', with its reference to Plato's shadows of the real, suggests that the elaborated codes, which allow us to inspect our own values, also give us the option of retaining some forms of positional control and some of the rituals that potentially unify cosmology, society and body.

Anti-ritualism simply substitutes another set of natural symbols for the ones it rejects. Two 'morals' then follow: 'first, the duty of everyone to preserve their vision from the constraints of the natural symbols when judging any social situation; second the opportunity of religious bodies to set their message in the natural system of symbols' (NS2: 170). That she states only three lines later 'beware…of arguments couched in the bodily medium' might seem an immediate subversion of her second point were it not for a concluding paragraph of criticism for Christian preachers who abjure the natural symbols of their faith to seek political power while religious symbols are taken over by the young who are politically quiescent (or, in terms of the earlier argument, whose revolt expresses only their alienation) (NS2: 170). The elaborated code which permits a dispassionate view of natural symbols is, finally, also the means to recognize the importance of natural symbols. This closing appeal to our capacity to reflect on our own circumstances to rescue us from either secularism or anti-ritualism is not without its problems. Presumably, a state of 'belief' that has undergone self-inspection in terms of the elaborated code is not the same as 'belief' in the restricted code. Can both be called 'belief' in the same sense? And, are 'belonging' and 'deciding-to-belong' the same? Our capacity to abstract ourselves from immediate social circumstances and objectify our situation is at issue in *Natural Symbols* just as much as it was in *Purity and Danger*.

RECEPTION

At once a treatise in theology and anthropology, a contribution to the discussion of social policy, and a link in a chain of 'spiritual autobiography', *Natural Symbols* was reviewed widely by theologians, sociologists and anthropologists. Leach's outburst apart, reviews of *Natural Symbols* tended to be constructive and admiring of the range of subjects the book attempted to tackle. However, anthropological reviews generally treated the book less favourably than others (reviews by Marwick NS2/Soc and Milburn NS1/JASO were critical, those by Burridge NS1/Man and Littlejohn NS1/NS while more favourable not uncritical). Unlike Leach, other reviewers did not claim the book impossible to understand, although they latched on to different parts of its argument and seem at times, understandably given the complexity of the original, almost to be reviewing different books.[2]

The affinity between *Natural Symbols* and the classifying urge in the Durkheimian tradition, and in modernist British anthropology more generally, was widely noted – as were certain intrinsic problems in this approach. Typologies suffer from a static bias and from the necessity to fit cases into unambiguous types. Reviewers noted Douglas's personal preference for clear boundaries, well-defined forms, hierarchy, tradition and lack of ambiguity in social organization and symbolic classification. Developing their point, they might have seen the theoretical apparatus itself (with its defined quadrants and rules) as a further reflection of Douglas's preferences. It would accord well with her general thesis to anticipate that a writer who preferred well-defined form in her social arrangements would seek the same characteristic in her theoretical mastery of the world. Adrian Edwards perceptively remarked a problem in the drive to unequivocal classification. If most societies were a bit of this and a bit of that, well structured in some respect and loosely organized in others, then classification would involve emphasizing one set of characteristics against the other; albeit both were typical of the same society. Some movement towards dealing with this argument is evident in Douglas's later reformulation of her thesis to deal with institutions rather than whole societies. What was true of social organization might also be true of the cosmologies classified: Catholic cosmology was expressed in a tradition of exegetical interpretation as much as in the symbolic communication of the restricted code of ritual. To stress only one side of the equation, that of ritual and tradition, necessitated downplaying the Christian traditions of prophecy and interpretation (NS1/NB: 430). Edwards gave the most specific and germane instances of static, typological bias.

Another group of comments addressed the pro-ritual, or anti anti-ritual, side of Douglas's argument. Because the basic dichotomy in Douglas's thought was one of form versus non-form, it was difficult for her to see modification to ritual, or criticism of particular rituals, as anything other than anti-ritualism. Thus, as Lurkings argued, she lacked a theory of changing ritual (NS2/ET). Edwards put the case more particularly. Her analysis of the Bog Irish, which he chided for not being empirically based, recommended that they cling to their traditions and rituals, and drew the moral that others ought also to cherish such restricted codes. But symbolic systems were best able to communicate when their restricted and verbally inexplicit codings rested on symbols that were able to connect up the entire range of the believer's social and religious experience. If the symbols did not do this then it might be better to change the symbols rather than recommend a return to tradition.

The more general case made against the dichotomous terms which anchor her evaluative argument is her tendency to argue as if whatever is not conducive to her is *ipso facto* opposed to her preferences. Thus liberalism seems to be conflated with anarchy, and Protestantism with sectarianism (NS1/BJS). Terry Eagleton, less enchanted than by *Purity and Danger* (see p. 100, n. 15), wondered why she rejected more radically reformed communal ritual and asked 'Is nepotism the only alternative to anarchism?' (NS2/Tab).

There are also some logical problems and inconsistencies in the argument. In general, these concern the failure to decide whether structured versus unstructured, and ritualized versus unritualized, are relative or absolute distinctions. Sometimes Douglas writes as if it were possible to evade social structural determination, at other times she eschews this possibility and treats social structure as something that may differ between societies but is never escapable. The same inconsistency applies to ritual: we could quote her to the effect that all societies have ritual, or to the effect that some do and some do not. James Littlejohn caught the sense of this double-bind most neatly:

The concept of ritual [in *Natural Symbols*] is…unstable. Among the numerous formulations given of it are: a restricted code, using either words, the body or objects as medium; statements celebrating social positions; symbolic action organising experience; actions such as sit-ins which don't in fact achieve anything. It is something of an anti-climax at the end of the book to read that after all 'the apparent anti-ritualism of today is the adoption of one set of religious symbols in place of another'; anti-ritualists have rituals of non-differentiation. If we cannot avoid the rituals social relations impose on us what is the problem? And if symbols control experience, what experience can we have which will permit us to control symbols? To say, in these circumstances, that we control symbols at will by 'resolving' to, seems to me to express the core of humanist philosophy. Verily, God is dead.

(NS1/NS: 697)

The anonymous reviewer in the *Times Literary Supplement* made a similar point when probably he (perhaps she) noted that science, bureaucracy and – the reviewer might have added – economic competition had their own rituals and thus should not be treated as unritualized (NS1/TLS, see also Deshen NS1/AJS). In fact, Douglas is inconsistent on this point, as I have noted, and to the extent that she exempts certain forms of social life from the precepts of structure and ritual in some passages of *Natural Symbols* actually regresses in terms of her own argument in *Purity and Danger*. Reviewers who urged her to recognize the importance of scientific thought in contemporary society, and more specifically the status of science as a symbolic statement of order (e.g. Littlejohn NS1/NS), anticipated a direction she would explore in later work. But we shall not be picking up the development of the group and grid model explicitly until Chapter 10, after we have followed its development by wide-ranging application to economics, risk and religion.

Notes

1 Other commentators, who thought that the reforms of Vatican II indicated an acceptance by the Church of a pluralized, 'anthropological' sense of culture, could quote John Paul II's 1983 address that 'the Church must give itself to the "long and courageous process of inculturation". But there cannot be inculturation unless evangelizers "adopt resolutely *an attitude of exchange and of comprehension*, in order to understand the cultural identity of peoples, ethnic groups, and the various sectors of modern society"' (Arbuckle 1986: 445, internal quote from John Paul II, *The Church is a Creator of Culture: Address to the Pontifical Council for Culture*, Sydney, ACTS, original emphasis).
2 Readers wishing to consult an original review might search out Edwards (NS1/NB) for the most penetrating Catholic response and Littlejohn (NS1/NS) for a reasoned anthropological appreciation.

Part III

EXCURSIONS AND ADVENTURES: 1970s–1990s

6 RITUALS OF CONSUMPTION

Publication of the two editions of *Natural Symbols* occurred either side of Mary Douglas's fiftieth year in 1971. During the last three decades of this century – with undiminished, even increasing, tenacity – she has applied the schema of grid and group in some fields, programmatically extended it to others, and refined the terms of the schema itself. The title I have given this part of her intellectual biography, 'Excursions and adventures', is meant to indicate some of the intellectual excitement which propelled Mary Douglas's several sallies out of conventional anthropology to colonize neighbouring disciplines. Each foray has an ethnographic character as she recounts her struggles to understand the customs of the natives who dwell in nutritional studies, economics, ecology or religious studies. There is, of course, the significant difference that in real ethnography there is always some sense, by definition, in which the natives have it right. Mary Douglas's visits were usually to tell the natives that they had it wrong. The next four chapters (Chapters 6–9) are devoted to three fields of application: economics and consumption, with special interest in the consumption of food and drink; risk analysis, with special attention to decision-making; and religion, with reference first to contemporary and then to archaic societies. The cross-currents between these interests are numerous, but I shall defer intensive consideration of these to my two concluding chapters in order to make a rapid survey of her most important works.

1970 was another turning year in Douglas's life, *Natural Symbols* was published and Mary Douglas was given a personal chair at University College London. It was also the year in which Daryll Forde retired to be replaced as head of the University College anthropology department by M.G. Smith. The academic staff and students were splitting into factions descended from the sociological trinity that I recall from my student days: Weberians headed by Smith, youthful neo-Marxists (whose ideas were to find expression in the journal *Critique of Anthropology*) and a scattering of Durkheimians led by Mary Douglas. Personality clashes fuelled intellectual differences, so that the department seemed a close analogy of the central African village riven by accusations of witchcraft described in *Natural Symbols*. Intellectually, it was exciting and, for students, not a little intimidating – the atmosphere often tense, and the rate of student attrition high.

Mary had attempted to move to the London School of Economics, but the chair in anthropology went instead to Ioan Lewis (also from University College). By the early 1970s, her children (the third born in 1956) were closer to completing their education, and her husband's career was reaching its peak with his appointment as Director of the Conservative Research Department in 1970. However, after Edward Heath was twice defeated in general elections during 1974, James Douglas was demoted to Associate Director, with Chris Patten (later Conservative Party Chairman and the last Governor General of Hong Kong) taking over as Director. Margaret Thatcher became leader of the Conservative Party in 1975, and the party began its move to the extreme – by post-war standards – right-wing, free-market position in British politics that it occupied throughout the 1980s. Under the influence of Sir Keith Joseph, the autonomy of the research department, which was associated with more 'progressive' Heathite policies, was curbed and its functions largely assumed by a number of right-wing 'think tanks' (Ramsden 1980). When James Douglas retired from the Research Department, and the Douglas children became independent, the pressing reasons for remaining in Britain were removed. But this is to run ahead; the move to the USA in the later 1970s belongs with discussion of Douglas's work on risk in the next chapter, although some of the developments in food research noted here are also of that period.

PRECEDENTS

In the early 1970s, Mary Douglas's attention turned to food and to consumption theory in economics. As a reader of *Natural Symbols* might anticipate, this work was to involve both application of theoretical argument and an urging of the policy implications that followed from her demonstration that food and consumption experts, of different stripes, collectively failed to appreciate the ritual qualities of everyday life. 'Man', as I quoted earlier, 'is a ritual animal.' Precedents for her interests in economics and politics are plentiful and consistent – from the study of the social teachings of the Church at school, through her Oxford first degree in Politics, Philosophy and Economics, to the numerous papers and reviews she produced in the first two decades of her professional life at University College (e.g. 1956a, 1958a, 1962a, 1967e, f, 1970j, 1971d). James, the dedicatee of *Risk and Blame*, was thanked for being 'tireless in [his] efforts to make [her] relate the discourse of anthropology to the discourses in economics and political theory' and for being 'impervious' to disciplinary boundaries (RAB: xii). However, the way in which she was to tackle economics is clearly inspired by the theoretical excursus of *Natural Symbols*.

The extraordinary range of interests Mary Douglas managed to address from 1970 onwards was possible only because she brought a common theory and methodology to bear upon them all. Explicitly, the theory is there for all to see: either in the different elaborations of grid and group, or in its later simplification as 'cultural theory' drawing on four ideal types. More diffusely, and as importantly, a consistent style of argument and presentation appeared. A theoretical adventure normally began by identifying prevailing misconceptions that were both intellectually and practically 'disastrous'. Nineteenth-century theories of magic played this role in *Purity and Danger*, as had the 'contempt of ritual' in *Natural Symbols*. Douglas then argued that these misconceptions told us more about the theorists proposing them, and the type of society in which they lived, than they did about the people they were supposed to be studying. Having, as it were, cleared the field by demolishing existing theories in terms of their contemporary social interestedness, she was then in a position to introduce her own theory founded in the primacy of social context. Douglas's arguments were always introduced oppositionally by the critique, and occasional ridicule, of existing theory. While this agonistic style was not the whole story – she also offered positive argument for her ideas – the technique was consistent enough to assure that each work was bound to offend some audience. Mary Douglas's sense that she was out of sympathy with her times and its intellectual movements, embattled with few supporters in a hostile sea of prejudice and wrong-headedness, is powerfully conveyed in this combative style. When, predictably, an infuriated response was elicited from the opposition, then, as predictably, her sense that she was misunderstood, under-appreciated and unrecognized was justified and strengthened.

The polemic accompanying Douglas's foray into economics was announced in an article for the *Times Literary Supplement* special issue on 'The state of anthropology' under the title of 'The exclusion of economics' (1973d/ITAV). Initially, she had anthropologists rather than economists in her sights, and she was particularly hard on the rejection of formal economic theory by a school of anthropologists who called themselves substantivists (by virtue of their interest in the substantive processes of production, circulation and consumption), 'With such high hopes and so little technical skill anthropology reached descriptive levels it had rarely plumbed before' (ITAV: 177). So it happened, according to her, that just as economists were looking to anthropology for help in an area they knew was weak – consumption theory – so anthropologists were 'too deeply enshrouded in their substantive home-spun to notice it' (ITAV: 180). A contemporary economic anthropology would study the pattern of social relationships served by the circulation of goods: such a programme would be 'exacting in its scope and power…[b]ut only stone age tools are ready for it' because the failure of anthropologists to attend to economists has 'left this one social science which claims to see mankind as a whole without an adequately developed theory of economics' (ITAV: 181, 182).[1] Later, disappointed by what she found there, Douglas's polemic would turn against economics.

Developing her interest in food and meals, Douglas argued that her analyses of classification systems could also be applied to the structure of meals in Western societies (1972b). The implications of this cognitive and classificatory approach to consumption were then explored in *The World of Goods* (1978b) which correlated social position and consumption style in a manner similar to the correlation of social situation and cosmology in *Natural Symbols*. If these correlations could be maintained, she argued, then the policy implications were broad, including the avoidance and relief of famines, health education and welfare policy. With these pieces in place, she was able to refocus her attention on the problems of creating viable communities in contemporary societies. Only certain types of community could produce public, or collective, goods for their members – indeed the capacity to produce these common benefits was one of their defining characteristics. In some respects, such communities might be analogized to the way in which homes functioned. A viable community was thus a way of being at home in a wider world, and 'cultural theory' was able to shed analytic light on choices people made, while going about their daily business, of the sort of society they were creating for themselves.

FOOD AND FESTIVITIES

To start at the beginning: the taking of food is the root of consumption. As Douglas puts it in an essay title: 'Food is not feed' (1977d/ITAV); food may nourish us, but we do not eat in order just to be nourished. Most people do not usually eat alone at irregular times and without the paraphernalia of seated eating. Nor do we eat what is best for us (according to whatever latest advice we attend to – or probably don't attend to). Mary Douglas's initial move on the hypothetical materialist position in consumption is now familiar to us. Treat food events as akin to little rituals: structured occasions in which certain components, combinations and behaviours are called for. As in all such occasions, the inappropriate, the gaffe, and the unacceptable illuminate the norm. Further, assume that if food events are like little rituals, then like rituals they involve communication:

> I first got interested in the ritual aspects of food around the age of five. [In my grandparents' home] I learnt to read off the days of the week from the lunchtime menu. Sunday was a roast, a chicken, leg of lamb, or beef or pork. It must have been a big roast, or we had very small helpings, as it served the next three days as well. Monday, cold with salad, Tuesday, shepherds' pie with cabbage or sprouts, Wednesday, rissoles with bubble-and-squeak, or curry. On Thursday a fresh start with liver and bacon. Friday was fish, Saturday was fishcakes or sausages and mash. Then we were back on roast.
>
> (1997a: 18)

An early programme of research on these lines, funded by the Department of Health and Social Security, was carried out by her student, Michael Nicod, in English working-class families. These families play the role of the Bog Irish in *Natural Symbols*. It is the conservatism of the habits of both groups that makes their ingrained behaviour a happy hunting-ground for structural analysis. Further analogy with *Natural Symbols* might be drawn in the controversy aroused by the research: a report published for a wider readership in *New Society* occasioned a question in Parliament about the expense of an allegedly pointless piece of investigation (1974a). Douglas vigorously defended the research (ITAV: viii; 1997a). The investigation of English working-class meal structure followed directly in the style of her analysis of the strict classification of animals, and of sacrifices for the temple, among the Israelites (1972b). A small number of perceptible contrasts in the qualities of food: hot versus cold, sweet versus savoury, solid versus runny, structured versus unstructured, was capable of classifying all the daily meals of the working-class family. The same contrasts were found to structure meals which marked weekly, annual and life-time events (Sunday dinners, Christmas and wedding meals); indeed the contrasts were more strongly marked than in the daily meal. Festive meals, like Christmas, brought everyday categories to a symbolic pitch: the wedding cake, Christmas cake and pudding with custard could be envisaged as sharing sensual properties and varying in their degree of sculptural form. This suggested an answer to the question why the British bought increasing quantities of biscuits when their demand for bread and cake was falling. The sensual and sculptural properties of the biscuit allowed it to operate as a condensed symbol (as the ending to a food event, like pudding or cake), and thus to occupy a variety of slots within the established structure of food events – even to be a minimal food event in itself (1975c).

Ethnographic fieldwork allied to structural analysis might seem a large hammer to take to a small nut, let alone a biscuit, but Douglas argued that both were required if nutritionists were to investigate how, why, where and when food events occurred so as to understand why people did not as a rule gratefully accept and act, 'in their own interest', upon scientific nutritional recommendations. In short, the nutritionists needed to find out what people's interests in eating were. The ethnographic and anthropological study of food events was subsequently to be refined with the help of a computer scientist, Jonathan Gross, to establish measures of 'culinary complexity' – in essence, the degree to which the food system (for instance, the different food items structured into menus) responded to events in the social world (for instance, to mark the passage of the week, the year and the life cycle) (1981a, 1984a, 1988a). What is to be read into a high degree of culinary complexity varies according to the social and economic circumstances of the household: high culinary complexity could indicate competition between the units staging food events, or it might reflect the economic stability of relatively independent households offering occasional hospitality (like the English working-class households studied by Nicod), or finally it could be a marker of the integration of households between which mutual invitations were frequent. On the same argument, low culinary complexity might result either from economic deprivation accompanied by high social pooling, or from social withdrawal. Only households with relatively low social involvement (either poorly integrated and/or non-competitive) would in principle be able to change their food habits according to nutritional advice without incurring high social costs (1984a). And such isolated households were in a minority.

A number of Douglas's early essays on food were run together under the title 'Food as a system of social communication' in her second volume of collected essays (ITAV; incorporating 1974a,b, 1977c,d). The point was not simply to produce an amusing 'after dinner anthropology' but to demonstrate that food was one of the mediums 'through which a system of relationships within the family is expressed' (ITAV: 86). Looking within families, rather than between households as above, the differentiation expressed through the food system could be compared with that found in the rest of the family social system. A typology of family food systems suggested that a highly structured food system might either correspond to a hierarchical family, or else reflect that conflicts within the family were resolved by catering for each member's preferences. Similarly, a relatively unstructured food system might either be consistent with unstructured family relations or conflict with it. Food problems (obesity, food fads, anorexia) should be contextualized not simply as nutritional problems, but as gestures referring to broader correlations between food events and the family social context in which they usually occurred. This analysis differed in subtle respects from that she had made in *Natural Symbols* and more often proposed in her abstract theorizing. Here, Douglas is suggesting that the *same* formal patterning of food habits means something *different* depending on its social embeddedness; more usually, she anticipates that social context and symbolic form covary.

On her transfer to the Russell Sage Foundation as Research Director in Culture, Mary Douglas both expanded this programme into a study of food and festivities in America by several researchers (see the essays collected in 1984a) and generalized it as a critique of the materialist bias in welfare and famine studies (1976a, 1982g, 1984c, see below). Various other papers announced the programme and sought collaboration (e.g. 1978e, 1979b,c, 1980b), while publicizing the results of a social contextualization of food habits for a wider public in the *Listener, Times Literary Supplement, Times Higher Education Supplement* (as well as 1974a; see 1977a–d, 1982g, 1983i, 1989g) and applying a similar perspective to drink (see the edited papers in 1987b).

WORLD OF GOODS: HOUSEHOLD CONSUMPTION

Research into food habits was the bridgehead for a broader programme of research into patterns of consumption on which Douglas embarked intensively during a year's leave of absence from University College in 1973–74, funded by a grant from the Social Science Research Council which allowed her to engage an econometrician, Baron Isherwood, as collaborator. *The World of Goods* (1978b) which resulted was, as its subtitle says, a step 'towards an anthropology of consumption'; but some of its character derived from being written against the background of the 'victory of monetarist theory', that most unsocial of economic orthodoxies and anathema to everything Douglas believed. I have already noted how Douglas prefaced her foray with a vigorous denunciation of the blinkers imposed by boundaries between disciplines, which has been a recurrent pet hatred whether of anthropology's relations with economics or with theology, sociology, philosophy, or whatever else. A 1976 paper condenses much of her argument about poverty: 'Goods are for mobilizing other people…Unless we know why people need luxuries and how they use them we are nowhere near taking the problem of inequality seriously' (1976a/ITAV: 23, 24).

To be destitute is to be wanting the minimum needed for survival, but to be poor is to be poorly connected through things to other people. It is to be unable to mount rituals of consumption. These are the bare bones of an argument expanded in *The World of Goods*,[2] which opens with another familiar ploy:

> There is obloquy for merchandising and guilt in ownership. A growing swell of protest against the consumer society sets the background to this book. Consumerism is castigated as greed, stupidity, and insensitivity to want. But what are we to do about it? If it is our moral responsibility to live more austerely, we are notably reluctant to do so…Overconsumption is more serious and more complicated than personal obesity, and moral indignation is not enough for understanding it.
>
> (WG: vii)

'Obloquy for merchandising' functions in *World of Goods* as 'contempt of ritual' had in *Natural Symbols*: by establishing the term from which an oppositional logic of the disparaged can be argued. Later essays in this vein have titles designed to make the same point: 'In defence of shopping' (1992i), 'The consumer's conscience' (1992h). Why do people consume? Conventional microeconomics assumes that rational individuals decide to consume a mixture of goods that maximizes their satisfaction. Consumption activity (what people buy) reveals the choices that have been made to allocate that scarce resource, disposable income, between different desirable ends (goods and services), not all of which the consumer can buy at once. At any moment, the pattern of decisions can be changed if the monetary values involved in deciding them alter. If income rises or falls, consumption patterns will have to be adjusted; if prices of goods and services change either together, through a general inflation or deflation, or relative to one another, then consumers are faced with changed conditions under which to exercise choice. All this is intuitively sensible, and economists are able to make predictions about short-term changes in patterns of demand for goods and services on the basis of information about prices and income. However, aspects of this reasoning caused concern to Mary Douglas.

Neoclassical microeconomic analysis takes the decision-making individual as an economic agent, and treats this agent asocially by concentrating on the way in which a rational agent would alter a set of consumption decisions in the light of changing conditions of availability, as represented by changes in price or disposable income. The complex motives of economic agents are redescribed as a set of interests (also, 1994f). Goods also are considered on a one-by-one basis: for instance, posing questions such as: what will happen to demand for cinema tickets if their price rises by 10 per cent? Neither of these simplifying assumptions appealed to Douglas's holistic theoretical proclivities, and we find her stressing instead the social character of consumption and the totality of goods and services consumed; which is almost the converse of her initial criticisms of substantivist, economic anthropology.

Microeconomic analysis is usually concerned with marginal decisions: what happens when consumers have to decide to change a pattern of consumption in the light of changes in existing prices and incomes? The relation between supply and demand determines the price of a good or service on the market; marginal changes in supply and demand are triggered by the price mechanism and, conversely, changes in price trigger changes in supply and demand. Economists tend to be interested in price behaviour rather than in what consumers do with the goods and services they buy. As a result they treat consumers' tastes as extrinsic to the model of price behaviour: analysis normally assumes tastes to be constant; changing tastes have effects within the model (by redrawing preferences and, thus, demand curves) but they cannot be accounted for by the model. The model simply assumes that consumers will attempt to maximize utility however their satisfaction arises. Different classes of goods may, however, be separated according to the price responsiveness of demand for them. Some things have to be bought even if the price for them goes up. Staple food is a typical example: a price rise may lead to a fall in demand, but this fall will be less than it would be for a luxury good; a rise in the price of basic goods may even lead to more, rather than less, of them being bought as consumers substitute greater quantities of staples for the items they can no longer buy at all. Together, these assumptions define a model of consumer rationality.

As Douglas notes (1987d), the idea that consumers derive diminishing marginal utility from increasing their consumption of a single good makes them the inverse analogue of the firm, for which costs of production (leaving aside economies of scale) tend to increase. The economists' model of wants meshes nicely with the theory of the firm to produce equilibrium prices, and economists value this theoretical elegance, not least for the neatness of its mathematical applications, despite the abstraction of the assumptions on which it rests.

Douglas's starting point begs quite different assumptions that are consistent with her two previous books:

> If it is said that the essential function of language is its capacity for poetry, we shall assume that the essential function of consumption is its

capacity to make sense. Forget the idea of consumer irrationality. Forget that commodities are good for eating, clothing and shelter; forget their usefulness and try instead the idea that commodities are good for thinking; treat them as a non-verbal medium for the human creative faculty.

(WG: 40–41)

This invitation is strongly reminiscent of that to forget everything except patterns of social relation in *Natural Symbols*; again we are asked initially to accept the proposition on methodological grounds ('bracketing away for the moment [the] practical uses [of consumption goods]'). And, again, the methodological advice will transpire rather to be an epistemological judgement (and part of the critique of materialist reasoning): 'Rituals are conventions that set up visible public definitions…Goods…are ritual adjuncts; consumption is a ritual process whose primary function is to make sense of the inchoate flux of events' (WG: 43).

But this ritual, like other rituals that anthropologists study, is not disinterestedly occupied with the making of meaning. 'Ultimately, consumption is about power, but power is exercised in many different ways' (WG: 63). *World of Goods* sets out to analyse consumption so that both its meaning and social context are highlighted.

Utility theory, Douglas quotes a critic, extracts the minimum of results from the minimum of assumptions. Consumption is the end of an economic process of which production is the mainstay; consumption is akin to the destruction of the goods and services produced, which are removed from the economic system so that production may continue. An anthropological model of consumption would question these assumptions. This inversion of the economic model was succinctly stated almost a decade later:

In economics the implicit assumption is that the origin of wants is to be found inside the individual's physical and psychic constitution. In anthropology, the implicit assumption is that wants are defined and standardized in social interaction…Put crudely, the reason anyone wants (physical needs apart) is for sharing with or showing or giving to someone else in recognition of similar gestures, gifts or services received in the past.

(1987d: 872, 873)

Assume that instead of the individual, the totality of culture is to be the object of analysis. Assume also that the household is to be envisaged not as the terminus of the economic system but as a productive unit: what it produces is a style of life for its members and a workforce that also engages in productive activity outside the household. In order to produce a style of life, the household needs goods and services. These goods and services are requisite to the task of creating an ordered, comprehensible and habitable environment. Goods belong to cate-gories, and their use in rituals of consumption serves to mark these categories (WG: 50–51). On this account, 'The most general objective of the consumer can only be to construct an intelligible universe with the goods he chooses' (WG: 43). The communicative functions of consumption are to pass on information about lifestyle to other members of the society, and to reflect back to the consumers themselves evidence of the character of the life-world they have created and inhabited. Since consumers do not create identical worlds, we need to be able to differentiate the kinds of information they are sending and receiving. A termi-nology is introduced to describe aspects of this information process: goods perform marking services for consumers; naming is assumed to be crucial to this; knowledge about naming can be shared; consumption events serve to prove, or test, naming. This articulation of the ideas of classification and ritual event is clearly cognate with the line taken in *Natural Symbols*; the third element as we would anticipate involves the social environment.

World of Goods employs a largely implicit and simplified version of grid and group analysis. Group describes demands on individuals emanating from the institutions to which they belong. Grid is the rule-governed environment in which individuals interact. Low grid is the position of extreme individualism. Seen this way, microeconomic analysis privileges the low grid, low group position where 'fair play' rules – in this case, to do with the operations of the market place – are accepted. However, microeconomic analysis must fail to appreciate the rationality of other positions. Low grid and group is inherently unstable because it is always rational for individuals finding themselves in a position of temporary advantage to attempt to consolidate their fortune by strategies of exclusion. In doing this they produce enormous disparities of wealth and power. If the powerless withdraw from the fray, they may either enter small enclaved groups or join the alienated masses. Ultimately, therefore, consumption is about power.

Seen in a social context, consumption enables different degrees of mastery over the social environment. Patterns of consumption can enhance the personal availability of the consumer, promoting linkage to others by staging consumption rituals, investing in technological linkage and in information services. These differences in mastery of the social environment can be addressed via scale and time. Scale describes both the extension of the range of contacts individuals can maintain, and the importance of the people to whom they are connected (an importance which partly depends, in its turn, on the scale of the contacts of these other people). Rather than 'consumption', this sort of expenditure can be redescribed as social 'investment' in the lifestyle of which the individual is a producer. Education, advice, communication linkage, information linkage, and so on, all belong with consideration of scale. Well-connected people are able to adjust to change, achieve a higher level of consumption and maintain their advantage.

The temporality of consumption is treated under two aspects: periodicity and time horizon. By analogy with studies of household production, it can be argued that less powerful members of a society find themselves landed with tasks that are highly repetitive and difficult to defer (think for instance of the busy mother and homemaker – shopping, cooking, caring, cleaning, washing…). The less technological linkage or income the household producer has at her disposal, the more she will be constrained by constant demands on her time that leave her little room for autonomy. What goes for some Western households is an even more marked condition for women farmers in many parts of Africa: they take responsibility for the repetitive tasks of finding firewood, cooking, weeding fields, gathering sauce ingredients, caring for children, and so forth, while their husbands assume tasks that are sporadic, involve spurts of energy, and generally command higher status (hacking down trees to clear a field, hunting, performing rituals necessary for the success of agriculture, etc.). Periodicity, then, is a measure of the degree to which a consumer can secure autonomy from the dull constraint of routine and begin to enjoy either the flexible use of time that will permit reaction to unpredictable circumstances, or the investment of time that will increase linkage and information.

The time horizon is treated rather differently. Douglas wants to argue, along with some consumption economists, that saving should not be seen as residual of consumption (what is left when the spending is done). Instead, individuals and groups will decide whether and how much to save in the light of expectations about the future, and these forecasts will be mediated by their social environment. Corporations that expect to exist in perpetuity, of which churches are an obvious example, may think in centuries, even eternity. Individuals belonging to groups in which close sociality is marked by open-handedness (she takes the classic account of drinking in mining communities as an example), or where expenditure is necessary to secure the linkage and information that will enable them to find work (she cites the example of casualized dockers), will not be able to give the same preference to the deferment of spending. Thus, although tastes may change, they cannot change in any direction but will have to be fitted into the periodicities and time horizons integral to a way of life. Consumption, contrary to classical, microeconomic theory, is ill-described as an individual decision unfettered by considerations other than means and personal preference.

WORLD OF GOODS: WELFARE ECONOMICS

The first part of *World of Goods* begins to outline the social mechanisms which establish and maintain status barriers between consumption groups. It also introduces an analogy with international trade that is critical to the arguments of its second part, which addresses social policy on the basis of an informational approach to consumption: highlighting issues of inequality, wealth and poverty to ask what can be done about them. This would be a disconcerting move for a readership that imagined Douglas as a 'conservative' thinker in the party political sense.[3] Douglas's views certainly are sociologically conservative, but not in a sense that can easily be reconciled with party loyalty. Her sympathies were entirely alienated by the conservative right of the Thatcher–Reagan years, whose antisocial, competitive market mentality was exemplary of her low grid–low group social form with its potential for social division, polarization, and reactive millennialism of the disadvantaged to narrow self-interest on the part of a successful and socially disengaged elite.

The ethnographic description of non-Western economies with distinct spheres of exchange, such as we saw in Chapter 3, introduces the main argument of the latter half of *World of Goods*. Spheres of exchange correspond to periodicities: the spheres ranked lower contain goods which are subject to daily routine transactions that excite little moral judgement.[4] Exchanges that occur in the prestige spheres have a lumpy, irregular character (e.g. brides for cattle, one woman for another, one shell ornament against the promise of another). Various characteristics of the spheres are important to Douglas: they are bounded, they consist of goods and services which are differently evaluated, they are differentially linked to the political process (as were raffia cloths in the Lele example), and they pose interesting questions about rational choice. For instance, why should Hausa women in Nigeria accumulate far more enamel pots than they will ever use for eating? In terms of a strategy of exclusion, it is rational to attempt to monopolize, or at least maximize, access to the high status goods of an upper sphere of transactions. Enamel pots are a prestige good for women, and transacted between women at marriages and inheritance, so to have many of them indicates a woman's standing and her capacity to take part in the social events for which enamel pots are prerequisite.

The next stage of the argument is to define some general types of consumption that will correspond roughly to the idea of spheres. The notion of a scale of consumption (WG: 111) is simplified to distinguish three profiles: small scale with a preponderance of routine tasks; medium scale with an improved technology lessening some constraints of routine, but still holding only infrequent major consumption rituals; large scale using technology or domestic labour to free itself from routine and holding frequent consumption rituals involving wide linkage but significantly not including as members those in the small or medium scale. This scaling of consumption roughly corresponds to three classes into which the typology of consumption goods is also simplified: a basic set of goods needed in all households, durable goods with a higher technological component, and a set of information services largely concerned with the enhancement of communication. The two triads are linked because basic goods predominate in small-scale consumption, technological goods are added in the middle scale, and the goods which enhance both the availability of the consumer to others, and the inflow of information from others to the consumer, are required by those with large-scale consumption. The train of reasoning that started from the ethnographic instances of spheres of exchange is particularly relevant to contemporary circumstances because the source of wealth has shifted from land to labour and now to knowledge.

Controversially, this typology is then linked by extended analogy to the international situation characterized by patterns and terms of trade. The point of the analogy is to generalize a mechanism by which initial disparities cause divergent patterns of economic growth: virtuous and vicious circles that lead to the rich getting richer while the poor get, relatively, even poorer. Industrialized, mechanized and urbanized societies are contrasted with those lacking these characteristics. 'To be rich means to be well integrated into a rich community...To be poor is to be isolated' (WG: 118). Linkage is the key concept here.

By analogy with linkage in production, one may look for forward and backward linkage in consumption activities. Since there is some degree of independence among them, technological, social and informational linkages are distinguished to do this. For instance, car workers invest their consumption in technological goods, miners in social goods and dockers in information. An arbitrary selection of indices has to be chosen to apply the schema, and Douglas and Isherwood choose three items, while recognizing that this choice will require continuous re-evaluation: the car (a technological good), the telephone (a social good), and a bank account (as an informational good).[5] The arbitrariness is obvious: for instance, if I live in a remote area poorly served by public transport, my car may be necessary to my social linkage, and my social linkage necessary to my gaining information. The purpose of the typology is clear, even if the allocation of particular goods to each class is arbitrary. Choices about consumption are patterned because they correspond to the requirements of living with other people in a definite type of social environment. Rather than castigate people for the senseless way they spend their money, investigators should ask themselves what type of sociality their consumption is designed to reproduce.

This is where *World of Goods* joins issues of welfare economics (the branch of the subject concerned with collective well-being in Western societies), and the consideration of the social causes of famine in parts of the Third World, as well as debates over improving people's dietary habits (and the frequent failure of health education programmes). In each case, Douglas begins from aversion to a widely construed category of materialist explanation she finds in most writings on these subjects (an echo of the opposition to 'medical materialism' in *Purity and Danger* with its projection of contemporary knowledge of the hazards of pork-eating in hot climates to Israelites). The overall conclusion to her book reiterates a moral stance that also concluded its 'Preface':

Each free individual is responsible for the exclusiveness of his own home, the allocation of his free time, and hospitality. The moralists who indignantly condemn overconsumption will eventually have to answer for whom they do not invite to their table, how they wish their daughters to marry, where their old friends are today with whom they started out in their youth. Goods are neutral, their uses are social; they can be used as fences or bridges.

(WG: xiv–xv)

there are gaps in social involvement which leave some households isolated and economically vulnerable. These gaps are not the result of particular capitalist production processes. We find them in other kinds of society. They arise from decisions not to share consumption rituals, not to invite to the home. They mark the boundaries of sharing and hospitality. [Because we fail to perceive exclusion] the problem of poverty in the midst of industrial plenty is seen solely as an outcome of the system of production, to be solved by redistributive legislation and state control. This book presents the complementary view. *The poor are our kith and kin. Not all our relatives are likely to be among the well-to-do.* If we do not know how the poor live, it can only be because we have selected against them in the constituting of our consumption rituals, and have declined invitations to join their celebrations.

(WG: 154, my emphasis)

The conclusion might be less allusive, but it points in the general direction that all Mary Douglas's policy statements take after *Natural Symbols*. *Purity and Danger*, I argued earlier, was the last of her works to end on a note of metaphysical transcendence. This perspective was replaced by a notion of social engineering: that most of our problems are problems of sociality, and their solution lies in changing the patterning of social relationships. The tone in which this solution is proposed, for instance in the sentences I have emphasized from the quotation above, still employ the inclusive 'we' and somewhat churchly language (as in 'kith and kin', and the general sentiment that the poor are always with us). Although the remedy is as firmly social as it is not socialist, it belongs close to that point in British post-war politics, when 'one-nation' Toryism and market-mediated socialism achieved consensus on the broad mixture of welfare and market economics appropriate to national government.

RECEPTION AND DEVELOPMENTS

Douglas's subsequent work has not diverged greatly from this scheme;[6] the more recent accounts of consumption, 'The consumer's conscience' or 'The consumer's revolt', return to the beginning of *World of Goods*, its 'obloquy for consumption' replaced by accusations of 'mindless consumerism' (1992h/OAO/TS). However, a decade's further thought finds consumption theory much more closely tied in to grid and group analysis (now known as cultural theory) than it was in *World of Goods* and enriched by the publication of Pierre Bourdieu's work on taste in French society (1981c).

Borrowing Arjun Appadurai's felicitous phrase (1986), Douglas argues that luxuries have 'semiotic virtuosity' by virtue of being able to mark events and persons as special. Consumerism is not mindless but reduces drudgery, as well as the close confinement of a local community that has its nose in other people's business. Do those who rail against consumerism really wish themselves to be subjected to the constraints that keep it in check?

> The basic choice is not between kinds of goods, but between kinds of society, and, for the interim, between the kinds of position in society that are available to us as we line up in the debate about transforming society. When we have made up our mind where we want to be aligned, do we have much free choice about the judgements we are going to make about goods?…No, our preference[s are] part of the bundle that we initially choose as we align ourselves in the political debate.
>
> (1992h, OAO: 53)

'Cultural theory' is concerned with choice, but that choice is largely about the company we desire to keep. Consumption goods allow the consumer to locate conducive others and maintain the type of collectivity he or she prefers. Bourdieu's account of French consumption patterns emphasized the way that criteria of taste reinforce social and economic classes, but Douglas seeks to broaden the types of society to which this approach might be applied, proposing – as by now we would anticipate – a fourfold classification:

Type 1 The individualistic society is marked by transactions constrained only by rules of fair play consistent with a free market.

Type 2 Socially isolated individuals might refuse any truck with power or authority living almost as hermits.

Type 3 The enclaved small group is a closely knit community resisting both neglect and domination by successful individuals of type 1. The cost of this lifestyle is its interference in individual lives.

Type 4 The last, and from its phrasing evidently preferred, form involves 'collaboration in a rationally integrated society. This pattern restricts opportunism for the sake of protecting categories and compartments it is prepared to defend' (1992h, OAO: 56–57).

This formulation is consistent with Douglas's previous ideas of community and hierarchy, but sharpened – particularly in its stern contrast between types 1 and 4 – in ways that must reflect the results of a decade of Thatcherite economic 'liberalism', during which, 'The Keynesian notion that poverty is a systems problem needing attention [has been] discarded by an enterprise culture which holds the individual poor to be personally responsible for their own misfortune' (1996c: xxi). The major theoretical development concerns the mileage Douglas has been able to extract from the economic conundrum of public goods (explored at length in *How Institutions Think* with reference to Mancur Olson, discussed in Chapter 10). Public goods are desirable for a community but their provision has to surmount the problem of the free rider. Since no one can be excluded from a public good (for instance, clean air), it is difficult to make individuals pay for them. It is also difficult to dissuade individuals from a private course of action in conflict with a public good. In terms of narrow economic self-interest, individuals should not 'rationally' contribute to, or respect others' rights to, goods from which they can most profit by behaving antisocially (Olson 1971 [1965]). Douglas takes the example of a public transport system: while individuals who live in a capital city may desire this to be efficient, they will still use private cars for their individual convenience even if by doing so they contribute to the inefficiency of the public system by congesting the roads. The provision of public goods involves some suspension or denial of an immediate private interest: either by giving up a short-term advantage or by making a payment that might be avoided. These disciplines are necessary, but they necessarily incite revolt or withdrawal. Communities, as agents, exact a payment from their members, and this payment may be onerous both economically and socially. The demands of the community chest and the private purse are antagonistic (1992h). Consumerism is an element of a highly competitive way of living; it is highly rational as a response to the demands of competition, but it has the effect of tearing down community boundaries and rendering the provision of public goods problematic. It is not consumerism that is irrational, but the simultaneous demand for private consumption and public goods. 'Rational behaviour puts its money where its mouth is and recognizes community levies for what they are' (1992h/OAO: 64).[7] The degree of collective will to produce public goods and the willingness to put up with coercion to this end express characteristics of the social form.

The moral that applies to the public domain also applies to the most intimate settings – the local neighbourhood and the family. Mary Douglas is unashamed to defend what some might consider bourgeois values: the corner shop to which one voluntarily pays over the odds so that it does not go out of business when a hyperstore is established within a car-ride of home (1987g, 1992h); the integrated family home run on complementary distinctions of gender and age (1991b). What appeals to her about hierarchy, on Douglas's rather specialized definition of it (see Chapters 10 and 11), is that its principles of organization are replicated from the smallest to the most inclusive levels. Thus, the family, the city and the polity might be integrated by the same distinctions, rituals and symbols (1972b, 1991b for the home; 1990b for the city; 1993c,d for the polity; 1992j for relations between men and women). Only within such forms of sociality, she argues, can meals and consumption goods carry the complex and differentiated meanings of which they are capable. In another social environment, the same goods would carry different, and even contrary, meanings. Douglas's work on environmental risk, and perceptions of personal risk more generally, follow immediately from this programme and its preferences.

As its subtitle had foreseen, *World of Goods* was later to be acknowledged as a foundational text in a new economic anthropology especially concerned with consumption.[8] Reviews at the time of publication, with the notable exception of Geoffrey Hawthorn's amusingly scabrous but finally unconstructive comments

(WG/LRB), were generally bland and none, that I have found, appeared in mainstream economics journals. That there was more to economic theory than Douglas and Isherwood had allowed (WG/SSJ) was certainly true, but a foothold for anthropological perspectives in consumption theory was established (WG/Soc). Douglas's next intellectual move, into risk analysis and environmental concerns, followed directly (but, in a fashion, largely unremarked) from the concern for collective goods and welfare broached in *World of Goods*. But reviews of *Risk and Culture* were to be anything but bland.

Notes

1 Douglas's 'Introduction' to the new edition of *World of Goods* notes that her hopes in 1973 of what she might find in economics were disappointed: 'The weakness of utility theory was a harsh surprise for the social anthropologist…She thought that if she went into it seriously enough, she would find nuggets to be polished up for an anthropology of wants' (1996c: xxv). Her attitude to previous economic anthropology mellowed in this light.

2 In spite of co-authorship, I treat this book as a continuation of the project defined in the last two chapters. Tone, style and argument seem to me identifiably Douglas. As I noted in the Preface, the chapters of Part 3 of this account will not follow their textual sources as closely as those of Part 2. My presentation of *World of Goods* reorders its argument substantially to bring out the features common to Douglas's approach to economics and other subjects.

3 This was recognized by Jonathan Benthall who revised his earlier judgement (1977) in the light of the 1980s (1991).

4 The Oxford influence on anthropologists' conceptions of spheres of exchange is substantial: Franz Steiner's early and brilliant paper on the comparative study of values was posthumously edited for publication by Paul Bohannan, whose studies of spheres of exchange among the West African Tiv became a classic instance of the approach (Steiner 1954b; P. Bohannan 1955).

5 These and other changes are frankly addressed in the 'Introduction' to the re-edition of *World of Goods* (1996c).

6 For instance, see her accounts of the behaviour of companies, trade unions and labour markets (1989c/RAB; 1990h/RAB).

7 A similar contrast between 'virtual market' and 'virtual community' is illustrated in a paper contemporary with that under discussion by the contrast between the hotel and the home (1989a).

8 Daniel Miller, whose opinion can serve as a touchstone of wider opinion in this respect, treated *World of Goods* relatively briefly in a book-length survey of the field as 'one of the most important recent examples' of anthropological studies of consumption (1987: 145). Eight years later, in an article-length survey, he reviewed the book at greater length and stated that 'The birth of the new anthropology of consumption may…unambiguously be dated to 1978–1979' with the publication of *World of Goods* (1978) and Pierre Bourdieu's *La distinction* (1979) (1995: 266).

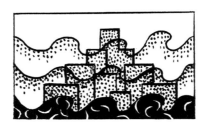

7 VERBAL WEAPONS AND ENVIRONMENTS AT RISK

BIOGRAPHICAL COUNTERPOINT

While Douglas's interest in environmentalism predates her move to the USA (1970e), in a variety of ways it was her change of job that catalysed her decision to make the linkages between classification and the environmental movement explicit (as she did in '*Purity and Danger* revisited' (1980c), summarized in Chapter 4). Her American period began with a year's sabbatical in 1977–78 as Research Scholar at the Russell Sage Foundation. Failing to secure a professorship in Chicago (to Victor Turner's distress as well as to her disappointment), she remained in New York as Director of Research on Culture at the Russell Sage Foundation – an organization that supported research into social, political and economic problems in America. Her first 'call for research' focused on the food programme surveyed in the last chapter (1978e). Aaron Wildavsky, who as President of the Russell Sage Foundation had secured her appointment, found his contract terminated by the time of her arrival – a circumstance (amusing to both in retrospect) that led to him occupying an office in the basement of the building while she moved into upper floor accommodation. Nonetheless, they collaborated to write *Risk and Culture* (1982b), which examined perceptions of risk with particular and sceptical focus on the worries of the American ecological movement. Until his death, Wildavsky remained an enthusiastic advocate of Douglas's cultural theories, applying them widely in his own work and co-authoring an account to popularize the method (with Thompson and Ellis 1990).[1] Douglas's contract at the Russell Sage Foundation lasted four years. In 1981, she moved to Northwestern University, just outside Chicago, to become Avalon Professor of Humanities: a joint appointment with the Department of Religious Studies. There she renewed her interest in explicitly religious and theological themes – with particular attention to contemporary, and specifically American, society – in ways that form the subject of the next chapter.

Not since the publication of *Natural Symbols* a decade earlier had a book of

Mary Douglas's raised reviewers' hackles as *Risk and Culture* would. Like that earlier skirmish with anti-ritualists, the book on the environmental movement was read as a polemic against dissenting groups – 'a neo-conservative critique of sectarianism' in the widely shared opinion of one reviewer (Weinstein RC/APSR: 204). Other critical reaction dwelled (among other things) upon the supposed cultural relativism, sociological reductionism or, even, un-American character (Boon RC/Rar) of the arguments proposed. Reviews appeared from an array of disciplinary positions and were largely American-authored – affording the novelty, for an anthropologist, of reaction from the 'natives'. Douglas felt herself and her co-authored book to have been widely misunderstood. Was the book too far ahead of its time, or too contrary to the ingrained assumptions of the risk-assessment field to be easily understood (Douglas RA: 2; RAB: 11)? Or, did the reviewers grasp the arguments but refused to agree with them? And, if the latter, was their opposition a function of reasoned academic misgiving, a reflex reaction to their own deeply committed positions, or a combination of the two? When academic works touch so closely upon personal convictions, a note of irascibility may be inevitable. But before broaching these issues, it is necessary to address the question of co-authorship.

AUTHORSHIP

Risk and Culture poses knotty problems to an intellectual biographer. Co-authorship is a striking feature of Mary Douglas's work, particularly after *World of Goods*; and collaboration is common where formal co-authorship is absent. However, the nature of her collaboration with Aaron Wildavsky is exceptional. Mary Douglas has always acknowledged how many of her own ideas have been borrowed, in more or less amended form, from academics with whom she has worked closely (Evans-Pritchard, Forde, Bernstein, and others) or who are the intellectual ancestors of her discipline (Durkheim and Mauss most generally – but also particular economists, social psychologists, philosophers, risk analysts, and so forth). She has been criticized frequently for yoking unlikely intellectual bedfellows together; so the commentator is bemused by the array of her sources more often than struggling to trace the ancestry of an idea. The majority of her more formal collaborations also pose few problems of intellectual copyright, since it is clear that Douglas has determined the main intellectual thrust of the joint research agenda. But the terms of her collaboration with Aaron Wildavsky – pugnacious political scientist and son of impoverished orthodox Jewish parents from the Ukraine (fondly described in Wildavsky 1975) – are more complicated. For all they remained close and loyal friends, each published subsequent accounts clarifying, at least to some degree, where they stood individually on the argument of *Risk and Culture*.

Mary Douglas's published versions of their collaboration credits Wildavsky with jibing her about the relevance of anthropological analyses of 'tribal' or 'ancient' societies to present-day societies (RA: 2; RAB: 10). '*He* was concerned to interpret a cultural change in contemporary America: the new awareness of technological dangers' (RA: 2, my emphasis). Given that application of anthropological analyses to 'modern' societies had been a leitmotif of Douglas's work, and that she credits her husband with constantly addressing the same question to her, Wildavsky must have been leaning on an open door so far as his general proposition was concerned. However, the immediate application of Douglas's ideas to contemporary American society – a topic on which she would have had no special expertise – does seem due to Wildavsky.

The two authors produced first drafts of different parts of the book, then read, commented upon and amended one another's work – so it cannot be assumed that either allowed the other to put ideas into print under joint authorship that they did not share. Nonetheless, the evidence of Douglas's other works on risk (*Risk Acceptability According to the Social Sciences* (1985a)), and of the first section of *Risk and Blame* (1992a), from which this third collection of her essays took its overall title suggests an agenda different in emphasis from *Risk and Culture*. Second-guessing responsibility for a collaborative work is not entirely fair, but *Risk and Culture* does find Mary Douglas rather far out on a very exposed limb; and while there is no evidence she particularly minded finding herself there, it is reasonable to question whether she would have got there alone.

Writing of collaboration for the *Journal of the American Political Science Association*, of which he was then President, Wildavsky pays lavish tribute to Mary Douglas: 'I gained not only a friend and a book but also an appreciation of her cultural theory that has guided my work ever since' (1986: 239). But, a few pages on, commenting on a book he wrote subsequently on risk, Wildavsky adds:

> While the earlier book [*Risk and Culture*] dealt with the social origins of risk *perception*, the new work is concerned with the *objective* aspects of risk: Which strategies should society follow to improve the health of its members? During the writing of *Risk and Culture*, I had to (compelled by my collaborator) leave aside interesting aspects of the debate over technological danger. While I liked and still like that book, I felt it wrong to leave the subject by decomposing the antagonists into their social categories without confronting the issue – Which sorts of actions make human life safer or more dangerous? – head on.
>
> (Wildavsky 1986: 245)

Douglas prefaces her own subsequent account of risk analysis with a stern health warning to the reader:

> [This book] is not about risks. Those who want to learn about the risks we face in the present day are advised to read no further. It is not about risk management. Those who want to learn how to handle risks of any kind should save their time and read no more. These notes are about

perception as treated in the various social sciences, and the particular focus is upon risk perception in the social sciences.

(RA: 2)

Here is the theoretical difference between the two authors at its starkest; and at its starkest it is difficult to reconcile. For instance, Douglas would certainly wish to argue that knowledge of risk perception empowers those who manage risks on behalf of society; that studies of perception and classification are relevant to how people choose to live is basic to the argument not only of *Natural Symbols* but of all the works that follow it. Moving from a strong programme for social control of cognition to active espousal of policy preferences raises several problems, but the most fundamental derives from the fact that any account of cognitive control is recursively subject to its own strictures. If there is no escaping social pressures for social actors, then no account of these pressures can claim to have escaped them either. Consideration of Douglas's various attempts to escape from this impasse belongs in Chapters 10 and 11, but the problem needs to be raised here because it underpins some of the differences between our co-authors. Mary Douglas recalled that some of Aaron Wildavsky's liking for cultural theory was

because it seemed to justify his prejudices: against hierarchy as a top-down, bureaucratic, oppressive form of government, and against sectarianism and political irresponsibility; this left individualism as the cultural bias with most in its favour…I myself like the theory of cultural bias because of its promise of objectivity…With such different outlooks it was extraordinary that we were able to collaborate [successfully].

(1996c: xxvii)[2]

Mary Douglas may be a little disingenuous here, since her own preference for hierarchy is explicit elsewhere. The upshot seems to have been a negotiated truce such that the political bias of *Risk and Culture* emerges as centrist, where the centre is seen as an alliance of market and hierarchy.

RISK AND CULTURE: THE PROBLEM STATED

I shall introduce *Risk and Culture* briefly before returning to it later in more detail; its opening sets the scene uncompromisingly:

The current consideration of risk has three peculiarities. The first is that disagreement about the problem is deep and widespread in the Western world. The second is that different people worry about different risks – war, pollution, employment, inflation. The third is that knowledge and action are out of sync: whatever programs are enacted to reduce risks, they conspicuously fail to follow the principle of doing the most to prevent the worst damage. In sum, substantial disagreement remains over what is risky, how risky it is, and what to do about it.

(RC: 1)

This pithy opening might well suggest to readers that the authors *are* about to tell them how to assess risks and how to bypass the peculiar circumstances of 'current consideration' which lead to such pervasive disagreement. If programmes 'fail to follow the principle of doing the most to prevent the worst damage', then there must be objective criteria against which this is demonstrable. But this is not, for the most part, what the book is about. Instead it is about the social genesis of the three peculiarities: in short, why people do not agree what is risky, or how risky it is, or what to do about it. These disagreements are set in a theoretical framework about the social control of cognition in order to argue that disagreement is inevitable when proponents of irreconcilable views are also advocates (wittingly or not) of competing forms of social life. But additionally, and in the style of *Natural Symbols*, the polemic of *Risk and Culture* has a particular adversary in its sights: the 'alarmist' splinter groups of the ecological movement in the United States are to *Risk and Culture* what the anti-ritualists were to *Natural Symbols* – the misguided results of failure to appreciate the determining effects of social context on their thinking. The controversial thesis proposed is that their constitution as 'small groups', characterized by strong group boundaries and weak internal grid (called sects here), impairs their ability to recognize risks in particularly disabling ways. The views of some elements of the ecological movement thus stand indicted by the way in which they organize protest. Before addressing the criticisms that have been voiced of this conclusion, we need to spell out the steps of the argument leading to it, and this is done most easily by relating it to Mary Douglas's earlier writings.

'ENVIRONMENTS AT RISK'

By now the reader will be familiar with the way Mary Douglas colonizes a new area of interest. At least a double assimilation is involved: the assimilation of an unfamiliar to a familiar field, allowing previous examples and issues to be rehearsed and reworked, and the assimilation of complexity within that field to variants identified elsewhere by reference either to grid and group coordinates or to exemplary social forms. The latter assimilation is particularly powerful because it enables her to reason from very broad analogy: for instance inferring the characteristics of a hierarchical (or strong grid and group) social form in contemporary American society from the same form described, for instance, in pre-colonial Africa. Her study of risk begins, quite explicitly, with moves of this type, prefaced by a consideration of 'cultural motifs' (see Chapter 8).

The most obvious resemblance between risk analysis and her previous work is lexical: pollution is the common term to her analysis of matter out of place in *Purity and Danger* and of hazardous waste in the environment. Furthermore, while risk has a technical sense that is probabilistic, involving 'chance', in ordinary parlance it tends to become synonymous with 'danger'. Once, 'In the preindustrial West, Christianity used the word *sin*…A major sin would be expected to unleash dangers on the community at large, or to afflict the sinner's nearest and dearest' (1990a/RAB: 25). But people cannot be held to account in contemporary societies by a doctrine of sin on which they cannot agree. 'Risk', in the negative sense of 'danger', retains the aura of science and potential calculability appropriate to modern discourse while functioning forensically as a blame-pinning mechanism:

> Being 'at risk' in modern parlance is not the equivalent but the reciprocal of being 'in sin' or 'under taboo'. To be 'at risk' is equivalent to being sinned against, being vulnerable to the events caused by others, whereas being 'in sin' means being the cause of harm…the risk rhetoric upholds the individual, vulnerable to the misbehaviour of the community…America has gone further down the path of cultural individualism, and so can make more use of the forensic potential of risk.
>
> (RAB: 28, 29)

Through this play of synonymy and antithesis, Douglas creates a new context, here called modernity, industrialism or cultural individualism, in which eternal verities, such as calling others to account for misfortune, can be seen to hold true in particular form. Her analysis of the situation depends on theoretical preferences and aversions we have noted previously: antipathy to materialist, idealist and individualist approaches – in each case widely construed – sympathy for holistic and sociological approaches – also widely construed; preference for policy approaches that favour communitarian values, and for the types of clearly demarcated organization celebrated in the formalities, or ritual, of differentiated social intercourse.

Most of the elements of this colonization, although not all of its implications, were in place by 1970 when Mary Douglas delivered a lecture at the Institute of Contemporary Arts in London, under the title 'Environments at risk', comparing ideas of threat in 'tribal' and 'modern' societies (1970e/IM). If both types of society, as she argued there, worried about threats to their environments caused by 'human folly, hate and greed' (IM: 230), was there any difference between tribalists and the ecology movement? She suggested there was and went back to the Kantian theme of self-knowledge, elaborated in *Purity and Danger*, and to a Lele parallel, in order to explicate it.

When she first began fieldwork Mary Douglas was congratulated on her good fortune in arriving during the short dry season. Chapter 3 has already explained why, but short repetition will serve to illustrate Douglas's knack for making connections. The reader may recall that by the standards of both Europeans, who disliked the humidity of wet season, and the neighbouring Bushong, who worked steadily all the year round, the dry season was cool. But for the Lele, who crammed most of their year's work into that period, the same season was hot. Climatically, there was little to choose between them in terms of temperature (one was hot and dry; the other hot and humid). If the Lele could have reorganized their work patterns to make their dry season less hectic, then they might have had different ideas about the relation between seasonality and climate. But to do that they would have needed a different kind of society. Doom ecologists also propose a value-laden account of time: specifically they tell us that time is running out.

> Among verbal weapons of control, time is one of the four final arbiters. Time, money, God, and nature, usually in that order, are universal trump cards plunked down to win an argument.
>
> (IM: 236)

Lele additionally believe that burning the bush on their farms causes rain to fall, and dilatory farmers try to persuade their more efficient neighbours to delay starting their fires, and precipitating the rains, until they can catch up. Lele beliefs and practices thus conspire to make the dry season both hot and stressful. Generalizing, *verbal* weapons of control are also *social* weapons of control. 'For no one can wield the doom points credibly in an argument who is not backed by the majority view of how the society should be run' (IM: 238).

In 'tribal' environments the breach of shared norms can lead to affliction for oneself or for closely related others: the adulterous Lele woman's conduct may menace her unborn baby, the stench from one fratricide among a group of Cheyenne hunters can warn off the game causing all the hunters to return home empty-handed. The same reckoning of accountability and blame applies to us, the 'moderns'. Because our scientists disagree, we have to decide whom we listen to. Our accusations that big businesses pollute lakes and rivers or poison children's food are directly analogous to accusations against wealthy old Lele polygamists, or against New Guinea big-men. The accusation that 'we', the rich nations, are menaced by the population growth of 'them', the poor nations, is analogous to blaming the poor for creating pressure on resources in Victorian society.

> It should be clear by now that credibility for any view of how the environment will react is secured by the moral commitment of a community to their particular set of institutions. Nothing will overthrow their beliefs if the institutions which the beliefs support command their loyalty. Nothing is easier than to change the beliefs (overnight!) if the institutions have lost support.
>
> (IM: 241)

This passage intercepts a conventional functionalist argument – about the mutually sustaining relation between ideas and institutions – at an unusual moment: functionalists in British anthropology tended to argue that beliefs had the effect of sustaining social institutions; Douglas stresses the other half of the causal loop, claiming that it is the ability of social institutions to command assent which underwrites the plausibility of beliefs that serve, among other things, to support those institutions. On this view, people's most fundamental beliefs concern the social institutions under which they consent to live, and their 'deepest emotional investment of all is in the assumption that there is a rule-obeying universe' (IM: 243).

> While a limited social reality and a local physical environment are meshed together in a single experience, there is perfect credibility for both. But if the society falls apart, and separate voices claim to know about different environmental constraints, then do credibility problems arise.
>
> (IM: 241)

Modernity is conflated here with differentiation (on the lines of the Durkheimian analysis proposed in *Purity and Danger* but later abandoned); but differentiation is represented as akin to society falling apart because a plurality of voices threatens community and the stability of belief. Having introduced so stark an antithesis between community and modernity, the argument cannot really develop, and the lecture turns to reiteration of the view that shared ideas uphold morality and promote the idea of an autonomous, rule-governed cosmos. So what can we do about our environmental worries? Three positive steps are proposed. First, our ability to reflect on our own behaviour may just rescue us (IM: 231). But second, and related to this, in reflecting upon our current anxieties we must recognize that without moral consensus we shall be unable to agree; and in order to achieve moral consensus we must scrutinize the value of our social forms (IM: 231, 246–47).

> In a sense the obvious risk to the environment is a distraction. The ecologists are indeed looking into an abyss. But on the other side another abyss yawns as frighteningly. This is the terror of intellectual chaos and blind panic. Pollution is the black side of Plato's good lie on which society must rest: it is the other half of the necessary confidence trick…We *must* talk threateningly about time, money, God and nature if we hope to get anything done. We must believe in the limitations and the boundaries of nature which our community projects.
>
> (IM: 245–246)

Third, looking to mainstream scientists for assistance may not help; they have their own professional biases, which partly result from the emotional commitment they have invested in system building. Solutions to grave problems are more likely to come from the margins of the science profession or from the areas where two or three specialisms meet. 'This', she remarks, 'is comforting' (IM: 246).

Germs of Douglas's later work are present in this piece composed in 1970; indeed, it is remarkable quite how much of her mature writing is foreshadowed very specifically in writings of that creative period. But, however stimulating the analogy between tribal and modern views of pollution, the conclusions she draws from the exercise are discrepant. The article argues that we should choose a form of society sufficiently structured to allow us to live with the dangers that face us without being terrified by them. But why are we more likely to achieve consensus about the social form we wish to live under than about assessments of ecological threat? Modern European history is a catalogue of disagreements and struggles over our preferred social forms. Second, the conditions which permit us to have 'self-knowledge' about the effects of our social forms seem to derive from the relatively less structured society the author would have us forego. To compound the problems, mainstream scientists are blinkered because they are fixed within the values of their scientific communities, and the author seems to take comfort from the fact that rogue scientists and disrespecters of disciplinary boundaries are less fettered. In order to reconcile her positions (at least in argument), it would seem that she needed to propose two accounts of knowledge: one for the mass (stressing the importance of community) and another for the intellectual elite (arguing that their creativity derived from lack of structure relative to everyday life and their willingness to ignore the conventionalized borders between disciplinary interests). But this type of distinction is not one she explores.

THE ACCEPTABILITY OF RISKS

Ecological discussion in the early 1970s largely revolved around the wisdom or folly of uncontrolled growth: both industrial growth and population growth. By the time of Douglas's later work, emphasis had shifted within the same agenda to the global threat posed by pollution. But how much had Douglas's analysis changed between the lecture given at the ICA in 1970 and *Risk Acceptability According to the Social Sciences* published fifteen years later? Certainly, the range of her reading in the field of risk analysis was vastly greater, but her theoretical framework had been refined rather than drastically modified. The questions pertinent to her writings on risk are almost identical to those she had already posed on consumption. How autonomous is the individual? What might be meant by rational choice? How does a society meet the challenge of the provision of public goods? And, most particularly, how can we think about social influences on risk perception? *Risk Analysis* was intended to review the existing literature on the state of this art, but Douglas begins instead by stating she found 'that art is in no state at all' (RA: 1). This opening salvo is also a defence of the

ideas published three years previously in *Risk and Culture* by means of a retalia-
tory strike on a social science literature which she considers largely vitiated by its
individualistic and psychologistic biases.

Risk and Culture had been, she tells us, a study in the sociology of perception (a
topic that includes the history, philosophy and sociology of science, as well as the
sociology of everyday life) (RA: 2); its aim was nothing less than a sociological,
cultural and ethical theory of human judgement (RA: 3). The crux of its argument was that particular risks are socially selected for attention. If the risk
professionals do not like the argument, do they have anything better to offer?
The risk analysis profession had hardly existed when Douglas delivered her
paper on 'Environments at risk' (1970e). Its growth had been an element of
'large cultural changes' during the intervening years. The growth of the risk
specialization had been achieved by recruiting scholars from other disciplines,
who brought their existing disciplinary baggage along with them. One result of
their individualistic bias was that risk and justice tended to be discussed in
different languages: the first in the mathematical language of free choice, the
second in English rhetoric. This distinction produced a hiatus that could be
bridged only by appeal to a sociological approach: a shift in perspective that is
signalled in the titles of Douglas's two books by the terms 'selection' and 'acceptability'. However, whereas 'Environments at risk' had started from the problem
scientists faced in making their judgements of risk credible to the public, fifteen
years later this problem is reversed:

> This story starts out with a need to understand why experts in industry
> and government cannot convince the public of the *safety* of new tech-
> nology. The generalized tendency of humans turns out to be quite the
> other way, not naturally timorous but rather overintrepid and difficult to
> persuade of the reality of dangers. But if the dangers in question are
> thought to be inflicted by a powerful minority (the industrialists) on a
> helpless majority, the sense of subjective immunity is not evoked. The
> difference is that the attitude to risks inflicted by others is political. The
> public considering new technology may not necessarily be afraid so
> much as angry. Risk perception may not be the issue at all, but indigna-
> tion at bamboozlement and exploitation. If so, we need to understand
> attitudes to blame.
>
> (RA: 33–34, my emphasis)

By arguing that perception and acceptance of risk are indissoluble from the
questions of who is perceived to be responsible for causing hazard to whom,
Douglas is able to argue from the familiar anthropological, and largely
Africanist, analogies of blame pinning and witchcraft accusations. The chapter
entitled 'Natural risks' closely echoes the earlier article on patterns of blame allocation. This permits another shift in argument, also prefigured in the 1970
article:

some would claim that the anthropologist's insights into stable cultures are irrelevant to modern society. After all, we are facing totally unprecedented technological dangers....if the focus is on the physical danger, the insights of anthropology would be irrelevant. However, the focus ought not to be on the danger but on the institutions if we are interested in public perception. The functional approach of anthropology insists that the expectation of dangers tends to be institutionalized so that it stabilizes and generally supports the local regime, whatever it may be.

(RA: 54)

A focus on one type of danger precludes attention to others: within institutions there are regular patterns of blame, and these function as mechanisms for renewing members' allegiance to the group through the threat of disaster. Three common patterns of blame can be distinguished: blaming the victim (for instance, the unmarried mother or sick person), blaming the nearest and dearest (the parents of a handicapped child, the mothers of rebellious children), or blaming an external enemy or agency (ancestors, nature). 'The question is not which dangers are most alarming but which explanations of misfortune are likely to function most effectively in the different kinds of society we might be able to identify' (RA: 59). At this stage of the argument, the problem of risk perception is assimilated to Douglas's overriding concern with institutional blinkers on thought. 'The well-advertised risk generally turns out to be connected with legitimating moral principles' (RA: 60).

In this recension of her theory, she begins by radically simplifying the types of society with which she is concerned to two: the closed, hierarchical, tradition-oriented community in which individuals are taught to subordinate their desires to the collective good, and a society committed to individual competition constrained only by rules of fair play which govern public showdowns. The first type of society is predicted to have a 'morally punitive and conciliatory cosmos' (RA: 62) reacting to human actions. Every cosmological sign will be the symptom of a human failing but, lest the 'load of guilt' prove impossible to bear, there will be rituals of expiation. The man-centred cosmos, on the other hand, will tend to be neutral. When fortunes wax or wane supporters will shift behind rising big men. Thus, '[c]ulture is the publicly shared collection of principles and values used at any one time to justify behavior',[3] without these verbal weapons, '[t]he rational agent of theory is deculturated' (RA: 67). How might this analysis be applied to current controversies?

The industrial use of nuclear power introduces the idea of gravely damaging effects following on very low probability events. Since it seems that human cognition normally works with a focus of medium probabilities, these dangers could be presumed to fall beyond the lay public's cognitive threshold.

(RA: 92)

154

If the 'lay public' is nonetheless alarmed this is because the 'institutional filter through which risks are perceived imposes a consistent distortion upon the probabilities' (RA: 92). At least two assumptions have been introduced to carry the argument further: we have to accept that the likelihood of nuclear accident can be measured objectively (in order to agree such an event is indeed a low probability), and we are also asked to accept that there exists a normal range of probabilities to which human cognition responds. Or at least we have to accept this of the lay public, which potentially courts a third assumption, I noted earlier, of a different set of cognitive cues for elite and mass intellects. Rather than explicate these complications, Douglas reintroduces a third form of voluntary association, distinct from what are now to be called bureaucracy (previously, hierarchy) and market (previously, individual competition):

> The full sense of the term community is a committed group in which individuals derive their life support and which bounds their commitments. The voluntary association seems to be an embryonic, partial or unfulfilled attempt at creating community – it is an association whose members are often able to boast more of having kept together than of having achieved anything in particular over the years.
>
> (RA: 95)

This less than even-handed introduction of a third organizational matrix signals the argument to come. De Tocqueville is credited with noting the relation between the ideal of equality and the widespread formation of voluntary associations in America. Douglas sees equality as an ideology that comes in to fill a power vacuum. Her images of disorder, bordering on anarchy, are strongly reminiscent of the terror-filled abyss into which she saw Western societies peer fifteen years earlier. 'Equality means all being jumbled together in the same constantly fluctuating crowd, without recognition, honor, or social standing, eyes coveting small prizes and resenting small inequalities' (RA: 96).

Rather than following de Tocqueville to see any benefit in the positive valuation of equality, Douglas's analysis now moves to consider the problems of provision of public goods under different types of social organization. Here she amends Mancur Olson's analysis, introduced in the last chapter, in a way I consider more closely in Chapter 10. Public goods can, analogously with her amended Durkheimian view of organized religion, be produced only within certain types of social organization. Their provision is possible under the types of regime that Douglas calls markets and hierarchy because individuals anticipate they will benefit from them. But voluntary associations are singled out as suffering particularly from 'a free-rider problem' – non-contributors cannot be prevented from benefiting from collectively produced goods. Reacting to this challenge, members of voluntary groups will attempt to draw the boundary around insiders and outsiders more clearly, and to make insiders' participation in the provision of collective goods statutory. In order to do this, voluntary organizations enlist a particular 'cosmic plot' behind a 'strategy of impeach-ment'. By analogy with the small, unstable village communities of central Africa, in which quarrels led to accusations of witchcraft in the community's midst, faction leaders in voluntary associations will be denounced for complicity in the ways of the outside world and become the scapegoats of collective failure. The 'doom-laden cosmos' is seen as part of the functioning of this particular organi-zational type, common to religious sects, communes, political lobbies, new political movements and public interest groups. Members of such organizations are likely to stress low probability, high risk outcomes that would go unremarked in forms of institution less hostile to the outside world or more hierarchically organized internally.

RISK AND CULTURE: THE ARGUMENT

This conclusion – that risk *perception* is tied to institutional form generally, and that predictions of doom are especially associated with the institutional form of the small voluntary group – can now be seen as Douglas's major contribution to the book she co-authored with Aaron Wildavsky and consistent with ideas she had been considering since the early 1970s.

Risk and Culture is specifically addressed to the contemporary American scene, and its argument is signposted in pithy chapter headings: for instance that of the Introduction – 'Can we know the risks we face?' This is the key question, and reviewers have not been entirely clear what answer the authors give to it. The authors' tone suggests they think that the American lay public is somehow unre-alistic about the risks it confronts. 'What are Americans afraid of? Nothing much, really, except the food they eat, the water they drink, the air they breathe, the land they live on, and the energy they use' (RC: 10). While life expectancy has been increasing, the general public – according to surveys – imagines life is riskier now than it was twenty years ago (RC: 2). But perhaps the public is justi-fied: while scientific advance does increase our understanding, it also shows us how much we do not know. To know all the risks that face us we would need to be omniscient (RC: 3). But rather than pursuing the question of whether we *can* know the risks we face, the book changes tack to note that people differ both in the risks they select to worry about, and in how much those risks worry them; their worry is seldom proportionate to the likelihood of a particular misfortune actually befalling them. This is the argument Douglas had worked out previously. But it is not clear whether that argument is capable of answering the question they started with: 'Can we know the risks we face?' Moreover, in arguing that some people worry disproportionately about some risks rather than others, the authors seem to concede that there is an objective measure of the risks we face.

In short, reviewers have been confronted with a problem of assessing just how relativistic the authors want to be about risk. And if relativistic, then relative to what? If we can never know risks objectively, but we nonetheless rank them and act upon our worries, then we might argue a strong case for the social construction of risk. But we couldn't argue that some people worried disproportionately, only that they worried differently, and that we would be inclined to side with fellow worriers whose social experience was most like our own. Perceptions of risk, and judgements of the acceptability of particular risks, would have to be seen as social constructs. But the authors do not allow that their argument is entirely relativist because they insist that risks are real: 'Plenty of real dangers are always present' (RC: 7). By some special pleading we might try to defend the view that risks are real but perceptions of relative riskiness are social constructs (though this would be difficult to maintain with any degree of theoretical parsimony – and might have to admit that social context affected expert scientific opinion differently from lay opinion), but this is not our authors' argument either because they both stress that life expectancy has genuinely increased in Western societies – and is susceptible to statistical measurement – and accept that the general public's ranking of specific dangers is at variance with the real likelihood of them being endangered. The authority of risk experts is impugned in terms of a sociological argument while it is implicitly accepted as the standard from which the non-objectivity of lay appreciation of risk is measured. Understandably, this has confused readers.

Perhaps the authors could have proposed a convincing case that allowed us to decide which experts we should believe, why we should believe them, and under what circumstances their opinions can be relied upon. But rather than doing this, they extend their sociological thesis to the scientific community in its entirety. Logically, this allows them to argue that the perception, ranking and selection of risks is always biased by sociological factors, so everyone suffers from it, scientists and lay people alike. But if they additionally want to argue that some institutional settings are relatively more biased than others, we either need to be convinced that there is a measuring rod of real risk or else we require that the special biases of organizational forms are revealed as intrinsic to those modes of organization. Despite appearing to favour departure from objectivity as a criterion of bias at some points, in fact the book more consistently develops the second argument.

Few commentators on *Risk and Culture* sought to dismiss Douglas and Wildavsky's sociological argument out of hand – although a number of them criticized the way it was applied – but they queried whether a sociological account of risk tells the whole story – both on the grounds that other factors ought to be allowed some part (and indeed are allowed to carry some of the burden of the argument), and on the grounds that if the authors really wanted to propose a single factor relativism, then their own argument would be caught recursively in it, strictly precluding them from drawing the conclusions they do. Douglas and Wildavsky basically conclude by asking us to trust the centre. But this is the obverse of Douglas's conclusion in 1970, that amateur scientists and the crossers of disciplinary boundaries (in short, the 'fringes') were more likely to produce solutions to our 'grave problems' (IM: 246). I shall return to these objections in conclusion after picking up the train of argument of *Risk and Culture* that I left pondering the question of how people select the dangers to which they attend.

Fear, our authors argue, is increasing; there is a loss of confidence in the environment. A cultural theory of perception that related some natural dangers to moral defects (RC: 7) would, on the argument also enunciated in 'Environments at risk', itself be part of the process of modernization; that process includes 'a burdensome responsibility either to refrain from politicizing nature or, if that is impossible, to recognize what is being said' (RC: 31). And what is being said? The risks that threaten Americans are of catastrophic proportions: they are involuntary, irreversible and hidden; they result from the use of technology by the major institutions of the society: the government and big business. In this, they are no different from some kinds of pollution beliefs. What sort of organizations are prone to such beliefs, and why should they have arisen when they did?

The argument takes the general form I explicated from Douglas's later book, 'The notion of risk is an extraordinarily constructed idea, essentially decontextualized and desocialized' (RC: 73). Or, in that recurrent Douglas image, 'Every form of social life, if it endures at all, digs its own channels of memory and its own shapes of amnesic spaces, just as important as memory, for allowing that social type to persist' (RC: 87). 'Cultural analysis does not ask about people's private beliefs. It asks what theories about the world emerge as guiding principles in a particular form of society' (RC: 89). For the purposes of the analysis the same three forms of society that we met in *Risk Acceptability* are delineated; two derive from the habitual contrast in Western thought between bureaucracy and market (RC: 90). In this instance, they are to be called hierarchy and individualism. Their virtues and drawbacks are distinctive: 'Individualism strongly believes in the maintenance of the whole exchange system as a prior value: any one individual who threatens it should be penalized' (RC: 101). Moreover, individualism is not too attentive to the casualties of the competition it organizes: 'This society is too hasty to be trusted alone with dangerous technology' (RC: 101). Hierarchy also believes in sacrificing the few to the good of the many. 'It is smug about its rigid procedures. It is too slow, too blind to new information. It will not believe in new dangers and will often be taken by surprise. It will accept large risks if they appear on a horizon beyond its institutional threshold of concern' (RC: 101). Thus the chapter title, 'The center is complacent'. This centrist alliance, as I remarked earlier, seems to have been a compromise between Douglas and Wildavsky's individual preferences.

On the grounds that the faults of these two are well known, the authors move, in the following chapter, to an analysis of the form of organization that they call 'sect', under the contrasting title 'The border is alarmed'. Sectarianism is contrasted to collectivism and individualism,[4] and initial illustrations of it are not taken from the environmental movement but from different Anabaptist groupings in America. Old Order Amish reject modern technology in the interest of maintaining separation and equality; but they must face up to the fact that this option restricts their potential resource base and necessitates restriction of farm size in order to maintain land availability. The cost of their preference for equality is paid in fissioning, often following internal allegations of worldliness. In this sectarian behaviour, they are analogous to the villages without entrenched hierarchies of central Africa, which regularly split acrimoniously following witchcraft or sorcery accusations. The Hutterites contrast point by point with the Amish; rather confusingly, in terms of the authors' working classification, they constitute a small hierarchy (see note 4). Indeed, every aspect of their organization is hierarchical: roles are multiple and clearly defined; each generation raises enough capital to allow the group to split, and the most up-to-date technologies are used to achieve this. On the point of splitting, the community is organized into two groups and both pack as if to leave for the new site; drawing straws decides which one will actually leave. Amish social forms cannot control internal jealousy as the more regulated Hutterite social institutions can. The Hutterites, with no private property, are a small hierarchy; the Amish are closer to a truly voluntary organization (or egalitarian enclave). And it is the latter who are in danger of dying out.

Very broad conclusions are drawn from this allegory of contrasting styles of organization, most notably the difficulty of providing public goods in organizations with a high degree of voluntariness. Sectarianism is a form of organization of the border rather than the centre. 'It would never be responsible or stable enough to maintain a center' (RC: 120). Sectarian politics, allied to denunciation of the centre, is now presented as a response to the voluntariness of association rather than its cause. The implication is that once people join single-issue organizations, presumably in order to make a point about these issues, they are also enmeshed in institutional settings which determine their subsequent political behaviour. The border needs to fear irreversible changes, caused by external threat, in order to maintain such cohesion as it possesses, and it is appropriate that nature (if not also time, money or God of Douglas's memorable 'trump cards') should be the agent of a threat to all of mankind.

The application of this model to the details of the American situation occupies only the chapters entitled 'The border fears for nature' and 'America is a border country'. The first of the two chapters is based upon research carried out by assistants under the supervision of the authors; judging by its references, the second chapter was initially drafted by Wildavsky.

'The border fears for nature' starts from premises that appear tautologous until their terms are specified:

> We expect that those [groups that exist to mobilize public concern] which show up as most hierarchical in their relation with each other and the outside world will also be making the more typically hierarchical selection of dangers. Those organized on voluntaristic,

egalitarian principles will make the sectarian selection of risks and justify their view of danger with a recognizably sectarian worldview.

(RC: 126)

This contrast is played out first between the Sierra Club, a 'hierarchical' conservationist organization, and Friends of the Earth, founded by secession from the Sierra Club to pursue a more activist and, it is claimed, alarmist approach. A number of problems attend the analysis at this point. The secession of Friends of the Earth from the Sierra Club, and the more aggressive stance its founder took on issues before he failed to be re-elected to the board of the Sierra Club, is said to evince a sectarian worldview. But this would really be contrary to the theory of correspondence proposed, since the sectarian worldview ought to be thinkable only within a sectarian organization rather than being the catalyst which brought it into existence. To argue further that Friends of the Earth is anti-bureaucratic, thus sectarian, but simultaneously closely controlled by an activist elite, seems to beg questions about the criteria of political control and administration that are supposed to differentiate sect from hierarchy. Despite documenting the very different degrees of involvement of members, officials, activists and supporters contacted by mailshots, the analysis also persists in treating the two environmental organizations as if these substantive movements could be conflated with their ideal types.

A second similar contrast is drawn between local people grouped to oppose the building of nuclear reactors and direct action alliances with their more egalitarian procedures.

Clearly, the activist groups conform more closely to the organizational practice of sects. Their strong barriers against the outside world are formed on the judgement that it is a waste of time to use legal and political processes to negotiate with central institutions or to participate in Nuclear Regulatory Committee hearings.

(RC: 147)

Umbrella organizations of environmental groupings, for instance the Clamshell Alliance of New England with ninety member organizations, represent sectarian and border characteristics in an extreme form. Such groups tend to conflate all environmental problems into a single stand against global evil, as the authors would expect of organizations that have strong boundaries but weak internal organization.

The following chapter asks why sectarian forces have grown so much stronger since the mid-1960s. Douglas and Wildavsky's answer attempts to argue both that America is historically strongly sectarian, and thus has always been a border country, and also that there are reasons why this sectarianism should have grown even stronger. Unhappily, most of the arguments proposed do not fall within the general theory outlined earlier in the book. For instance, because the American states predated the nation, and it was contentious 'whether there would be a center', the chapter argues that the USA is sectarian on account of its history in the same sense that the Amish and the Clamshell Alliance are sectarian. The term is applied immediately to the small cabals who run electoral processes in the major political parties, and then to the Democratic Party 'requiring the most precise percentages of blacks, Hispanics, youth, women, and other ethnic and biological groups to receive representation in proportion to their numbers' (which could as well be argued an index of high grid) (RC: 156). Leaving aside the proposition that America has been sectarian historically, why has there been a recent growth of sectarianism?

America enjoyed a great increase in wealth in the immediate post-war period. A large proportion of its population entered higher education (including a 'significant racial minority' (RC: 159)). Since the supply of graduates outstripped the need for them in the industrial sector, they went into the service sector. 'The economic boom and the educational boom together produced a cohort of articulate, critical people with no commitment to commerce and industry' (RC: 159). On no particular evidence, it is argued that hierarchy is less necessary to the production of ideas than it is to the production of goods, thus 'the boundary between service and production becomes one between border and center' (RC: 160).[5] A further loss of respect for the centre ensued because of Vietnam and Watergate; meanwhile the civil rights movement provided an exemplar for the type of organization which fuelled the environmental movement.

> Black people were always a bone lodged in the throat of American individualism. They couldn't be swallowed whole and the American value system could not breathe freely with them stuck in a peculiar place.
>
> (RC: 163)

This unattractive passage is developed into the thesis that everything about the civil rights movement was thereby ennobled, but in the rejection of white leadership by black movements:

> a cadre of white activists, accustomed to leadership and trained to represent deprived groups, was left out of work and free to lead the fight against the risks perpetrated by giant corporations and big government on the public at large.
>
> (RC: 164)

Eventually, the public interest groups organized by these militants were able to raise funds by mail order membership and through gaining tax-deductible status for their members' contributions, as well as public subventions to part finance law centres and subsidize lobbying. The border thus gets the centre to pay for its activities and 'the political views of the border are predictably on the left' (RC: 169).

161

These headless groups can be politically potent. They are numerous, small, and unencumbered. They travel light. They are difficult to defeat because there are so many of them, and they do not stay in one place (or one shape, for that matter) for too long. Beaten down here, they rise elsewhere.

(RC: 172)

Yet it is proposed that people support these groups through mailshots simply on the basis of their offering a sectarian analysis of events (an explanation which should be disallowed by the very cultural theory proposed). From being incapable of organizing a decent-sized religious organization, sectarians emerge from Wildavsky's chapter capable of menacing the entire fabric of American society:

The biggest and most immediate risk [of sectarian dominance] would be to the civic rights of the individual, not merely the risk of being born a second-class citizen in a hierarchy or of becoming one of the human derelicts which litter the market place but the risk of being classified as evil, a malefactor outside the protection of the law.

(RC: 182)

The need to engage closely with this argument is obviated by none of it deriving from the cultural theory it is supposed to apply. Instead, the analysis of American society is based on a series of factors quite exogenous to cultural theory. Why Mary Douglas allowed her name to appear as co-author of a chapter expressing views attached so tendentiously to her cultural theory is, I suppose, only explicable in context of the terms of her collaborative relationship with Wildavsky. But, on the grounds that both these views and the arguments used to support them are quite unlike any she has published under her sole authorship, I pass the buck on treating them as part of her intellectual biography.

CRITICAL REACTIONS

Risk and Culture was widely and critically reviewed in several disciplines, including anthropology, politics, law, the sciences and religion. If few reviewers endorsed its argument entirely, none entirely dismissed it. Wishing to preserve the book's sociological insights, critical reaction carefully split up the argument along fault lines that were interpreted differently. Conceding the overall case that social and cultural dimensions had been excluded from risk analysis, several reviewers questioned whether simplification of social forms to three types could in principle cope with the complexity of US society successfully or whether, in practice, the model had been applied even-handedly. Clearly, most reviewers were more sympathetic to environmental concerns than they thought the authors to have been, and suspected that characterizing all environmental protest as sectarian skewed treatment of dangers that they also felt to be real and urgent. How to assess or deal with change in the nature of dangers facing industrial societies seemed a key issue, so I shall deal with this before broaching other criticisms in order of their ethnographic specificity.

To understand her latest intellectual foray, several reviewers were prompted to review Douglas's earlier work, some of them at length (Boon RC/Rar; Kaprow RC/AA), but it was a reviewer for the *Journal for the Scientific Study of Religion*, perhaps predictably, who went straight to the heart of the parallel between the analyses of religion and science she proposed. Thomas Robbins noted that:

> The authors contend that today's vehement controversies over environ-mental and ecological pollution constitute the basic form of church–sect conflict in modern America.
>
> In the modern world science has replaced God as the source of explanations and threats. Science and technology are easily perceived as demonic and nature becomes a symbol of special purity to be vindi-cated against pollution, as God has continually been vindicated by sectarians against corruption and worldliness.
>
> (RC/JSSR: 188)

The productivity of a church–sect division in Douglas's thought is readily attested (as I have shown in relation both to *Purity and Danger* and *Natural Symbols* in Chapters 4 and 5), but the effect of applying the schema by analogy to envi-ronmental lobbies in a scientific culture is problematic; the relation between science and religion is a hoary problem but, unhappily, one we cannot entirely pass over for that. At its simplest, most reviewers argued that environmental risks, however much their exact riskiness can be disputed, are real. In the course of an otherwise highly sympathetic review, the philosopher Ian Hacking notes an 'alarmingly unrealistic tone…*Risk and Culture* sometimes hovers near the anthro-pological fallacy of thinking that everything we perceive is a cultural artifact. Every once in a while the reader has to cry out that some pollution is real' (RC/NYRB: 32; see also Daniels RC/AAPSS: 237, and Kaprow RC/AA for two of many expressions of similar concern). To an atheist, it might seem evident that the difference between pollution beliefs in religious and scientific cultures is that one is true and the other is not. A theist might be less sure of the distinction, and a complete relativist might eschew it altogether. Any anthropolo-gist wishing to understand a way of life could suspend judgement in order to report on what people apparently believe. But it is difficult to see how a contribu-tion to risk analysis in our own societies can be made while bucking the question of the reality of the risks we face. Presumably, if the writers do avoid asbestos dust but are not worried about mixing milk and vegetables in their diet (as are Hima pastoralists who furnish one of the examples taken up by Hacking, see also RC/ABFRJ), the reader is entitled to ask whether their relativism is cosmetic more than practical. But, as I have already argued, Douglas and Wildavsky cannot be arguing the 'suspension of disbelief' line familiar from interpretative ethnographies, because they could not then argue that some groups in American society are more unduly alarmed than others. For a contemporary readership, this is not quite the same kind of judgement as saying that some groups are more God-fearing than others – though it looks so similar. In which case, the analogy between environmental groups and religious sects can only be partial – both in the sense that these groupings differ in themselves just as much as they are similar, and in the observation that a single-issue environmental group is not as a rule the encompassing setting of a person's life that membership of a sect may be. Sects, after all, are examples of total institutions (as are central African villages).

Even accepting Douglas and Wildavsky's general case that market and hierarchy are social forms typical of the 'centre', and sect-like social forms are typical of the 'border', if the low probability events that contemporary society is capable of manufacturing for itself are real, then it may be beneficial to have groups of people particularly sensitive to their danger and sufficiently active to keep these dangers in general view; the proliferation of such groups to match the proliferation of dangers may be a plus (Hacking RC/NYRB: 41; Boon RC/Rar: 112–13). Again, it seems that Douglas and Wildavsky's preference for the centre betrays some, even implicit, judgement of their own about the reality of environmental risks.

However, there are several good reasons to distrust the equation of the opposition – centre versus border – with that of hierarchy plus market versus sect. First, Douglas and Wildavsky refine their own argument – both by seeing America as a 'border country' and by grading sects in terms of degree of hierarchy – but they do not respect their own strictures in reaching their centrist conclusion. As several reviewers comment, there are just as good grounds to remark sect-like organizations close to the heart of power, and just as arguably exaggerated fears (for instance, of Soviet nuclear threat) arose within the hierarchy.

Beyond the issue of the centre-versus-border mapping of social groupings lies the question of the adequacy of the three social types to map American variety (Agar RC/AQ), or their mutual exclusivity. James Boon's doubts about the mutual exclusivity of the three social forms is another in a long line of criticisms of the tendency to see people's social commitments as being confined to a single type of organization. But, as he notes, it is difficult to equate broad penumbral support for environmental movements such as Friends of the Earth – by people who may only respond to mailshots – with commitment to living according to the communal regulations of sects like the Hutterites or Amish. Supporters of environmental movements might, on other counts, be model hierarchs or market competitors. Douglas and Wildavsky's argument concludes by likening single-issue environmental groups to contenders in a struggle to displace the present holders of power from the centre – an eventuality they view with foreboding of a new puritanism. But this not only treats everything not explicitly supportive of the centre as dissent, but goes on to characterize all dissent as sect, and finally endows the residual category created in this fashion with a unified purpose.[6] Why, Boon asks in the spirit of Douglas and Wildavsky's argument, are the authors so alarmed (RC/Rar: 111–16)?

Apart from detecting a note of right-wing Republican partisanship in the book (fair comment, so far as I can tell, and presumably attributable to Wildavsky's politics), at least two reviewers questioned whether the USA was really exceptional. Miriam Kaprow argued that the environmental movement was in fact stronger in Western Europe than in the USA, while Gerald Steinberg notes that if the voluntarism of association in America, which so impressed de Tocqueville by contrast with Europe, still distinguishes the two continents, then Europe should have no environmental movements at all (Kaprow RC/AA; Steinberg RC/JAS).

Law practitioners had particular problems with the practical consequences of the thesis of *Risk and Culture*. If the motivation of litigants was always 'socio-genetic' then it might be argued that the victims were always in the wrong; but this is to fall into the 'genetic fallacy' of considering that '[t]he validity of a belief can be tested by investigating the characteristics and motives of those who hold it' (RC/ABFRJ: 406). In related vein, the reviewer for the *Ecology Law Quarterly* asked whether the inhabitants of Harrisburg or Three Mile Island had suddenly become border people when they reacted litigiously to the threats to which they had been exposed. More generally, the reviewers thought that the risk-imposers and their strategies for evading accountability (like filing for bankruptcy) had been under-explored in the analysis.

John Adams, a sympathetic commentator who draws heavily upon the insights of risk perception analysis, nonetheless drew attention to the neglect of individual agency in the account proposed in *Risk and Culture*. Reasoning in the main from his study of transportation regulation, rather than from the risks imposed by big business, he noted that risk-takers acted upon their perceptions of risk as if to maintain an acceptable level of risk: for instance, the safety premium derived from seat-belt legislation might be converted into higher speed. Furthermore, the voluntariness of risk, which is mentioned by Douglas, might be more important than she allowed: Greenpeace protesters might accept great personal risk in their efforts – direct sea-borne actions for instance – to forestall global risks (Adams 1995). Suggestions on these lines should have been conducive to Douglas in the light of her espousal of 'active voice' social theories (Chapter 10).

This list of objections to the theses of *Risk and Culture*, although by no means comprehensive, is substantial.[7] So it may seem perverse to conclude by noting that the reviews are also in large measure supportive, and even where they are critical show the reviewers to have repaid the authors' efforts with attention and reflection. As I noted above, approbation often came in the form of sympathetic reading – distinguishing the intention of the argument from its execution, or trying to discriminate the positions of the co-authors. The general ambition to supply a social dimension to arguments about risk – arguments that had tended previously to veer widely between science and statistics on the one hand and individual psychology on the other – as well as the particular insight that perceptions of risk correlate with the organization and control of social groups, received a general welcome (see Bellaby 1990; this applied equally to Douglas's subsequent book, some technical limitations aside, Glasner RA/SR; Macgill RA/EPA; Seabright RA/TLS). The substantive application to the American case, as well as the particular lesson the authors draw for that country, were as convincingly challenged.

Risk and Culture is the monograph which clearly announces Douglas's move from grid and group theory to 'cultural theory' – although the move is neither permanent nor unequivocal. In many ways the two methods are almost identical since reasoning from four exemplary types of social form, which is distinctive of 'cultural theory', is also the implicit form that Mary Douglas's argument occasionally takes when explicitly framed by the continuous variation of grid and group, as for instance in *Natural Symbols*. But 'cultural theory' seems more readily to invite Douglas to conflate the analytic and synthetic terms of her reasoning, so that one instance of something called hierarchy is immediately applied to another instance called the same thing but from a different time or place. This form of reasoning by analogy directly contravenes strictures Douglas resolved to impose on her own practice in *Natural Symbols* when she decided to respect the *ceteris paribus* rule and compare the bias of examples that were related culturally, or historically, or both. Narrowing the schema to three types (hierarchy, individualism and sect – the fourth term 'mass alienation' is oddly absent from this analysis) may enhance its comprehensibility and ease of application to the complexities of contemporary life, but this is achieved at the cost of drastically simplifying the ways in which sociality can be conceived. Thanks to the wish to derive complex varieties of risk perception from social context, the account of risks is correspondingly impoverished. Argument by stereotyping is not in itself altogether bad, and recognizing three or four social types is clearly an improvement over schemes with only two types. But in Weberian sociology, the classic site for ideal types constructed either logically or historically, the method was justified by virtue of illuminating connections and drawing the analyst's attention to how far substantive social processes *departed* from their ideal typifications. Douglas and Wildavsky tend to do the opposite; they appeal to substantive cases to exemplify (even prove) the connections established in their logical types. Such a procedure makes it easy for prejudices about ideal types to be transferred unalloyed to substantive cases.

Risk and Culture makes a compelling theoretical case for the sociological contextualization of risk perception, even if its methodology is debatable. However, if one of the authors' ambitions was for their argument to be noticed (and in the light of the muted reception of *World of Goods* this might seem reasonable) then the result of their strategy – measured in column inches of review and citation – would have to be judged a triumph.

Notes

1 I met Wildavsky only once. Knowing I was writing this account, he paid Mary Douglas a generous tribute that I recently discovered he had also committed to an unpublished paper: 'Until coming across cultural analysis, I had no independent stance for viewing the world…I had values [but] I lacked…a theory of my own I could use to come to my own conclusions about anything that seemed important' (1987 'From economy to political culture. Or why I like cultural analysis', as quoted by Ellis and Thompson 1997: xiv). Wildavsky credited Mary Douglas with allowing him to become a more creative scholar. For more on cultural theory, see his last collection of essays, Wildavsky 1997.

2 Douglas's account of Wildavsky's political preferences is echoed by Ellis and Thompson, 'the pathologies and contradictions of egalitarianism…interested (even obsessed) Aaron…[who] never hid his personal preference for competitive individualism, nor his dislike of radical egalitarianism (except in small doses)' (Ellis and Thompson 1997: xvii).

3 The different senses of culture in Mary Douglas's use are examined in Chapter 10.

4 Collectivism seems to have replaced hierarchy, which in turn was a synonym for bureaucracy. This latest terminological shift is triggered by the recognition that some sects are hierarchical (a view ignored in *Risk Acceptability* where sects are all treated as egalitarian). The frequent changes in terminology for the four types of social environment reflect the degree of work the terms are being asked to do. Douglas later noted that the use of sect, with pejorative overtones, was unfortunate and that enclave was a better term to describe a group encapsulated within a wider society. This might suggest a distinction between hierarchical and egalitarian enclaves. However, Douglas wishes to specialize the term enclave for egalitarian groups, which additionally may be sectarian if their self-definition is largely by rejection of the social environment in which they are enclaved. What would otherwise be hierarchical enclaves are simply to be called 'hierarchical groups' (Douglas 1996b: xix–xxi).

5 The reader may recall that, in *Natural Symbols*, Douglas had argued the contrary: that hierarchy was a conducive setting for finely differentiated ideas.

6 The reader may recall similar criticisms of Douglas's tendency to lump together all shades of anti-ritualism in *Natural Symbols*.

7 A reader particularly interested in these might also want to look up John Holdren's review and the ensuing exchange of letters (RC/BAS, Douglas 1983j), and compare the mutual appreciations of Shrader-Frechette (1991) and Douglas (1993m). For further critiques, see Downey (1986), Boholm (1996).

HAZARD

8 RETURNING TO RELIGION – IN THE CONTEMPORARY WEST

RELIGION AND RITUAL AS ANALOGIES

Judged solely by the titles of her published works, Mary Douglas's interest in the anthropology of contemporary religion might seem to have lain dormant during the dozen years between the publication of *Natural Symbols* in 1970 and *Risk and Culture* in 1982.[1] Her writings explicitly devoted to religious topics were few, while her energies were engaged by the analysis of food and consumption theory (Chapter 6), risk and justice (Chapter 7), and the elaboration of grid and group, later cultural, theory (Chapter 10). However, as she, and all commentators on her work, agree this diverse work is synthesized, in the last analysis, by recurrent resort to Durkheimian antecedents.

Putting the point starkly as a peg on which to hang some nuance, if Marxist analyses favour analysis of religion in economic terms, and Weberian writers commonly emphasize religion's political implications, then we could say that Mary Douglas, on the contrary, analyses both economics and politics by analogy with religion. One of the particularities of Durkheimian sociology is usually taken to be a holism which is both ontological and methodological. Societies are assumed to constitute an order of reality different from the otherwise asocial individuals who make them up. This is so because societies furnish individuals with their categories of cognition and evaluation: by virtue of belonging to particular social groupings individual members of society share ideas of how their life-world is organized and how they ought to behave towards one another within that world (whether or not they do so). Pursuing this line of thought, the contrastive relation between society and individual tends to disappear: there is no such creature as the asocial individual; humanity is possible only within society; human variety is social variety. An urgent question logically follows: what form of society best serves our potential humanity? If it is assumed that society provides human beings with the reference points, both cognitive and moral, to find their way around in the world, then you might argue (especially if you have lived through the political turmoil of Durkheim's life) that it is incumbent on us to promote forms of society attuned to our economic and political realities. Durkheim eventually argued that contemporary 'moral individualism' should not be atomistic, as methodological individualism is, but rest instead on a shared attitude of sacralization of individual rights and responsibilities consistent with an increasing division both of labour and of roles within complex societies.

Comparing the political attitudes of writers living in different epochs is contentious; nonetheless it is not unfair to say that Douglas's reading of Durkheim's theory is more socially conservative than its author's. From Durkheim she takes the argument that our ideas and morality are produced collectively, and she shares his antipathy to Anglo-Saxon, nineteenth-century utilitarianism. Seen in this light, our shared ideas are the most social possession we have. In many societies, both historically and comparatively, these shared notions have been sacralized by hedging them around with celebrations and interdictions of a religious character. Religion is, therefore, the most social of all human collective accomplishments. 'Religion', Douglas says approvingly in review of a new translation of Durkheim's *The Elementary Forms of the Religious Life* (1915), 'is the prime example used to illustrate the [Durkheimian] revolution in cognitive science and philosophy' (1996i: 467). Elsewhere she explains:

> Religious disagreement is the richest material for cultural analysis. Debates which originate in quite mundane issues tend to become religious if they go on long enough. Durkheim said that religion is the consciousness of consciousness. Certainly a religious debate goes straight to first principles…A religious debate parades transcendental reasons at the outset.
>
> (1987e/RAB: 271)

An incommensurability of 'transcendental reasons' might be another way of typifying the differences Douglas seeks to demonstrate in distinguishing four archetypal forms of sociality in her 'cultural theory'. Douglas, thus, follows Durkheim's lead to find in religion the exemplary social phenomenon, but she does not entirely follow him in seeing moral individualism as a contemporary form of religion. Contrary to Durkheim's main thrust,[2] she argues that we should value the richness of differentiation and analogy possible in a complex cosmology (for instance, one in which transubstantiation is thinkable, Chapter 5). But in order to have this kind of cosmology we have to consent to live in the form of society that undergirds it, one also richly integrated by virtue of the differentiation of its parts. This sort of vision is central to her idealized account of the social form she calls 'hierarchy'. How far this rather formal preference can be specified practically is a problem to which I turn in the concluding chapter.

Durkheim thought that secular moral individualism went hand in hand with an increasing division of labour and with the definition of a growing proportion of social relations contractually. Like many turn-of-the-century writers, he was able to read the traces of nineteenth-century notions of evolution into a theory that was otherwise conceived in terms of binary categories. I noted some trace of Durkheimian evolutionism in Douglas's *Purity and Danger* (1966a), but by the time of *Natural Symbols* (1970a), and consistently thereafter, her antipathy towards explanation in terms of secularization, or towards privileging the division of labour in explanation, grew markedly. She argues instead that Durkheim got things only half right. The half he got right was in connecting the experience of strongly bounded, and internally differentiated, social groups with the sacralization of society; where he was wrong was to associate the decline of this form of experience with an evolutionary plot. Instead, she asserts that human *social* experience is fundamentally unchanging historically. There are 'secular savages' whose lives are every bit as unsacralized as those of contemporary cut-throat entrepreneurs; but there are also religious communities in contemporary society whose members' lives are integrated into cosmologies as complex as any anthropological exemplar of primitiveness with which Durkheim chose to illustrate an earlier stage of social evolution. Durkheim's agnosticism and Douglas's Catholicism obviously play some part in explaining the difference, as does Douglas's repeated reaffirmation of the hubris in believing that there exist a primitive 'them' and a modern 'us' who are really so different from one another – a view which might be made in terms of a humanist vantage but equally accords with the potential of all human beings for salvation.

But just as marked as these 'religious' themes is a more explicitly political ambivalence that Douglas expresses in terms of ideas of order and disorder. These attitudes distinctly harden. Some of her earlier work was relatively optimistic about the consequences of transcending the normal order of categories of thought (as, for instance, in the last chapter of *Purity and Danger*, 1966a), or about the scientific advances that might come from the borders of scientific endeavour (in the concluding paragraphs of 'Environments at risk', 1970e). Her later writings evince increasing antipathy to forms of organization that are relatively undifferentiated or egalitarian, often portraying these types of society and their cultures as potentially anarchic, hardly worthy of the names society or culture. Durkheim's moral individualism, premissed on a shared commitment to the equal rights of ethical individuals, is hardly explored in a positive light, leading some commentators to question her willingness to envisage challenges to existing norms, or indeed any form of protest, in terms other than disorder. She attempts to be even-handed, but hardly needs to confess that, 'My own preference has emerged as an idealized form of hierarchy' (1989d/RAB: 266).

This digression from the texts that are the subject of this chapter begins, I hope, to clarify the far from neutral senses in which Douglas's apparently non-religious works are, nonetheless, inspired by analogies with religious ritual and myth as the preeminently social phenomena that illustrate the sources and consequences of humans' capacity to share and celebrate their classification of the world. The religious bias in her approach to the sociology of knowledge (and I use the term 'bias' non-pejoratively to describe her style of thought) is extended to other areas of collective life which produce their own shared classifications and the rituals to mark them. Mary Douglas thus differs from a majority of social theorists, including many fellow-travelling 'cultural theorists', in not seeing religion as a derivative feature of social life. However, this tends to introduce a double standard of judgement: to the extent that they are usually devalued as sensual expressions of everyday lives, she tends to celebrate the small delights of the rituals of eating, shopping and housekeeping; but when these affirmations of domestic solidarity are weighed against the sacralization of broader social commitments, she can inveigh against the individualism of an 'emancipatory' culture.

From this vantage it is worth returning to some of the ideas previously summarized. *Purity and Danger* had already suggested an analogy between money and ritual which was later developed more theoretically:

> By the Keynesian revolution money has to some extent been tamed and put to service. A parallel ritual revolution lags behind. Ritual has so far only been denigrated. It is time for it too to be grasped and its creative potential to be understood.
>
> (1966b/ITAV: 38)

World of Goods, and the essays on similar subjects, are informed by the idea that goods and services are bought to enable and mark social intercourse; they make visible the categories of culture and allow everyday life to be celebrated. To rail against consumption, just as to criticize ritual, reveals only the impoverished social concerns of the critic. For how else is sociality to be made manifest and celebrated among us?

CULTURAL MOTIFS

It is difficult to imagine what social commentator other than Mary Douglas would be so attuned to religious harmonies as to base her analysis of risk on the similarity between that term in social accounting and ideas of sin and taboo in religion (Douglas 1990a/RAB; 1992e/RAB). One of her most explicit statements of the analogy employs the 'idea of the cultural motif', which elsewhere she traces to Scandinavian writers on religion whom she claims also to have influenced Evans-Pritchard (with Perry 1985c). A quotation from that article illustrates not just the notion of the cultural motif but Douglas's own suppositions about the way cultures cohere:

> It becomes clear that the apparent logical coherence of a set of religious ideas in a particular civilization is not due to the simple application of logical rules of noncontradiction. They seem logically coherent, first because they rest upon consistent institutional forms and second because a set of analogies has been constructed upon them.

These analogies create coherence by extending words and logical operations from one context to another. Overlapping and repeating, such
analogies impose a complex ordering on experience where confusion
would otherwise reign.

(1985c: 426–427)

Here, she clearly moves on from her sense, in *Purity and Danger*, that contemporary societies had lost this earlier coherence. Risk, like sin or taboo, is a cultural
motif, with sufficiently broad and ambiguous senses to recur in the different institutional settings of a complex society and to offer a means to allocate
responsibility for events that occur within it. Where the risk concept is well established it functions as a 'groove' (that favourite Douglas image) into which debate
within a community always flows and, by flowing that way, deepens the channel
it uses. But the cultural motif of risk has shifted its sense. The nineteenth-
century idea of risk was associated with benefit (the disinclination of people to
take unrewarded risks meant that entrepreneurs were justified in reaping profit
from undertaking ventures that might not succeed). Nowadays, risk is generally
associated with cost (so that risk is what justifies the payment of compensation
for harm). It might be suggested that

the risk concept would have come to the fore in politics because probabilistic thinking is persuasive in industry, modern science, and
philosophy....However, the risk that is a central concept for our policy
makers has not got much to do with probability calculations. The original connection is indicated only by arm-waving in the direction of
possible science: the word *risk* now means danger; *high risk* means a lot
of danger.

(1990a/RAB: 23–24)

So why not just call it danger? 'The new sense of the word *risk* works because it
can be strongly biased to emancipation' while retaining 'the aura of science' and
the 'pretension of a possible precise calculation' (RAB: 24, 25). Particularly in
America, which she treats as the extreme form of an industrial democracy based
on ideas of individual emancipation, most misfortune is believed to occur either
because people put themselves at risk (through a dangerous lifestyle) or because
others have put them at risk. The latter makes American life peculiarly litigious
(RAB: 17). Within a scientific worldview, risk is a blame-pinning device similar to
witchcraft elsewhere. Accusations of risk call the powers that be – bureaucracy
and big business – to account. Although risk is avowedly a secular and not a religious concept, analogically it does what religious ideas (sin as the cultural motif
of Christianity, or *tabu* in some Polynesian cultures) did previously: unifying
diverse elements of experience and allocating responsibility when things go
wrong (1997b; in press, 'Religious taboo'). Even the apparent appeal to science is
not so great a difference; often scientists can be found to support both sides of an

argument. But the social correlates of the cultural motif of being *at* risk are opposite to those of being *in* sin or *under* taboo. Sin and taboo express the vulnerability of the community to individual misconduct, but it is the individual who is 'at risk' from the community. Given Douglas's assumption that dangers are allocated within the environment so as to support valued institutions, she might go on to argue (as one reading of Durkheim would permit) that contemporary ideas of risk justly reflect the institutional importance of notions of moral individualism. In fact, although she insists upon the interpenetration of social forms and the ideas that sustain them, she does so in a way that remains ambivalent about moral individualism. Theories of risk are religion-like in their scope and function, and they indeed correspond to the characteristics of contemporary society, but these characteristics are agonistic, and a risk motif serves only to accentuate them. Risk is a commodifying, symbolically impoverished, and inhuman way to conceive of human relationships.

But to characterize entire national societies uniformly (albeit some parts of her argument can be read like this) goes against the grain of Douglas's recognition (for instance, in *Risk and Culture*) that plural forms of sociality exist within modern nations. Industrial democracies in general depend on individual competition, and on holding people accountable for their own fortunes and misfortunes. This process necessarily throws up an underclass of failures whose existence can be hidden residentially, occupationally or both. This is the society that she envisaged in *Natural Symbols* as split between two quadrants of the grid and group diagram: the successful eschewing some social controls by virtue of their low grid and group constraints, and the unsuccessful groupless but strongly constrained (prone to occasional millennialism). The upshot she perceives is for the stigmatized to be blamed for their own misfortunes, and for their reaction to be to stigmatize the stigmatizers in their turn. The cultural motif of risk in a society committed to equality eventuates in the unsuccessful being blamed for their failure, and those considered to have failed holding the powers that be responsible for their ills. The problem is not that risk fails to offer a framework which makes everyday life comprehensible – justifying fortune and misfortune, allocating blame, and holding others to account – it does these things all too well but in doing so reflects and accentuates the values of a form of society already based on agonistic struggle and multiple exclusions.

As I explore in greater detail in Chapter 10, Douglas's analysis commits her to distinguishing two levels, or definitions, of culture. The idea of cultural motif belongs with a definition of *culture as classification and cognition*: a level of analysis which, at its simplest, can be considered normally to be unavailable or irrelevant to the social actors engaged in the hurly-burly of everyday life. *Culture as contention* – meaning the arguments brought forward by social actors to support their beliefs, explain their fortune and misfortune, and hold the world to account by pinning blame (whether on themselves, others, or some inhuman agency) – is by definition explicitly stated. Thus, people can share a presupposition – like 'risk' in American culture – which they employ to make disparate claims. The interplay between implicit supposition and explicit argument is crucial to explaining how, why and when presuppositions change. Douglas's use of the phrase 'cultural bias' does not always respect this distinction, which I would argue is necessary for her theory, with the result that bias in the classificatory culture is sometimes analogized to bias in the culture of contention: a step which needs to be taken cautiously (Chapter 10).

To return to our texts: Douglas's analysis of risk might seem quite consistent with an account of secularization in contemporary society. Even if it is pseudo-scientific in practice, the risk motif performs social purposes analogous to those of religion and thus displaces religiously transcendent explanation. But in fact she has taken a diametrically opposite view, vigorously arguing that institutional-ized religion is not consistently on the wane either in the West or elsewhere. Whether this view can be reconciled with the argument that risk is the broad cosmology of a globalizing form of industrial democracy, is a question to which I return after setting out her critique of the secularization hypothesis.

CONTEMPORARY RELIGIOUS DIVERSITY

Douglas's publications explicitly dealing with religion resumed around 1981 when she left the Russell Sage Foundation and took an appointment as the Avalon Professor of Humanities at Northwestern University as 'part of that insti-tution's intent to connect the social sciences to the humanities. One part of the agenda was to engage anthropology and comparative religion in professional conversation' (1985c: 410 fn.). This chapter concerns that half of the conversa-tion concerned with contemporary society; the next chapter looks at the other half carried on, increasingly since her retirement from a teaching position, with Old Testament scholars.

Douglas's contribution to a 1982 edition of *Daedalus* represents her considered view of the fate of institutionalized world religions (1982e, 1983a). 'The effects of modernization on religious change' is Mary Douglas at her most vigorously critical, subjecting theories in the sociology of religion to examination. As anthropological inquisitor among the theologians and sociologists, she is on devastating form, cheerfully dissecting the theories on offer.

Douglas's distrust of the narrative that modernization and secularization go hand in hand is long-standing: after *Purity and Danger* she had emphasized the anomaly that 'secular savages' posed to the 'primitive' beginnings of an evolu-tionary story; a story in which believers in 'modern' society were no less out of place. Douglas's account of modernity – insofar as this story interests her – tends to emphasize that moderns potentially have the capacity to reflect comparatively and historically on human social forms and are in the position, again potentially and if only they can resist the snares of what is self-evident in their own societies, to evaluate the merits and drawbacks of different social forms. Borrowing from Robin Horton she describes this as the capacity of 'a culture to view itself…from a meta-level' (1983a: 42); embracing this possibility is one of the several senses she gives to the movement from 'passive' to 'active voice' theories (1979a/ITAV). Because this meta-level view becomes available through the lens of Douglas's own theory, she has tended to counter disbelief in her theory in terms of the theory itself. Those not socially positioned to accept her ideas will predictably not do so. While this is indeed what the theory anticipates in broad terms, as an argument it is uncomfortably close to that line of defence in psychoanalysis which also claims to explain why people resist theoretically disclosed truths of their own lives. Douglas's writings from the early 1980s on theology and the sociology of religion claim these disciplines were hampered by a conventional wisdom which predicted that trends of modernization and secularization went together, interrupted only by occasional outbreaks of short-lived, cultic enthusiasm. She sets out to show not only that they were wrong, but why they were wrong and, given that the sources of their wrong-headedness are explicable, why they were predictably wrong.

Religious studies, Douglas argues, singularly failed to spot the revival of the traditional religions in our times; the list of oversights is long and grave: the role of the Catholic Church in Poland, the rise of Christian fundamentalism in America and Islamic fundamentalism in the Middle East, religiously defined wars in Ireland and Lebanon, and the support of radical Catholic priests for revolutionary movements in South America are but a few instances. Specialists in religious studies failed to see that these facts went contrary to their thesis relating modernity and secularism because they were saddled with a limiting and wrongly conceived definition of religion. Failing to account for the present, they made even less plausible future prognoses. Their failures relate directly to their social positions: as relatively autonomous, professional thinkers, they are predictably unsympathetic to public forms of ritual. They not only claim these to be in decline when they are not, they actually recommend their abandonment. Their assessment of modernity is biased, in part because their appreciation of pre-moderns is a caricature. All this is plain in three consistently misleading assumptions they bring to the study of religion:

1   They believe that religion is somehow 'good for the human psyche', and build this integrative function into their definitions. The objections to this are numerous: people are not always better off with religion ('a lot of religious behavior…is widely regarded as emotionally restrictive, bigoted, fanatical, or psychotic' (1983a: 26)); religion may divide people as easily as unite them; anthropologists have abundantly demonstrated that people vary in religiosity and some are not religious at all; finally, there is no evidence that there has been a decline from previous standards of piety (1983a: 29). In short, people do not necessarily need religion.

2   Specialists believe we moderns are different from others because, rather circularly, of modernization. But every society believes it is unique. Admittedly, science, bureaucracy and technology have changed society, but

they have not necessarily caused the decline of religion. Combining the first two assumptions, by arguing that religion is both good for the psyche and in decline, raises an 'anxious problem'. If belief in a religion of public rituals has become impossible for modern man so that religion cannot sacralize social institutions, then it is suggested that we instead cultivate interior spiritual awareness to assure our psychic health. But the several strands of this argument are equally fallacious.

(a) Science has reduced the explanatory appeal of religion. But, Douglas argues, science and religion have specialized in different sorts of question. Moreover, our reliance upon specialists makes us more, rather than less, like those societies in which initiation is requisite to acquiring certain sorts of knowledge. We are constantly subjected to the advice of experts who reason from premises we do not presume to understand in terms of theories we cannot comprehend. But we accept their advice in the name of science. Although religion is not alternative to science, science certainly engenders awe which some have argued (though wrongly in Douglas's view) is a characteristic of religion.

(b) Moderns have greater choice. Moderns certainly love to tell themselves so. But our view of primitive society is stereotyped, and it flatters us into believing that there are not 'grooves' into which our thoughts and actions tend to run. Tongue in cheek she asks, 'Where is free choice? Our Viking ancestors had much more of it, free to spend a few years in Greenland, nip back to Scandinavia to help a political ally, or join a raid on Britain' (1983a: 35). Elsewhere, she included the Vikings with other people who rather than being risk averse actually sought out risks (1992e).

(c) Modern society is run bureaucratically. This means we cannot possibly know the millions of other people with whom 'we march in columns through the vision of those responsible for our lives as so many statistics'; but then we wouldn't have known them anyway (1983a: 33). It may be true that bureaucratic manipulation leads to crises of identity, but crises of identity are also part of the biographies of the saints. In some ways, bureaucratic regulation brings us closer to the stereotypical idea of the small, closely regulated community in which behaviour was normatively governed but which was 'congenial' to religious belief (she cites ancient Byzantium or the fifteenth-century Vatican as examples) (1983a: 34).

(d) We are no longer dependent on nature. But in one of its senses the idea of nature is a cultural convention; technological changes mean that the boundary between nature and culture is now defined differently. It is difficult to see how this, rather than our social relationships, can have determinant effects on our religiosity.

Accentuating a previous gambit, Douglas is willing to argue the possibility that the experience of humans in technologically advanced and bureaucratically regulated societies is actually converging with that of pre-industrial people: science deepens the wonders of nature, while the struggle to wrest a living from impersonal forces goes on – albeit nowadays against bureaucracy. By this point, she is amusing herself by standing the thesis of modern exceptionalism on its head. Most of the constructive side of her argument is contained in her third major criticism.

(3) Culture is capable of being somehow autonomous of society, and is becoming increasingly so in modern times. 'The spirit moveth where it listeth', as Douglas tartly summarizes the position (1983a: 29). This is not an assumption, she retorts, supported by an anthropological approach (particularly her own) which asks who in society supports or rejects a cultural viewpoint.

In fact Douglas has detected in the sociology of contemporary religion most of the types of analysis and the attitudes she likes least: including the explanation of periodic religious enthusiasm in terms of compensation, or deprivation, which she had decried in *Purity and Danger* and *Natural Symbols*. In an echo of the 'contempt of ritual' in *Natural Symbols*, Douglas generalizes that religious sociology indulges a 'bias against public religion' (1983a: 29). From previous experience we know that this is not an accusation she will pursue lightly. Two distinguished American sociologists are picked out for particular censure: Peter Berger and Daniel Bell.

As a writer whose work she had previously reviewed with sympathy and admiration (1970k), she rounds on Berger in sorrow more than anger. Berger had recently proposed a distinction between the religious traditions of West and East Asia. In Douglas's recension, Berger suggested that the East Asian religious tradition developed continuously from a vision of human experience in a sanctified life-world. This outlook held out the prospect of an individual interior transcendence which rendered personality irrelevant. By contrast, in the West Asian tradition there occurred a break with the previous tradition at the point when humans confronted a personified God in terms of the sorts of enduring moral responsibilities that obtained between themselves. This encounter had the effect of individuating people and occasioning a rupture between humankind and cosmos. Berger's recommendation that Westerners look eastwards in order to heal this breach particularly perplexes Douglas. How could a writer whose previous work had emphasized the close fit between a society, and the ideas plausible within it, imagine that an outlook can be transplanted in this way? His suggestion reveals a bias towards interiorized religion and away from that currently less favored mystic incorporation [which] implies more public celebration, more expressive rituals, more emphasis on instituted sacramental channels. *It attracts supporting theories of mutual interdependence, and tends to transform the spiritual realm into a model of what the consecrated society would be like.* Furthermore, according to this doctrine in its highly developed forms, individuals should not all expect to play the same roles: in an organic system the head and the hands perform different functions. Within this doctrinal form there is often the idea that great sanctity is exceptional. Yet thanks to the mystical incorporation of individuals, the sharing of grace evens up the inequities between people or over time, the spiritually well-endowed providing a welfare fund from which benefits flow to the rest.

(1983a: 28, my emphasis)

In contrast to Berger's sacralization of the individual who withdraws from society, Douglas offers a restatement of the hierarchical and communal model, what she calls here the 'consecrated society'; and her use of the image of a 'welfare fund' of spirituality echoes the analysis of collective or public goods, better provided under some social forms than others, that becomes increasingly crucial to her comparison of the desirability of the social types between which her readers are asked to choose. She continues:

By contrast [with mystic incorporation], the doctrines of self-transcendence are more egalitarian, more individualist, and more optimistic about the human potential for sustaining great spiritual achievement. It seems obvious that the latter religious trend, however well it thrives in the East, also matches the favored principles of an achieving society organized in a democracy dedicated to the freedom and equality of individuals.

(1983a: 28)

Berger thus stands accused of simply going with the flow. Self-transcendence, as a form of religiosity – like risk as an idiom relating individuals – is compatible with emancipatory, Western democratic social forms. But if risk (and its litigious practices) and self-transcendence (presumably requiring social withdrawal) are both symptoms of Western social forms, how do we decide who will choose one and who the other, or whether it is possible to choose both at once? Douglas develops her argument about self-transcendence in an almost contemporary article to which I turn shortly. So far as I know, she has not explicitly addressed the relationship between her analyses of risk and religion in contemporary American society, although it is not difficult to imagine how she might argue reactions to the shared cultural motif of risk were refracted through the life-forms of differently organized religious groupings.

Douglas's second target is Daniel Bell's attempt to drive a wedge between society and culture: the former driven by efficiency and the latter by expressive concerns. Bell's argument that the relation between these two is typically disjunctive is predictably provocative to Douglas who holds the contrary view. Apart from trying to show how Bell contradicts himself, Douglas reinterprets two of his examples to show how close is the correlation between contemporary culture, and contemporary political and economic processes. As the economy becomes dominated by its service sector, so there is an axial shift to the control of power through knowledge. Women become bankers and scientists and enter the learned professions, while men's control over female sexuality and the family is eroded. Changing sexual morality is far from autonomous of changes in the organization of society. So far as the autonomy of cultural production in a narrower sense goes, Douglas taxes Bell with, what is in effect, an elitist preoccupation with high culture. Antinomian values are predictable on the part of artists outside the power structures of society, but mainstream culture is distinct and different.

> Soap opera, TV commercials, weekly magazines, musicals, mystery stories, and situation comedy give another impression altogether – of care for clean clothes and floors, love of good food and elegant service, concern for law and property, laughter at complex, entwined situations, and a passionate interest in individual freedom and individual success.…The endless search for pleasure that Bell takes as a feature of modernism sounds like the familiar complaint against other people's mindless consumerism.
>
> (1983a: 40)

The phrase 'mindless consumerism' takes us back immediately to the defence of shopping and consumption. Bell is elitist and Berger is unsociological. Douglas's argument is not with shoppers or proponents of public ritual, whom she wishes to defend, but with the kill-joys who either think they know better or else wish to deny life its sensuous, social basis.

Taking the texts on risk, religion and consumption together, we find Douglas arguing that contemporary social forms permit the spread of a risk cosmology, *and* the growth of self-transcendence as a religious ideology, *and* competitive consumerism, but none of the antitheses to these terms is ruled out: so there is also a resurgence of more fundamentalist forms of religion, *and* a maintenance of traditional religious communities, *and* a rejection of consumerism. This might seem like an anything goes account, but that would be incompatible with everything Douglas believes about the consistency between culture and social environment. Ordering this variety is the job of grid and group, or cultural theory. How well it is able to do this we examine in Chapter 10, but one aspect of her argument, about disengagement from social commitment, is made in an essay which picks up directly from the themes we have been examining here.

CONTEMPORARY SCEPTICISM: THE SCHOLARS' TREASON

Douglas's article published first under the title 'Pascal's great wager' and later, in slightly amended form, under the descriptive title 'The social preconditions of radical scepticism', is particularly allusive and dense (1985b/RAB, 1986c). Its subject is both anti-foundational accounts of knowledge, and the social positions of those who espouse such theories. Douglas suggests that the denial of a knowable reality is a recurrent motif: not just the property of some modern and postmodern theorists but also of Eastern religious traditions. But this aversion to foundations is credible only for the occupants of particular social environments; it is not an option for those presently exercising power or for those who wish to influence how power is wielded in the future. In Douglas's hands this line of argument becomes at once a denunciation of intellectuals who refuse to enter social commitments, an explanation of why they feel disinclined to do so, and another championing of her belief in the ontological primacy of sociality.

Pascal, Douglas recalls, argued that religious scepticism was a bad bet: the consequences of ending in heaven or hell for eternity were incommensurable, so there was nothing to be lost by believing (or at least living as if one believed) even if the likelihood of the belief being true was slight. Readers might assume that living as if one believed was the sceptic's choice, but Douglas does not interpret her chosen fable that way. For her, radical scepticism implies refusal to accept any foundational account of reality. Douglas herself argues a long way towards this position but then stops just short of it. Our thoughts, she claims, may logically follow from one another but, in order to think at all, our experience has to be organized into cognitive categories. These categories are shared by virtue of our living in society (her usual Durkheimian argument). If thought categories are social conventions, then by acting upon our desire to live in a particular type of society we also select to abide in the sort of world people make there. This is a standard Douglas opening move, and difficult to interpret until we know just how far she means to push the thesis of social determinism of cognition, and just how much latitude is to be allowed our ability to choose the form of society in which we live. The bigger the claim, the more problems she will face in sustaining it (Chapters 10 and 11). For immediate purposes, I am more interested in the way she develops her narrower argument about the relation between religious and social commitment. As in the previous article we examined, her passion is mostly oppositional.

As Douglas sees it, Pascal's choice derived from his already having classified his options: either believing in reality or living in uncertainty. If we allow that this binary distinction exhausts the options, then we might agree that

> [Pascal's] real *enemies* are not the Protestants, Jews or Muslims, nor even the Jesuits and academicians against whom he inveighs, but the pronouncements of radical sceptics. In this choice of problem, *he poses*

an option which is more contemporary than the choice between denominational religious forms.

(1985b/RAB: 237, my emphases)

Pascal came down on the side of the realists as, she claims (recuperating what is broadly Berger's distinction above), has the Western tradition historically. For instance, the Scottish philosopher David Hume was a sceptic not about empirical reality but only about our ability to know it definitely. The Eastern traditions, she generalizes, came down on the side of illusion. The point of this stark dualism lies in her further argument. Following a Buddhist sceptic, 'radical scepticism is feasible but not stateable'; the complete sceptic about reality simply refuses to join any of the terms on which anyone else wants to talk about the world. From here she derives a continuum of scepticism, according to the willingness to keep a dialogue going: at one extreme is the small community marked by unquestioned belief (whether in primitive or modern societies), somewhere in the middle she places the religiously plural society in which beliefs have to be made axiomatic because they are contested, and at the other extreme the radical scepticism of those who have renounced the world. The position people occupy, she asserts, has to do with power and revolt against its claims; all the points along the continuum are occupied in contemporary society. Berger's Eastern inner spirituality is already with us, but it belongs in a particular social niche.

> Many students of religion display a bias against the idea that an individual human being receives and sustains his religious beliefs in a social medium. But can they seriously discount the possibility that *God, having made man a social being, allows His Face to be seen only through a distorted lens, through the medium of the society which men themselves create?* To say Yes, belief and society go together, to concede this, would endorse a further element in Pascal's argument. For he did not think that belief comes by a decision to believe. At issue in his wager is the idea that belief comes by living in the company of believers. He did not discount social influences. So there is a further implication for theology: *could it be that the virtuous activity of avoiding damnation could entail making the society which best images God?*
>
> (RAB: 237–38, my emphases)

Although posed as questions, one cannot help but wonder how closely the phrases emphasized above reflect Douglas's own beliefs (see Chapter 11). Referring darkly to the 'subversive energies that lie dormant in religious doctrines on the nature of reality' (RAB: 242), Douglas begins to fill in her scale of scepticism, with particular attention to the historical occupants of its radically sceptical pole. Gnostics in the second century and Brahmans renouncing claims to secular power in India are to be found there. More recently she notes the similar position of young Russian radicals in the 1830s and 1840s, and of the

English highbrows reviled by George Orwell almost a century later. All found themselves confronted by unacceptable, arbitrary power they were unable to challenge. Following the ideas of Foucault, Marx and Freud, she claims that contemporary intellectuals are opposed to institutions as such. The foundations of all the disciplines are being undercut, their internal logical operations shown to rely on the way resemblance is already recognized in the world. 'In what sense do *we* form an excluded elite?' (RAB: 250, my emphasis). At the national level she decides the parallel is weak. But in global terms, in the North facing South, 'we' also are wedged between imponderable machineries and suffering masses, we feel guilt, and despair and mouth the right sentiments while clinging to our few privileges. If we choose subjective idealism, there will be no sustained support to 'heal the widening divisions'. 'One by one the great logicians of our day [Wittgenstein, Quine, Goodman] are coming out with the same kind of answer. The ultimate and only authority for the way the universe is divided up has to be the community' (RAB: 251). 'To my naïve eye the probable value of deciding to live by a simple faith in reality seems high' (RAB: 252).

A passage appended to the second published version of the argument (but omitted from the reprint in RAB) recognizes the oddness, in a sociological essay, of what has gone before: 'to end at this point would turn the argument into a sermon' (1986c: 85). Addressing scholars of religion, she recapitulates that people's ideas of reality are contingent on their sense of the futility or immorality of wielding power, and this sense depends on their place in a particular social structure. At this point we explicitly rejoin Mary Douglas's own commitments: to differentiated, hierarchical organization, to social inclusiveness and responsibility, and to complexly demarcated styles of thought and action – in short, to form, and especially to form as realized in the Roman Catholic Church, or organizations analogous to it in these terms.

DEBATES WITHIN THE CONSECRATED SOCIETY

These commitments become substantive in Douglas's occasional contributions to the life of her own religious community which she has urged consistently to cherish its symbols and internal differentiation. The role of women in the Church has particularly preoccupied her, and the ordination of women is a subject on which she has written more than once – and noticeably dispassionately in comparison with her earlier writings on the Second Vatican Council (perhaps because the case for women priests had been rejected by the 'Sacred congregation on the admission of women to the priesthood' in 1976).

In an essay originally entitled 'The woman–priest problem: a cultural analysis' (1987e/RAB 'The debate on women priests'), Douglas employed the apparatus of cultural theory's ideal types of social environment in order to relate the different reasons expressed for the desirability of the ordination of women to the very diverse social contexts of those who proposed them. The argument in favour of ordination of women may issue from people who otherwise are divided in terms of their commitment or opposition to hierarchy. Post-Vatican II reforms had disbanded pre-existing communities of nuns, which were hierarchical and fitted into the larger hierarchy of authority of the Church. Some women sought ordination because this space in a hierarchical order was no longer available to them; effectively, they had been thrust into an undifferentiated and competitive world outside the convent that offered them a less meaningful social setting. Unlike them, other women might be anti-hierarchical as such. For them, as egalitarians, a hierarchical Church might not be an appropriate home at all. As she put it subsequently, 'Catholic doctrine…bears witness to the hierarchical bent for argumentation and a cumulative, incorporative style of thought' (1996e: 36).

Douglas's advice to the Roman Catholic Church instances her general understanding of hierarchy. The Church might elaborate the gender symbolism of the relation between a male God and female Church in order to convince women who want to be priests that procreative imagery is a natural symbol, or exemplification, of the nuptial mystery (1987e/RAB). Perhaps, like some African counterparts, as she has suggested in both the *Catholic Herald* (1988d) and to the Catholic Theological Association (1996e; and noted in the *Tablet*, 16 September 1995, p. 1183) women might be advised better to lobby for a women's organization empowered with the right to veto decisions taken by men; Third World Catholic societies accustomed to 'hierarchy and gendered organization in their own traditions' might correspondingly be more open to the suggestion of a 'high-powered women's commission'.

Parallels between the positions of African and European women are prominently explored in an article on 'Hierarchy and women's voice' (1992j), which is also one of Douglas's most extended discussions of hierarchy. There she begins from a question of the sorts of societies in which women, and other disadvantaged categories, are rendered mute. How is dialogue suppressed? By suppression of the right to association she responds. The answer must be institutional: granting women (and other muted – or simply overridden – groups) the space within a differentiated, hierarchical system in which they can articulate their voices in terms of complementary, and relative, differences. These differences are relative, because they depend upon a focus and level of activity, and complementary because they may be construed symbolically as necessary to one another. In a dispersed and egalitarian society (she takes the East African Hadza gatherer–hunters as example), women may depend on mother–daughter ties and women's solidarity against actual male threats. In hierarchical societies, like some of those of Western Cameroon, women's associations organized in parallel with those of men under the leadership of distinguished women elders wield countervailing powers to ridicule men and hold them to account for wrongs visited on women, while extolling the intrinsic virtues of womanhood. Hierarchy permits claims to be expressed as claims to 'spheres of authority' rather than in terms of individualized equality. Sadly, in her consideration, individual equality for contemporary women serves only to endorse an ideology of market-mediated competition in which individuals are conceived as producers and consumers of goods, and in which self and other, and men and women, are strongly dichotomized. The complex social differentiations of hierarchy are matched by a cognitive style of complementary dualisms, ranked and subject to inversion and recombination; and one recalls how *Natural Symbols* had argued that hierarchical, rather than egalitarian, forms of organization were able to support a complex life of the intellect.

With the North/South divide again in mind, Douglas has also written (for the *Tablet*) on the disappearance of the devil, hell, damnation and angels from the Catholic West, and the move towards a monotheism in which believers as individuals commune with an increasingly benign and loving God. She counsels the Church not to move too quickly to suppress the manifestations of evil recognized in African churches; when Westerners lived in small communities they also believed in such possibilities and used that belief to hold one another to account (1990i; cf. 1955c). With 'no community umbrella offering to shelter us; no one is trying to make us conform to community standards' (1996e: 29).

Douglas's occasional writings, often addressed to a Catholic public, offer intriguing glimpses of an applied anthropology different from what that phrase normally means: a social anthropologist using her professional resources to contribute to discussions of the direction of her own community. These excursions also help explain the emotional commitment she has made to the top right-hand (high grid/high group, or hierarchical) quadrant of her diagram of social types. And, as we have seen already, this preference is transferred analogically from religion to risk, consumption and welfare economics. In this sense, then, Douglas's comparative and wide-ranging anthropology has consistently been engaged and committed to contemporary cultural critique, and has as consistently espoused a formal, somewhat abstract, hierarchical vision of social inclusion, differentiation and complementarity. Ideas to which I shall return in conclusion.

Notes

1 Although this was a time when her ideas were being digested in religious studies and theology; see Wellbourn 1970, Pyle 1973, Isenberg and Owen 1977, Richard 1984, Arbuckle 1986.
2 Though possibly in accordance with his preference for incorporation into modern equivalents of guilds mediating between the individual and the State, itself consistent with the social teachings of the Roman Catholic Church on subsidiarity, explained in Chapter 2.

9 RETURNING TO RELIGION – IN THE OLD TESTAMENT

PURITY AND DANGER REVISED

Mary Douglas's fascination with the Old Testament as an ethnographic source was stimulated, she claims, by its use as a standard reference for her Oxford lecturers;[1] however, it developed into something more talismanic – her name permanently linked to the celebrated analysis in *Purity and Danger* of the dietary rules of Leviticus, and each stage of her theoretical development mirrored in a revised analysis of some aspect of Israelite ethnography.

Douglas had noted a parallel between Lele and ancient Hebrew attitudes of avoidance to ' "unnatural behaviour" in animals' as early as her 1957 article on the religious symbolism of animals (1957a; IM: 32). Although the argument was famously expanded in *Purity and Danger*, her use of Old Testament sources remained in the service of a general argument that – in terms quoted more fully earlier:

> [T]he only way in which pollution ideas make sense is in reference to a total structure of thought whose key-stone, boundaries, margins and internal lines are held in relation by rituals of separation.
>
> (PD: 42)

In a spirit of self-criticism, she returned to this analysis in two papers contemporary with revision of her argument between the first and revised editions of *Natural Symbols* (and republished together in the section of *Implicit Meanings* concerned with 'The *a priori* in Nature'). Editorializing her own work, she notes that

> in writing on Hebrew cosmology [in *Purity and Danger*] I had done the very thing that the rest of the book was written to stop. It was an analysis of a system of ideas with no demonstration of its connection with the dominant concerns of the people who used it for thinking with.
>
> (IM: 207–208)

And rereading Edmund Leach's essay on 'The legitimacy of Solomon' 'brought home...with a resounding thud something which Old Testament scholarship had been agreed upon for a very long time...that the Pentateuch was full of concern for the evils that flowed from marriages with foreigners' (IM: 208). Tracing a general analogy between animal classification, food rules and sexual mating required, as she put it, something of a 'conversion' to alliance theory in the analysis of kinship.[2]

The first of the two essays, 'Deciphering a meal' (1972b/IM: 249–75) suggests not only conversion to alliance theory but slight softening in her attitude to structuralism more generally. Initially, she analogizes food to language, and then meals to poems. 'If food is treated as a code, then the messages it encodes will be found in the pattern of social relations being expressed' (IM: 249). With a nod in the direction of Lévi-Strauss's structural analysis in *Mythologiques*, she immediately notes problems with his method: the failure to relate codifications of foods to the social relations that give rise to them, and the undisciplined generation of binary pairs without reference to their relative importance or syntagmatic (sequential) relations. Accepting that the 'analogy with linguistic form...is limited in relevance' (IM: 251), she goes on to a variant of the analysis of British and French meals that we explored in Chapter 6 and concludes that

> the meaning of a meal is found in a system of repeated analogies. Each meal carries something of the meaning of other meals; each meal is a structured social event which structures others in its own image.
>
> (IM: 260)

This idea leads her to another analogy – that of versification. Jewish meals, governed by the Mosaic dietary rules, were – she begins to suggest – akin to cosmic poems. Recent articles by Ralph Bulmer (1967) and Stanley Tambiah (1969) (both of which she had anthologized in *Rules and Meanings* 1973b) suggested 'a strong analogy between bed and board' in the classification of animals among both Karam in New Guinea and Thai peasants. The patterns of rules categorizing animals corresponded in formal terms to – indeed, might even be projected from – the patterns of classification of affines and kin. In *Purity and Danger*, Douglas had been satisfied to conclude (in terms quoted above) that pollution ideas make sense in reference to a total structure of thought – but this is only an exhortation to holistic analysis. Following Bulmer's reproach, she now criticizes her erstwhile textual approach for lacking an ethnographic basis that would tie it to people's social environment. Why would the Jews have had such strict rules that resonated so widely in their lives? And why, unlike Karam and Thai, should their rules not liken eating to sex but repeatedly compare the table and the altar, and analogize the ancient Israelites to their own domestic animals?

Before tackling Douglas's answer, we might notice a couple of developments that have been slipped into the argument. From arguing that meals – for instance, set pieces like Sunday or Christmas dinner – intensify the codings of everyday meals, Douglas has moved to the idea that classification of foodstuffs analogizes the classification of the agents involved in social actions or, more exactly, that analogy exists between the formal patterning of gastronomy and the formal patterning of kinship and affinity. The highly abstract nature of the correspondence suggested – effectively that between the overall designs of two patterns of relationships – is signalled in her use of Venn diagrams to represent patterns of inclusion and exclusion in the classifications she detects. As I noted above, formal patterns of relationships are not treated as equivalently powerful, since it is assumed that the formal properties of, say, animal classification or edibility can be treated as projections of the patterning of social relations – as if they had been traced from this masterplan (and not vice versa). This position is a subtle restatement of the argument Durkheim and Mauss proposed in their essay on 'primitive classification' and relies in part on arguments from cognitive consistency.

In *Purity and Danger* Douglas had already examined how Jewish classification distinguished three spheres (of land, air and water) and assigned animals to one of these as their proper habitat – simultaneously specifying the characteristics appropriate to creatures in each element that they might be edible. Water creatures need fins and scales (swarming things are inedible), but all water creatures are unfit for the altar to which only domesticated animals can be offered. To be edible, creatures of the air must have wings and two legs and moreover not belong to a named subset of birds, which has proved problematic to interpret but probably consists of birds that consume blood (thus falling foul of a further rule to separate blood and meat).[3] Only two birds are suitable for the altar: turtle-doves and pigeons. Of the land creatures, quadrupeds with cloven hoofs which chew the cud are fit for the table. Additionally, the first-born of these animals are to be presented to the priests and may be offered on the altar if they are unblemished.

Israelites are distinguished from other humans by the covenant between God and Abraham, and analogously their livestock is distinguished from all other animals. The first-born of all the Israelites are Levites, consecrated to temple service; but they may serve in the temple only if they are without blemish. The criteria of fitness of people and animals for the temple are, thus, isomorphic. In fact, the entire classification is concerned with purity expressed through the rigorous application of categorical criteria of separateness to things and to people. The states of purity of the Jewish people, their animals and their land are made homologous and, more than this, the patterning is 'metonymic' with the 'Promised Land' as its basic point of reference.

> The sanctity of cognitive boundaries is made known by valuing the integrity of the physical forms. The perfect physical specimens point to the perfectly bounded temple, altar and sanctuary. And these in turn point to the hard-won and hard-to-defend territorial boundaries of the Promised Land.
>
> (IM: 269)

187

Where the metaphysical scheme fails to fit with nature, the Jews rejected or avoided the anomalies produced. 'Israel is the boundary that all the other boundaries celebrate' (IM: 269). Following Edmund Leach's lead (Leach 1969) – in fact, following this lead along a path she will later disavow – Douglas notes the recurrent railing against foreign marriages and finds here another ground on which the pig might be multifariously reviled by Israelites. Not just a classificatory anomaly and indiscriminate feeder – even of carrion – the pig is reared by outsiders as food, might be offered at the banquet of an Israelite betrothed to a foreigner, and 'by these stages comes plausibly to represent the utterly disapproved form of sexual mating and to carry all the odium that this implies...The common meal, decoded, as much as any poem, summarizes a stern, tragic religion' (IM: 272). This identification of metonymic relation for Jews between the pig and the outsider as sexual partner allows Douglas to find common ground with Bulmer's characterization of the cassowary – as akin in its mediation of the categories of cultivated and wild to the Karam sister's child who is both cross-cousin and potential affine – and with Stanley Tambiah's analysis of an analogy between the feckless boundary-crossing of the otter and inappropriate behaviour on the part of a Thai son-in-law. This conclusion, however, opens a new problem for Douglas: wherein lies the perception of similarity?

'Self-evidence' (1972c/IM), written at the same time as the previous article, takes up one aspect of this conundrum: how 'sameness' seems culturally variable and is yet everywhere recognized to be an intuitive or gut reaction.[4] Like intuitive 'deciphering' of a meal, 'self-evidence' – or intuition more generally – is not to be contrasted with rationality but 'anchor[ed]...in the experience the individual has of the logical properties of social forms' (IM: 281). The advance over the preceding paper is that Douglas explicitly sets out to delineate different social forms and their correlates. In a recurrent turn of phrase she tells us:

> the emotions are channelled down the familiar grooves cut by social relations and their requirements of consistency, clarity and reliability of expectations...the intuition of the logic of these social experiences is the basis for finding the *a priori* in nature...This is the level of experience at which the guts reaction of bewilderment...is strengthened by potential fury, shock and loathing.
>
> (IM: 280–81)

From this vantage, she returns explicitly to the attitude accorded to mediators – but now in comparative perspective. In her earlier article, Douglas had already sought to demonstrate that the pig in the Hebrew scheme of things belonged in a taxonomic class of one (an animal that was cloven-hoofed but not cud-chewing). If, following Durkheim and Mauss as well as Lévi-Strauss, taxonomy organizes nature so that social rules are mirrored and reinforced by this reflection, and if boundary-crossing is forbidden, then it is comprehensible that both marriage and animal classification should conform to an intuitive reaction of disgust against the crossing or confusion of boundaries. 'What fellowship has a wolf with a lamb?', asked Ecclesiasticus (IM: 310).

Using the same correlation, we would note that Lele enjoin marriage between cross-cousins, and the Karam's semi-complex system of prohibitions tended to scatter marriages. The pangolin, that mediator *par excellence* for Lele, is treated positively; while the Karam's attitude to the cassowary mirrors the ambiguities of their relations with their own cousins. Expectations of exchanges between different human communities, on the one hand, and exchanges between humans and animals, on the other, are morally evaluated in terms of their isomorphism.

The Israelites' rules tended to encourage close marriage. Israelites did not distinguish between cross and parallel cousins,[5] and they were allowed to marry first cousins on either side.

> Here is a people who prefer their boundaries to remain intact. They reckon any attempt to cross them a hostile intrusion. They expect no good to come of external exchange and have no rules to facilitate it…A people whose experience of foreigners is disastrous will cherish perfect categories, reject exchange and refuse doctrines of mediation.
>
> (IM: 304, 307)

At what stage in their historical experience might Israelites have decided that mixing with foreigners was disastrous? The answer has only some elements of the response Douglas was to offer when returning to these issues over a decade later. Again following Leach, she noted that particular worries seem to revolve around the position of half-blooded Israelites; like anomalous animals they failed to satisfy the membership criteria of a single classificatory category unequivocally. The editorial work of the Priestly Code, known as P, was begun by small groups of scholars during the Babylonian exile and lasted until the end of the fifth century BC. However, Leviticus 11 and Deuteronomy 14, the chapters concerned with animal classification, are held to predate P and simply to have been incorporated by the exiled scholars out of respect for the past. Douglas believes this is unfair to P, now characterized as an individual, who

> went on calmly applying the analogy of purity to the rules of the camp, the altar, the body and also to animal kinds…In his theology there could be no conflict between logic and holiness.
>
> (IM: 308)

P, therefore, is the logician of a people apart:

> A group of humans that sees itself as a distinct species will not need to mirror in nature their society seen as a system of regulated transactions with other humans.
>
> (IM: 311)

These two essays are not less imaginative for being, in Douglas's later opinion, erroneous in serious respects. Together they constitute ingenious statements of one of the stronger versions of isomorphism between social experience and classifications that she has tried to establish on the basis of the logic of inclusion and exclusion. At several points they uncannily foreshadow her re-entry to the same issues from the middle 1980s. However, the intervening period had seen further modifications to her theoretical battery which we need to itemize provisionally in order to proceed.

RETURNING TO THE OLD TESTAMENT

Theoretical developments

As I write, Mary Douglas's recent contributions to Old Testament scholarship include a monograph on the Book of Numbers and several articles, including provisional re-analyses and a monograph in press on the Book of Leviticus, all published since 1993 and representing work begun in earnest in the late 1980s after her professional retirement. Because this productive stream shows no sign of drying, the remainder of this chapter concerns a work in progress that may eventually address the entire Pentateuch (the first five books of the Old Testament: Genesis, Exodus, Leviticus, Numbers and Deuteronomy). Douglas's initial interest in mining the Old Testament for appropriate examples, which then became a vehicle for theoretical rethinking, has eventually become the main focus of her work – to the extent that she contemplates devoting part of her eighth decade to learning Hebrew (in press, 'Why I have to learn Hebrew').

Before presenting something of their argument, it may be helpful to summarize some ways – other than with respect to the sheer detail of their involvement with the Old Testament – in which Douglas's recent ideas differ from those in her earlier writings.

1   What Douglas and her circle call 'cultural theory' comes in more than one version. The version that underpins her monograph on the Book of Numbers predicts that a single 'culture' or 'classification' will be given different slants, or 'cultural biases', depending upon the social organization of the group within society using it. The vocabulary to describe this relation still needs to be made consistent, but the difference it makes to her previous analysis is clear. Instead of a Jewish community that speaks with a single voice, the version of cultural theory used in *In the Wilderness* (1993a) persuades her to look instead for contention among groupings with rival political visions. The idea of the Jews as a 'distinct species' (see above) is now presented as a position among others, that triumphs only in the later Mishnaic period. The dating of the redaction of the Pentateuch (and of the books of Ezra and Nehemiah) becomes even more crucial. Other than in

the textual sources that are themselves under analysis, there are few clues to the immediate social and political environment in which the editors (P) did their work that might help identify the contemporary interest groups. Despite these difficulties, the first point of which to take note is that 'cultural theory' altered the way Douglas thought about social positionality by making plurality a normal expectation.

2 Her development of the notion of 'cultural motif' (discussed in Chapter 8) brought greater complexity in a second respect: recognizing the specificity of the symbolic. Key symbols, and clusters of symbols, preoccupy her later far more than her earlier work. On closer inspection Douglas decided that the Biblical doctrine of defilement turns out to be highly unusual in that it is scarcely coercive for the general populace (quite the obverse of the apt illustration of a universal tendency that *Purity and Danger* portrayed it, and especially unlike hygiene (IW: 21)). Equally unusual was the aniconism of Jewish religion: monotheism as such is not uncommon, but a God who could not be imaged, who tolerated no other gods, and in whose name an exhaustive purity code was enforced, was and is (IW: 27).

3 Cultural theory specified that differing social positions should correlate significantly with – and even explain – the different biases in the appeals those occupying them made to cultural motifs in explanation and justification of their courses of action. It was therefore incumbent on the analyst to identify a diversity of interests and associate them with different shades of worldview. To do this required a more precise specification of historical context than she had risked previously. Accepting that the final redaction of the Pentateuch occurred between the destruction of the first temple in 586 BCE and the edict of Cyrus allowing the remnant of the Jews to return to Jerusalem, Douglas goes further and identifies the priestly party as editors of the Pentateuch and attributes to them a universalist doctrine of purity which was opposed to a theory of the defilement of the foreigner and outsider which she associates with some elements of popular thought, or the party of government, or both. Implicitly, the five books of the Pentateuch recorded the propaganda of the priestly faction, while the books of Ezra and Nehemiah represent something of the ideas of their government opponents. By the time of its redaction, the Pentateuch already referred to events that had occurred many centuries before – but these events had a particular immediacy to a people returning to the promised land. The return is therefore the context in which to read the Pentateuch as a contemporary document. However, the books of Ezra and Nehemiah – which purport to record events contemporary with the return – seem to be datable to the fourth or third centuries BCE, that is, two centuries later. The Pentateuch is historically a product of the community that was to build the Second Temple in Jerusalem, while Ezra and Nehemiah are reconstructions of this period on the part of authors looking back from the situation that prevailed two centuries later.[6] It is to that later period we should attribute intense

concern with Jewish exclusivity in both marital relations and access to the land.

4   Why had this not been realized before? Douglas's boldest notion is to break with any residual, universalizing structuralism and propose instead that the books of the Pentateuch shared with much other literature of the ancient world a compositional framework based on a ring. This structure would have been realized by the priests, noted by their informed readers and listeners, but become opaque to later commentators after the destruction of the Second Temple. Only by reading the Pentateuch through the genre conventions of its own compositional structure is it possible to restore to it the meaning its priestly editors had intended and its contemporary readership recognized.

These emphases on social positionality, cultural motif, cultural or political bias, and the genre characteristics of the Old Testament sources – or rather the relations between them – constitute, to my mind, the theoretical originality of Douglas's later body of work on Jewish history. Now, to look at her arguments in closer detail.

The Pentateuch as historical account

When the exiles returned after forty years in Babylon, Judah had become a province of the Persian Empire and was surrounded by kingdoms to which it was genealogically related in terms of the account of the first two books of the Pentateuch. As Douglas sees the situation, most prominently at stake between the returnees and those who remained behind would have been two issues: access to land and the type of relations which should prevail between Judah and its neighbours. The exact identity of the redactors of the pre-existing traditions of the books is thus crucial, since they will have edited the, largely received, materials at their disposal with an eye to their own biases in political matters. What were these materials and how might the editors' hand be detected in its arrangement?

The first five books of the Old Testament, known as the Pentateuch (five scrolls in Greek) or the Torah (law in Hebrew), have conventionally been treated as an integrated work. After recounting the creation and the flood in the early chapters of Genesis, the narrative is concerned with Abraham and his descendants. The five books cover a period that begins with the covenant between God and Abraham, by which Abraham's descendants are promised the land of Canaan, and ends with the death of Moses just before the promised land is entered. If the historicity of the events is conceded in general terms, then they occupy at least six centuries to the death of Moses in 1250 BCE. However, in the form in which we know it, the Pentateuch is generally reckoned to be the work of priestly editors working during the fifth century BCE – at least seven hundred years after the events described. (A parallel contemporary project would be concerned with British history between 650–1250 AD.) Technically their editorial work is called 'redaction'. 'Redaction criticism', as a branch of Biblical scholarship, has among its aims the dating of the redaction of the texts we now possess and the attribution of elements of them – often on internal grounds of language, style, lexicon, internal reference, and so forth – to the lost texts on which the editors drew. The difference between the date of the events recalled and the date of redaction is, as I noted above, crucial to Douglas's argument.

She follows recent redaction criticism to argue that the priestly editors of the Pentateuch were working at the time of the building of the Second Temple. This followed the return of the exiles who had been sent to Babylon after Jerusalem had fallen to Nebuchadnezzar II and been destroyed. When Cyrus, king of Persia, defeated the Babylonians, he encouraged the exiles to return home and rebuild Jerusalem, the capital of Judah (the southern kingdom), which became a Persian province under the rule of a *satrap*. A couple of important considerations follow. The redaction of the Pentateuch took place under circumstances that could not help but evoke the earlier exile of the Israelites and their previous return to the promised land culminating in the building of the First Temple by Solomon. The story of the covenant had a particular salience. Moreover, the redaction took place amidst the concerns attendant on the return of exiles to a community which was not extinct. Douglas particularly detects problems about the allocation of land between the exiles and those who had remained. Her assumption is that the political situation contemporary with the redaction will be reflected in the way in which the ancient history of the Israelites is recalled and motivated. This, of course, is no more than a standard assumption about the interestedness of historical accounts in contemporary politics, and one familiar to ethnohistorians. Thus, she dismisses her own previous assumption that the purity regulations simply reflected an enclaved society as facile – matters were far more complex. Furthermore, her own procedure of excising only the dietary laws (or, subsequently, dietary laws plus temple regulations) comes to seem arbitrary. The Pentateuch needs to be seen as a whole in the context of its date of redaction – some of the evidence for which can be found in other books of the Old Testament recounting the circumstances of the Second Temple community.

All this implies putting the Pentateuch into a context, and especially into the political context of its redactors rather than that of the actors who appear in the narrative. This, again, is standard anthropological method, especially as developed in Africa with reference to oral histories, and is not inimical to historical reconstruction but essential to detecting the interestedness of source materials (see 1993l).

We need to recap briefly some of the contents of the books of the Pentateuch. Genesis begins with the creation, fall and flood before following the fortunes of Abraham who journeys from Ur to Canaan, the land his descendants are promised by God. He is then forced into Egypt by hunger. Eventually he bears Isaac, whose sons are Esau and Jacob. Jacob (Israel) rather than his elder brother is heir to the promises made by God to Abraham. Jacob has children by his wife Rachel and her handmaiden Leah. Joseph, Rachel's long-awaited first son, is sold into slavery in Egypt and eventually joined by the remainder of the family which lives in Egypt for four centuries. Genesis depicts the twelve sons of Jacob as the ancestors of the tribes of Israel and traces the descent of other peoples of the known world from Noah.[7] The Pentateuch can thus speak of contemporary political relations through the idiom of patrilineal genealogy – again a familiar idea for Africanist anthropologists of Douglas's generation (see Chapter 3).

Exodus opens when Joseph's people have been in Egypt for 370 years and have become slaves. Moses and Aaron are descendants of Jacob. God visits plagues on Egypt to assure the liberation of his people, eventually killing the first-born sons of Egypt. Escaping through the parting seas, the Israelites set up the tabernacle. The first-born of Israel thus belong to the Lord, but they are redeemed against the Levites who will become the priests of Israel but henceforth will no longer be numbered among the tribes to inherit the promised land. The Israelites wander for forty years in the Sinai peninsula and receive the Ten Commandments.

The remaining three books, Leviticus, Numbers and Deuteronomy, continue the narrative and detail the terms of the covenant between God and Israel. Leviticus recounts the detailed laws given to Moses by God on Mount Sinai. It takes its name from the fact that it was Aaron and his descendants who administered the laws and tended the tabernacle assisted by the other Levites. Numbers resumes the narrative of Israel 'in the wilderness' (its Hebrew title), beginning two years after the escape from Egypt and ending on the eve of entry into Canaan when Moses dies before entering the promised land. Numbers, therefore, shows the fulfilment of the promises made by God in the first two books. It takes its name from the numbering, or counting, of the tribes of Israel recounted both towards the beginning and at the end of the book. Deuteronomy hardly figures in Douglas's account to date, so it is enough for us to note that this book records Moses' final addresses to Israel prior to entry to the promised land, applying the laws stated in Exodus, Leviticus and Numbers to settled life in Canaan.

Ring composition

There has never been much doubt that the Pentateuch may be seen as a unity for all that it is made up of different genres of narrative, genealogies, laws, instructions about rituals, poetry, etc. Douglas would like to demonstrate a tighter unity to the Pentateuch than has previously been recognized, and has so far proposed rereadings for Leviticus and Numbers. In both cases she detects evidence of 'ring composition'. Contrary to accusations of incoherence, repetition or logical weakness on the part of the priestly scholars for the way in which they cobbled together extant texts into the received versions, Douglas proposes that 'the Book of Numbers is a work of consummate artistry' (1994a: 194) and 'Leviticus has undoubtedly an elegant literary form. Like a mosaic, or a Cosmati pavement' (1993f: 128).

Ring composition is a demanding poetic technique and all too likely to appear chaotic to anyone not attuned to its method (learn the exotic conventions – another familiar anthropological point). The thematic materials in a ring composition are unified by their arrangement. The idea is simple in its essentials – and this is all I have space to discuss – but the reader may easily envisage how complexly these essentials can be made to ramify. The materials set out at the beginning of a poetic construction are rejoined at its end – thus the 'ring'. Because ring composition involves the arrangement of units of text, it is particularly useful as a technique for the task of the Pentateuch redactors: selecting and organizing existing texts and traditions. Without independent access to these earlier texts we cannot know how the redactors selected their materials, we can however ask why they arranged things as they did. The ring form is particularly suited to exploring an issue by exemplification and analogy. A question can be set out in the beginning and rejoined with new insight at the end. Thus the beginning and ending will be crucial. Douglas calls the final passage a latch, since it closes upon the opening – like an epilogue, which resolves a question stated initially by returning to it.

Ring composition not only closes the beginning and end of a text on to one another but governs the techniques for navigating between these two points. The intervening materials are divided into two halves which develop outwards from the opening and then back towards the conclusion. The 'turning point', where the direction of the narrative is reversed, is particularly important and may reiterate in some condensed form the content of the entire cycle. Diagrammatically, the materials can be set out counter-clockwise on a page in two columns (for Numbers, see Diagram 1). The left-hand column lists the textual units downwards from the beginning to the turning point; the right-hand column works upwards from the turning point to rejoin the opening section. Arranged in this fashion the textual units can also be read laterally, in what Douglas calls parallel 'rungs': such that a section on the outward journey towards the turning corresponds to a section on the homeward leg. Once it is conceded that the textual materials of a ring composition can be conceived and arranged in this fashion, then it is evident that there are various ways to read them: not just from beginning to end, but in terms of the opening and latch compared to the turning point, or across the rungs. The sophistication that Douglas detects in the redaction adds great complication to this simplified account; for instance, individual textual units may themselves be arranged as small ring compositions, and the internal organization of units can take different forms – repetition, inversion, and so forth. I shall have to ignore these details which are very consequential for specialist scholars deciding the plausibility of her analysis. I shall also have to ignore another issue likely to preoccupy specialists – the identification of the units of text that have been subject to ring composition (a subject on which Douglas sought specialist help). Evidently this is crucial, the textual units are of highly disparate length, and it is the distinction between them (in terms of subject matter, genre, or via a recurrent introductory phrase) that allows the

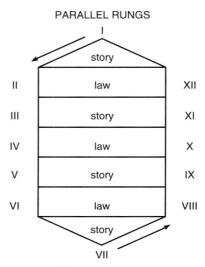

Diagram 1 Parallel rungs in the Book of Numbers

Source: *In the Wilderness*: 117, diagram 2

analysis to proceed (Crenshaw IW/Rel; IW/CBQ). But since our interest is with Douglas's analysis let's concede her the technical points to see what she seeks to demonstrate. I shall follow with two examples: first her provisional reanalysis of Leviticus, because this has been a recurrent theme of her writings, and then her completed project on the Book of Numbers, which actually furnishes an easier example of the method.

Leviticus again[8]

Whereas her earlier analysis of Leviticus concentrated on the rules of edibility and purity – presenting the book as the product of obsession with purity on the part of a grim logician – Douglas's reading of the book as a whole leads to different conclusions (1993e, f, 1994c, 1995f, g). As a book of rules put together by priestly editors – a manual, we should note, and not the description of an everyday set of behaviours – Leviticus is liberal in many respects:

> the book insists over and over again that the poor and the stranger are to be included in the requirements of the laws. In saying, 'Love the stranger as thyself' (Lev 19: 34) the rules of Leviticus are applied to every person.
>
> (1995f: 240)

On this and other evidence, the work of redaction seems attributable to priests who favour a policy of coexistence or even solidarity with such neighbours as Samaria. Perhaps they reflect in part the opinions of those who remained behind when the rest of the community went into Babylonian exile.[9]

Leviticus explicates the Laws given to Moses to govern the covenant, or solemn and binding agreement, between the Lord and Israel. Obligations are recognized on both sides and signalled in the 'ending turn' (the penultimate chapter) which expatiates on the righteousness of the Lord. The ending matches the turn of the entire book which is concerned with the righteousness of the people. The exact terms of the covenant are, as it were, enclosed between these two statements of its overall purpose. The outward leg of the book is predominantly concerned with regulations governing the relations between the people of Israel and the Lord, and the various categories of sacrifice they must make to him either because some things are his in principle or because things can be dedicated to him as a way of making amends. The classifications of edible animals, and the sub-classification of animals fit for the altar, are only a small part of this overall regulation which also covers sexual relations, birth, and diseases which disfigure the form of people and animals (blemishes of various kinds), and conditions which confound the inside and outside of people (menstruation, birth, suppuration all treated together). The homeward leg of the book concentrates on the responsibilities of the priests applying the same rules to their bodily condition and to the condition of sacrificial animals, specifying the condition of their wives and noting the occasions in the calendar on which atonement is to be made. Reading the book as a ring composition reveals that various of its themes are pursued in parallel: thus the bodily condition of the people of Israel is taken up in the parallel section on priests; specific blemishes requiring sacrifice are mirrored in a section detailing the occasions on which atonement is to be made. This summary greatly understates the complexity of the analysis, but let us see where it leads.

If Douglas's analysis is correct then Leviticus should be read analogically in terms of the comparisons it implies. These analogies give coherence to the worldview. The book can be understood to say that the covenant demands righteousness on the part of the people which will be reciprocated justly by God's righteousness (ending turn and turn). Things that already belong to God must be offered to him on regular occasions of atonement, they are His as the land is His. Other things, not already His, can be dedicated to Him to atone for sins of commission or for regular ('natural') punctuations of correct order. How is this order and its breaching conceived? Douglas argues that the idiom involves the idea of a covering and its tearing; atonement is making good a rent in the fabric of the covering. In order to make reparation, God has given people blood. They may not ingest blood or eat animals that themselves eat blood. The covering contains blood; thus, the preoccupation of the book with blemishes and with (what is translated as) leprosy: a range of conditions of suppuration (see Lewis 1987; Douglas 1996f). Fat, stipulated as an offering to God, is also conceived as a kind of covering. Thus, there is a series of coverings: fat, the skin, the temple, all of which may be subject to rending which has to recovered, and this is what sacrifice achieves.

Contrary to her previous analysis of Jewish separatism, Douglas notes that arguments about membership of the congregation seem to be absent from this book, which is a disquisition on wholeness and blood, and the sources of uncleanness ranging from contact with unclean things, to blemish, suppuration, moral transgression and idolatry – all presented as analogous to one another. Even the forbidden animals can be accounted for in terms of doctrines of blood and blemish. By specifying herbivorous animals as the proper kind of meat, and further detailing cloven-hoofed, cud-chewing quadrupeds as quintessential of these, the priestly editor has guarded against ingestion of blood, even against ingestion at one remove by consuming predators or carrion-eating creatures. These injunctions seem to account equally for the precluded animals and birds. To go further requires explication of the sense of blemish, which 'means some-thing superfluous or something lacking, or crushed, broken or cut' (1993f: 125); whatever is not 'meet' in the Old English sense. Douglas suggests that forbidden species not covered by the injunction against eating blood have something lacking or superfluous about them that would be included in the sense of blemish. To eat them would be an injustice additional to those they already bear (1993e: 20–21); rather than being reviled as abominations, the 'forbidden' animals are stricken 'objects of divine compassion and sympathy' (1996f: 101, 105). Boldly, Douglas suggests the priests' purpose in this account is to present a negative theology, at variance with populist theories of defilement:

> The body is a theological microcosm: the blemished, bleeding, leaking, suppurating, torn body, now presented as a woman, now a man, now as garment, then a house, now as an imperfect priest, now an inadequate offering, and then climaxing as the sanctuary defiled, is an image of Israel in the horrible condition she would be in, if unsanctified.
>
> (1993f: 129)

Numbers

Once the ring composition of Numbers has also been detected it is easier to read it and Leviticus together. Numbers fulfils the covenant and expectations of the earlier books of the Pentateuch. Most that happens in it has been preordained; the genealogical structuring around descent from Noah of the peoples neigh-bouring the Israelites – some cursed, others like the Israelites in some respects – can be shown to foreshadow the way events are going to turn out. A brief résumé of the compositional structure of Numbers is required before we can pursue the analysis.

In Douglas's reading (IW), Numbers consists of twelve main sections which are much more readily discernible than was the case for Leviticus (see Diagrams

THE BOOK IN A RING

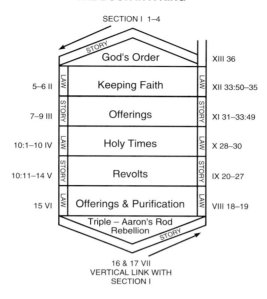

Diagram 2 The Book of Numbers in a ring

Source: *In the Wilderness*: 118, diagram 3

1 and 2). Stylistically distinct sections dealing with eternal law (in which only Moses or Aaron is named) alternate with sections of story (which have spatial and temporal parameters, action and plot). The division into twelve sections has been related by the editor to the twelve-month year, with especial significance accorded to the seventh month and, thus, the seventh stage of the composition. Sections I and VII form a continuous narrative which is begun as the opening of the book and continued in its turn. If these two sections are placed as the beginning and turn, then the other ten sections can be arranged as five stages setting out and five coming back (in similar fashion to Leviticus), yielding five rungs of paired sections. The rungs are also tightly structured: the first, third and fifth rung are law rungs, while the second and fourth are narrative rungs.

If this is the basic structure, then how does it illuminate the sense of the content? Section I involves three numberings: first, of the people of the twelve tribes to inherit the land who are distinguished from the Levites (symbolically the first-born of the Israelites) and protectors of the tabernacle. Then, the families of Moses and Aaron are told to stand apart because they are in charge of the sanctuary. Third, the families of the Levites are numbered, among whom the descendants of Kohath are singled out by being referred to first despite not being first-born. They are not to come near the tabernacle. Each numbering is accompanied with warnings of the dire consequences of failure to respect these separations. These warnings are fulfilled in section VII when there are three rebellions: the first – of the Kohathites on behalf of the Levites against Aaron's authority – eventuates in the earth swallowing up the Kohathites, the leading Levites and the Reubenites. Then the leading men of the tribes of Israel are consumed by fire. When the people complain of this holocaust, they are consumed by plague until God's wrath is averted by Aaron's waving the censer. After these rebellions have been quelled, Aaron tells the heads of the twelve tribes to put their names on their rods. Left overnight in the tabernacle, the rod of the Levites bearing Aaron's name bursts into bloom. The twelve tribes numbered in the beginning are thus substituted by the two rods: of Judah and of Aaron. Since all rods have been in Aaron's charge this signals the ascendency of the priests (and of God) over Judah. The axis between sections I and VII halves the Book of Numbers. An unpaired, thirteenth section, slightly anomalous in being both law and narrative, relates to both sections I and VII and closes the ring with a significance we shall address at the end of this chapter.

The relations between sections I, VII and XIII both halve the Book of Numbers and produce its textual closure. The rungs of paired stories (rung 2: sections III–XI; rung 4: sections V–IX) are made up of four narratives to which I shall turn, albeit briefly, after discussion of the law rungs.

The three law rungs (rung 1: sections II–XII; rung 3: sections IV–X; rung 5: sections VI–VIII) relate back to the legal stipulations made in Leviticus. Indeed, the laws in Numbers are likely to seem ill-organized, repetitive and somewhat haphazard read outside their broader organizing framework. Read as rungs, Douglas generalizes that the first and third rungs are respectively concerned with the negative cult involving defilement and purification; the intermediate second rung is concerned with the positive cult detailing the holy days of the formal cult.

Rung 1 deals in section II with the boundaries of the land and especially its defilement by shedding blood through homicide; in section XII it deals with the exclusion of lepers from the camp, with adultery and contact with corpses.

Rung 3 (the epicentre of the book, confirming to Douglas's mind that the entire book is centred in the law rather than its narrative structure) announces the occasions on which trumpets shall be used (sections IV and X).

Rung 5, section VI outlines the rules for preparing sacrifice, emphasizes that all (Israelite and stranger alike) are to be subject to the same law, and distinguishes inadvertent from deliberate sin – the deliberate sinner to be utterly cut off. The corresponding section VIII outlines why holy things are dedicated to the priests and Levites, how various rites of purification are to be carried out (for Israelites and strangers alike), and emphasizes that the unclean person must be cut off from the congregation (like the intentional sinner). Both sections conclude that these laws are eternal; they are to be recalled for all generations.

The first and fifth rungs summarize the negative side of the priest's duty: the necessity to atone for sin (make whole and cover). The middle or third rung concerns the positive duties when trumpets are used to call men to arms or to celebrate one of the many festivals.

The two story rungs (consisting of the paired narrative sections III and XI, V and IX) elicit a complex analysis which we can follow in part only. The stories are sequential (III, V, IX, XI). The first of them describes the dedication of the altar before the events of I; each of the leaders of the tribes brings the same offerings (which have been described in Leviticus). The Levites are purified and presented as a gift to Aaron from the Lord. The Passover is celebrated on the fourteenth day of the second month and God guides them in the wilderness as a cloud by day and a fire by night.

In section V the people are grumbling about eating manna and missing the meat they could have eaten in Egypt. Miriam and Aaron rebel against Moses' authority, and Miriam is shamed by God with leprosy, a punishment later commuted to exclusion from the camp. Spies bring false reports of grasshoppers and giants in Canaan. God's curse on Israel is followed by their defeat at Hormah.

The third of the story sections (IX to match V) occurs after the three rebellions which Douglas treats as the turning point of the Book of Numbers (VII). Miriam dies and the request for water is answered by the miracle of water from the rock. Then Aaron dies, and the Israelites are victorious at Hormah. Further complaints are met by fiery serpents and the well of water. Then more victories, and the remarkable episode when King Balak of Moab sends for Balaam to curse his enemies, but Balaam is able only to repeat God's blessings three times. Israel again deserts the Lord by idolatry and is redeemed by the slaying of Cozbi and Zimri. The new census is taken.

The fourth story section (XI to match III) begins with war against Midian and the slaughter of the Moabite women who have seduced the men of Israel. Tribute is given to the Lord for victory. Reuben and Gad are granted their land east of Jordan for fighting against the Canaanites. Moses summarizes their settings out.

The thematic development involves a change of mood from defeat through to victory. The first rung shares the theme of reciprocity between the people and the Lord which opens the stories, and both stories end on the theme of setting out. In section V the Lord has cursed his people, but during section IX he renews his promise to them through Balaam.

Aside from its structural cohesion, the Book of Numbers also employs recurrent metaphors. Notably, Israel is often imaged as a female character. Misdeeds recurrently involve women or are occasioned by them. However, women are not treated as impure as such, rather (as discussed in Chapter 8):

> Thoroughgoing hierarchists believe that gender polarity means that women are only inferior in an inferior context, and that their role is to represent the whole against sectional interests.
>
> (IW: 198)

Miriam's apostasy against her own brother Moses is thus made to stand for the people as a whole, and her punishment with leprosy mirrors the gravity of her crime in the most utter defilement of her body. Yet she was forgiven even as the Lord would forgive Israel's repentance (IW: 203).

All that has been foretold in the earlier books comes to pass, and specifically the blessings and cursings of Jacob on his sons: Reuben, eldest son of Jacob and Leah, was cursed for seducing his father's concubine; his descendants (sons of Peleth) join Korah's revolt against Moses. Simeon and Levi were cursed for their attack on Schechem; Zimri, the Simeonite, dies for his – unspecified, or unnameable – shocking behaviour with a Midianite woman near the tent of meeting. Levi's descendant Aaron supported his sister Miriam's revolt against Moses. However, Jacob blessed Judah and Joseph, whose descendants Caleb and Joshua were the only members of their generation who survived to enter the promised land; Judah meant Jerusalem to contemporary readers while the remnant of Joseph (or Joseph's younger son Ephraim) was Samaria (or Schechem) the historic capital of Israel which, although destroyed by the Assyrians, remained home to some who claimed to be co-religionists with those at Jerusalem. The genealogy proves a sure guide to the outcomes depicted in Numbers, since Edom, to the south of Jerusalem – although it denies Moses' people passage – is not attacked because it consists of the descendants of Esau, Jacob's older brother. Once all the promises are fulfilled, the stage is set for Balaam's praises.

According to Douglas, Ezra and Nehemiah, as the party of government allied to the Persians, are corrupt local officials returned from exile and owing their positions to the Persian Empire. The priests, and redactors of the Pentateuch, represent the people who have remained the intervening forty years in Jerusalem – a settled community with close ties to its neighbours (including Samaria) which construes the inclusiveness of the covenant generously. These themes are satirized in the story of Balaam. The donkey threatened by its rider, Balaam, for stopping before the angel of the Lord is Israel. If Balak is the Persian Emperor, then Balaam must be his provincial governor. When he opens his mouth to find he can utter only the praises of Israel, Balaam names Judah and Joseph (Jerusalem and Samaria) together.

From the books of Nehemiah and Ezra, we know that, as a returnee governor of Judah appointed by the Persian emperor, Nehemiah along with the priest Ezra favoured the exclusionary interpretation of the covenant. Ezra forbade intermarriage between the people of Israel and the people of the land; and the books of Ezra and Nehemiah seem to record what we would now call an 'ethnic cleansing', since Ezra assumes the right on behalf of the Persian Emperor Artaxerxes to confiscate the lands of any man refusing to renounce his foreign wife and children (1994c: 288–89). The 'seed of Israel' is restricted to mean only the returnees, the remainder finding themselves accused of defilement. By contrast, Leviticus and Numbers, as priestly documents, propose an alternative politics, stressing intention and repentance, and the equality of all in the eyes of God.

Tentatively, Douglas identifies the opposition to Ezra–Nehemiah with Eliashib, the high priest and apparently not one of the exiles. The story of Balaam could serve as Eliashib's version of the events that Nehemiah recounts. And the politics of the priestly redactors might explain the inclusion of the problematic thirteenth section of the Book of Numbers, a legal passage in narrative mode which previous commentators have thought to be little more than a tacked-on afterthought. Moses is asked by the sons of Joseph (the people of Ephraim) to adjudicate a concern they have about what happens to the property of five daughters (who have inherited in the absence of sons and might subsequently marry outside their tribes), when the Jubilee – involving remission of debts – comes around. Will their property be added to that of their husbands' people? The Jubilee, involving remission of debts and slavery, is mentioned not in Numbers but in Leviticus. However, the women's inheritance seems to have nothing to do with debt and, therefore, with the Jubilee. Nonetheless, Moses replies by commending them for having raised the issue and repeats four times that inheritance is not to be transferred between the tribes of Israel.

In fact the issue of the Jubilee is far from clear-cut in biblical sources; should it be celebrated every fifty or seventy years? And when was the last? A jubilee of sorts was held during Nebuchadnezzar's siege of Jerusalem, but the slave owners reneged on it once the siege was lifted. Implicitly, Nehemiah seems to be celebrating a jubilee in returning the land to the exiles. Nehemiah's railing against those who married foreign wives is likely to involve the same people against whom claims for the return of land are being lodged. Douglas suspects Nehemiah appropriated land from the descendants of the sons of Jacob who had not gone into exile. Thus the injunction – to return to everyone what was their right – needs careful exegesis: is it to refer only to the exiles or to all the sons of Jacob? This final peroration latches with the opening in which the inheritances of the tribes of Israel had been stated. Numbers and Leviticus are, Douglas argues, 'utterly opposed to any theory of hereditary taint' (1994c: 291), indeed the 'priestly editors appear as universalising theologians teaching a brand of liberation theology' (1995h: 14).

Numbers is a book of triumph and forgiveness whose message was lost after the destruction of the Second Temple when the fashion for literary parallelism had given way to metric verse, and the political climate had changed as Samaria competed with Jerusalem and the dream of reunification as well as praise of unity began to ring hollow (1995h: 23). Parallels with the range of political positions occupied in contemporary Israel may be implicit in Douglas's account, but they are certainly not lost on her.

CONCLUDING NOTE

I have touched upon only some of the broader points of Douglas's historical ethnography of fifth-century BCE Jerusalem and am not competent to evaluate the finer points of criticism to which it has been subjected.[10] However, I hope my account is sufficient to demonstrate how much she has become – as in relation to several other disciplines previously – something of a specialist in the field she thought to visit. More remarkably, we see a theory-led, radical rethinking of what is probably – to judge by reprints and references – the most famous of her ethnographic tableaux, or paradigms in the Kuhnian sense of exemplary demonstrations. Scholars who continue to refer to the thirty-year-old analysis of *Purity and Danger* as if it were Douglas's last word on the subject should at least recognize that the famous 'abominations' of Leviticus are, in Douglas's later view, not abominations at all, and that the 'message' of the editors of Leviticus is not one of ethnic exclusivity.

The resolution of her theoretical insights in terms of the competing interests of hierarchical, inclusive priests, and sectarian, divisive politicians reiterates a dominant binarism in her own thought which we need now to examine in more detail.

Notes

1 Old Testament sources were important generally to the Oxford transmission of social anthropology because Robertson Smith was taught as so important a precursor of Durkheim (see Chapter 2). Mary Douglas also recalls the particular impact of a paper on the relation between 'enslavement and the early Hebrew lineage system' – derived from his doctoral dissertation – which Franz Steiner delivered to the 1948 international anthropology conference (see Chapter 3), which she also attended (published posthumously as Steiner 1954a).

2 Douglas's earliest antipathy to structuralism seems to have mellowed as it was domesticated in the form of a more sociological 'Anglo Saxon' structuralism, the broadest terms of which she shared with, for instance, E.R. Leach and V.W. Turner. In this sociologized form, structuralist methodology became a more or less common intellectual property of British-trained social anthropologists of the period.

In French, 'alliance' has the same sense as in English but foregrounds the more occasional English meaning of 'marriage'. At the time of its introduction, French structuralist, 'alliance' theory (emphasizing exchange of women between in-laws) was seen as opposed, rather than complementary, to British functionalist 'descent' theory (emphasizing inter-generational relations between parents and children). Contemporary kinship theorists generally incline to seeing the articulation of affinal exchange with inter-generational relations as critical, thereby undercutting the antagonism between the two schools.

3 For other efforts to resolve the identities of the birds of Leviticus and thus the principles of their classification, see Carroll 1978, Hunn 1979, Bulmer 1989, Douglas 1993e.

4 The conundrum of the conventional character of similarity is developed further by Douglas in response to the work of the philosopher Nelson Goodman (see Chapter 10).

5 Cross cousins are children of an individual's parents' opposite-sex siblings, and parallel cousins are children of their same-sex siblings. The distinction has been crucial to anthropological analyses of preferred and prohibited partners cross-culturally.

6 J.D.Y. Peel has dubbed as 'presentism' the tendency of anthropologists to index historical accounts to the period of their production and/or promulgation rather than to the period to which they overtly aver (Peel 1984). Douglas has so far proposed a more presentist approach to the Pentateuch than she has to Ezra and Nehemiah; although an article published since *In the Wilderness* suggests movement in the direction of greater even-handedness (1995g: 280–81).

7 The genealogy describes the position of the enemies/neighbours also: the sons of Noah's son Ham (Egypt, Ethiopia, Babylon, Assyria) and of his cursed son Canaan; Ammon and Moab who are collaterally related to Abraham through the offending Lot (who was seduced by his own daughters); and Edom (Idumea) who are descendants of Jacob's elder brother Esau.

8 The reader deserves to be warned that in a published discussion, Mary Douglas has announced a revision of her account of the poetic structure of Leviticus in her monograph on the subject (Douglas, in Sawyer 1996: 57).

9 We are confronted with slight inconsistency in that Douglas attributes to the priestly editors a politics that is compatible with their remaining in Judah, and therefore empathizing with others who also stayed behind (1994c: 286), and a poetics that may have been current in Babylon (1995f: 256). The discrepancy can be resolved, though the number of options for doing so underlines just how little evidence of contemporary political and social organization there is to go on.

10 Readers interested in specialist review could conveniently start with the review colloquium (IW/Rel) and move on to the proceedings of a symposium (Sawyer 1996). Reception of *In the Wilderness* tended to divide scholars on disciplinary grounds: regional historical specialists tended to dwell, predictably, on points of fine interpretation; some of them appeared hostile to a theoretically driven and speculative reading as such (IW/Int, Smart IW/Rel). With differing degrees of enthusiasm, specialists in other disciplines, times or places – and a minority of regional specialists – applauded the novelty and excitement of Douglas's analysis. Strong support for Douglas's evidence of ring composition has come from the classics scholar Kathryn Gutzwiller, who was also alone in recognizing that Douglas had demonstrated the serviceability of the compositional technique by using it in her monograph (Gutzwiller IW/Rel).

Part IV

CONSERVING ANTHROPOLOGICAL MODERNISM

10 DO INSTITUTIONS THINK?

THEORETICAL MARGINALITY

Even her detractors concede that Mary Douglas is a sparkling essayist: her critical machinery embellished with mischievous turns of phrase, and her own insights developed through arresting analogies.[1] There is no doubting she has enlivened debate in the many fields where she has ventured. Grander theoretical ambitions, on the part of someone gifted as epigrammatarian and disciplinary trickster – I lose count of the reviewers who have likened her role to that of the transgressive but endearing Lele pangolin – have been treated less sympathetically. Aside from legitimate scholarly criticism, there has been an occasional note of disdain. In explanation, it could be suggested that Douglas simply had the misfortune to strive for theoretical clarity and system-building when many members of her discipline had concluded these objectives were either unattainable, undesirable, or both. But the postmodern turn against grand narratives has as many detractors as supporters among anthropologists. Or, perhaps her political preferences, broadly if idiosyncratically conservative at a time when the discipline has liked to think itself radically egalitarian (see Chapter 11), have been to blame. There is something to this argument, but there would be more to it were there evidence that her critics had attended closely to her political ideas. Less consequential factors may also have played their part: system-building has been the proper preserve of dour men rather than witty women; and in the expectation of criticism Mary Douglas has often got her retaliation in early. Relations between her supporters and detractors, and between herself and both, may have become matters of loyalty and commitment to an unhelpful degree. Mary Douglas can certainly be 'difficult' when roused, but her male contemporaries were hardly easy, and their foibles occasion affectionate reminiscence. Mary Douglas does not pretend to dispassion or distance in relation to her work – her ironies and wit are superficial rather than evidence of a fashionable questioning of the value of what she, or anthropology as a discipline, is capable of doing, and her Oxford education has left no trace of donnish coolness towards her work.

All these factors played their part, but I want to focus this chapter – dealing with the elaboration of Douglas's theories during the couple of decades subsequent to the publication of *Natural Symbols* – on an alternative explanation for the relative marginality of her ideas in her own discipline, at least in the English-speaking world.[2] The 'British' school of anthropology of the decades between, roughly, 1930–1970, distinguished itself from its 'American' and 'French' counterparts by a concern with the 'social'. Minimally, this meant that explanation involved putting matters into 'social context'. How the 'social' was to be defined, and quite what constituted an adequate account of social 'context', were open to dispute, but to ignore social context was, in the conventional wisdom, plain bad methodology or evidence of the baneful influences of either American 'cultural' anthropology or French 'idealism'. Because Mary Douglas has continued to develop the terms of British anthropology typical of its modernist, or socially contextualizing, phase she has attracted every variety of criticism to which that paradigm is open. Some American cultural anthropologists have berated her for failing to redeem all the promises of social contextualization (e.g. Geertz HIT/NR); some British anthropologists have considered her to be working within an obsolete paradigm; fellow British 'social' anthropologists have criticized her particular developments of an approach they broadly shared. Mary Douglas's consistent effort to clarify the premises of explanation from social context have probably compounded her problems. Few anthropologists eschew explanation from social context in an *ad hoc* manner but, like all theories of relevant context, a theory of social context is difficult to formalize. Like other contexts, social context is potentially unbounded. When there is something in particular to explain, enough context can be brought to bear to explain it in a way that seems adequate; but, when we are talking about explanation by social contextualization as such, quite how much context is adequate is endlessly disputable. Mary Douglas's theoretical writings pushed the method of British social anthropology to a logical extreme at which both its strengths and weaknesses became evident. This, to head off misunderstanding, I consider a service: all methods have strengths and weaknesses, and their judicious application is helped by knowing what these are.

In referring to Mary Douglas's grand theory I may be employing a phrase she would dislike; her ideas are more often presented in the guise of method rather than theory, and synthesis rather than innovation; as she writes of grid and group in *Essays in the Sociology of Perception*, 'The object is not to come up with something original but gently to push what is known into an explicit typology that captures the wisdom of a hundred years of sociology, anthropology and psychology' (1982c: 1). It is little more than convenient fiction to separate theoretical elaborations from practical applications in her writings subsequent to *Natural Symbols*. Not only are the applications occasions for theoretical elaboration, but texts that appear to be exercises in theoretical stock-taking also have their immediate and more substantial problems. The two theoretical texts I examine most closely here are sides of a single coin in this respect. *Cultural Bias*

(1978a/ITAV), slightly predating Douglas's move to the United States, is also concerned with the problem of social withdrawal; *How Institutions Think* (1986a), preceding Douglas's return to the United Kingdom, is additionally a meditation on social solidarity and on justice. Together the two texts show Mary Douglas concerned, not only to conserve the theories of social anthropological modernism, but also to draw out their implications in the interests of a (small c) conservative ideology.

INTENTIONS

In a series of useful overviews, James Spickard distinguished three different formulations of Mary Douglas's grid and group methodology and a further recension in her 'neo-functionalist' cultural theory (Spickard 1984, 1989, 1990, 1991). He envisages her moving between these relatively distinct positions, albeit her overall project has retained a recognizable shape. Douglas's response to his 1989 article suggested he may have been 'too kind' in noting only three versions, she would have had to confess to many more – always supposing she 'were to use the word "version" as he does' (Douglas 1989b: 171). The barb suggests that she would not use the word this way; as she goes on to explain, her consistency follows from what she has been trying to achieve rather than from any particular one of her explicit formulations. Broadly, I shall fall in with her self-assessment; I shall, as Aram Yengoyan has advised, attempt to read 'with' her rather than 'at' her (ITAV/Know). As Spickard rightly recognizes, Douglas has moved on theoretically, but she has left little behind in doing so; the new recensions are amplifications, clarifications, methodological innovations sometimes presented as correcting past errors, but she has not reneged on her original ambitions. What were these?

Mary Douglas has never described herself other than as an anthropologist; her scant respect for conventional disciplinary boundaries is of a piece with this – her effort, post-1970, has been to colonize other specialisms in the name of anthropological method. Douglas's justification for this is simple: anthropological method is better than those on offer elsewhere. When she talks of anthropological method to outsiders, Douglas is using shorthand for the method she defends against other contenders within the subject. I have laboured the sources of Douglas's anthropological method already, but the reader may forgive the briefest synthesis.

Douglas's Oxford training was in a particular recension of Durkheimian sociology: holistic, anti-idealistic, and sociological in a strong sense. 'The central task of anthropology [according to Evans-Pritchard's teaching] was to explore the effects of the social dimension on behaviour' (IM: 212). This programme was being realized in Africanist ethnography, and the precedents for Douglas's excursions into other times and places are invariably to be found in analogies from African anthropology (in large part the ethnography of the 1930s–1960s). To these methodological antecedents, Douglas has allied strongly held personal beliefs, most evidently in her defence of ritual (Chapter 5) and of hierarchical organizations (under her specialized definition of hierarchy – see Chapter 11). Personal preferences and intellectual method are united in the priority (ontologically, epistemologically, methodologically and morally) accorded to a relatively autonomous general conception of sociality and to the more specific conditions under which human sociality can be organized so as to yield an optimal (but never utopian) form of life. From this perspective, it is indeed the case that rather than moving from position to position, Douglas has always occupied the same position. Her work has concentrated on how best to occupy that position, how to defend it from alternatives, and how to explore its ramifications in neighbouring disciplines. In detail the developments have been numerous, complex and occasionally perplexing: diagrams redesigned, new terms introduced to replace old ones, other terms redefined, arguments restated with fresh twists, but fundamentally Douglas's presuppositions have been consistent. Human beings are social creatures; the single most important context of their lives is other people; different forms of society support different systems of belief, and morality. But how is this assumption of the coherence between social environment and ideas to be turned into more than a banality?

We have met many of the initial steps in the argument previously so I need only recap. Subsequent to *Purity and Danger* (1966), Douglas had rejected developmental accounts of history that required different theories to be proposed about 'primitives' and 'moderns'. In order to discount social scale, she emphasizes instead immediate social context – in other words, the relatively unmediated experience of living with other people. *How Institutions Think* is titled in ironic tribute to Lévy-Bruhl's *How Natives Think* (1926); for like Evans-Pritchard, Douglas believes Lévy-Bruhl posed an interesting question entirely wrongly. The answer to 'how natives think' is 'no differently from everyone else'; the answer to how everyone thinks is, by and large, institutionally.

For the detail of her arguments, Douglas draws upon a wide range of favoured sources – anthropologists, sociologists, philosophers, psychologists, educationalists, linguists, historians, theologians; the heroes and traitors of her account increase in number over the years, but she remains loyal to the earliest recruits to their ranks. But her use of these sources subordinates them to intellectual habits of her own, the first of which might be summed up most abstractly, generally and crudely as a penchant for order. Intellectual order is a human requirement; more social order is preferable to less; Douglas's method itself is an ordering. Order is form, in the senses of both clarity and propriety; theoretical assumptions and personal preferences coalesce. But the repeated imposition of criteria of well-orderedness on her materials leads to complicated arguments. Take the idea of form; the apparent antithesis of form is formlessness. But all form is defined against a ground of the formless, so there is a sense in which form presupposes non-form. Criteria of classification produce anomaly, since some items either fail to qualify for inclusion in a class, or satisfy some of the characteristics for inclusion in more than one class. Anomaly is thus consequential on classification; what doesn't fit is just as much part of the classifying exercise as what does. The complementary of both form and non-form is energy (the term recurs page by page in *How Institutions Think*). Energy is life, social life, but it needs to be channelled into 'grooves' that have been cut and deepened by earlier energies. Whether this is for good or bad depends on the design of the channels. Thus, Douglas's highly abstract concern for form, order or structure which appears to be static and typologizing actually imparts a large part of the internal momentum to her theoretical explorations.

A second Douglas penchant, already remarked repeatedly, is to embed all her intellectual borrowings into social context. Ideas do not 'float free', for the channels into which they flow have been created by a thought style embedded in a social form. Like the tendency to reiterate the antithesis form–formless, or order–disorder, the effects of this very general habit of thought are diverse. Sometimes the reference point for social contextualization is the environment of the thinker from whom she is borrowing (or whom she is berating). On other occasions, social context may refer to the social situation under study. The neglect of social factors is always castigated as disastrous; more positively, social factors are often described as explanatory. The negative version of the argument is relatively easy to establish – simply by demonstrating that something which could have been explained has not been, or that some error in reasoning might have been avoided had social factors not been ignored. Justifying the positive form – that social factors explain – is more complex: the social factors have to be specified and distinguished from what they are to explain, and the exact way in which they explain things has to be stated. Because Douglas's habit of referring back to social context is so ingrained, she is forced to deal with the enormous explanatory weight she puts on the idea of society. Two particular problems have to be faced: the first is a temptation to so expand the scope of the idea of the social that it becomes difficult to distinguish between social factors and what they are supposed to explain. If she does succeed in limiting the scope of the social, and making it convincingly explanatory, then she becomes liable to a second charge: that of sociological reductionism.

With these two rather general considerations in mind – the reiteration of the trope of order–disorder and the recourse to social context – I turn to consideration of the elements of Douglas's theory in more detail under the following headings: first culture – as cognition, shared classification, and contention – and then social context.

COGNITION, CLASSIFICATION AND CONTENTION

Cognition: Douglas accepts Durkheim's formulation of the problem of human cognition as her starting point. Following Kant, Durkheim (1915; also Durkheim and Mauss 1903) argued that individual sense impressions could not explain the comprehensible character of the world. Thought required organizing categories which were *a priori*, or prerequisite, to cognition rather than its result. These categories had to be shared to a sufficient degree that people inhabited the same world and could communicate with one another about it. Without such categories the world would be entirely confusing – either continuous and without classes, or wholly discontinuous, composed of distinct and ungeneralizable sense impressions (for our immediate purpose, it doesn't much matter which). Since Durkheim tended to polarize the individual and society as explanatory terms, and because he had already ruled out the individual as the source of shared classifications, the conclusion that society was the source of *a priori* categories was foregone. Quite what this conclusion meant depended on what was to be made of terms like 'source' and 'society'. In the strongest version of the argument, Durkheim argued that the first logical classes were classes of people, and that other phenomena were modelled on these classifications of people (thus people with moieties or lineages might also model their environment on a lineage or moiety system and so forth). As a thesis, this has the advantage of being vigorous but the disadvantage of being rather perplexing by virtue of conflating several steps in an argument and leaving out most of the connections that would allow any judgement of its credibility. Douglas starts from the same premiss as Durkheim and is thus obliged to deal with many of the problems he failed to face. I want to unpack only a few of these as a preamble to discussing her solutions.

The negative implications of the thesis of the social character of the *a priori* are the least interesting and most straightforward to discuss, although both Durkheim and Douglas use them freely in the critical sections of their work. Durkheim, the reader may recall, was concerned among other things to establish the autonomous standing of sociology as an intellectual discipline. Social facts were, he argued, irreducible to facts about individuals. Thus the attempt to build models of society from facts about individual human beings was erroneous and doomed to failure. A number of current approaches shared this individualist fallacy: utilitarianism which tried to derive social solutions from individual preferences (themselves socially given), attempts to reduce social phenomena to individual psychological states (themselves shared within society), attempts to account for religion in terms of faulty individual reasoning (also shared), and so on. The critical side of Durkheimianism is strongly represented in Evans-Pritchard's Cairo essays that influenced Douglas (Chapter 2). While she updates Durkheim's analysis in some of its philosophical aspects, with the help of Wittgenstein, Quine and Goodman (as explained below and Chapter 11), Douglas fundamentally retains Durkheim's argument – that failure to recognize the social foundedness of individuals is pernicious – as her passport into disciplines of more individualistic persuasion.

While useful to browbeat the socially purblind, this does not erect a positive argument. We can admit that neglect of the social (however defined) may be an error, without agreeing how much to anticipate of the social as an explanatory term. Douglas generally attends to two types of work. Following Bartlett's ideas (which she controversially suggested to have been central to Evans-Pritchard's own thinking, Chapter 2) she emphasizes the selectivity of human attention. We tend to recall what is familiar given our cognitive schemata and to reject what is unfamiliar – human beings are conventional creatures. This is especially apparent in the efficiency of memory (as she notes following Halbwachs, 1980d/ITAV). At different times, Douglas has used various metaphors to make this point: talking of 'filters on our perception', 'muffled ears', 'blinkers', a 'thought style', or 'bounded rationality'. The point is that cognition, or thought, or perception, are strongly conventionalized; since this is necessarily the case, there is no point castigating the fact as such. Without conventions we would be unable to classify at all. Two questions follow: where do these conventions come from and what sort of conventions are preferable?

Douglas's general answer to where schemata come from is that the broad categories of our thought are embedded in the social world in which we move. But this involves a number of active arguments. We actively seek cognitive consonance between elements of our experience. And in doing this we seem to know instinctively, 'self-evidently' ('in our guts'), when something doesn't fit. Thus, 'out of place-ness', or going contrary to 'the nature of things', comes from a failure of the implicit worldview to embrace all the applications to which we put it. Douglas's point here is akin to the capacity of native speakers to identify well-formed utterances in their language without being able to explain why they are such. The principles used to put phenomena under covering categories are sensed as much as known. Although the terms she has used to make this point over the years have been modified, the basic point has not. Something like a drive to realize consistency in our apprehension of the world is posited as a human universal. This explains the centrality of classification in Douglas's account of thought style, since we can only think on the classes and attributes which have been assigned to our social and cultural environment. If the basic categories of this environment – time, space, people, nature, Gods – do not come from individuals they must come from society. This line of argument refines the senses of 'collective' without introducing major considerations not already implicit in our use of that term.

Culture as shared classification and cultural motifs: Douglas does not always distinguish between, what I have called 'culture as classification' and 'culture as contention', although her later works require the distinction and do suggest it (somewhat inconstantly). In Douglas's theoretical practice classification and contention as dimensions of culture interact, and this is why they need to be separated heuristically.

If entities do not belong naturally in classes (or if in principle we have no unmediated access to natural classes) then, by definition, entities belong in classes only by reference to criteria of class inclusion and exclusion. For social beings, this requires implicit agreement over the criteria of difference and sameness by which classes are constructed. But sameness and difference are also conventional. Quine, Wittgenstein and Goodman are, she argues, at one on this point (1992c). Where do these conventions come from? To say we receive them as members of society does not add much, since calling them social only reiterates the fact they are shared. How are the differences to be grounded? They cannot be: except that they are conventional, traditional, or depend on a 'form of life'; which is only to say again that they are shared. Douglas is convinced but unsatisfied. If similarity, difference and classification depend on forms of life we ought to be able to say something more. For instance, classification necessarily produces anomalies. But anomalies are treated differently in different cultures. If cognition presupposes classification, and classification presupposes criteria of sameness and difference, and if all these depend on the social, then their variation (or some part of that variety) should correlate with variations in the social – otherwise our reasoning is at best banal or tautological, and at worst a matter of simply playing with synonyms for 'shared'. Douglas's account of the different statuses of the revered pangolin among Lele and the despised pig among Hebrews – albeit she later modified her interpretation of the Hebrew ethnography – was designed to demonstrate just such a correlation between social factors (in this case the regulation of marriage) and features of classification (the attitude taken towards anomalous creatures) (Chapter 9). More generally, she wants to argue that biases in cognition and classification (what she sometimes calls 'implicit cosmology') and biases in social organization correlate with one another. The term 'bias' is important here, since it signals her recognition (but again somewhat inconstantly) that synchronic analysis is unable to account for differences among societies highly disparate in time or space. Bias refers instead to the relative differences apparent when we compare the way in which a single society changes over time or, what may boil down on occasions to something rather similar, the differences among otherwise cognate societies.

Because culture as classification is analogical, one area of classification can be transposed on to another so that similar principles are put to work across cultural domains. Classification is characterized by an economy of effort, because what is familiar is used as a template for understanding the less familiar. Durkheim had argued that the organization of human relations was the foundational analogy for other systems of classification, and constituted their source in two senses. Douglas sometimes writes as if Durkheim and Mauss's (1903) account of 'primitive classification' was unproblematic and simply needed extension to 'modern' societies. This is not the case; if it were there would have been little point in her own efforts to establish a viable way of arguing the Durkheimian thesis. The Durkheimian argument – that the first logical classes were social classes – is, as Rodney Needham noted many years ago, simply a non-answer to the question it is supposed to address (Needham 1963, also Segal HIT/JR). The idea of a category of people already presupposes what it is supposed to explain: the source of categorization. The fact that people are classed cannot be granted a more privileged status than the fact that time, space, natural phenomena or whatever are classed, and certainly not on the basis of a putative story about which came first. Even if it were the case that social classification in some sense came first, it is dubious whether this would carry any serious implications for the analysis of contemporary societies. Durkheim's other argument – that society is an originary, in the sense of an ever-present, cause – is closer to Douglas's usage. Her formulation of society, as a small-scale local setting of others with whom a subject interacts regularly, suggests social context as an urgent environment of other people to be dealt with. It is this small-scale sense of society, she seems to be suggesting, that is the source of people's gut sense about the rightness and wrongness of categorization. To understand how this occurs we need to explore her second sense of culture.

Culture as contention concerns holding other people to account: making them responsible agents in terms of established cultural classifications. Granted the way the world has been categorized – and the sorts of difference and sameness to be found there – others can be blamed credibly, or exculpate themselves with some hope of being believed, or shift agency to outsiders, the dead, God, nature, or whatever. Culture as contention is people arguing explicitly with one another about what matters to them. It is about their wielding the big sanctions available in their culture of classification and its motifs: God, time, money, witchcraft, taboo, pollution. These can be called upon in the hope of being believed because they are already built into the design of the classified world; no use appealing to witchcraft among the scientists or bacteria among the witch-fearing. Will they be believed in particular cases? This depends on the precise circumstances in play. Thus, there are two sets of biases at work: one is to do with the character of the classifying culture (what are its cultural motifs, where does it erect boundaries, how are these boundaries sanctioned, etc.?), the other concerns the culture of contention (when and on whom can an accusation of witchcraft be pinned?). Over time, bias in the classifying culture will be affected by the frequency and significance of bias in the culture of contention.

Douglas has proposed various terms to describe this approach: a 'forensic' approach to risk and blame, or a 'social accounting' approach to analysis. Although subsequently extended, for instance to the analysis of risk in Western societies, the approach is strongly marked by the precedent of studies of witchcraft accusations in Africa. Witchcraft, in terms repeated often by analysts of Africanist ethnographies, explained misfortune and did so by identifying (ambiguously) human agents – often kin or co-residents – who could be accused credibly of attacking their victims. Africanist ethnographers noted that patterns of accusation or suspicion varied between African societies, so that suspected witches might be overwhelming male in some societies but female in others, marginal in some societies and powerful in others, kin in some places and affines in others…and so on. The patterns might change: on return to the Lele, Douglas found that the accusations of sorcery, which used to be aimed credibly at old men trying to wield authority, had become more random with the collapse of gerontocracy (Douglas 1996f: 98). Typifying the patterns of likely and credible accusation told the analysts a lot about the social tensions within the society under study, and the way in which recurrent social processes – like the fissioning of villages or lineages – were typically achieved.

Douglas's espousal of culture as explicit contention slightly post-dates her analysis of culture as classification. Or, more accurately, both ideas are there from the outset but the dimension of contention gradually becomes separated from that of classification and attributed increasing importance. This occurs as part of her espousal of an active voice in social analysis (ITAV). In reaction to accusations of sociological reductionism – presenting human beings as little more than programmed automata – Douglas renewed her emphasis on the knowledgeable activities of the social agents who reproduce either the same or modified social forms through their actions. Over the long term, her favoured metaphors for social analysis seem to have been drawn even-handedly from religion and economics. But it is noticeable that when she discusses culture as classification the analogy with religion comes most readily to mind, whereas when she writes of culture as contention the economic metaphor suggests itself. Thus, she envisages social actors behaving in an immediate social environment which offers them various costs and benefits. The cost structure of their setting results from previous actions, so that in planning and executing courses of action there can be some assessment of the likelihood of different outcomes being achieved. Culture as classification describes the relatively taken-for-granted (doxic, in Pierre Bourdieu's term) setting for the action; culture as contention describes what is to be contested in terms of classificatory culture. But both formulations of culture are embedded in particular forms of society. In less varied societies, it may be permissible to underplay the difference between these two levels of cultural bias. But when Douglas argues in relation to the cultural motif of risk both that the culture of the United States is individualistic and egalitarian in its bias, and that some groups in the United States are individualistic and egalitarian relative to others, such a distinction is clearly necessary.

Recursively, then, the argument throws explanatory responsibility back onto dimensions of the social. Quite how convincing is Douglas's theoretical synthesis can be judged only in terms of the case she makes for dimensions of the social to perform all the work asked of them.

DIMENSIONS OF THE SOCIAL: CHARTING GRID AND GROUP[3]

To recap, credibility depends on social experience at several levels of specificity: humans are social creatures, their cognition is consequential on their sociality, analogic correspondences are drawn between social and worldly designs so that the culture of classification differs inter-societally, via specific cultures of contention, arguments draw on these analogies and reinforce them differently in the practice of everyday life, cultures of contention react upon one another (markedly so in complex societies). Social context is therefore originary in several senses: the ontological grounds of humanity, the variable grounds for cultural difference, the specific site of social activity and of reactions between social groupings. The nub of Douglas's theoretical effort in recent years has been to specify the sense of the social dimension and to decide quite how much can be asked of it as an explanatory tool.

Let us note for later reference (see Chapter 11) that all activity has a social context, therefore there is no 'news from nowhere', no absolute freedom from social context; opposition to institutions as such is futile. Any theory of social context is proposed from a social context. In this sense, a theory of social context must also be self-justifying, since it has to be presented as something more than another predictable, and probably interested, emanation of its circumstances of enunciation. Because a theory of social context has to address us from some-where on the social map, there is logical necessity (as well as intellectual honesty) in Douglas's declarations that she addresses her readers from loyalty to the insti-tutional forms she characterizes as hierarchical. This does mean that advocacy of her theory is necessarily associated with promotion of the virtues of being in only one of the contexts the model sets out to describe; we have already seen how another exponent, Aaron Wildavsky, began from a different point of prefer-ence.

Douglas's methodological problems become acute once she begins to distin-guish consistently between types of immediate social context in order to demonstrate how beliefs and social environment might correlate. Most simply she has to decide how the social is to be disengaged in order that its operations can be specified, what it is to be credited with determining, and how it is supposed to do this. This job is assigned to the two dimensional model of grid and group, of which we have already seen two recensions in the editions of *Natural Symbols* (1970 and 1973).

The more consistently defined dimension, group, was initially to measure membership of enduring social groups. Group referred, in the first edition of *Natural Symbols*, to the experience of a bounded social unit (NS1: viii). By contrast, grid consisted of the rules that related people to one another through ego-centred networks. Grid controlled the flow of behaviour by defining proper relations based on sex, age, seniority, etc. The first of a series of grid and group diagrams was introduced in which the strength of grid was plotted vertically and that of group horizontally on intersecting axes (NS1: 59, diagram 5). This diagram suggested that grid and group could be present or absent, but it was succeeded on the following page by a diagram in which the axes were both posi-tive (NS1: 60, diagram 6) (see Diagram 3 below):

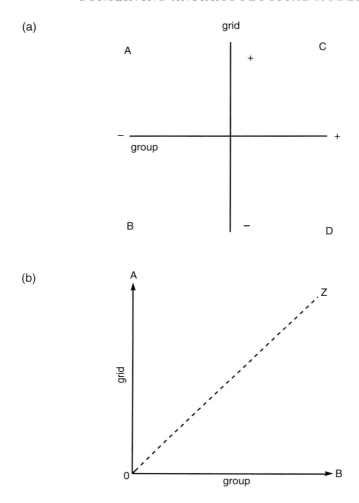

Diagram 3 Grid and group in the first edition of *Natural Symbols*

Source: (a) NS1: 59, diagram 5; (b) NS1: 60, diagram 6

The effect was confusing: diagram (a) suggested grid and group were on/off qualities (thus group might be found with grid or without grid, grid with or without group, and both might be entirely absent), but diagram (b) suggested that grid and group varied only in strength. The confusion might not be worth mentioning, except that Mary Douglas has herself worried about where the 'zero' point on such a diagram ought to occur, and how it ought to be construed.

The grid and group analysis of *Natural Symbols* was concerned to align cosmologies and attitudes to ritual in different sorts of societies. Diagram 3(a) is repeated later in the book with its quadrants filled predicting the cosmological and ritual biases of its occupants (see Diagram 4).

The two positions of strong group on this diagram will change little – C: where grid and group are positive, we find a complex cosmos regulated by ritual (the hierarchists of later works); D: where grid is negative but group positive are found dualist philosophies in which good and evil war against one another in a battle of witchcraft and counter-witchcraft (the later enclavists or sectarians). The low group side of the diagram is soon redesigned, but in 1970 we find – A: where grid is positive but group absent, the competitive, success oriented cosmology (the market society but also its casualties, later to be split); B: where grid and group are absent, a correspondingly benign and unstructured cosmos with personal religion and weakly condensed symbols (a form which does not occupy its own quadrant in later versions). The basic intention of the diagram, if we read 'with' it, is that mapping combinations of the importance attributed to group and individual relations will yield predictions about the bias to be found in cosmology and ritual. The correlation sought is between systems of social control, in the broadest sense, and the attitudes of those subjected to them.

The two dimensions, not maintained consistently throughout the text of the first edition of *Natural Symbols*, drew on an antithesis then prominent in British anthropology: between the focus on recruitment to corporate groups of the Africanist ethnographic tradition, and the slightly newer transactional movement with its focus on entrepreneurship, networks, quasi-groups, patron–client relations, and so forth, which sought to bring the decisions of the actor back into focus. The second edition of *Natural Symbols* changed the definitions of grid and

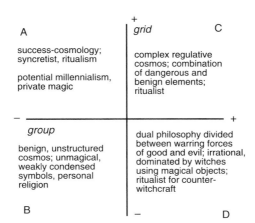

Diagram 4 Types of cosmology according to the first edition of *Natural Symbols*

Source: NS1: 105, diagram 9

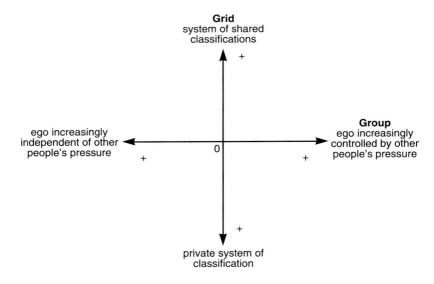

Diagram 5 Grid and group in the revised edition of *Natural Symbols*
Source: NS2: 60, diagram 4

group substantially. Although this is the edition most frequently reprinted, James Spickard rightly notes that later development of the theory was closer to the spirit of the first edition. In the second edition, group was redefined as pressure to consent, which an individual either exerted or was subjected to. Grid was to subsume not only the rules governing behaviour with other people but the scope and coherent articulation of the symbolic system in general. The three diagrams reproduced from the 1970 edition of *Natural Symbols* were replaced by a single diagram (see Diagram 5) in 1973.

All four extremes were labelled positively and a zero point added at the intersection of the two axes. It is unsurprising that the diagram correlating cosmology and attitude to ritual disappeared because, as Spickard noted, adding the coherence of the classification system to the grid dimension – contrary to Douglas dubbing both grid and group 'social dimensions' (NS2: 58) – really left nothing to be determined by the mapping of grid and group. The antithesis between public and private classification on the grid dimension was entirely unhelpful and never developed. The second edition of *Natural Symbols* is, for all the importance of that work in her intellectual biography, not a place I would recommend someone trying to understand the mechanics of her theory to begin. The same schema had a further airing in Douglas's inaugural lecture as Professor of Anthropology at University College (delivered November 1971, published in extract 1971b, and in full in IM). But despite interesting asides, and some further development of arguments about cultures of contention, this attempt also fell into narrow circularity by virtue of defining one of its dimensions as order, classification and the symbolic system as if this was not almost the same thing as cosmology.

The pamphlet *Cultural Bias*, almost unreviewed before anthologization (1978a/ITAV), represents an attempt to specify the grid/group coordinates and solve some of the methodological problems of Douglas's earlier accounts. The account she offers there is virtually unchanged in the edited volume *Essays in the Sociology of Perception* (1982c). Experience, as she puts it in *Cultural Bias*, is to be divided into implicit cosmology and social context. By implicit cosmology she means those beliefs and values which may be used to justify action, 'the ultimate justifying ideas which tend to be invoked as if part of the natural order'; grid and group are respectively concerned with individuation and social incorporation and describe social context (ITAV: 190; 1982c: 5). Group is again treated as the unproblematic dimension, defined by the strength of its boundary, and the rights and obligations that are imposed on members. Grid, which is 'much more difficult' (ITAV: 202), is defined residually as 'every remaining form of regulation' experienced by the individual (1982c: 3). With the help of James Hampton, whose research was supported by an SSRC grant, Douglas had attempted to disentangle and clarify some of the dimensions of grid regulation and to make grid and group measurable (see Hampton 1982).[4] Four interrelated dimensions of grid were proposed:

(a) Insulation: the strength of the social classifications governing behaviour (such as age, seniority, gender, etc.). Where insulation is strong, the further three criteria may be irrelevant.
(b) Autonomy: the degree to which individuals enjoy independence in making decisions (for instance over disposition of time) affecting themselves.
(c) Control: the degree to which individuals control the decisions of others.
(d) Competition: the degree to which individuals who score highly in terms of personal autonomy and control over others are subject to competition among themselves.

As Douglas summarizes,

> The intention is to establish a dimension on which the social environment can be rated according to how much it classifies the individual person, leaving minimum scope for personal choice, providing instead a set of railway lines with remote-control of points for interaction. Strong grid, defined in this way, is in itself not difficult to assess. The problems arise in assessing how the move down towards zero takes place, and where to place zero.
>
> (ITAV: 202)

While restatement of grid as a dimension of personal regulation other than through incorporation clarifies matters, the problem of a skewing towards the extreme cases remains. In the language of the grid and group diagram, this is part of the problem of conceiving the move towards zero. The extreme types of organization that the method is supposed to depict are not difficult to grasp, and by the early 1980s they had found the positions on the 'social map' they were to maintain from hereon (see Diagram 6).

(C) high grid and group depicts a hierarchical total institution – externally bounded and minutely regulated and differentiated internally; (D) high group with low grid depicts an organization committed to boundedness but without strong rules for internal differentiation – for instance, egalitarian communes. (C) and (D) have survived from *Natural Symbols*. (A) low grid and group now refers to a competitive environment in which individuals eschew group membership and compete subject only to rules of competition – as, for instance, in individual sports; (B) high grid and low group depicts the 'atomized subordination' of those who do not belong to well-articulated groupings and are constantly subject to coercive regulation that limits their autonomy. (A) and (B) had been conflated in *Natural Symbols*. As 'ideal types' these four extremes can be thought through to locate their abstract consequences. This strategy, which was present in Douglas's writing from the outset, is the one favoured in her later development of cultural theory. However, this move simplifies much that was methodologically interesting in the grid/group formulation.

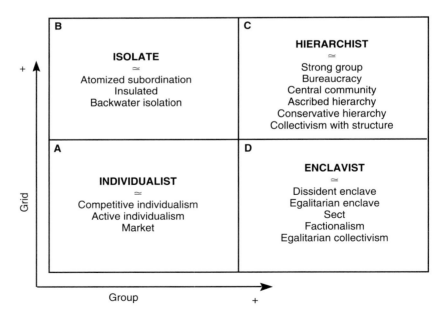

Diagram 6 Some synonyms for the four quadrants of grid and group

Source: 1978a, 1982b,c, 1990d, 1993c, 1994h, 1996b

Grid and group criteria, particularly the former, are difficult to specify with economy in the abstract, but this may be an attraction or deterrent depending what one anticipates of typologies and methodological clarification. At the very least, the complexities of grid and group reveal the simple-mindedness of schemata that oppose individual to society. The problems of the 'move towards zero' in the grid dimension are indicative of some of these interesting complexities. With reduction in the dimension of insulation, the three remaining dimensions of grid yield three versions of its zero point: in terms of autonomy, the hermit might seem the zero point; in terms of control over others, the unscrupulous despot might seem like the zero point; and in terms of competition, the zero point might be occupied by the rule-governed perfect competition of neoclassical economists' depictions of the capitalist market-place (and this third option in fact comes to occupy the quadrant nearest zero grid and group in Douglas's later work, see Diagram 6).

What applies to the zero point of measurement applies, equally of course, to deciding what is to count as the top end of the same scales. The problem is acute in the abstract, because the three instances do not seem to be measuring the same thing; and, unless grid and group are measuring variation consistently, it cannot be argued that the axes of the diagrams are scalar; instead we would be dealing with four distinct types of sociality. In substantive applications, informed by a reasoned application of the *ceteris paribus* rule to limit the scope of comparison, it would be possible to decide how the dimension is to be specified most appropriately. Case-by-case definition of relevant grid and group criteria would detract from grander comparative ambitions, which require the typological dimensions to be maintained consistently, but it does have the great virtue of forcing an investigator to think clearly and explicitly about the parameters of a comparison of social contexts. Without the *ceteris paribus* rule, there is a constant danger of close comparison falling into loose analogy. In its complex form, grid and group seems a useful methodological device to inform comparison of biases within related cultures (historically or comparatively); indeed, I think it is the fullest elaboration of what was implicit in the project of social contextualization of mid-century British social anthropology.

HOW INSTITUTIONS THINK: A PREQUEL

Despite the fact that various of her descriptions of the grid and group method do suggest a limited theoretical ambition, I doubt that Mary Douglas would be satisfied with merely methodological encomium. *How Institutions Think* (1986a), her most recent book-length theoretical work resulting from a lecture invitation at the end of Douglas's American period, contains an ambitious statement of what she now prefers (other than in this book) to call 'cultural theory'. Aside from the ironic echo of Lévy-Bruhl I noted previously, her title also reflects the lessons of her work on consumption, risk, and religion in contemporary Western societies over the preceding decade. Rather than societies, or immediate social environments, she approaches social context via institutions – a recognition that the bases for comparison between pre-colonial African peoples with relatively uniform organizational regimes, typical of *Purity and Danger* or *Natural Symbols*, need to be rethought so as to apply to societies in which institutional forms are more diverse.[5] Continuing in the vein of *Risk and Culture*, one of the central concerns of *How Institutions Think* is with 'latent groups' in modern societies: groups which may be organized around particular issues with no expectation of becoming the setting for an individual's entire life, or indeed for persisting longer than the issue they address remains cause for concern. Although much of the reasoning which informed the grid and group formulation remains, the terms themselves are absent. This may be unsurprising: because their group-like characteristics are so slightly developed, latent groups are anomalous in terms of grid and group typology.[6] Nonetheless, they clearly fall under the heading of institutions.

How Institutions Think begins in retrospective review of her work in the two decades since *Purity and Danger*. This, Douglas says, is the book she should have written first to clarify the premises underlying the others. It is difficult to disagree with her judgement that she had been trying since the mid-1960s to 'understand the theoretical and logical anchoring that I would have needed to present a coherent argument about the social control of cognition' (HIT: ix). She had additionally sought, I have suggested, arguments to support her own preferences for solidarity, order, role discrimination, complementarity, social inclusion and symbols of transcendence. Whereas *Cultural Bias*, written in the Britain of the 1970s, had articulated these concerns with special attention to the problem of withdrawal, *How Institutions Think* appears to have been sharpened by exposure to American society under the Reagan presidency:

> Writing about cooperation and solidarity means writing at the same time about rejection and mistrust. Solidarity involves individuals being ready to suffer on behalf of the larger group and their expecting other individual members to do as much for them. It is difficult to talk about these questions coolly. They touch upon intimate feelings of loyalty and sacredness.
>
> (HIT: 1)

How Institutions Think is, apart from a methodological treatise, a meditation on ideas of justice, solidarity and collective provision for individual needs. If ideas of justice and ethical conceptions are bound to forms of society, how do rational individuals decide upon the sacrifice of their own interests? Rational choice theory founders upon the problem of solidarity, only being rescued at the cost of redescribing every disinterested motive as self-serving behaviour. But Douglas does not reject rational choice theory. Instead she attempts to synthesize the two senses of culture in her previous work that I have distinguished as classification and contention. How to reconcile understanding of the givenness of classificatory culture with, to coin a contrast, the 'takenness' of cultural contention has been at the heart of much modernist anthropology and sociology.

Presented as restatement, *How Institutions Think* actually revises some of Douglas's previous positions. The book seeks a seamless argument about the relationship between institutional forms and epistemological foundations. The succession of examples and edifying tales that occur on the way were appreciated by reviewers who bestowed the usual epithets on the work: 'a sparkling project of a sparkling mind' (Ian Hacking HIT/LRB), a 'remarkable agile mind' (Frederick Bailey HIT/AA), 'an abundance of erudite thoughts and provocative anecdotes' (Michael Kearl HIT/AJS). However, Ian Hacking also suggested, Douglas 'dances over an amazing array of topics…The effect is some sort of intellectual hopscotch', and another philosopher, Alan Ryan, who had sympathetically reviewed her previous books, likened *How Institutions Think* to the 'nest of a bower bird…one can see the attractions of the items thus collected, but their order remains obscure' (HIT/NS). The anthropologist Clifford Geertz's view was uncompromising: 'rich in opinion, emphatic in style, and interested in virtually everything, she has come to instruct', but the instruction transpires to consist of 'one undeveloped comment after another' (HIT/NR).

Like some others of Douglas's books, *How Institutions Think* wears its architecture on the inside, but a careful reading reveals coherent progression in an argument that develops in several strands simultaneously.[7]

The book's introduction and conclusion are both concerned with issues of collective solidarity. Why do people make willing sacrifices when they could remorselessly pursue their narrow self-interest? A closely related question is introduced: what are the rational foundations of socially shared notions of justice? The introductory chapter briefly explores these issues in a story concerning a party of five speleologists trapped by a rock fall. All would have died had they not agreed to kill and eat one of their number chosen by throw of a dice. The man who suggested this course had second thoughts about taking part, but he is the one chance selects, and his colleagues hold to their original agreement and eat him. When the survivors emerge from temporary entombment, the morality of their action is subject to competing legal judgements. But the judges cannot agree, because they reason from different premises: individualist, egalitarian and hierarchical. The analogies that seem relevant to the judges derive from their commitments to different ways of life, and these forms of social life differ in their attitudes towards individual sacrifice to the collective good – here literalized. As Emile Durkheim argued, 'Classifications, logical operations and guiding metaphors are given to the individual by society. Above all, the sense of a priori rightness of some ideas and the nonsensicality of others are handed out as part of the social environment' (HIT: 10).

The reaction of 'outrage' to collectively cherished ideas is explicable only by the strength of commitment to a group sharing those ideas. Ironically, Douglas notes, Durkheim's argument was borne out when his own analysis aroused hostility for seeming to suggest there existed a group mind which subordinated the sovereignty of individual reason. But Durkheim meant his comments to apply only to societies organized by resemblance (the mechanical solidarity of *The Division of Labour in Society* (1896)); modern, organically solidary, societies were integrated through the division of labour and, as part of this division of labour, science could largely be exempted the strictures of social determination. Douglas wishes to 'update' this argument about the social sources of cognition by making it apply to all forms of society. She turns to an account of the identification of syphilis by the Polish epidemiologist Ludwig Fleck. Fleck argued that the venereal diseases separated today were distinguished both because there was a public demand for attention to this cluster of illnesses (rather than others which killed more people), and because investigators in different research groups changed their laboratory practices in response. The breakthrough was a collective rather than individual accomplishment. Adopting and modifying Fleck's terminology, Douglas applies the phrase 'thought world' to a social grouping that shares its 'thought style'. Science worlds may be contrasted with art worlds, music worlds, or presumably as many thought worlds as it seems useful to distinguish. Each has an institutional setting and competes with other thought worlds with which it shares an embeddedness in the context of a wider thought world and its institutions. Social groupings are therefore associated with thought styles – of varying degrees of generality – and vice versa. But what mechanisms more precisely explain the nature and extent of the relationship between the two? And to what extent is one justified in attributing the capacity to 'think' to institutions?

Douglas suggests a double stranded view of social behaviour to accommodate the cognitive or classificatory view of culture as classification, which she sees as answering 'the individual demand for order and coherence and control of uncertainty', and the transactional view of 'individual utility maximizing activity described in a cost-benefit calculus' (HIT: 19). A second chapter, entitled 'Smallness of scale discounted', partly restates familiar arguments against driving a wedge between the sorts of societies traditionally studied by anthropologists and sociologists. But it does this through a prolonged analogy between the economists' concept of a public good (which I discussed in Chapter 6) and the anthropological idea of social order. The point of the analogy is not just to dispute that social order in small groups is any less problematic than it is in larger groups (hence the chapter title, see also Douglas 1985e) – and thereby to end the illusion that the problem of solidarity is somehow solved simply by smallness of scale – but also to explore the subversive potential of the notion of the 'public good' applied to theories of self-interest.

In a witty and influential book first published in 1965, *The Logic of Collective Action: Public Goods and the Theory of Groups*, the American economist Mancur Olson used the example of the public good to show the insufficiency of shared self-interest as grounds for the achievement of collective welfare. Moreover, he did this while accepting, for the sake of argument, the limitations of the economists' notion of individual, self-interested rationality. A pure public good is conventionally described in terms of its characteristic differences from a pure private good:

1   The supply of a public good is not diminished by individual consumption of it (e.g. the supply of clean air is a public good in the sense that it is there for all to breathe).
2   A public good can only be provided collectively because,
3   no consumer can be excluded from consumption of it.

From these characteristics stem the problems of provision intrinsic to pure public goods. The most important of these for Douglas's argument bear directly upon the subject of self-sacrifice. It is only worth my contributing to a public good if I know that everyone else will do so (if they do not my contribution is wasted). However, this problem of contribution is exacerbated by the fact that if everyone else does contribute then it is in my narrow self-interest not to do so, since I cannot be denied access to what is provided collectively and will maximize personal benefit by making no contribution to it. It is this problem of the 'free rider' that Douglas chooses to stress. To recall a couple of her local examples, suppose that all Londoners want a decent public bus service; then they ought to take their private cars off the road and allow the buses to run on schedule. But the more who act in this way the greater the incentive to the renegade car user to benefit privately from a clear run into the city. Or, suppose the residents of Highgate value their corner shops, then they will need to accept paying the slightly higher prices that prevail there rather than driving to their local hyper-markets (1992h/OAO/TS). In practice, there are few goods that can be described as pure public goods; most are subject at least to diminishing marginal utility as demand for them rises (thus a public park becomes less attractive to the extent it becomes congested by users). But if pure public goods are rare then so are pure private goods. Consumption of most goods produces externalities, as anyone who doesn't share their close neighbours' musical tastes will readily attest. The ability to produce public goods has to be assured collectively (for instance, through compulsory tax collection sweetened by appeals to common interest in the provision of services). If there are numerous other elements of collective life that share the characteristics of public goods to some degree, then the idea of the public good speaks directly to Douglas's opening declaration of interest in why individuals are ready to suffer on behalf of a larger group, and why they can expect others to do the same for them. Highly structured organiza-tions are often designed to serve precisely these purposes (every regiment its hero, every church its martyr), but how are public goods (or the public good) to be produced in latent groups? Lacking sanctions or incentives, such groups can organize on only a short-term, unstable, probably single-interest basis (the glance back to environmental groupings is clear). 'The scale of latent groups in modern society is vast; the consequences of their failure to coalesce are momentous' (HIT: 24).

Given Douglas's definition of latent groups, the first half of the statement is undeniable; all purpose, encompassing social groups are indeed rare in the contemporary societies. Why the existence of latent groups has momentous consequences is partly tackled in the following chapter, 'How latent groups survive', which transpires to be a defence of a particular brand of functionalist explanation and a discussion of the development of 'the most elementary forms of society' (HIT: 45).

On Douglas's account, a functionalist argument basically requires two elements.[8] One is the idea of circularity: behavioural patterns exist that sustain a pattern of collective organization, which in turn reproduces the same behavioural patterns, which in turn sustain the collective organization – and so on, and so on. In other words, a functionalist argument requires a causal loop that explains the persistence of patterns of activity that tend to stabilize the matrix responsible for generating them. The second criterion of a functionalist argument is that this causal loop goes unrecognized by the social agents who make it happen. They undertake the actions that sustain the causal loop for other reasons. Douglas's particular examples of functional explanation have been disputed by both ally and critic (Bailey HIT/AA, Hacking HIT/LRB, Thompson *et al.* 1990: 211, fn. 31). The requirement that the effects produced by patterns of behaviour be unintended, and go unrecognized, by those who produce them is particularly problematic: intentions are difficult to decide (direct questions about them after the event elicit responses that must, in the first instance, be treated as *post hoc* rationalizations), these reasons may vary depending whom one asks and when, and people's understanding of the intentionality of their actions is subject to rapid redefinition as self-consciousness about the circumstances of action changes. Douglas's overall argument probably requires only the softer condition that elements of institutional organization and the ideology that accompanies them can be argued to cohere.

Douglas's favoured case is the type of organization, by now familiar to us, which she refers to elsewhere as sect, enclave or small group – and here as latent group.[9] The choice of example in this context is partly motivated by her construction of an argument about the 'origin of the social order' (HIT: 41). Each type of social grouping 'thinks along certain grooves; it has a mind of its own' (HIT: 40). A latent group may begin with an egalitarian commitment to a certain goal; members do not wish to give up much individual autonomy. Leadership will tend to be weak, because members have few weapons at their disposal other than the threat to leave. But in order to maintain equality of contribution to their collective effort, they will need to institute a boundary between members and outsiders. This is the only available solution to the 'free-rider' problem. But the strong boundary has the additional effect of polarizing the relation between the social grouping and its social environment. Without differentiated internal sanctions (because of weak leadership), the social grouping will periodically be beset by internal factionalism revolving around the betrayal of founding principles; this can only be resolved by secession, thus reinforcing the pattern of weak leadership. Douglas's point is that the pattern of thought about the organization of the group follows from individual actions but is an effect of the structural weaknesses of the form of organization (or, rather, attempts to compensate this weakness): to that extent this thought style is constructed collectively. A loose analogy with the public good can be argued in that the jointness of this thought style disguises the consequentiality of their own contribution from each member (HIT: 41); 'hidden sequences catch individuals in unforeseen traps and hurl them down paths they never chose' (HIT: 42). A cognitive or thought style, Douglas wants to generalize, is necessarily a public good because it is produced collectively. For economists, 'free-riders' are those who benefit from a public good without contributing to it, but contribution to a thought style is more subtly produced. Although this somewhat strains the analogy, the counterpart mechanism is that 'the elementary social bond is only formed when individuals entrench in their minds a model of the social order' so we need 'to think of the individual mind furnished as society writ small', 'the whole process of entrenching a theory is *as much* social as it is cognitive' (HIT: 45, my emphasis).

At this point, Douglas equivocates between the stronger and weaker versions of her thesis. She proceeds to argue, in keeping with the title of Chapter 4, 'Institutions are founded on analogy', that a social grouping is usually justified by 'a formula that founds its rightness in reason and in nature'. This is the 'cognitive process at the foundation of the social order' (HIT: 45). Whether the other half of her thesis – 'that the individual's most elementary cognitive process depends on social institutions' (HIT: 45) – necessarily follows can be decided only when we know more precisely what she means by 'elementary' and 'depends'. That many institutions are defended in terms of their fit with a theory of what the world, or human nature, is really like is undeniable: think, for instance, how 1980s laissez-faire economics (of the Thatcher–Reagan stripe) appealed to a self-evident and naturalized account of human propensity to self-interest, drawing the 'truck and barter' of human nature from Adam Smith while ignoring the 'moral sentiments'. The formal structure of social classification, as Douglas puts it, is found by analogy 'in the physical world, or in the supernatural world, or in eternity, anywhere, so long as it is not seen as a socially contrived arrangement' (HIT: 48). She offers familiar ethnographic examples: of analogy between the complementarity of right and left and that of male and female, or between mental and physical work and the head and hand. Cognitive conventions are granted credibility by their use in pursuit of social interests, thus they become adopted generally. This argument develops the half of her thesis that the disputable legitimacy of institutions is usually grounded, in some way or another, with respect to other things that are analogous and less disputable. The 'effort to build strength for fragile social institutions by grounding them in nature is defeated as soon as it is recognized as such. That is why...the hold of the thought style upon the thought world has to be secret' (HIT: 52–53).

Granted that institutions are naturalized, and that people's behaviour is comprehensible only if their institutional commitments are taken into account, it does not immediately follow, as the title of Chapter 5 has it, that 'institutions confer identity' in the sense of relations of sameness among things and people. We need to follow this part of the argument with care. Things are not assigned into categories by the givenness of similarity; rather sameness depends upon the properties selected as relevant. What follows?

> [1] For discourse to be possible at all, the basic categories have to be agreed on. [2] Nothing else but institutions can define sameness. [3] Similarity is an institution. [4] Elements get assigned to sets where institutions find their own analogies in nature. [sub-clause 1] On the one hand, the emotional energy for creating sets of analogies comes from social concerns. [sub-clause 2] On the other hand, there is a tension between the incentives for individual minds to spend their time and energy on difficult problems and the temptation to sit back and let the founding analogies of the surrounding society take over.
>
> (HIT: 55, square brackets mine)

This is a dense passage. We might let pass the idea that some degree of agreement on classificatory categories is prerequisite to people understanding what one another are talking about. The second sentence [2] only asserts what we need to demonstrate, while the third [3] unhelpfully changes the sense of institution from its reference to social groupings. The fourth sentence [4] seems to risk circularity, so we need to focus on its two sub-clauses. First, social concerns create a demand for explanation which is met by creating analogies. Douglas goes on to reiterate Fleck's conviction that social demand for attention to the problems of sexually transmitted diseases influenced the focus of research and led to innovation in scientific classification. The second sub-clause claims that the path of least resistance is to fall into comfortable analogies. 'Thinking as usual' goes on most of the time; without institutional specialization (for instance, scientific specialization) people's interests tend to be dominated by their social concerns. Scientific communities are not insulated either but react to the concerns of their wider social environment; however, in reacting to these concerns they may produce specialized classifications which resist those of the wider society. Thus, a scientific classification may identify relations of similarity between things differently from the wider culture. Scientific classification is not simply a deeper version of a socially inspired classification, because socially inspired classification does not have the quest for knowledge as its overriding objective. It is not evident that this sequence of steps produces the strong argument that Douglas wants it to. Instead, it throws the burden of possible explanation onto the credibility of differentiating social dimensions and correlating these with a diversity of levels of shared and disputed classification.

Although this chapter wants to demonstrate that similarity is conferred by institutions, what it actually demonstrates is that classificatory schemata develop in social contexts – not the same thing. The problem is to decide how strong an argument is being proposed: that the kinds of relations of similarity and difference recognized in institutional arrangements are analogous to those recognized more generally, that similarities and differences are institutions, that differences are only energized when authority and classification coincide, or that institutions confer difference. The chapter concludes modestly by promising to show that 'Even the simple acts of classifying and remembering are institutionalized' (HIT: 67).

'History emerges in an unintended shape as a result of practices directed to immediate, practical ends' (HIT: 69–70). School textbooks on history need to be rewritten regularly because our interest in the past reflects our current sense of where we are and what is problematic about the way we came to be there. Evans-Pritchard (as I discussed in Chapter 2) demonstrated how many generations of their ancestors Sudanese Nuer have to forget, despite the depth of their genealogical account of descent through men. The stable upper levels of Nuer genealogy define the foundational events and broadest categories of common descent defining their society. The proximate genealogy is vital because that defines kin and affines, tells people whom they can marry, from whom they will inherit, and how they stand in relation to the cattle debts so crucial when forty head of cattle are equivalent to a person in calculation of marriage and blood debts. But in the middle of the genealogy there is no pressing reason to recall ancestors who therefore fall into a black hole of memory. Direct analogy is drawn with Robert Merton's writings on multiple discovery in science: given the way that funding and recognition are parcelled out to scientists, originality is highly valued. So, normally reasonable scientists find themselves involved in squalid arguments about who discovered what first. 'Forgotten discoverers are like a lot of forgotten [Nuer] ancestors' (HIT: 77). Moving on, not accidentally in the light of her conclusion, to Kenneth Arrow's voting paradox (which demonstrated that majority voting would not necessarily lead to an agreed ordering of policy priorities), Douglas argues that rediscovery of this puzzle (simultaneously by Arrow and Duncan Black), and forgetfulness of its original instantiation (by the French philosopher Condorcet 160 years previously), is only explicable by factors in the social environment: Condorcet's demonstration was soon to lack relevance to a France in the throes of revolution but became compellingly relevant to a democratic America.[10] A speculation becomes established only when it coheres with accepted methodologies, shared interests and naturalized analogies (HIT: 90).

The book closes in on its quarry: that according so much power to institutionalized thought affronts any commitment to individual freedom of thought.

> Institutions systematically direct individual memory and channel our perceptions into forms compatible with the relations they authorize. They fix processes that are essentially dynamic, they hide their influence, and they rouse our emotions to a standardized pitch on

standardized issues. Add to all this that they endow themselves with rightness and send their mutual corroboration cascading through all the levels of our information system. No wonder they easily recruit us into joining their narcissistic self-contemplation. Any problems we try to think about are automatically transformed into their own organizational problems. The solutions they proffer only come from the limited range of their experience. If the institution is one that depends on participation, it will reply to our frantic question: 'More participation!' If it is one that depends on authority, it will only reply: 'More authority!' Institutions have the pathetic megalomania of the computer whose whole vision of the world is its own program. For us, the hope of intellectual independence is to resist, and the necessary first step in resistance is to discover how the institutional grip is laid upon our mind.

(HIT: 92)

This rousing passage follows directly from noting a parallel between her account and that of Michel Foucault. Institutions appear to possess the reach and influence of Foucault's conflated concept of power/knowledge. To answer to the question she poses of Foucault – how may the theory explain its escape from the determination of all thought by institutions? – she relies upon the insight of the theory itself. The escape from social determination rests on the recognition of social determination (an argument we shall examine in more detail in the following chapter). Douglas's trans-historical, cultural theory is itself the vehicle that allows us to objectify institutional thinking. Addressing her American audience in that familiar inclusive form, Douglas cautions that

When all the great thinkers of a period agree that the present day is like no other period, and that a great gulf divides us now from our past, we get the first glimpse of a shared classification. Since all social relations can by analyzed as market transactions, the pervasiveness of the market successfully feeds us the conviction that we have escaped from the old non-market institutional controls into a dangerous, new liberty. When we also believe that we are the first generation uncontrolled by the idea of the sacred, and the first to come face to face with one another as real individuals, and that in consequence we are the first to achieve full self-consciousness, there is incontestably a collective representation. Recognizing this, Durkheim would have to concede that primitive solidarity based on shared classification is not completely lost.

(HIT: 98–99)

What are these shared classifications? Douglas draws on the example of Ian Hacking's study of the growth of social statistics during the nineteenth century (see also her review 1991f), to remark the sheer diversity of human kinds that were generated by burgeoning techniques of statistical normalization. These relabelled and newly prominent kinds of people began to behave differently in the light of fresh categories of self-ascription becoming available; they thus behaved in an opposite fashion to microbes mutating after exposure to treatments designed to control them: 'life outside of human society transforms itself away from the labels in self-defense, while that within human society transforms itself towards them in the hope of relief or expecting advantage' (HIT: 101).

> But individual persons do not control the classifying. It is a cognitive process that involves them in the same way as they are involved in the strategies and payoffs of the economic scene or in the constitution of language. Individual persons make choices within the classifications. Something else governs their choices, some need of easier communication, a call for a new focus for precision. The change will be a response to the vision of a new kind of community.
>
> [As people attempt to exercise or evade control] they make new kinds of institutions, and the institutions make new labels, and the label makes new kinds of people.
>
> (HIT: 102, 108)

At this point we could imagine the argument directly rejoining that of grid and group theory to specify how particular forms of social and ideological environment tend to cohere. We might even anticipate a restatement of Douglas's own preferences for hierarchical institutions and well-articulated classifications. Instead, she closes by scoring a final point against the prevailing wisdom of the times.

It might be comforting to imagine that institutions were like well-oiled machines: they coped with the minutiae of existence allowing people to attend to bigger questions. Douglas believes precisely the opposite: institutions make life and death decisions, distracting their members by immersing them in the procedural or tactical details of foregone designs. Although contemporary writers are usually willing to accept Durkheim's thesis that the sacred is socially constructed, they are resistant to the idea that justice, as David Hume suggested, is an artificial virtue, and contemporary ideas of equality are conventional and not natural or universal principles. On the contrary, we ought to recognize the history of contemporary Western egalitarianism, remind ourselves that other societies have naturalized no such principles, and (returning eventually to the story of the speleologists) admit that there is glaring disparity between the formal and substantive versions of our egalitarian outlook. When kidney dialysis was first introduced, facilities for treatment were in chronically short supply. The Seattle Artificial Kidney Center established a confidential committee to decide whom to treat of the impossibly large number of potential patients. Their decision depended on reaching a judgement on the relative worth of lives to be preserved. Had the occasion demanded, the President of the United States would have been rushed to the head of the queue – and it is unlikely that this would have occasioned protest in the name of equality. When resources are scarce, institutional thinking therefore makes life-and-death decisions in the United States just as much as when some live and others die if famine strikes elsewhere.

Having argued herself to this relativistic understanding of justice embedded in institutional arrangements, Douglas proceeds to begin to argue her way back out of it. Part of the argument is familiar: by making the connections between institutions and attitudes visible their spell is broken, and the functional loops can be viewed dispassionately (whether this would be so in the case of the American President is not evident). However, Douglas's argument also requires that functional loops be maintained. For if, as she contends, our choice lies between institutional arrangements, then the arrangements we choose must still entrain the consequences we have learnt to predict. Moreover if, in her own phrase from *Cultural Bias*, no one is in social terms entirely off the map, then the choice of institutional arrangement must be made from a culturally biased position. By analogy with her analysis of scientific communities, she might argue a role for the thought world and style of specialists in her own social epistemology. To the extent that such social thinkers (like scientists) are responsive to wider social environments, yet to some degree insulated from demands for standardized cognitive conformity, then they may be in a relatively privileged position to develop more adequate models of social behaviour. From this view of intellectuals as relatively disinterested follows a well-trodden path that Douglas here, as elsewhere, eschews.

Douglas's second retreat from relativism might come as more of a surprise (although it stems from the same hesitation as her account of the reality of dangers). She argues that we can judge between systems of justice on objective grounds in terms of such criteria as the reality of their assumptions and the consistency of the system as a whole. 'It is as straightforward to study human systems of justice objectively as it is to measure the length of human feet from heel to toe' (HIT: 121). Curiously, among her examples she notes that a system of justice cannot both assume people to be in two places at once and correspond to reality. In my local cultural practice, I would readily assent to the proposition; but the argument is curious in this context because it is not relativistic: elsewhere Douglas has argued that ideas of the person are cultural constructs, and in some African cosmologies – for instance those that take witchcraft to be a reality – people can palpably be believed simultaneously to be asleep in their huts and abroad in the form of animal avatars. Simply telling believers that they are wrong may conform to received opinion elsewhere but is inconsistent with an argument from the socially shared construction of reality. Ian Hacking worries about similar examples in recent European history of 'efficient, pertinent non-arbitrary coherent [systems of 'justice'] co-ordinated with vast amounts of empirical data that have been internalised in the social fabric, and which have been or are monstrous, not to mention unjust' (HIT/LRB: 18).

CLOSING THOUGHTS

Mary Douglas can be impatient with carping of this sort, as we shall see in her exchange of views with John Skorupski in the next chapter, but the logical coherence of her views does bear importantly on deciding quite how strong a version of social embeddedness of ideas she wishes to propose. Can she reconcile her views on the institutional government of thought with occasional asides about the objectivity of dangers or justice? Only, one would think, by arguing that the capacity for objectivity is greater from some position on the social map (or perhaps from several positions that differ in relation to the matter in hand). Failing to address these issues would leave her open to the objection Clifford Geertz voices of *How Institutions Think.*

> The central question...is just how settled, how exceptionless and universal, how strong Douglas wishes her argument to be...The result of [her] vacillations between hard and soft versions of Durkheimian sociologism is that Douglas's vocabulary for describing the relation between 'thoughts' and 'institutions' is vague and unstable. Thinking 'depends' upon institutions, 'arises within' them, 'fits' or 'reflects' them. Institutions 'control' thought, or they 'shape', 'condition', 'direct', 'influence', 'regulate', or 'constrain' it. Thought 'sustains', 'constructs', 'supports', or 'underlies' institutions...
>
> Sociologists of knowledge...have all been caught between asserting the strong form of the doctrine – that thought is a sheer reflex of social conditions – which nobody, themselves included, can really believe, and the weak one – that thought is to some degree influenced by social conditions and influences them in turn, which hardly says enough for anyone to want to deny it.
>
> (HIT/NR: 36–37)

Douglas and Geertz are old adversaries in review (his most celebrated collection of essays receiving a trenchant reception for its lack of sociological insight, 1975e). *How Institutions Think* is a manifesto for Douglas's more detailed methodological writings discussed earlier in this chapter. Manifestly written combatively, and in large part as critique, the book is short of the detailed argument that would distinguish the forms and levels of the social dimensions or cultural configurations it argues to be the contexts of all our thinking. Fundamentally, I suggested at the outset, a theory of context as such, as opposed to a method to theorize context in some substantive case, is enormously challenging – perhaps unfeasible. If so, supposing we are convinced by the general argument for the importance of the social embeddedness of thought, we need to seek the best theory of social context available in a tradition of such theories: a theory that defines and explores avenues of investigation, offers to refine its terms, invites our selection among its methods, reasons its virtues relative to other theories, has relevant applications and so forth. On these and other grounds, I feel that Mary Douglas's writings represent the most coherent development of, to restate my introductory comment, the mid-century project of British anthropology as a socially contextualizing form of enquiry. Agreeing with this does not mean agreeing with everything Mary Douglas writes; if for no other reason than that she often disagrees with herself.

In substantive applications, Douglas's writings usually require at least two types of refinement: in relation to the social and the cultural. She seems to wish to explore the effects of sociality on two distinguishable but interrelated conceptions of culture. According to what she calls the social accounting approach to culture (what I have distinguished as culture as contention), explicit reasons are offered for action and inaction, people are made accountable for misfortune and risk, blame and reward are meted out. Comparing social situations that are similar in many other respects, she contends that formal differences in social organization will show up in different patterns of cultural contention. This strikes me as a reasonable hypothesis for any investigator to explore. *Cultural Bias* is mostly concerned with this idea of culture as contention. *How Institutions Think*, for the most part, takes up the other formulation of culture: culture as classification. Here, argument is concerned with both the 'origins' (in the sense of recurrent sources) of elementary forms of sociality, and with the general grounds on which we identify shared classifications and motifs in cultures. The biases of implicit classificatory culture and explicit cultures of contention are dynamically related. The two (or perhaps more) conceptions of culture can be correlated with dimensions of the social. Particular institutional arrangements may, for instance, both share a wider classificatory culture and support distinctive cultures of contention. Douglas's later formulations explicitly recognize that institutional cultures, particularly in mass societies, may be defined oppositionally, and through reaction and alliance. Diagrams from Douglas's recent account of the person illustrate this (Douglas 1994h/TS: 45, figure 2.2; 1994j/TS: 89, figure 4.2; the latter rearranged here into a quadrant, see Diagram 7 below).

In urging her general thesis of correlation between cultural bias and institutional form, Douglas increasingly favours argument in terms of four extreme types. In application, I previously suggested, this can invite conflation between what can reasonably be called 'ideal type', despite Douglas's antipathy to Max Weber, and ethnographic instance. But nothing prevents anyone stimulated by her method from revisiting the open-ended dispute about the definition and calibration of the grid dimension. If the anthropological study of contemporary mass society is not to dissolve into high level cultural generalization at one extreme, and individual case study at the other, some method for attending to associational variety is essential. Mary Douglas is unique in having translated a theoretical agenda from its fully professional application, both intensively and comparatively in a non-Western setting (central Africa), into a comparative methodology applied in, especially, the United Kingdom and the United States, but with a claim to more general viability. Even her marginality to her own disci-

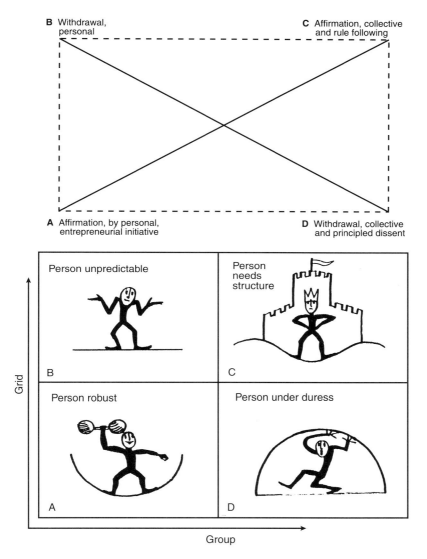

Diagram 7 'Opposed cultural bias and alliance' and 'Myths of person and cultural bias'

Source: TS: 45 and 49

Note: Drawings by Pat Novy rearranged into quadrants

pline, with which I began, has begun to recede as the extent and difficulty of this project have been appreciated fully.

Notes

1 She has 'an astonishing capacity to see connections that, once indicated, are obvious but have not before been noticed', noted Frederick Bailey in a review largely devoted to the logical errors of *How Institutions Think* (HIT/AA).

2 Reviews, other than by anthropologists who subscribe to 'cultural theory', have been more hostile in Britain and America than in continental Europe, where Douglas has been the subject of interviews (e.g. Douglas 1994k,l) and her ideas closely studied (e.g. Reis 1996). Luc de Heusch has consistently promoted knowledge of Douglas's ideas in France (1964, 1971). In Britain and America, her work has received more intensive attention outside her discipline than within it (e.g. Hargreaves Heap and Ross 1992; Sawyer 1996).

3 The first half of this title is borrowed from a working title Mary Douglas originally intended, but never used, for a volume of her collected essays.

4 Measurability has always been important to Douglas, who wants linkages to be hypothesized in cultural theory in ways that are empirically testable.

5 Douglas's own Lele ethnography in fact deals with diverse institutional forms, which de Heusch was able to characterize as existing with primary reference either to time or space (see Chapter 3). Some of this complexity can easily be lost when comparing African peoples as entities.

6 The reader may recall that Douglas and Wildavsky were criticized for treating latent groups by analogy with bounded enclaves that made far-reaching demands on their members (Chapter 7).

7 My review of the book on publication made a poor job of locating the argument which occasions fellow feeling for others who also missed it (HIT/AT).

8 A diagrammatic representation of processual linkages between Lele economy and social organization prefigured most of this argument thirty years previously (1962a/ITAV: 170).

9 As numerous critics of the analysis in *Risk and Culture*, and essays of that period, pointed out, conflating latent groups (which might make slight demands on the individual) with sects (which might demand total commitment) was methodologically suspect.

10 One form the paradox takes is that in voting, say, for the programmes of two political parties by simple majority, people are not necessarily expressing preference for all of either of their policies.

11 THE SECRET CONSCIOUSNESS OF INDIVIDUALS AND THE CONSECRATED SOCIETY

COMMITMENT

An eminent philosopher once remarked that, in order truly to understand the central doctrines of an original thinker, it is necessary, in the
first place, to grasp the particular vision of the universe which lies at the
heart of his thought, rather than attend to the logic of his arguments.
For the arguments, however cogent and intellectually impressive, are, as
a rule, only the outworks – the defensive weapons against real and
possible objections on the part of actual and potential critics and opponents. They illuminate neither the psychological process by which the
thinker in question came to his conclusion, nor even the essential, let
alone the sole, means of conveying and justifying the central conception
which those whom the thinker seeks to convince must grasp, if they are
to understand and accept the ideas that are being put forward.

(Berlin 1990: 161)

In his essay on Joseph de Maistre, to whom I return below, Sir Isaiah Berlin
immediately notes that the opinion of this 'eminent philosopher' seems over-
stated in the case of some highly rationalist thinkers; nevertheless, the
conclusions of many writers, especially those whose influence reached beyond
academic circles, are not best approached through the narrow path of the arguments they used to support them.

They may use arguments – indeed they often do – but it is not by these,
whether valid or invalid, that they stand or fall or are justly estimated.
For their essential purpose is to expound an all-embracing conception
of the world and man's place and experience within it, they seek not so

much to convince as to convert, to transform the vision of those whom they seek to address, so that they see the facts 'in a new light', 'from a new angle', in terms of a new pattern in which what had earlier seemed to be a casual amalgam of elements is presented as a systematic, inter-related unity. Logical reasoning may help to weaken existing doctrines, or refute specific beliefs, but it is an ancillary weapon, not the principal means of conquest: that is the new model itself, which casts its own emotional or intellectual or spiritual spell upon those who are converted.

(Berlin 1990: 161–62)

This evocative description of a style of thought captures my own reaction to prolonged immersion in Mary Douglas's work. The arguments supporting her views are invariably erudite and often plausible, but they are like Berlin's defensive outworks: the overawing protection of the keep, a difficult route, in many respects, to follow to the centre – albeit, this is the route posted for us to follow. The outworks are not all brutally military, they are also embellished with baroque gestures, adorned with appealing secluded groves, and elaborately constructed ornaments. Mary Douglas's work is often amusing – full of wit in the older and newer senses of the term. The esoteric and everyday are juxtaposed to produce a frisson of recognition akin to the structure of the joke, where something in common suddenly connects previously distinct perceptions. But the playfulness is never frivolous: to recognize that, for instance, performance of ritual is analogous to the contemporary consumption of what some, naively we learn, call luxuries is to begin to accept a view of the world in which both 'ritual' and 'luxuries' are necessary because of social circumstances they mark. The defence of ritual is also the defence of a form of life, and my argument has been that we need to seek the experiential grounds for Mary Douglas's championing hierarchical, differentiated and inclusive forms of sociality early in her biography: in the encounter between post-war Oxford anthropology and the young Mary Tew, formed at the Sacred Heart Convent, that was crystallized in her mid-career decision to turn her attention to her own society and its current travails.

The works of her period of transition (*Purity and Danger* in 1966, *Natural Symbols* in 1970 and 1973, *Rules and Meanings* in 1973) represent, on this reading, her struggle to devise an anthropological modernism conducive to her opposi-tion to reputedly modernizing trends in contemporary society: in the Catholic Church particularly, but also in an antagonism to formality, deference and ritual more general in society. The keep, to return to Berlin's metaphor, is home to a tension in her relation to different strands in modernism. The distinguished American sociologist, Lewis Coser, in a warm appreciation of one of her books, drew on another of Isaiah Berlin's characterizations of intellectual style:

following a fragment of an obscure Greek poet, Archilochus, which says 'the fox knows many things, but the hedgehog knows one big thing', Sir

Isaiah Berlin…suggests that there are thinkers who have a wide range of interests and concerns, who move from one topic to another, while others are content to dig ever deeper into one major area of interest…Mary Douglas is very much a fox.

(HIT/Socy: 86)

His view, echoed by many others, is I think right and wrong. The extravagant range of Mary Douglas's, not passing, but intensive interests, her absolute refusal to be deterred by disciplinary boundaries, and the teeming fertility of her liberal cultural imagination are startling. Not a feminist in any conventional sense, Mary Douglas has nonetheless brought to anthropology the feminine concerns of her middle-class environment: with the house, its meals and upkeep, with domestic rituals of cleaning and of marking events with friends and family, with shopping and the fate of the ironmongers at the corner, with the female body, its boundaries, exudations and its care. Writ larger, these same concerns can be extended to the wider society, its welfare, and its solidarity, summed up in its capacity to produce public goods. All this, expressed in her singularly arresting style of pithy aphorism, might seem to denote the fox. But, like the hedgehog, Douglas has known one big thing; these outworks are less defensive fortifications than the organic outgrowth of the way in which she has explored her big idea. Her liberal cultural imagination has been disciplined by the conservatism of her sociological imagination.

The consensus we noted among anthropologist reviewers, that *Purity and Danger* was a 'modern' work, was as complete as their consensus that *Natural Symbols* was not. But the referents of 'modern' shifted in these evaluations from theoretical grounds to social implications. *Natural Symbols* was not only a book about the Roman Catholic reforms of Vatican II, or a critique of anti-ritualism, it was also – I suggested on the basis of her semi-autobiographical essays of the period – the book that allowed her to set her personal concerns in a wider pattern. The implications of her recognition, that the secret consciousness of individuals was furnished as society writ small, stemmed from emending a strand of social anthropological modernism as a critique of social modernity. Only a society and culture 'worthy of the name' could promote a thought style capable of resolving social questions urgent in the second half of the twentieth century. This is the source of her sociological, and political, conservatism. Like few anthropologists of her own time, Mary Douglas has articulated a general and explicit vision of the society in which she lives and of the society she would prefer to live in. The invitation to share this vision is urgent and insistent and cannot fail to be akin, in Berlin's terms, to a conversion – after which facts known before cannot seem quite the same. It is an invitation bound to divide opinion, just as other invitations with so many implications have in the past. To conclude, I shall explore some of these implications as they touch upon the relations between Mary Douglas's anthropology and religion, the nature of anthropological understanding she proposes, and her own moral commitments.

CATHOLICISM AND ANTHROPOLOGICAL MODERNISM

Adam Kuper's succinct account of British anthropology since Malinowski is now sub-titled 'the modern British school' (Kuper 1996). He demonstrates that anthropological modernism, like other modernisms, has been a contested ground, riven by dispute. After Bronislaw Malinowski's 'discovery' of intensive, local participatory research, British anthropology became modern in its self-estimation by turning its back on evolutionary theories and redefining its future. This change had several strands: a relativistic, non-evolutionary estimation of cultural difference (at least when compared to that prevalent in the wider society) was allied to social and cultural holism. Explanations of local social or cultural features took the form of close translation and contextualization (theoretically with respect to some 'whole' of which the feature was a part). This became thinkable only by virtue of intensive local research, an enhanced understanding of the variety of cultures and societies of a wider region, and the discovery of useful, middle-range theoretical and methodological devices (for instance, in Africa, devices to disaggregate and interrelate notions of witchcraft, descent, marriage, residence, and so forth). As the Oxford anthropologist Franz Steiner recognized anxiously and repeatedly (Adler and Fardon 1999), these gains in sophistication of insight tended to emphasize the particularity of the features of local societies; they actually made comparison more difficult. Modern social anthropology programmatically still advertised itself as a project concerned with the comparative study of human societies, but was practically fractured by the fact that its desires to particularize and generalize worked against one another.

By the time Mary Douglas left Oxford, the assumption that social organization might be the privileged ground for a project of comparative anthropology was already on the wane there; her own work is the most substantial continuation of that project. Why has she stuck with it so single-mindedly? Modernism has been centrally concerned with both the assertion and denial of the stability of our objects of study. Mary Douglas, I would suggest, has strongly invested in the stability of personal and collective identities, and she has done so for reasons that go beyond the academic.

Take the case of biography and autobiography: the master conceit of intellectual biography, that is to say a narrative of a subject unfolding from protean to developed form over a lifetime's work, has been subject to criticism from those who would prefer to stress the exigencies, inconsistencies and contingencies of a life. Both versions can lay respectable claim to modernist status: in the classical modernist idea of the bounded, individuated self, or in the high modernist self of James Joyce's *Ulysses* or Robert Musil's *Man without Qualities*. Perhaps the modernist self is best defined in the tension between these two versions. It has been difficult for Mary Douglas's intellectual biographer to resist a narrative of the unfolding self. Douglas may almost accidentally have become an anthropologist; professional opportunities that might have been given her narrowly passed her by (chairs at the LSE and Chicago for instance); but the impression, looking back, is that the line of intellectual least resistance was the one she in fact took. The accidents seem just that: contingent features of the life. In seeing her this way, one is falling in with the way she likes to see herself. Mary's predilection for prefacing new works, or responses to criticisms, with biographical accounts of the development of her thought underscore the importance to her own sense of a life's work of the idea of unfolding development. Rebuttals of critics frequently consist of recapitulations of her theories, their origins, and – most importantly – her intentions however imperfectly realized. Her emotional involvement in a life's work, already a fraught area for any professional anthropologist, gathers a clutch of further investments from articulations that involve commitments to religion, community and the quality of family and everyday life. This sturdy self-perception, though not devoid of its anxieties, imparts a sense of identification with the momentum of the life and work: a circumstance which she, literally, figures in her sister's cartoon of a structured individual inhabiting a structured world (Chapter 10, Icon and Diagram 7). Subjects who feel themselves inconsistent or inconsequential, she argues, do so because their social contexts do not favour a robust sense of self. If the consciousness of individuals is structured (analogously and processually) within the institutions they inhabit, then retentive memory, differentiated thought and conceptual complexity are possibilities only because a social environment enables them. In order to benefit from these, it is necessary to accept commitment to the restrictions and self-sacrifice such institutional environments impose on those who dwell there. Douglas's religious and social commitments are key to this.

One way to appreciate the character of post-war British anthropology is to start from the tensions within the post-war Oxford Institute of Social Anthropology. Quite how radical were Evans-Pritchard's views on the possibility of comparative anthropology has been a matter of unresolved debate. I like to see Oxford in those years poised between particular versions of British social anthropological modernism and British anthropological deconstructionism. Both tendencies were present, and the tension between them was not immediately apparent. If, in Mary Douglas's case, the social modernist strand proved more conducive than the deconstructionist, in another distinguished scholar, Rodney Needham, the opposite happened. But either position leant upon the other in various ways, and frequently by repudiation. In different Oxford 'products' the mix turned out differently again, but always in relation to this tension which gave them a family resemblance.

Oxford social anthropology after the war is generally accepted to have been the route through which particular interpretations of the classics of French sociology of the Durkheimian school entered the mainstream of British anthropology via Radcliffe-Brown, Evans-Pritchard and a stream of translations and commentaries. Oxford was also remarkable for the number of Catholic converts who were prominent in the Institute – and some who were not Catholics were members of other world religions. Given the more general prevalence of atheists and agnostics among anthropologists (as among sociologists), this fact is notable and has, indeed, been noted often. The flaw in accounts that have both recognized Oxford Catholicism and Oxford Durkheimianism is to have jumped to the conclusion that there is therefore such a thing as a Catholic Durkheimian Oxford Anthropology. This strikes me as mistaken because there are several ways of being influenced by Durkheim, and even more of being Catholic. This is to deny, not that there are some elective affinities, but that they need be the same in each case. The Catholicism of Oxford anthropologists was predominantly that of adult converts choosing a religion of transubstantiation; for Mary Douglas, as a cradle Catholic, the choice was to retain commitment to the institutions of her upbringing. Her personal experience spoke in concert with Robertson Smith's and Durkheim's theoretical dicta that their practices predisposed people to believe (for converts one might crudely reverse the formula, see also Evans-Pritchard 1962).

Steven Lukes' masterful study of Emile Durkheim summarizes a discussion of Durkheim's *The Elementary Forms of the Religious Life* that took place in 1914 at a meeting of the Union des Libres Penseurs et de Libres Croyants pour la Culture Morale. This was only three years before Durkheim's death and represents something like a final word on his part and, unusually, as Lukes alerts us, Durkheim allowed himself to 'indulge in prophetic speculation' (Lukes 1973: 514).

> Addressing himself first to the non-believers in the audience, he argued that religion was not simply to be seen as a system of ideas, but as primarily a 'system of forces'. The man who lived religiously was not just someone who saw the world in a certain way, knowing what others did not know: he was a man who felt within himself an extraordinary power, a 'force which dominates him, but which, at the same time, sustains him and raises him above himself', giving him greater strength to face life's difficulties and enabling him to bend nature to his will. Such a sentiment was too universal and too constant to be an illusion; an illusion could not last for centuries.…It was moral forces that were in question; and for the non-believer seeking to render religion rationally intelligible, the only possible source of such moral force was to be found in the coming together of people.…Turning next to the believers present…They might certainly believe there to be another, higher religious life, with a quite different origin, but perhaps they could agree that there were religious forces within us and outside us that we could call into existence, indeed could not avoid arousing, by the very fact of thinking, feeling and acting in common.
>
> Recently an orator had gestured prophetically at the heavens, saying that they were emptying and urging his hearers to turn their gaze towards the earth and look after their economic interests. This had been called impious, but for Durkheim it was simply false: 'No, there is no reason to fear that the heavens will ever become quite empty; for it is

we ourselves who fill them. And so long as there are human societies, they will provide from within themselves the great ideals for men to serve.'

(Lukes 1973: 514–16)

Not only are most of the sentiments here akin to those Mary Douglas *might* herself have written, the rhetorical strategy of the final, direct quotation, is remarkably close to the trope Douglas *actually* employs in the 1980 lecture entitled '*Purity and Danger* revisited' (quoted at the beginning of Chapter 4). Durkheim continued by arguing that Western societies were undergoing an 'intermediary period' caused by profound disturbance following an earlier equilibrium: this was a 'period of moral indifference which explains the various manifestations that we see every day, in anxiety and sorrow' (Durkheim quoted in Lukes 1973: 516–17). But forces emerging among the working class, however obscure their aspirations, boded the crystallization of a new higher justice. 'Will [these new ideals] remain general and abstract, or will they be linked to certain persons who incarnate them and represent them? That will depend on historical contingencies that one cannot foresee' (Durkheim quoted in Lukes 1973: 517). Here, Durkheim and Douglas might part company, the first favouring a moral individualism and the second an incarnational theology. But the train of reasoning is similar. And well it might be if we reach back to the influences that antedate them both.

Durkheim, as is well known, became a secular Jew, but it is not paradoxical to describe his sociology as Catholic. In many respects, Durkheim can be seen as heir to problems, though not answers to them, bequeathed him by Auguste Comte. Robert Nisbet is a commentator who tends to emphasize these connections. Auguste Comte (1798–1857) was the son of Catholic and Royalist parents. Influenced by Saint-Simon (with whom he broke), the Enlightenment, and early nineteenth-century French Catholic conservative reaction to the Enlightenment, he derived an interest in order and stability. Nisbet summarizes an early work, 'Prospectus of the scientific works required for the reorganization of society' of 1822:

In this learned and original piece, Comte set forth germinally most of the ideas that he later incorporated in his more systematic works. He disclosed his underlying vision of a Europe disorganized and alienated by the forces of modernism – nationalism, centralization, religious dissent, secularism, revolution – that had broken up the consensus of the Middle Ages without producing anything to replace it. The prime requirement of the modern age, he declared, was a new philosophy, one rooted in science, that would do for the present and future of Europe what Christianity had done in the medieval period, that is, serve as the basis of intellectual certainty, moral consensus, and social stability. Comte had no use for the democratic ideas of the

247

Enlightenment and the French Revolution. He saw in them metaphysical fallacies that could only subvert the social order. It was his attack on the Revolution and its equalitarian ethos that made him, for all his anti-Catholic, antimonarchist ideas, a favored name of the extreme right in French politics at the end of the 19th century.

(Nisbet 1967: 100)

Douglas would explicitly reject the Comtian programme, both in its evolutionary scenario and its summoning of a brave new world. But she inherits something of his terms of reference, and some of his intellectual tools: including a programmatic role for positive sociology – for instance, in the capacity for meta-reflection on society described in *Purity and Danger* and often thereafter, as well as the division into a statics and a dynamics typical of grid and group analysis. In Comte's positivist society there would be neither equality nor popular democracy; its underlying theme would be consensus and internal articulation of interests, dominated by hierarchy and ritual. Positivism would, in scientific fashion, carry on the work of Catholicism. With reason, his work has been called by some commentators 'Catholicism without Christianity'.

The life of Joseph de Maistre (1753–1821) overlapped with that of Comte (1798–1857); in turn Comte died the year preceding Durkheim's birth, and Douglas was born in 1921, four years after the death of Durkheim. Four lives carry us from a man who was already in mid-life when the French Revolution broke out to a woman living at the end of the second millennium and announcement of the end of modernism. Little surprise if there might be continuities among the differences between them.[1] Maistre came of a noble family and underwent a Jesuit schooling, he fled the revolution to exile. In 1819, he published his *Du Pape* which, according to the *New Catholic Encyclopaedia*, became the 'charter' of Ultramontanism (Mercier 1967). 'From the premise of papal infallibility Maistre, as a political philosopher, draws positive conclusions in the hope that a stable order based on divine law will be restored in Europe' (Lombard 1976: 43). The early-nineteenth-century date is roughly contemporary with the foundation of the Society of the Sacred Heart to meet a need for the Christian education of young women in the wake of the French Revolution.

Maistre's counter-reformation position was part of an intellectual stance which became available only in the wake of the Reformation and Enlightenment. It is a variety of Catholicism stressing ritual, hierarchy, authority – particularly that of the Papacy – and social order. To see it as merely reactionary would be to simplify. Maistre 'attacked eighteenth-century rationalism with the intolerance and the passion, the power and the gusto, of the great revolutionaries themselves' (Berlin 1990: 109). To the question, 'Who is the enemy?', Berlin has Maistre reply:

All those who throw dust in the eyes of the people or seek to subvert the appointed order. Maistre calls them 'la secte'. They are the disturbers and subverters...all those...who put faith in individual reason or the

248

individual conscience; believers in individual liberty or the rational organisation of society, reformers and revolutionaries: these are the enemy of the settled order and must be rooted out at all costs. This is 'la secte', and it never sleeps, it is forever boring from within.

(Berlin 1990: 119)

To believe that society is an outgrowth of a social contract is absurd: society must antedate the possibility of contract. To believe that men merely maximize pleasures and minimize pain is to fly in the face of historical evidence.

[Society] rests on something much more elemental, on perpetual self-sacrifice, on the human tendency to immolate oneself to the family or the city or the church or the state, with no thought of pleasure or profit, on the craving to offer oneself upon the altar of social solidarity, to suffer and die in order to preserve the continuity of hallowed forms of life.

(Berlin 1990: 123)

Isaiah Berlin stresses the apocalyptic potential of the irrationalism he finds in this stance. But without the violence and darkness of Maistre's sombre vision, there is another route, via Comte and Durkheim to Douglas, for which to speak of society is to imply religion, and to speak of the individual as prior to society – or to religion – is a nonsense. And for the individual to find herself or himself at home in society is simultaneously to beg the question of the cognitive, moral and ethical parameters which might be functional in such a society. Elemental self-sacrifice of the individual is common to all three writers. In the final chapter of Douglas's *Purity and Danger*, the theme appears in sacrifice and transcendence; in the later works, it is explored in the apparently more mundane conundrum of the public good which rational, self-seeking individuals both require and are unable to supply for themselves. But this secular problem also raises the problem of the reality of collective obligation.

Comte and Durkheim differ from Douglas and Maistre in that their solutions are not theistic and look to a future unlike our present or past.

Durkheim's mind was one of fascinating paradox. Politically liberal (he was an active Dreyfusard), he nevertheless constructed his sociology around the conservative values of solidarity and consensus; religiously agnostic, he became the author of the most convincing demonstration of the indispensability of religion to society ever written by a social scientist; utterly dedicated to science and to ethical neutrality in the study of human phenomena, he nevertheless made the moral element primary in all of his studies; a pluralist in his view of authority and a cosmopolitan in culture, he became known in World War I (in which he lost a son and many lifelong friends) as an ardent French nationalist.

(Nisbet 1967: 1121)

Once the framework of grid and group was put in place in *Natural Symbols*, Douglas definitely turned her back upon the evolutionism which was one of the possibilities of *Purity and Danger*, and I interpreted as a residual legacy of Durkheim and Comte.[2] The discounting of scale in *How Institutions Think* was the last nail in the coffin of evolutionism or the argument that modernization, secularization, or rationalization could really identify fundamental differences in contemporary societies. The supposition of a relatively unchanging human nature is implied in the narrowing of focus to patterns of sociality within institutions. Human nature may differ, but it differs consistently in accordance with a limited number of social environments. Since institutional settings are in principle few in number, human societies seen from this viewpoint are preordained to shift around and between the available coordinates of grid and group but never to escape the map on which these movements are plotted, nor to redefine it. Revolution is no more than a predictable shift within already specified parameters.

This is sociologically the most fundamentalist of the classical modernist projects that might have been derived from the confluence of religious and sociological influences found in Oxford anthropology after World War II. It is not the only project that could have been derived: a number of others grew from the same nexus in the 1960s, and traces of some of them feature briefly, later to disappear, in Douglas's earlier works.

One option was to work to define cognition as transcendent in terms either of a sociology of knowledge, or of a transcendent theology. Instances will have to be outlined rather briefly – although their implications are germane to my later discussion of 'relativism'.

Rodney Needham (1963), in the far-reaching intellectual deconstruction of Durkheim and Mauss's *Primitive Classification* to which I have referred repeatedly, points to a logical error in the argument that classification of social categories can solve the origin of classification as such. Rather, he points out, social classification presupposes, thus cannot explain, shared categories. Pursuing this line of argument led him to explore universal tendencies in classificatory thought.

Another riposte to social reduction might be found in Godfrey Lienhardt's *Divinity and Experience* (1961) in which experience is the key term of analysis. The final chapter of this book, detailing the acceptance of death by the master of the fishing spear, struck Douglas forcibly. The closing pages of her own *Purity and Danger* drew explicit Christian parallels between the death of the spearmaster, and the 'sorrowful mysteries' of that redeeming 'kingly victim' the Lele pangolin, in terms of 'men's common urge to make a unity of all their experience and to overcome distinctions and separations in acts of atonement', and of the 'power for good released by [the pangolin's] dying' (PD: 170, 171).[3]

Not of Oxford pedigree, but very much a fellow traveller of the period (and the provider of another example to the conclusion of *Purity and Danger*), is Victor Turner, whose later work on ritual is founded upon an antithesis between structure and anti-structure that is not dissimilar to the tension between Douglas's master images of order and disorder, category member and anomaly, form and formlessness. For Turner, anti-structure is realized in the liminality of certain types of human encounter which, generalizing from van Gennep's insights into the central phase of rites of passage, deconstruct the distinctions of status and hierarchy definitional of mundane life. Rather than emphasizing, as does van Gennep, the way in which these unstructured experiences prepare for the reintegration of individuals with changed statuses back into mundane life, Turner envisages them as intimations of communitas, the immediate apprehension of common transcendent humanity. Like Douglas, Turner also wrote articles questioning the liturgical reforms of Vatican II (Turner 1972; Deflem 1991). In my view (which I suspect would not be general in my discipline), Turner is a far less complex thinker than Douglas, which (along with the amenability of his theory for opposition to institutions as such) may explain why his ideas have exercised the more obvious mainstream influence within cultural anthropology.

Douglas's path from the Oxford confluence consisted in clear differentiation of the concept of sociality into types of social environment to which should correspond modes of cognition, experience and shared expression. How to do this, and how to apply the theory, was open to revision and negotiation; that this was what had to be done was not. The question was not *whether* social environment determines thought style but *how* it does so.

Mary Douglas's antipathy to schools of thought she found either idealistic or utilitarian is expressed vigorously and often. However, it is one thing to root out idealism, utilitarianism and all their works, another to instate a wholly sociological form of understanding. The three terms do not exhaust the field of potential explanations. Arguing that ideas emanate from particular social environments (however defined), and that they are part and parcel of the social environments in which people accept them, dispute them, assert them or whatever else they do with them, does not in itself give social environment a determining role – it only suggests that whatever argument we propose should not ignore social factors. Her attempts to strengthen the argument are open-ended and recursive – constantly worrying at previous formulations. An argument about culture as classification is, not entirely consistently, refined by distinguishing a strand of the argument concerned with culture as explicit contention. Grid and group coordinates are refined, then temporarily put aside in favour of formulation in terms of the ideal types of cultural theory. The ideal types are subject to relabelling and splitting (as in the replacement of 'sect' by egalitarian enclaves and small hierarchies). Criticism of sociological determinism finds response 'in the active voice'. And so on. The numerous attempts to produce a stronger argument about the social dimension of thought evidence her commitment to defending such an argument rather than a fixed preconception, more definite than the critique of theories neglectful of the social, of how this is done best. Douglas is dogmatic about her ends but open-minded about her means. Commitment to the end is justified by the contribution she believes meta-reflection on the sociality of our shared thought style will make to our ability to choose rationally among social arrangements that compete for our loyalty. Professional philosophers have found all this hair-raising.

IN WHAT SENSE IS MARY DOUGLAS A RELATIVIST?[4]

An analysis of the sort proposed in Douglas's later writings requires two kinds of truth standing to be interrogated simultaneously (in the course of which the distinction between them can become difficult to maintain). The first truth standing refers to the instances bracketed for analysis (beliefs in secular or religious pollution, witchcraft, risk or whatever); the second concerns the status of the analysis, or bracket, itself. I start by specification of the second problem.

If the analysis suggests that ideas emanate, however they do so, from social circumstances, then how is its own status to be defended? Surely it cannot escape the bracketing moves it deploys to show other thought styles to be either analogous formally to the social setting in which they are found, or constrained by the terms of argument employed strategically within the institutional settings of which they are part? It is easy to apply this argument crudely to Mary Douglas's thought. The grid and group framework, or cultural theory's typology of exemplary social forms, are highly ordered ways of looking at the world entirely consistent either with Mary's membership of (or preference for) highly ordered institutions, or with her contestatory position within them. I do not see why she should object to this argument; as we have seen, she makes a case (in *Natural Symbols* and *Risk and Culture*) for the particular advantages of hierarchy in facilitating a differentiated thought style.

In *Purity and Danger*, and on occasions subsequently, she appeals to a different argument. Rather than privileging any position on the social map, this foregrounds the capacity for social map-making; in other words, the objectivity of Douglas's theory allows us to reflect upon the social determination of thought in a way unavailable to those not in possession of this means of insight. We are able to be conscious of the social conditions of our own consciousness because we have a tool which allows us to transcend limitations which have been imposed on the self-consciousness of others. Our willingness to objectify ourselves in this way derives from our sharing an elaborated code of expression. This sounds a large claim, but the same general type of claim is begged by any other theory that aspires to escape the trap of a reflexive relativism in order to claim insight into their situation of which social agents are necessarily, and to their detriment, ignorant. Commentators on *Natural Symbols* noted that combining the two arguments (objectifying social situations and their associated thought styles in order to decide to occupy one quadrant) invited two sorts of problem. First, we seemed to be asked to suspend the social determination of belief (in order to choose), and then apply it again (once we had chosen), so that our beliefs again flowed from our social location. Second, this notion of choice made it difficult to know what status to give our beliefs. If, for instance, we chose to enter a hierarchical social space for social reasons, in what sense could we then claim to 'believe' doctrines, say natural symbols, which we found there? Mary Douglas has responded, as in 'Pascal's great wager' (1985b), that beliefs result from activity in common regardless of the motives for entering into them. Social investigations might show this to be so in some substantive cases; whether there exists any convincingly principled philosophical answer is dubious. Mary Douglas employs a rhetoric of relativity, especially when arguing oppositionally, but it is unhelpful to think of her as a relativist in short. Relativist rhetoric is generally used in anthropology either in a positive sense – to mean the opposite of judgemental – or in a negative sense – to mean devoid of moral principle; the result is that arguments about relativism in anthropology tend to generate more heat than light. A narrower discussion would specify quite what is to be considered relative to what else and under which circumstances.

In the late 1970s, the philosopher John Skorupski undertook a close reading of a passage from the preface to *Implicit Meanings* in which Mary Douglas sets out her stall for a 'sociology of perception' (the title of the edited volume 1982c). Although widely quoted by analysts, this is one of Douglas's more rhetorical pieces of writing and not a reliable guide to her theoretical practice (Spickard 1984: 156). Skorupski rigorously notes a slippage in her argument and tries to establish what she would need to hold in order for the slippage to make sense. Some of the ensuing cross-purpose between Skorupski and Douglas results from his warranted but literal reading of a single passage, and her response by reference to her practice. Skorupski constructs a figure he calls 'our relativist', who is charged with the responsibility of producing the strongest available argument to connect Douglas's statements. Imagining that she is 'our relativist', Douglas coins 'our philosopher' in riposte, and the mutual misunderstanding is total. But Skorupski's strongly relativist reading provides a professional philosopher's vantage from which to describe the situated relativisms to which Douglas does subscribe.

Summarized, the passage Skorupski examines contains the following statements (1979: 151–153):

1　Around the beginning of this century Durkheim demonstrated the *social factors controlling thought*.
2　But he argued this only for peoples with mechanical solidarity (where the society consisted of an assortment of similar units, e.g. lineages or clans). He exempted our own society from his theory because of his belief in the objectivity of scientific thought.
3　As a result the thesis about *social determination of knowledge*, which involved the *sociological determinism* or *social construction of reality*, was applied only to one type of society.
4　To apply the same insights to all societies would involve a *thoroughly relativized theory of knowledge*. But relativity is a threat to cognitive security.

5   Quoting Douglas, 'Were truth and reality to be made context-dependent and culture-dependent by relativizing philosophy then the truth status of that philosophy itself is automatically destroyed.' The 'only security lies in the evolution of the cognitive scheme, unashamedly and openly culture-bound, and accepting all the challenges of that culture'.

Skorupski begins by questioning whether a relativist is well advised to deny truth values. Relativism only requires that truth is relative to something: an overall theoretical framework or set of core statements, for instance. The assertion that the world is round simply has to be construed as 'relative to whatever it is to which the truth value of all our assertions is relative' (Skorupski 1979: 154). Following this argument might suggest that relativism is a transcendental doctrine, in the sense that if all our statements are relative to something, including our statements about those statements, then it becomes strictly impossible to say what they are relative to. The regression need not be entirely uninteresting, but the line of argument would be incompatible with sociological determinism, and Skorupski wants to find a line of argument that would both allow Douglas to be both a relativist and an advocate of the social determination of knowledge.[5]

Instead, the relativist needs to assume that every worldview contains a core of statements of a rather high order of generality, other statements having a truth value relative to these. The core statements are not properly speaking true or false at all. A statement may therefore be true relative to one worldview, false relative to another, and part of the core of a third (a triad formally analogous to Pierre Bourdieu's orthodox, heterodox, doxic distinctions – acknowledged consensus, acknowledged dissensus, and, in Douglas's terms, the self-evident or implicit).

Next, Skorupski moves on to consider the argument articulated under the banner terms: social determinism, social control of cognition, or social construction of reality; he notes that the causal account of a belief does not give us any information about its truth or falsity.[6] Because of the specialized nature of scientific enquiry in contemporary Western societies, it seems evident to Skorupski that contemporary scientific findings cannot be derived easily from their social organization. Durkheim got around this problem not by arguing that primitive cosmologies were true relative to their own cognitive parameters, but rather that they were less cosmologies than symbolic representations of the social order in which they occurred. At this point Skorupski's notion of truth in part diverges from Douglas's – by true Douglas normally has to mean that something has the status of truth (or self-evidence) for particular people belonging to a particular culture. But she also requires Skorupski's stronger sense of true in relation to her own theory.

Skorupski's move on knowledge is, for similar reasons, from a different direction from the anthropologist's. For something to be true, he argues, it must be related causally to the object it purports to refer to. If a belief is related causally to social structure and not its reference object, then it cannot be said to be knowledge. Again, this is not immediately germane to the way anthropologists use the idea of knowledge – simply to mean what people know (though deciding what they know, and on what grounds, is less than simple). But Skorupski's conclusion – that a worldview contains beliefs secured only by the stability of the social relations which generated them – comes closer to the mark. He adds to this the idea of underdetermination of knowledge by experience. If certain beliefs are socially secured, then others will be experientially related to these. The problem that then ensues is that, if we cannot know the truth of the core statements, we are prevented from interpreting the truth of the statement that other statements are relative to these.

The only route from this morass, he argues, is via assertibility conditions: no statements could be true or false unless the truth of some is given. Unfortunately, this conclusion derives directly from our requiring it. Following it, the boundaries of worldviews are constituted, so to speak, 'from the inside' (1979: 173) by conventional limits on what one questions and how one 'goes on'.

Douglas refuses to engage with these issues on Skorupski's terms: noting an over-reified conception of worldview, a poor selection of core statements, a refusal to allow the knower a role in knowing, and a mistaken identification of herself with 'our relativist'; 'I find the philosophical discussion quite dizzying, like a Victorian parlour game devised by Lewis Carroll' (1979d: 179). Her reply asserts both that you *can* choose between worldviews (a view reiterated in *How Institutions Think*, and discussed in the preceding chapter), and that all constructions or worldviews, even scientific ones, are comparable with respect to credibility. Douglas continues, 'I am interested in finding criteria for agreeing, *within our world view*, that among other core structures some are not as good as others' (1979d: 180, my emphasis). Yet she also proposes that truth and reality are not directly relevant to anthropologists' discussions.

> Knowledge is related to meaning at the level of analysis at which particular meanings connect with one another, to make a coherent inter-dependent set, each part guaranteeing the place of the others. The testing by experience of each part of a set provides some of the grounds of its claim to be entered as belief and knowledge in a world view, and its coherent relation with the rest of the set probably provides the rest.
>
> (1979d: 181)

Finally, the core statements which have to be unassailable in Skorupski's version of relativism are insufficiently general, they should refer to the structure of social relations and are abstractions of the type: inclusion, exclusion and hierarchy – which constitute cultural bias (1979d: 186).

Douglas's response refers to at least three levels of analysis: the first, the ethnographic, consists of ethnographers' reports of what are taken to be knowledge and truth in a particular society. In terms of ethnographic method, each society has its own relative knowledge and truth in this sense. Second, her anthropological method requires that regimes of knowledge and truth in reported societies are relativized to their social arrangements with especial attention to their coherence in terms of such abstractions as inclusion, exclusion and hierarchy, etc. Third, comparing a series of such analyses, 'we' may agree that some core structures are better than others. What she means by relativism (or her answer to the question: relative to what?) is not the same in these three stages. Moreover, the whole procedure could start over again: reporting 'our' agreement about core structures, relativizing that agreement to our social context, comparing a range of such cases (and, if need be, starting over again).

John Skorupski, unable to fit Douglas's reply into any of his relativist categories, responded that Douglas was not a relativist if she believed worldviews can be compared as she suggests. She gives no argument for relativism, and so there is not 'radical relativism, but only radical-sounding metaphor' (1979: 192).

The exchange, marked on the face of it by pronounced mutual irritation, actually takes us some way towards narrowing down a version of relativism to which Mary Douglas might subscribe. Douglas argues for less than her rhetoric sometimes suggests, and less in some places than in others. The exchange with Skorupski is roughly contemporary with such second thoughts on 'cultural bias' as, for instance, the later amended demonstration of analogy between rules regulating food and marriage among Karam, Lele, Thai, and in Leviticus that we examined in some detail at the outset of Chapter 9. If anything, subsequent development has made her thought even less relativistic (in Skorupski's sense) while developing her theories of cultural bias at the level both of classification (where it is largely secured by analogy, exemplification and self-evidence) and contestation (where a functional argument is used to explain mutual reinforcement between a form of life and the arguments that occur within it). As well as refining her conception of culture, Douglas has also added explicit recognition of institutional complexity and individual agency to her account. As we saw in relation to *Risk and Culture*, these developments mostly occur within a theory of credibility (or social construal) rather than a theory of truth. And credibility is more often approached as a question of relative bias than a question of belief in short. Her occasional asides about the realities of kinds of dangers, or the objective measurability of systems of justice, at least *ought*, if Douglas is to be consistent, to be relativized to the social positions from which they are enunciated. This does not preclude attributing them a current truth status if, as in *How Institutions Think*, Douglas is willing to privilege knowledge acquired in particular social settings for some purposes (for instance, scientific knowledge among those acting on social concerns but, to a degree, insulated from some of the pressures towards cognitive conformity).

Douglas's relativism is thus relative to an initial set of entrenched circumstances – in short, relative to the *status quo ante*. This is small-'c' conservatism of an analytic type. Realizing this, 'we' are able to witness the extent to which institutions do the thinking for us ('we' in this context being anyone willing to accept the analysis). In a neutral sense, we are all able to think clearly about these matters with a little help. However, having accepted this invitation, 'we' are able to pursue things a little further. But in doing so we break the frame of the foregoing analysis.

On inspection, some types of institution seem able to deliver an experience of life that others cannot provide, and this life quality may be very wide ranging, including, for instance, the capacities for intellectual insight and collective well-being. The message is therefore twofold, acceptance of the theory opens an opportunity for reflection, reflection convinces us of the superiority of hierarchy, the experience of hierarchical organization then predisposes us to construct a worldview in which problems will be more easily susceptible to solution. The argument, from a more general reading of Douglas, fits rather ill into the categories of Skorupski's discussion, based on a textual fragment, because that excerpt does not allow him to see the diverse grounds of the relativisms proposed. Sociological determinism has to be, as it were, suspended temporarily to allow the moment of insight that will allow its hegemony to be reinstalled. Philosophically, this is indeed a difficult argument to make convincing. Without this final step, the argument might be justified in the terms of 'our relativist' of Skorupski's creation, but it would not be Mary Douglas's emendation of the sociology of knowledge.

ANTHROPOLOGY AS A MORAL ENQUIRY

Why is it necessary for Mary Douglas to, as I put it, break the frame of her non-evaluative sociological relativism? And where does this leave the theological and political questions which shadow the anthropological? If we again itemize the aversions and preferences of Douglas's sociology the list would run something like this: anti-individualism and anti-utilitarianism (the question of individual sacrifice to the collective good cannot be addressed from here); anti-idealism (the social is foundational and ideas do not float around freely); against empty gestures of disaffection (those who have views to express should organize and beware reflecting only the marginality of their own condition, whether that be expressed in terms of collective millennialism or socially uninvolved scepticism); anti-revolutionary (for sociological determination is inescapable, no use simply being against institutions – for all that she occasionally appears ambivalent about their inescapability).

Since Mary Douglas believes a majority of contemporary thinkers fall into one or more of her categories of aversion, this is the litany of someone embattled, out of sorts with her times and society – temperamentally, religiously, socially – almost an outsider to a present viewed with regret (Turney 1988, 1996). This perceived loss of collective life is common to French, broadly 'Catholic' in the sense of my earlier discussion, social thought. Society may

Photograph 9 Mary Douglas at home in 1997
Source: © Pat Novy

appear an earthly reality, but in Mary Douglas's hands its connotations are less mundane; and this is why some commentators who bracketed her as a right-wing thinker were thrown by her abhorrence of Thatcherite values in the 1980s. In the simplest recension of the group and grid theory, there are but four social forms: individualism, isolation, hierarchy and sect. Individualism, devoid of sacrifice, is a deformation of society. Isolation involves abrogation of social responsibility. Hierarchy and sect are in Manichaean relationship. Both are strong on form, but sect is short on internal content. It is validated by the boundary separating it from a wider society. Internally, it is marked by recrimination and schism. It supports collective dissent from social inclusion. Hierarchy is socially encompassing, strongly formed internally, based on authority and division of responsibility. Although each is antithetical to the others, alliances are possible. Thus, isolates and sectarians may ally in terms of their dissent from the terms of wider social inclusion. This 'negative diagonal' of Douglas's diagrammatic representation (1993d; see Chapter 10, Diagram 7) sums up most that she views with foreboding in contemporary society: an alliance of socially irresponsible dissent. The 'positive diagonal' allies individualism with hierarchy: both involved, though differently, in claims to power. Heavily weighted towards hierarchy, this is the alliance she prefers, though without great optimism either that it will prevail or that the outcome of its alliance will be utopian.[7] The 'secret consciousness' of individuals rests in the fact that their internal mental furniture, the forms in which their thought is set, are analogous to those of the institution in which their thinking is done. Biases in forms of association correspond to biases in forms of moral commitment.

However, there is also a utopian strand, or aesthetic preference, to Douglas's social thought. This is to be found in the idealized form of hierarchy, with its distinctions and reversals of levels of responsibility between custodians of the sacred and the secular, its social inclusion, differentiations of status along lines of complementarity, its complex symbolic life, and the system of justice which might be a property of this social arrangement and the structured persons that inhabit it (1993c). This is the quadrant on the social map she feels most conducive to resolving social issues in ways that are long term, holistic and subtle.

I have stressed how a theological and anthropological argument reconverge – they became distinguished after the counter-Reformation and pursued separate trajectories via de Maistre, Ultramontane Catholicism and the Sacred Heart convents (on one side) and from de Maistre, to Comte, to Durkheim, to the Oxford Institute of Anthropology's sociological modernism, on the other. Mary Tew and Mary Douglas must have heard these themes set to different arrangements numerous times – and recognized the fragments. She has never stressed her own originality, but rather her proclivity to gather those who had something to say to one another, 'who would have agreed if only …'. Where did the proclivity to hear the music come from? The Sacred Heart Convent, on her own account, seems to hold a key. Perhaps the convent teaching of St Thomas

Aquinas[8] contrasting the substantive and accidental attributes of forms might have played a part: the substantive defining forms to be what they are, and thus being necessary; the accidental describing non-necessary attributes of forms. Her predisposition to formal analysis and highly formal imagery, in text and figure, is consistent: Venn diagrams, 'grooves', inclusion–exclusion, hierarchy, graphs with crossed axes, diagonals, and so on. Enormous diversity is distilled into relatively simple criteria of form.

In its stress on sociality, cultural variety, comparison, anti-utilitarianism, empiricism, anti-idealism – Mary Douglas's is a classic expression of British anthropological modernism of the second half of the twentieth century. But its further articulations are more individual. If anthropology, in the old philosophical sense, is the quest for human nature, or 'the secret consciousness of individuals', and theology a quest for the nature of God, then in Mary Douglas's writings, society is elicited as a third. God, having created man as a social animal, allows His face to be seen only through a distorted lens, that of society. The consecrated society, where life is an expressive ritual and individual sacrifice and pain are called forth and made meaningful, best images God (paraphrased from my direct quotations in Chapter 8). At least, that is my speculation of what might lie within a keep of the kind Isaiah Berlin envisaged for us.

Notes

1 Some of these connections are suggested in the section 'French and English liberalism compared' of Douglas 1993c: 507–10.
2 The evolutionary narrative – from mechanical to organic solidarity – of Durkheim's *Division of Labour*, and also present in *Purity and Danger*, is undercut by recognizing 'secular savages' in technologically less complex societies, and social solidarities in technologically more complex societies. Apparently, the evolutionary narrative is thereby rewritten as a typology (that of grid and group). However, the division of labour cannot be entirely discounted by this strategy. The reformulation of *How Institutions Think*, where attention is shifted from society in aggregate to a plurality of institutional frameworks, reinstates a measure of complexity between types of society. In her Introduction to *Essays in the Sociology of Perception*, Mary Douglas noted that she had been forced (rather reluctantly) to recognize that individuals are members of institutions that differ in their range *and* in their characteristics (measured by grid and group). She gave the example of the businessman running his home hierarchically as a refuge from the competitive environment of his working life (1982c: 12–13). The implicit invitation to examine the complexities of identities defined by the cross articulations of multiple, and differently defined, memberships and exclusions is one she takes up only occasionally.
3 Mary Douglas also took the unusual step (in terms of the series' conventions) of persuading Godfrey Lienhardt to allow her to republish his essay, 'The situation of the death among the Anuak', in her edited conference papers from the Association of Social Anthropologists (Douglas 1970b).
4 James Spickard (1984) provides a more detailed discussion of the philosophical grounds of Douglas's project than I can here. However, I do not follow his attribution to Douglas of 'individualist' rather than 'hierarchical' preferences, despite the pair society–individual being as essential to her thought as it is for all Durkheimians.

5 Skorupski also discounts a second possible relativism (self-referential relativism) on the grounds that it could not lead to the social determination of knowledge by virtue of that claim also being relativized in its turn. For present purposes, this argument is subsumed under transcendental relativism, since its relationship to social determination poses similar practical problems. However, the recursive character of Douglas's appeals to the social dimension, and her emphasis upon credibility rather than truth, do impart elements of self-referentiality to her account.

6 An obvious comparison would be the Marxist equivocation over ideology on the same grounds; for instance, Jorge Larrain has strongly argued that ideology is not of necessity false (1979).

7 Thompson and Ellis suggest that Douglas's cultural typology now rests upon discriminating attitudes to power and authority rather than upon types of social relation (Ellis and Thompson 1997: 4). Although I find this difficult to accept, since they have worked closely with Mary Douglas over a long period, I am willing to be convinced. Clearly, attitudes to power and authority are supposed to be distinct in the four quadrants of the grid and group diagram, but their remaining distinct depends upon their functional relation to differing forms of social life (as argued in *How Institutions Think*). So, I would have thought that its social dimensions remain paramount to the theory as Mary Douglas presents it.

8 Thomas Beidelman perceptively remarked a relation between Douglas's notion of dirt/disorder, as intrinsic to classification, Aquinas's view of the necessity of sin, and Durkheim's of the social necessity of crime (PD/Anth: 908).

REFERENCES

Adams, John (1995) *Risk*, London: UCL Press.

Adler, Jeremy (1992) 'The poet as anthropologist: on the aphorisms of Franz Baermann Steiner', in E. Timms and R. Roberson (eds) *Austrian Studies III: Psychoanalysis in its Cultural Context*, Edinburgh: Edinburgh University Press.

—— (1994a) ' "The step swings away" and other poems by Franz Baermann Steiner' (trans. and introduction by Jeremy Adler), *Comparative Criticism* 16: 139–60.

—— (1994b) 'Special bibliography: the writings of Franz Baermann Steiner (1909–1952)', *Comparative Criticism* 16: 281–92.

—— (1994c) 'An Oriental in the West: the originality of Franz Steiner as poet and anthropologist', *Times Literary Supplement*, 7 October, pp. 16–17.

—— (1995) 'Die Freundschaft zwischen Elias Canetti und Franz Baermann Steiner', *Akzente* 42(3): 228–31.

Adler, Jeremy and Fardon, Richard (forthcoming 1999) 'Introductions' to *Franz Steiner: Selected Writings*, 2 volumes, Oxford: Berghahn, Studies in Methodology and History in Anthropology.

Anderson, Perry (1968) 'Components of the national culture', *New Left Review* July/August 50: 3–57.

Anon. (1995a) 'New model of the church', *Tablet*, 16 September, 249(8093): 1183.

Anon. (1995b) 'The hundred most influential books since the war', *Times Literary Supplement*, 6 October, p. 39.

Appadurai, Arjun (1986) 'Introduction: commodities and the politics of value', in Arjun Appadurai (ed.) *The Social Life of Things: Commodities in Cultural Perspective*, Cambridge: Cambridge University Press.

Arbuckle, Gerald A. (1986) 'Theology and anthropology: time for dialogue', *Theological Studies* 47(3): 428–47.

Beidelman, T.O. (1974a) *A Bibliography of the Writings of E.E. Evans-Pritchard*, London: Tavistock.

—— (1974b) 'Sir Edward Evan Evans-Pritchard (1902–1973). An appreciation', *Anthropos* 69: 553–67.

—— (1974c) *W. Robertson Smith and the Sociological Study of Religion* (Foreword by E. Evans-Pritchard), London and Chicago: Chicago University Press.

Bellaby, Paul (1990) 'To risk or not to risk? Uses and limitations of Mary Douglas on risk-acceptability for understanding health and safety at work and road accidents', *Sociological Review* 38: 465–83.

Bennett, Jackie and Forgan, Rosemary (eds) (1991) *There's Something about a Convent Girl*, London: Virago.

Benthall, Jonathan (1977) 'Grasshoppers and cattle', *Spectator*, 12 February 1988, p. 8.

—— (1990) 'Christianity and British anthropologists', unpublished paper for Network of Christian Anthropologists, New Orleans, American Anthropological Association, 1 December.

—— (1991) 'Address on the occasion of Mary Douglas's seventieth birthday', unpublished, University College, London, 26 March.

Berlin, Isaiah (1990) 'Joseph de Maistre and the origins of fascism', in Henry Harding (ed.) *The Crooked Timber of Humanity*, London: Fontana.

Bernstein, Basil (1971) *Class, Codes and Control. Vol. 1: Theoretical Studies Towards a Sociology of Language*, London: Routledge and Kegan Paul.

—— (1975) *Class, Codes and Control. Vol. 3: Towards a Theory of Educational Transmission*, London: Routledge and Kegan Paul.

Bohannan, Laura (1949) 'Dahomean marriage: a revaluation', *Africa* 19(4): 273–87.

Bohannan, Paul (1955) 'Some principles of exchange and investment among the Tiv', *American Anthropologist* LVII: 60–69.

Boholm, Åsa (1996) 'Risk perception and social anthropology: critique of cultural theory', *Ethnos* 61(1–2): 69–84.

Bourdieu, Pierre (1979) *La distinction: critique sociale du jugement*, Paris: Editions de Minuit. English trans. 1984.

Bowen, Elizabeth (1978) 'Introduction' to Antonia White [1933] *Frost in May*, London: Virago.

Boyle, Katie (1991) 'Katie Boyle', in Jackie Bennett and Rosemary Forgan (eds) *There's Something about a Convent Girl*, London: Virago.

Bulmer, Ralph (1967) 'Why is the cassowary not a bird? A problem of zoological taxonomy among the Karam of the New Guinea Highlands', *Man* NS 2(1): 5–25 (reprinted in Douglas (ed.) 1973b).

—— (1989) 'The uncleanness of the birds of Leviticus and Deuteronomy', *Man* NS 24(2): 304–20.

Burton, John (1992) *An Introduction to Evans-Pritchard*, vol. 45, Fribourg: University Press, Studia Instituti Anthropos.

Carroll, Michael P. (1978) 'One more time: Leviticus revisited', *Archives européennes de sociologie* 19(2): 339–46.

Coyle, Dennis J. and Ellis, Richard J. (eds) (1994) *Politics, Policy and Culture*, Boulder CO: Westview Press.

Curran, Charles E. (1986) 'Official Roman Catholic social teaching' and 'Subsidiarity, principle of', in James F. Childress and John MacQuarrie (eds) *A New Dictionary of Christian Ethics*, London: SCM Press.

Deflem, Mathieu (1991) 'Ritual anti-structure, and religion: a discussion of Victor Turner's processual analysis', *Journal for the Scientific Study of Religion* 39(1): 1–25.

De Heusch, Luc (1981) [1964] 'Social structure and praxis among the Lele of Kasai', in L. de Heusch *Why Marry Her?*, Cambridge: Cambridge University Press/Paris: Editions de la Maison des Sciences de l'Homme.

—— (1971) 'Préface', to Mary Douglas *De la souillure: essai sur les notions de pollution et de tabou*, Paris: François Maspero.

—— (1991) 'Hunting the pangolin', *Man* NS 28(1): 159–61.

—— (1996) 'Petite histoire d'une grande anthropologie', review of Goody (1995) *Social Anthropology* 4(3): 299–302.

Downey, Gary L. (1986) 'Risk in culture: the American conflict over nuclear power', *Cultural Anthropology* 1(4): 388–412.

Durkheim, Emile (1915) [1911] *The Elementary Forms of the Religious Life*, trans. J.W. Swain, London: Allen and Unwin.

Durkheim, Emile and Mauss, Marcel (1963) [1903] *Primitive Classification*, trans. (with Introduction) Rodney Needham, London: Cohen and West.

Eagleton, Terry (1967) 'Politics and the sacred: city on the hill, dung of the earth', *Commonweal*, 29 December, pp. 402–6.

—— (1970) *Exiles and Emigrés: Studies in Modern Literature*, London: Chatto and Windus.

Eakin, John Paul (1985) *Fictions in Autobiography. Studies in the Art of Self-Invention*, Princeton NJ: Princeton University Press.

Edwards, Adrian (1972) 'V.W. Turner: a pathbreaker in the forest of symbols', *Clergy Review* LVII: 410–18.

Ellen, Roy (1994) 'Comment: "Hunting the pangolin" ', *Man* NS 29(1): 181–82.

Ellis, Richard J. and Thompson, Michael (eds) (1997) *Culture Matters: Essays in Honour of Aaron Wildavsky*, Boulder CO/Oxford: Westview Press.

Evans-Pritchard, E.E. (1937) *Witchcraft, Oracles and Magic among the Azande*, Oxford: Clarendon Press.

—— (1940) *The Nuer. A Description of the Modes of Livelihood and Political Institutions of a Nilotic People*, Oxford: Clarendon Press.

—— (1951) 'The Institute of Social Anthropology', *Oxford Magazine*, 26 April, pp. 354–60.

—— (1956) *Nuer Religion*, Oxford: Clarendon Press.

—— (1959) 'The teaching of social anthropology at Oxford', *Man* (July, note 180) 59: 121–24.

—— (1962) 'Religion and the anthropologists' (Aquinas Lecture 1959), in *Essays in Social Anthropology*, London: Faber.

—— (1965) *Theories of Primitive Religion*, London: Oxford University Press.

—— (1970) 'Social anthropology at Oxford', *Journal of Anthropological Society of Oxford* 1(3): 103–109.

—— (1973) 'Fifty years of British anthropology', *Times Literary Supplement*, 6 July, p. 763.

—— (1981) *A History of Anthropological Thought*, André Singer (ed.), London: Faber.

Evans-Pritchard, E.E. and Fortes, M. (eds) (1940) *African Political Systems*, London: Oxford University Press for International African Institute.

Forde, Daryll (ed.) (1954) *African Worlds*, London: Oxford University Press for International African Institute.

Forde, Daryll and Kaberry, P.M. (eds) (1967) *West African Kingdoms in the Nineteenth Century*, London: Oxford University Press for International African Institute.

Forgan, Rosemary (1991) 'Introduction', in Jackie Bennett and Rosemary Forgan (eds) *There's Something about a Convent Girl*, London: Virago.

Fortes, M. and Dieterlain, G. (eds) (1965) *African Systems of Thought*, London: Oxford University Press for International African Institute.

Goody, Jack (1995) *The Expansive Moment: the Rise of Social Anthropology in Britain and Africa 1918–70*, Cambridge: Cambridge University Press.

REFERENCES

Greene, Graham (ed.) (1934) *The Old School: Essays by Divers Hands*, London: Jonathan Cape.

Gunneman, Jon P. (1986) 'Business ethics', in James F. Childress and John MacQuarrie (eds) *A New Dictionary of Christian Ethics*, London: SCM Press.

Gutzwiller, Kathryn (1996) 'Comments on Rolf Rendtorff', in John F.A. Sawyer (ed.) *Reading Leviticus. A Conversation with Mary Douglas*, Sheffield: Journal for the Study of the Old Testament Supplement Series no. 227, Sheffield Academic Press.

Hale, Sheila (1977) 'Closely observed brains', *Harper's Bazaar and Queen*, January, pp. 70–73, 144.

Hampton, James (1982) 'Giving the grid/group dimensions an operational definition', in Mary Douglas (ed.) *Essays in the Sociology of Perception*, London: Routledge and Kegan Paul.

Hargreaves Heap, Shaun and Ross, Angus (eds) (1992) *Understanding the Enterprise Culture: Themes in the Work of Mary Douglas*, Edinburgh: Edinburgh University Press.

Harrison, Henry (1918) *Surnames of the United Kingdom*, London: Morland Press.

Hastings, Adrian (1991) *A History of English Christianity 1920–1990*, 3rd edn, London: SCM Press.

Hayes, Patricia (1991) 'Patricia Hayes', in Jackie Bennett and Rosemary Forgan (eds) *There's Something about a Convent Girl*, London: Virago.

Hinnant, C. (1987) *Purity and Defilement in Gulliver's Travels*, London: Macmillan.

Holt, Hazel (1990) *A Lot to Ask: a Life of Barbara Pym*, London: Macmillan.

Hornsby-Smith, Michael P. (1987) *Roman Catholics in England: Studies in Social Structure since the Second World War*, Cambridge: Cambridge University Press.

—— (1991) *Roman Catholic Beliefs in England: Customary Catholicism and Transformations of Religious Authority*, Cambridge: Cambridge University Press.

Hunn, Eugene (1979) 'The abominations of Leviticus revisited', in Roy Ellen and David Reason (eds) *Classifications in their Social Context*, London: Academic Press.

Isenberg, Sheldon R. and Owen, Dennis E. (1977) 'Bodies, natural and contrived: the work of Mary Douglas', *Religious Studies Review* 3: 1–17.

Kenny, Michael G. (1987) 'Trickster and mystic: the anthropological persona of E.E. Evans-Pritchard', *Anthropology and Humanism Quarterly* 12(1): 9–15.

Kolde, T. (1911) 'Sacred Heart of Jesus, devotion to', in S.M. Jackson (ed.) *The New Schaff-Herzog Religious Encyclopedia*, New York/London: Funk and Wagnalls.

Kristeva, Julia (1982) *Powers of Horror: an Essay on Abjection*, New York: Columbia University Press.

Kuklick, H. (1991) *The Savage Within: the Social History of British Anthropology 1885–1945*, Cambridge: Cambridge University Press.

Kuper, Adam (1996) *Anthropology and Anthropologists: the Modern British School*, 3rd edn, London: Routledge.

Labanyi, Jo (1996) 'Typologies of catastrophe: horror and abjection in Daimela Eltit's *Vaca Sagrada*', in Anny Brooksbank Jones and Catherine Davies (eds) *Latin American Women's Writing: Feminist Readings in Theory and Crisis*, Oxford Hispanic Studies, Oxford: Oxford University Press.

Larrain, Jorge (1979) *The Concept of Ideology*, London: Hutchinson University Library.

Lethbridge, Lucy (1994) 'Among the outward, visible signs …', *Catholic Herald*, 15 April, p. 6.

Lévi-Strauss, Claude (1963) [1962] *Totemism*, Harmondsworth: Penguin.

Lévy-Bruhl, Lucien (1926) [1922] *How Natives Think*, trans. Lillian A. Clare, London: Allen and Unwin.

Lewis, Gilbert (1987) 'A lesson from Leviticus: leprosy', *Man* NS 22(4): 593–612.

Lewis, I.M. (1991) 'The spider and the pangolin', *Man* NS 26(3): 513–25.

Lienhardt, Godfrey (1961) *Divinity and Experience: the Religion of the Dinka*, Oxford: Clarendon Press.

—— (1974) 'E-P: a personal view', *Man* NS 9(2): 299–304.

Lodge, David (1980) *How Far Can You Go?*, Harmondsworth: Penguin.

Lombard, Charles M. (1976) *Joseph de Maistre*, Boston: Twayne Publishers.

Lukes, Stephen (1973) *Emile Durkheim. His Life and Work: a Historical and Critical Study*, Harmondsworth: Allen Lane.

McBrien, Richard P. (1987) 'Roman Catholicism', in M. Eliade (ed.) *The Encyclopedia of Religion*, vol. 12, London: Macmillan.

McCarthy, Mary (1963) [1957] *Memories of a Catholic Girlhood*, Harmondsworth: Penguin.

MacLysarght, Edward (1972) *Irish Families*, Dublin: Allen and Figgis.

Mack, John (1997) 'Kuba art and the birth of ethnography', in Enid Schildkrout and Curtis A. Keim (eds) *The Scramble for Art in Central Africa*, Cambridge: Cambridge University Press.

Mars, Gerald (1982) *Cheats at Work: an Anthropology of Workplace Crime*, London: Unwin.

Mercier, L. du S. C. (1967) 'Maistre, Joseph Maric de', in *The New Catholic Encyclopedia*, vol. 9, New York: McGraw-Hill.

Middleton, J. and Tait, D. (eds) (1958) *Tribes without Rulers: Studies in African Segmentary Systems*, London: Routledge and Kegan Paul.

Miller, Daniel (1987) *Material Culture and Mass Consumption*, Oxford: Basil Blackwell.

—— (1995) 'Consumption studies as the transformation of anthropology', in D. Miller (ed.) *Acknowledging Consumption*, London: Routledge.

Moell, C.J. (1967) 'Sacred Heart, devotion to', in *The New Catholic Encyclopedia*, vol. 12, New York: McGraw-Hill.

Needham, Rodney (1963) 'Introduction', in R. Needham (trans.) E. Durkheim and M. Mauss [1903] *Primitive Classification*, London: Cohen and West.

—— (1975) 'Polythetic classification: convergences and consequences', *Man* NS 10(3): 349–69.

Newman, J. (1967) 'Rerum novarum', in *The New Catholic Encyclopedia*, vol. 13, New York: McGraw-Hill.

Nisbet, Robert (1967) 'Comte, Auguste' and 'Durkheim, Emile', in *The New Catholic Encyclopedia*, vol. 4, New York: McGraw-Hill.

O'Leary, April, RSCJ (1992) *Living Tradition. The Chronicle of a School: Roehampton–Woldingham 1842–1992*, Woldingham School.

Olson, Mancur (1971) [1965] *The Logic of Collective Action: Public Goods and the Theory of Groups*, Cambridge MA/London: Harvard University Press.

Peel, J.D.Y. (1984) 'Making history: the past in the Ijesha present', *Man* NS 19(1): 111–32.

Pitt-Rivers, Julian (1971) [1954] *The People of the Sierra*, 2nd edn, Chicago/London: University of Chicago Press.

Platt, Steve (1988) 'Light in dark places', *New Society*, 27 May, 84(1326): 18–20.

Pyle, E.H. (1973) 'Mary Douglas on symbolism and social situations', in A. Cunningham (ed.) *The Theory of Myth: Six Studies*, London: Sheed and Ward.

Pym, Barbara (1994) [1984] *A Very Private Eye: the Diaries, Letters and Notebooks of Barbara Pym*, Hazel Holt and Hilary Pym (eds), London: Macmillan.

Radcliffe-Brown, A.R. and Forde, Daryll (eds) (1950) *African Systems of Kinship and Marriage*, London: Oxford University Press for International African Institute.

Ramsden, John (1980) *The Making of Conservative Party Policy. The Conservative Research Department since 1929*, London/New York: Longman.

Reid, Donald Malcolm (1990) *Cairo University and the Making of Modern Egypt*, Cambridge: Cambridge University Press.

Reis, Ria (ed.) (1996) *De Schoonheid van Mary Douglas, Focaal: Tijdschrift voor Antropologie* 28 (Themed Issue).

Richard, Lucien (1984) 'Anthropology and theology: the emergence of incarnational faith according to Mary Douglas', *Eglise et Théologie* 15: 131–54.

Richards, Audrey (1939) *Land, Labour and Diet in Northern Rhodesia: an Economic Study of the Bemba Tribe*, London: Oxford University Press for International African Institute.

—— (1950) 'Some types of family structure amongst the central Bantu', in A.R. Radcliffe-Brown and Daryll Forde (eds) *African Systems of Kinship and Marriage*, London: Oxford University Press for International African Institute.

Rodgers, Silvia (1996) 'On the shelf: *Purity and Danger*', 'Reviews of classics', *Sunday Times*, 8 September, 7: 9d.

Sawyer, John F.A. (ed.) (1996) *Reading Leviticus. A Conversation with Mary Douglas*, Sheffield: Journal for the Study of the Old Testament Supplement Series no. 227, Sheffield Academic Press.

Shrader-Frechette, Kristin (1991) 'Reductionist approaches to risk', in Deborah G. Mayo and Rachelle D. Hollander (eds) *Acceptable Evidence: Science and Values in Risk Management*, New York/Oxford: Oxford University Press.

Skorupski, John (1979) 'Pangolin power' and 'Our philosopher replies', in S.C. Brown (ed.) *Philosophical Disputes in the Social Sciences*, Sussex: Harvester Press.

Spearing, A.C. (1980) '*Purity* and Danger', *Essays in Criticism* 30: 293–310.

Spickard, James V. (1984) 'Relativism and cultural comparison in the work of Mary Douglas: an evaluation of the meta-theoretical strategy of her grid/group theory', unpublished PhD thesis, Graduate Theological Union.

—— (1989) 'A guide to Mary Douglas's three versions of grid/group theory', *Sociological Analysis* 50(2): 151–70.

—— (1990) 'Worldview, beliefs and society: Mary Douglas's contribution to the study of human ideas on ultimate reality and meaning', *Ultimate Reality and Meaning: Interdisciplinary Studies in the Philosophy of Understanding* 13: 109–21.

—— (1991) 'A revised functionalism in the sociology of religion: Mary Douglas's recent work', *Religion* 21(2): 141–64.

Srinivas, M.N. (1973) 'Itineraries of an Indian social anthropologist', *International Social Science Journal* 25: 129–48.

Steiner, Franz Baermann (1954a) 'Enslavement and the early Hebrew lineage system', *Man* 54, no. 102: 73–75 (reprinted in Steiner 1999, vol. 1).

—— (1954b) 'Notes on comparative economics', *British Journal of Sociology* 5(2): 118–29 (reprinted in Steiner 1999, vol. 2).

—— (1956) *Taboo*, (ed.) Laura Bohannan (with Introduction by E.E. Evans-Pritchard), London: Cohen and West. (Reprinted: Pelican (1967), Steiner (1999, vol. 1).)

—— (1992) *Franz Baermann Steiner*, Michael Hamburger (trans. and Introduction) *Modern Poetry in Translation: Special Issue*, New Series no. 2, London: King's College, London.

—— (1999) *Franz Steiner: Selected Writings*, 2 vols, Jeremy Adler and Richard Fardon (eds), Oxford: Berghahn, Studies in Methodology and History in Anthropology.

Tambiah, Stanley J. (1969) 'Animals are good to think and good to prohibit', *Ethnology* 8(4): 429–59 (excerpt in Douglas (ed.) 1973b).

Thompson, Michael, Ellis, Richard and Wildavsky, Aaron (1990) *Cultural Theory*, Boulder CO: Westview.

Turner, V.W. (1972) 'Passages, margins, and poverty: religious symbols of communitas', *Worship* Part I: 46(7): 390–412; Part II: 46(8): 482–94.

Turney, Jon (1988) 'Profile: Out of tune with the rest of the group', *Times Higher Education Supplement*, 25 November, pp. 11, 13.

—— (1996) 'Mary Douglas', in Sian Griffiths (ed.) *Beyond the Glass Ceiling: Forty Women whose Ideas Shape the Modern World*, Manchester: Times Higher Education Supplement/Manchester University Press (revision of Turney 1988).

University Gazette (University of Oxford), vols 79–83 (1949–53), Annual Reports of Institute of Social Anthropology 1948–49, 1952–53; Lecture Lists for Faculty of Anthropology and Geography.

Vansina, Jan (1978) *The Children of Woot: a History of the Kuba Peoples*, Dawson: University of Wisconsin Press.

—— (1987) 'The ethnographic account as a genre in Central Africa', *Paideuma* 33: 432–44.

—— (1994) *Living with Africa*, Madison: University of Wisconsin.

Welbourne, F.B. (1970) 'Mary Douglas and the study of religion', *Journal of Religion in Africa* 3(2): 89–95.

Werbner, R. (1990) 'South-Central Africa: the Manchester School and after', in Richard Fardon (ed.) *Localizing Strategies: Regional Traditions of Ethnographic Writing*, Edinburgh: Scottish Academic Press.

White, Antonia (1978) [1933] *Frost in May* (with Introduction by Elizabeth Bowen), London: Virago.

—— (1934) 'A child of the Five Wounds ("Lippington")', in Graham Greene (ed.) *The Old School: Essays by Divers Hands*, London: Jonathan Cape.

Wildavsky, Aaron (1975) 'The richest boy in Poltava', *Immigrant Parents and Native Children, Society*, November/December, 13(1).

—— (1986) 'On collaboration', *PS*, Spring: 237–48.

—— (1997) *Culture and Social Theory*, Sun-Ki Chai and Brendon Swellow (eds), New Brunswick NJ: Transaction Publishers.

Woodman, Thomas (1991) *Faithful Fictions: the Catholic Novel in British Literature*, Buckingham: Open University Press.

Wuthnow, R., Hunter, J.D., Bergesen, A. and Kurzweil, E. (1984) 'The cultural anthropology of Mary Douglas', in *Cultural Analysis: the Work of Peter L. Berger, Mary Douglas, Michel Foucault, and Jürgen Habermas*, London: Routledge and Kegan Paul.

APPENDIX 1
Mary Douglas: a bibliography 1950–98

Given the variety of genres and journals in which Mary Douglas has published, this bibliography is unlikely to be exhaustive. Publications by year are in the following order:

1 Books
2 Edited books
3 Articles in journals
4 Chapters in books
5 Review essays and book reviews
6 Letters and ephemera

Essays reprinted in Mary Douglas's collected essays – sometimes under different titles – are indicated as:

(IM)   *Implicit Meanings* 1975
(ITAV)   *In the Active Voice* 1982
(RAB)   *Risk and Blame* 1992
(OAO)   *Objects and Objections* 1992
(TS)   *Thought Styles* 1996

Mary Douglas's Lele fieldwork photographs were given to the Ethnography Division of the British Museum in 1997. 'Photos', below, indicates illustration with original ethnographic photographs.

TEW, MARY

1950

a   *Peoples of the Lake Nyasa Region*, in Daryll Forde (ed.) *Ethnographic Survey of Africa, Eastern Central Africa*, Part I, London: Oxford University Press for International African Institute.

b   'Elicited responses in Lele language (Belgian Congo)', *Kongo-Overzee* 16(4): 224–27.

DOUGLAS, MARY

1951

a   'A form of polyandry among the Lele of Kasai', *Africa* 21(1): 1–12.
b   'A further note on funeral friendship', *Africa* 21(1): 122–24.

1952

a   'Alternate generations among the Lele of Kasai', *Africa* 22(1): 59–65.
b   Review of Elizabeth Colson and Max Gluckman (eds) *Seven Tribes of British Central Africa*, *Africa* 22(1): 81–82. (Reply by Colson and Gluckman in *Africa* 22(3): 271–74.)
c   Review of Monica Wilson *Good Company: a Study of Nyakusa Age Villages*, *Africa* 22(3): 282–83.

1953

a   *A Study of the Social Organization of the Lele of Kasai*, DPhil thesis, University of Oxford.

1954

a   'Native treatment of leprosy in the Belgian Congo', *Medical Press*, 17 March: 251–52.
b   'The Lele of Kasai', in Daryll Forde (ed.) *African Worlds. Studies in the Cosmological Ideas and Social Values of African Peoples*, London: Oxford University Press for International African Institute.
c   Review of Max Gluckman *Rituals of Rebellion in South-East Africa* (Frazer Lecture, 1952), *Man* LIV, no. 143: 96.

1955

a   'Social and religious symbolism of the Lele of Kasai', *Zaire* 9(4): 385–402 (1 photo), reprinted in Y. Cohen (ed.) 1974 *Man in Adaptation*, vol. II, 2nd edn, Chicago: Aldine. (IM)
b   'The environment of the Lele', *Zaire* 9(8): 802–23. (7 photos)

c   'The Devil in Africa', *Contemporary Review* 187: 338–42.

d   Review of G.W.B. Huntingford *Ethnographic Survey of Africa: East Central Africa. Part VIII: The Southern Nilo-Hamites*, and P.T.W. Baxter and Audrey Butt *East Central Africa. Part IX: The Azande and Related Peoples of the Anglo-Egyptian Sudan and Belgian Congo, Man* LV, no. 93: 77.

e   Review of Mary Smith *Baba of Karo: a Woman of the Muslim Hausa, Africa* 25(2): 195–97.

1956

a   (and Daryll Forde) 'Primitive economics', in Harry Shapiro (ed.) *Man, Culture and Society*, Oxford: Oxford University Press, reprinted 1960, New York: Galaxy Books.

b   Review of Mgr J. Cuvelier and L. Jadin (eds) *L'ancien Congo d'après les archives romaines (1518–1640), Africa* 26(1): 84–86.

1957

a   'Animals in Lele religious symbolism', *Africa* 27(1): 46–58 (3 photos), reprinted in J. Middleton (ed.) 1967 *Myth and Cosmos*, Garden City, New York: Natural History Press. (IM, photos replaced by drawings)

b   'The pattern of residence among the Lele', *Zaire* 11(8): 819–43, reprinted in S. and P. Ottenberg (eds) 1960 *Cultures and Societies of Africa*, New York: Random House.

c   Review of M.I. Finley *The World of Odysseus, Man* LVII, no. 12: 13–14.

d   Review of J. Clyde Mitchell *The Yao Village. A Study of the Social Structure of a Nyasaland Tribe, Africa* 27(3): 290–92.

1958

a   'Raffia cloth distribution in the Lele economy', *Africa* 28(2): 109–22, reprinted in George Dalton (ed.) 1967 *Tribal and Peasant Economies*, New York: Natural History Press; Bobbs-Merrill reprint series in social science A-410. (ITAV selectively as section of 'Money')

b   Review of Marcel Griaule *Méthode de l'ethnographie, Africa* 28(4): 374–75.

1959

a   'Age-status among the Lele', *Zaire* 13(4): 386–413.

b   'The Lele', in Adrian Hastings (ed.) *The Church and the Nations*, London: Sheed and Ward.

c   Review of William Watson *Tribal Cohesion in a Money Economy*, *Man* LIX, no. 270: 168.

d   'The spirit of contradiction', review of V.W. Turner *Schism and Continuity in an African Society*, *Zaire* 13(3): 295–300.

1960

a   'Blood debts and clientship among the Lele', *Journal of Royal Anthropological Institute* 90(1): 1–28.

b   Review of Robert Briffault *The Mothers*, Audrey Richards *Chisungu*, *British Journal of Sociology* 11: 391–92.

c   Review of Ruth Slade *The Belgian Congo: Some Recent Changes*, *Man* LX, no. 220: 175.

d   Review of Elizabeth Colson *Marriage and the Family among the Plateau Tonga of Northern Rhodesia*, *Africa* 30(2): 196–97.

e   Review of Luc de Heusch *Essai sur le symbolisme de l'inceste royal en Afrique*, *African Affairs* 59, no. 234: 63–64.

1961

a   (and Daniel Biebuyck) *Congo Tribes and Parties*, (Preface by A.I. Richards), London: Royal Anthropological Institute, Pamphlets, no. 1 (49 pp.).

b   Review of Jacques Binet *Le mariage en Afrique noire*, *Africa* 31(1): 93–94.

c   Review of Elizabeth Marshall Thomas *The Harmless People*, *Africa* 31(1): 195–96.

d   Review of Paul Bohannan (ed.) *African Homicide and Suicide*, *African Affairs* 59, no. 239: 196–98.

1962

a   'Lele economy compared with the Bushong: a study of economic backwardness', in P. Bohannan and G. Dalton (eds) *Markets in Africa*, Evanston IL: Northwestern University Press, reprinted as 'The Lele – resistance to change', in E.E. LeClair, Jr and H.K. Schneider (eds) 1968 *Economic Anthropology: Readings in Theory and Analysis*, London: Holt, Rinehart and Winston, and (under original title) in G. Dalton (ed.) 1971 *Economic Development and Social Change: the Modernization of Village Communities*, American Museum of Natural History NY: Natural History Press. (ITAV)

b   Review of I.G. Cunnison *The Luapula Peoples of Northern Rhodesia: Custom and History in Tribal Politics*, *Africa* 32(3): 297–98.

c   Review of W.P.F. Burton *Luba Religion and Magic in Custom and Belief*, *Africa* 32(4): 409–10.

d   Review of A.W. Wolfe *In the Ngombe Tradition: Continuity and Change in the Congo, Man* LXII, no. 223: 141–42.

1963

a   *The Lele of Kasai*, London/Ibadan/Accra: Oxford University Press for International African Institute. (xiv + 286 pp.; 9 photos; pbk 1977; microfilm OCLC 34591346)

b   'Tribal policies for the old', *New Society* 25 April: 13–14. (1 photo)

c   'Techniques of sorcery control in central Africa', in John Middleton and E.H. Winter (eds) *Witchcraft and Sorcery in East Africa*, London: Routledge and Kegan Paul. (Reprinted 1978)

d   Review of Georges Brausch *Belgian Administration in the Congo, Man* LXIII, no. 64: 59.

e   Review of P.W.J. Ganshof van der Meersch *Congo, Mai–Juin 1960: rapport du ministre chargé des affaires générales en Afrique, Man* LXIII, no. 65: 59.

f   Review of Alan P. Merriam *Congo: Background of Conflict, Man* LXIII, no. 66: 59–60.

g   Review of J. van Wing, SJ *Etudes bakongo: sociologie-religion et magie*, 2nd edn, *Man* LXIII, no. 67: 60.

h   Review of August Verbeken *La révolte des Batetela en 1895: textes inédits, Africa* 33(1): 77.

i   Review of Daniel Biebuyck *Les Mitamba: système de mariages enchaînés chez les Babembe, Africa* 33(1): 79–80.

j   Review of L. de Sousberghe *Pactes de sang et pactes d'union dans la mort chez quelques peuplades du Kwango, Africa* 33(1): 82.

k   Review of Max Gluckman (ed.) *Essays on the Ritual of Social Relations, Africa* 33(3): 271–72.

1964

a   (ed.) *Man in Society. Patterns of Human Organization*, London: Macdonald; Garden City NY: Doubleday Pictorial Library; revised US edn 1968, Englewood Cliffs NJ: Responsive Environments Corporation. (Author of: Chapter 3 'Scale and organization'; Chapter 7 'Work and wealth'; Appendix: 'How societies are studied: the work of the anthropologist'.) (367 pp., 3 Lele photos)

French: *Les sociétés humaines, exemples de leur organisation*, trans. Armand Biancheri, Larousse: Paris.

b   'Matriliny and pawnship in central Africa', *Africa* 34(4): 301–13.

c   'Taboo', *New Society*, 12 March: 24–25.

d   Review of Pierre Elshout *Les Batwa des Ekonda, Africa* 34(3): 287.

e Review of Bronislaw Stefaniszyn *Social and Ritual Life of the Ambo*, *Africa* 34(4): 387–88.

1965

a Review of Georges Balandier *Sociologie actuelle de l'Afrique noire*, 2nd edn, *Man* LXV, no. 46: 58–59.

1966

a *Purity and Danger. An Analysis of Concepts of Pollution and Taboo*, London: Routledge and Kegan Paul (viii + 188pp.); 2nd imp. with corrections 1969, 1970; Pelican edn with corrections 1970, reprinted 1976; Routledge paperback 1978, 1980; Ark paperback 1984, reprinted 1985, 1986; Routledge reprints 1991, 1992, 1993, 1994, 1995 (viii + 193 pp.); US edn New York: Praeger 1966, 1970.

Dutch: (1976) *Reinheid en gevaar*, Utrecht and Amsterdam: Het Spectrum.

French: (1971) Anne Guérin (trans.) *De la souillure. Essai sur les notions de pollution et de tabou*, preface Luc de Heusch, Paris: Maspero, Bibliothèque d'Anthropologie. Reprints: (1981) Editions Maspero, Fondations; (1992) new edition with author's 'Preface' (see 1992e), Paris: Editions de la découverte, Textes à l'appui.

German: (1985) *Reinheit und Gefährdung*, Berlin: Dietrich Reimer Verlag (paperback Suhrkamp). Author's 'Introduction' to German translation also published as (1984) 'Profane Verunreinigung', *Freibeuter* 22: 24–34.

Italian: (1975) Alida Vatta (trans.) *Purezza e pericolo. Un'analisi dei concetti di contaminazione e tabù*, Bologna: Universale paperbacks, il Mulino. Reprint: (1993) new edn with author's 'Introduction' (see 1992e), Bologna: il Mulino.

Japanese: (1972) *Kegare to Kinki (Pollution and Taboo)*, Tokyo: Schichosa.

Portuguese: (1970s, exact date not known) *Pureza e perigo*, Editora Perspectiva: Brazil, São Paulo.

Spanish: (1973) *Pureza y peligro*, Madrid: Siglo veintuno de España sa; reprint: (1991) new edn with author's 'Introduction' (see 1992e).

Swedish: (1997) Arne Kallrén (trans.) *Renhet och Fara: En analys av begreppen orenande och tabu*, Nora: Nya Doxa.

Forthcoming translations: Serbo-Croat (Zemun: Biblioteka XX Vek); Finnish (Vastapaino); Korean (Hyundai Meehak Press); Norwegian (Pax); Russian (Kanon).

Widely excerpted, for instance:

Roland Robertson (ed.) (1969) *The Sociology of Religion*, Penguin Modern Sociology Readings, Harmondsworth: Penguin, as 'Primitive thought worlds' (Chapter 5).

William A. Lessa and Vogt, Evon Z. (eds) (1979) *Reader in Comparative Religion: an Anthropological Approach*, 4th edn, New York: Harper and Row, as 'The abominations of Leviticus' (Chapter 3).

b   'The contempt of ritual', *New Society*, 31 March, 23–24. (ITAV selectively under this title as section of 'Money'.)

c   'Population control in primitive groups', paper presented to Association of British Zoologists' Annual Meeting, 8 January 1966, *British Journal of Sociology* 17(3): 263–73; reprinted in A.H. Halsey (ed.) 1977 *Heredity and Environment*, London: Methuen. (ITAV)

d   Review of Igor de Garine *Les Massa du Cameroun: vie économique et sociale*, *Africa* 36(1): 93.

e   Review of Jan Vansina *Le royaume kuba*, *Africa* 36(1): 105–107.

f   'Straw men stand and fight', review of Elizabeth Marshall Thomas *Warrior Herdsmen*, *New Society*, 19 May: 28.

g   'Another of the Comedians?', review of Francis Huxley *The Invisibles*, *New Society*, 28 July: 166–67.

1967

a   'Witch beliefs in central Africa', *Africa* 37(1): 72–80.

b   'If the Dogon …', *Cahiers d'études africaines* 28, 7(4): 659–72. (IM)

c   (with Martha Harris: psychology) 'The family circle: anthropology',

      1: 'Brothers and sisters', *New Society*, 15 June: 872–73.

      2: 'Grandparents', *New Society*, 22 June: 917–18.

      3: 'In-laws', *New Society*, 29 June: 950.

      4: 'Aunts, uncles and cousins', *New Society*, 6 July: 10–11.

d   'The meaning of myth with special reference to "La geste d'Asdiwal"', in E.R. Leach (ed.) *The Structural Study of Myth and Totemism*, Association of Social Anthropologists, monograph 5, London: Tavistock. (IM)

e   'Primitive rationing', in R. Firth (ed.) *Themes in Economic Anthropology*, (Association of Social Anthropologists, monograph 6), London: Tavistock. (ITAV as section of 'Money'.)

f   Review of Paul Einzig *Primitive Money in its Ethnological, Historical and Economic Aspects*, 2nd edn, *Man* NS 2(2): 317.

g   Review of David Aberle *The Peyote Religion among the Navaho*, *Man* NS 2(3): 482–83.

h   Review of M. Fortes and G. Dieterlen (eds) *African Systems of Thought*, *Africa* 37(3): 352–53.

i   Letter to *The Times* concerning student unrest at LSE, 21 March: 13.
j   Letter to *New Society* commenting on an article by H. Dick, 25 May: 775.

1968

a   'The relevance of tribal studies', proc. 11th Annual Conference of Society
     for Psychosomatic Research, 'Disorders of sex and reproduction: psychoso-
     matic aspects', 10–11 November, Royal College of Physicians, London,
     Journal of Psychosomatic Research 12(1): 21–28. (IM 'Couvade and menstrua-
     tion')
b   'The social control of cognition: some factors in joke perception', *Man* NS
     3(3): 361–67. (IM 'Jokes')
c   'Dogon culture – profane and arcane', *Africa* 38(1): 16–25.
d   'Nommo and the fox', *Listener*, 12 September, 80: 328–30.
e   'The contempt of ritual' (St Thomas Day lecture for Dominicans at
     Blackfriars, Oxford), *New Blackfriars*, Part 1: June, 49: 475–82; Part 2: July,
     49: 528–35.
f   'Pollution', *International Encyclopedia of Social Sciences*, vol. 12, New York:
     Macmillan/Free Press. (IM)

1969

a   (and Phyllis Kaberry) (eds) *Man in Africa*, London: Tavistock Publications.
     (xxvii + 372pp.)
b   'Is matriliny doomed in Africa?', in Mary Douglas and Phyllis Kaberry (eds)
     Man in Africa, London: Tavistock Publications.
c   'Social conditions of enthusiasm for heterodoxy', in Robert F. Spencer (ed.)
     Forms of Symbolic Action, proc. 1969 Annual Spring Meeting of American
     Ethnological Society, Seattle: University of Washington Press; reprinted in
     V.W. Turner (ed.) *Symbolic Action*, Seattle: University of Washington Press.
d   'Which witch?', review of Lucy Mair *Witchcraft*, *New Society*, 7 August:
     222–23.
e   Letter in 'Virgin Births' controversy, *Man* NS 4(1): 133–34.

1970

a   *Natural Symbols. Explorations in Cosmology*, London: Barrie and Rockliff/Cresset
     Press. (xvii + 177 pp.)

     UK: (1973) rev. 2nd edn: (pbk) Pelican; (hbk) Barrie and Jenkins; both
     including Introduction to Pelican edn (219 pp.); reprint: Pelican (1978) of
     1973 edn; republication: Routledge (1996 hbk/pbk) of Pelican/Barrie and
     Jenkins, 2nd edns, with new Introduction (xi–xxx). (xxxvii + 183 pp.)

USA: (1970) 1st edn New York: Pantheon Books; 1972 reprint of 1st edn New York: Random House; 1982 republication (pbk) of 1st edn with new Introduction (pp. xix–xxvii), New York: Pantheon Books. (xxvii + 177pp.)

All translations are of 2nd edn:

Danish: (1975) Kirsten Poder Hansen (trans.) *Naturlige symboler*, Nyt Nordisk Forlag Arnold Busck.

Dutch: (1976) *Wereld-beelden*, Utrecht and Amsterdam: Het Spectrum.

German: (1974) Eberhard Bubser (trans.) *Ritual, Tabu und Körpersymbolik. Sozialanthropologische Studien in Industriegesellschaft und Stammeskultur*, Frankfurt: Fischer Verlag.

Italian: (1979) *I simboli naturali. Sistema cosmologico e struttura sociale*, Torino: Einaudi.

b   (ed.) *Witchcraft Accusations and Confessions*, Association of Social Anthropologists Conference, King's College, Cambridge, 3–6 April 1968, monograph 9, London: Tavistock Publications. (387 pp.)

Italian: (1980) *Stregoneria: confessioni e accusi*, Torino: Einaudi.

c   'Heathen darkness, modern piety', *New Society*, 12 March: 432–34. Reprinted as 'The myth of primitive religion', *Commonweal*, 9 October, 92(2): 41–44. (IM 'Heathen Darkness')

d   'Smothering the differences – Mary Douglas in a savage mind about Lévi-Strauss', *Listener*, 13 September, 84: 313–14.

e   'Environments at risk', lecture, Institute of Contemporary Arts, London, *Times Literary Supplement*, 30 October: 1273. Reprints in: Jonathan Benthall (ed.) 1972 *Ecology in Theory and Practice*, New York: Viking Press; Jonathan Benthall (ed.) 1972 *Ecology, the Shaping Enquiry*, London: Longman. (IM)

f   'Preface' and 'Introduction: thirty years after *Witchcraft, Oracles and Magic*', in Mary Douglas (ed.) 1970b: xi–xxxviii.

g   'The healing rite', review of V.W. Turner *The Forest of Symbols* and *The Drums of Affliction*, *Man* NS 5(2): 302–308. (IM)

h   Review of Ernest Gellner *Saints of the Atlas*, *Journal of Anthropological Society of Oxford* 1(2): 101.

i   Review of Harvey Cox *The Feast of Fools: a Theological Essay of Festivity and Fantasy*, *Man* NS 5(3): 560.

j   Review of Claude Meillassoux *Anthropologie économique des Gouro de Côte d'Ivoire*, *Africa* 40(1): 87–88.

k   Review of Peter L. Berger *A Rumour of Angels*, *New Society*, 9 April: 610.

1971

a   'Do dogs laugh? A cross-cultural approach to body symbolism', proc. 14th Annual Conference of Society for Psychosomatic Research on 'Psychosomatic disorders of voluntary movement', *Journal of Psychosomatic Research* 15: 387–90. (IM)

b   'In the nature of things (on man and his place in nature)', *New Society*, 9 December, 480: 1133–38. (Excerpt from Inaugural Lecture, University College London, November 1971; IM full version)

c   'Schon's Utopia', *Listener*, 3 June, 85: 710–11.

d   Review of Richard M. Titmuss *The Gift Relationship: From Human Blood to Social Policy*, *Man* NS 6(3): 499–500.

e   Review of Isaac Schapera *Rainmaking Rites of the Tswana Tribes*, *Man* NS 6(4): 712.

1972

a   'Introduction' to English pbk edn (trans. M. Sainsbury) of Louis Dumont *Homo Hierarchicus*, St Albans: Paladin. (IM 'Louis Dumont's structural analysis')

b   'Deciphering a meal', *Daedalus*, Winter, special issue on *Myth, Symbol and Culture*: 68–81. (IM)

c   'Self-evidence', Henry Myers Lecture of Royal Anthropological Institute, *Proc. Royal Anthropological Institute*, 1972–73: 27–44. (IM)

d   'Symbolic orders in the use of domestic space', in P.J. Ucko, R. Tringham and G.W. Dimbleby (eds) *Man, Settlement and Urbanism*, proc. Research Seminar in Archaeology and Related Subjects meeting, Institute of Archaeology, London University, 1970, London: Duckworth.

e   'Humans speak', review of Basil Bernstein *Class, Codes and Control*, vol. 1, *Listener*, 9 March, 87: 2241. (IM)

f   Letter concerning 'In the nature of things' (Douglas 1971b), *New Society*, 6 January: 31.

1973

a   'Introduction' to rev. 2nd edn of *Natural Symbols*, Harmondsworth: Penguin. (see 1970a)

b   (ed.) *Rules and Meanings. The Anthropology of Everyday Knowledge*, Harmondsworth/Baltimore: Penguin. (319 pp.) (Reprinted 1977.)

c   'Torn between two realities', *Times Higher Education Supplement*, 15 June. (IM 'The authenticity of Castaneda')

d   'The exclusion of economics', *Times Literary Supplement*, special issue on 'The state of anthropology', 6 July: 781–82. (ITAV) e   'Food as a system of communication', report to Department of Health and Social Security, November. (ITAV)

f   'The Tablet Notebook: E. Evans-Pritchard', *Tablet*, 20 October: 999.

g   'Critique and commentary', addendum to Jacob Neusner *The Idea of Purity: The Haskell Lectures, 1972–73. Studies in Judaism in late antiquity from the first to the seventh century 1*, Leiden: Brill.

h   'Breaking boundaries', (anonymous) review of Robin Horton and Ruth Finnegan (eds) *Modes of Thought: Essays on Thinking in Western and Non-Western Societies*, *Times Literary Supplement*, 14 September.

i   Review of Luc de Heusch *Le roi ivre ou l'origine de l'état*, *Man* NS 8(3): 495–96.

j   Review of P.H. Gulliver *Neighbours and Networks*, *Bulletin of School of Oriental and African Studies* 36(3): 733–35.

1974

a   (and Michael Nicod) 'Taking the biscuit: the structure of British meals', *New Society*, 19 December, 637: 744–47.

b   'Food as an art form', lecture, Royal Anthropological Institute, London, 30 May, *Studio International*, September, 188: 83–88. (ITAV)

c   'Lying and deceit, conference report', *Times Higher Education Supplement*, 8 March; reprinted in *Rain*, May–June, 2: 1–2.

d   Letter concerning review of R. Willis *Man and Beast*, *Times Literary Supplement*, 4 October: 1079.

e   Letter concerning Essex University Enquiry Report, *The Times*, 3 August: 13d.

1975

a   *Implicit Meanings. Essays in Anthropology*, London/Boston: Routledge and Kegan Paul. (xxi + 325 pp.) (Reprinted 1978, 1979, 1984; Routledge 1991, 1993)

     Italian: (1985) Eleanora Bona (trans.) *Antropologia e simbolismo. Religione, cibo e dinaro nella vita sociale*, Introduction by Luisa Leonini, Bologna: il Mulino. (Selected essays from IM and ITAV.)

b   'In the nature of things', inaugural lecture, University College London, 1971. (First complete publication in IM; shorter version as 1971b.)

c   'The sociology of bread' (with discussion), in Arnold Spicer (ed.) *Bread: Social, Nutritional and Agricultural Aspects of Wheaten Bread*, London: Applied Science Publishers.

d   (and James Douglas) 'English translation of "The Introduction to *Les Nuer*" by Louis Dumont', in J.H.M. Beattie and R.G. Lienhardt (eds) *Studies in*

Social Anthropology: Essays in Memory of E.E. Evans-Pritchard, Oxford: Oxford University Press.

e 'The self-completing animal', review of Clifford Geertz, *The Interpretation of Culture*, *Times Literary Supplement*, 8 August: 886–87.

1976

a 'Relative poverty – relative communication', in A.H. Halsey (ed.) *Traditions of Social Policy: Essays in Honour of Violet Butler*, Oxford: Basil Blackwell. (ITAV 'Goods as a system of communication')

b Letter concerning move of Royal Anthropological Institute library, *The Times*, 5 August: 15.

1977

a ' "Beans" means "thinks" ', *Listener*, 8 September, 98: 292–93.

b 'O reason not the need!', *Listener*, 15 September, 98: 330–31.

1977a/b reprinted as 'Why do people want goods?' in Shaun Hargreaves Heap and Angus Ross (eds) *The Enterprise Culture: Themes in the Work of Mary Douglas*, Edinburgh: Edinburgh University Press.

c 'The food art exhibition', catalogue notes, Cambridge Festival, July. (ITAV)

d 'Introduction', in Jessica Kuper (ed.) *The Anthropologist's Cookbook*, London: Routledge and Kegan Paul; New York: Universe Books. (ITAV 'Food is not feed')

1978

a *Cultural Bias*, Royal Anthropological Institute occasional paper 35, London: RAI. (59pp.) (Versions as Frazer and E.M. Wood lectures 1977; US publication: Atlantic Highlands: Humanities Press.) (ITAV)

b (and Baron Isherwood) *The World of Goods. Towards an Anthropology of Consumption*, New York: Basic Books. Reprints: (1979) London: Allen Lane (193 pp.); (1980) Penguin Education (xi + 228 pp.); (1982) New York: Basic Books (xi + 228 pp.); (1996) London: Routledge, rev. edn with new Introduction (xxvii + 169pp.).

Italian: (1984) *Il mondo delle cose. Oggetti, valori, consumo*, Bologna: il Mulino.

Spanish: (1990) *El mundo de los bienes. Hacia una antropología de consumo*, Mexico: Grijalbo, Consejo Nacional para la Cultura y las Artes.

c 'Judgements on Sir James Frazer', *Daedalus*, 'Generations', Fall: 151–64. (ITAV) d   'Introduction to *The Illustrated Golden Bough* by Sir James Frazer', Mary Douglas (general editor), abridged and illustrated by Sabine MacCormick, Garden City: Doubleday/ Rainbird.

e   'Culture: structures of gastronomy', in *Annual Report and Call for Research Proposals*, New York: Russell Sage Foundation.

     French: (1979) 'Les structures du culinaire', *Communications* 31: 145–70.

f   Review of David Bloor *Knowledge and Social Imagery*, *Sociological Review* 26(1): 154–57.

1979

a   'Passive voice theories in religious sociology' (1978 Paul Douglass lecture), *Review of Religious Research*, Fall 21(1): 51–61. (ITAV)

b   (and Ravindra S. Khare) 'International commission on the anthropology of food: statement on its history and current objectives', *Social Science Information* 18(6): 903–13. (See 1980b.)

c   'Accounting for taste', *Psychology Today* 13(2): 44–45, 48 & 51. (Based on 1978e.)

d   'World view and the core', in S.C. Brown (ed.) *Philosophical Disputes in the Social Sciences*, Sussex: Harvester Press/New Jersey: Humanities Press. (Reply to John Skorupski, 'Pangolin power', pp. 151–76, with Skorupski's further response, 'Our philosopher replies', pp. 188–94.)

1980

a   *Evans-Pritchard*, Glasgow: Fontana Modern Masters (pbk), Harvester (hbk) (140 pp.); *Evans-Pritchard: His Life, Work, Writings, and Ideas*, New York: Viking Press. (x + 151 pp.)

b   (and Ravindra S. Khare) 'International commission on the anthropology of food and food problems', *Appetite* 1(4): 317–20. (Also published in: (1980) *Ecology of Food and Nutrition* 10(1): 63–64.)

c   '*Purity and Danger* revisited', lecture, Institute of Education, London, 12 May, *Times Literary Supplement*, 19 September: 1045–46.

d   'Introduction: Maurice Halbwachs (1877–1945)', in Francis J. Ditter and Vida Y. Ditter (trans.) Maurice Halbwachs *Collective Memory*, New York: Harper and Row. (ITAV)

e   Review of Peter Brown *The Making of Late Antiquity*, *Religious Studies Review* (April) 6(2): 96–99. (ITAV 'The debate on the Holy')

f   Letter concerning 1980a *Evans-Pritchard*, *New Society* 53: 187.

1981

a   (and Jonathan Gross) 'Food and culture: measuring the intricacy of rule systems', *Social Science Information* 20(1): 1–35; also in (1981) *Journal for Anthropological Study of Human Movements* 1(3): 139–65.

b   'Nature et pureté', *Le débat*, Editions Gallimard, March, no.10.

c   'High culture and low', review of Pierre Bourdieu *La distinction: critique sociale du jugement*, *Times Literary Supplement*, 13 February: 163–64. (ITAV 'Good taste')

1982

a   *In the Active Voice*, London/Boston: Routledge and Kegan Paul with Russell Sage Foundation. (xi + 396 pp.)

    Italian: (1985) Eleanora Bona (trans.) *Antropologia e simbolismo. Religione, cibo e dinaro nella vita sociale*, Introduction by Luisa Leonini, Bologna: il Mulino. (Selected essays from IM and ITAV.)

b   (and Aaron Wildavsky) *Risk and Culture: An Essay on the Selection of Technical and Environmental Dangers*, Berkeley/London: University of California Press. (ix + 221 pp.); (1983 pbk): cover carries sub-title *An Essay on the Selection of Technological and Environmental Dangers*; translations: Italian.

c   (ed. and introductions) *Essays in the Sociology of Perception*, London/Boston: Routledge and Kegan Paul with Russell Sage Foundation. (viii + 340 pp.)

d   'Introduction', to US pbk of 1st edn of *Natural Symbols*, New York: Pantheon Books (see 1970a).

e   'The effects of modernization on religious change', *Daedalus*, Winter, 111: 1–19; reprinted in *Daedalus* special issue *Three Decades of Daedalus*, Summer 1988 (117): 457–84, and in Douglas and Tipton (eds) 1983a; excerpt as: (1982) 'Bureaucracy as rain god', *Psychology Today* 16(8): 12.

f   'Guest editorial: the future of semiotics', *Semiotica* 38(3/4): 197–203.

g   'Viewpoint article: foodstuff', *Times Literary Supplement*, 4153, 5 November: 1216.

1983

a   (and Steven M. Tipton) (eds) *Religion and America: Spiritual Life in a Secular Age*, Boston: Beacon Press (xiii + 290 pp.). (Largely based on winter 1982 issue of *Daedalus*.)

b   'Social anthropology in the 1980s: a symposium – Asynchrony', *Rain* 56: 7–8.

c   'An appreciation of Meyer Fortes', *African Studies Newsletter*, Northwestern University, 11 February.

d   'How to make identity problems disappear', in Anita Jacobson-Widding (ed.) *Identity: Personal and Socio-cultural. A Symposium* (Acta Universitas Upsaliensis: Uppsala Studies in Cultural Anthropology), Uppsala/Stockholm: Almqvist and Wiksell; Atlantic Highlands Jersey: Humanities Press.

e   'Perceiving low probability events', in James Douglas, Mary Douglas and Michael Thompson *Social Choice and Cultural Bias*, collaborative paper 83–84, International Institute for Applied Systems Analysis AQ-2361, Laxenberg, Austria. (RAB 'Muffled Ears')

f   'Foreword', to Howard Kunreuther and Joanne Linneroth (eds) *Risk Analysis and Decision Processes: the Siting of Liquified Energy Gas Facilities in Four Countries*, New York: Springer Verlag.

g   'Morality and culture', review of A. Mayer (ed.) *Culture and Morality*; R. Needham *Circumstantial Deliveries*; P.R. Sanday *Female Power and Male Dominance*; M. Midgeley *Heart and Mind*, *Ethics* 93(4): 786–91.

h   'Little room for the anthropologist', review of Robert Cassidy *Margaret Mead: A Voice for the Century*, *Nature*, April 302: 759–61.

i   Review of Gillian Feeley-Harnik *The Lord's Table: Eucharist and Passover in Early Christianity*, *American Ethnologist* 10(1): 178–79.

j   Letter 'Risk assessment', *Bulletin of Atomic Scientists* 39(7): 58–59. (One of two letters from MD and Aaron Wildavsky concerning review by John Holdren of *Risk and Culture*, followed by response, *op. cit.*: 59–60.)

k   Letter concerning food and nutrition education, *Times Literary Supplement*, 4170, 4 March: 215.

1984

a   (ed.) *Food in the Social Order. Studies of Food and Festivities in Three American Communities*, New York: Russell Sage Foundation. (xi + 292 pp.)

b   'Comment on Jose Carlos Gomes da Silva "Versants de la pollution"', *L'Homme*, July–December xxiv (3–4): 127–29.

c   'Fundamental issues in food problems', *Current Anthropology* 25(4): 498–99.

d   'Standard social uses of food: introduction', in Mary Douglas (ed.) 1984a: 1–39.

e   'Obituary of Victor Turner (died 19 December 1983)', *Rain* 61: 11.

f   'Betwixt, bothered and bewildered', review of E.R. Leach and D. Alan Aycock *Structuralist Interpretation of Biblical Myth*, *New York Review of Books*, 20 December: 43–46.

    Italian: (1985) 'Il santo vero. Riflessioni sull'idea del sacro in Durkheim', *Intersezioni* 3: 431–43.

    German: (1987) 'Heilige Wahrheit – Uberlegungen zu Durkheims Begriff des Heiligen', *Das Heilige, sein Spur in der Moderne, Athenäum*, 428–40.

g   Review of Elvin Hatch *Culture and Morality*, *Ethics*, June 94(3): 517–20.

1985

a   *Risk Acceptability According to the Social Sciences*, New York: Russell Sage Foundation (115pp.). UK edn (1986) London: Routledge and Kegan Paul; US pbk (1986) New York: Basic Books.

Italian: (1991) *Come percepiamo il pericolo: antropologia de rischio*, with new Preface, Milan: Feltrinelli. (Italian Preface in English as Preface RAB 'Risk and danger'.)

b   'Pascal's great wager' (address to American Academy of Religion, 1983), *L'Homme* 93(xxv)1: 13–20. (RAB 'Credibility') (Reprinted with slight additions as 1986c.)

c   (and Edmund Perry) 'Anthropology and comparative religion' (with reply by J. Neusner), *Theology Today*, January 41(4): 410–27.

d   'Concealing and exposing', review of Valerie Steele *Fashion and Eroticism*, *Times Literary Supplement*, 4310, 8 November: 1254.

e   Review of M. Taylor *Community, Anarchy and Liberty*, *Ethics* 96(1): 189–191.

f   Review of C. Perrow *Normal Accidents: Living with High-Risk Technologies*, *Contemporary Sociology* 14(2): 171–73.

1986

a   *How Institutions Think* (Frank W. Abrams Lectures, 1985), Syracuse NY: Syracuse University Press. (xi + 146 pp.) (UK (1987) London: Routledge and Kegan Paul)

French: (1989) Anne Abeillé (trans.) *Ainsi pensent les institutions*, with Preface by Georges Balandier, Paris: Usher.

Italian: (1990) Pier Paolo Giglioli and Carla Caprioli (trans.) *Como pensano le istituzioni*, with Introduction by Pier Paolo Giglioli, Bologna: il Mulino.

German: (1991) *Wie Institutionen Denken*, Suhrkamp.

b   'Lita Osmundsen and the Wenner–Grenn foundation: an appreciation', *Current Anthropology* 27(5): 521–25.

c   'The social preconditions of radical scepticism', in John Law (ed.) *Power, Action and Belief. A New Sociology of Knowledge?*, Sociological Review Monograph no. 32, London/ Boston: Routledge and Kegan Paul. (Version of 1985b with slight additions.)

d   'Institutionalized public memory', in J.F. Short, Jr (ed.) *The Social Fabric: Dimensions and Issues*, American Sociological Association Presidential Series, New York: Sage Publications.

e   Review of L. Jayyusi *Categorization and the Moral Order*, *Ethics* 96(3): 633–35.

f Review of Marvin Harris *Good to Eat: Riddles of Food and Culture*; Stephen Mennell *All Manners of Food: Eating and Taste in England and France from the Middle Ages to the Present*, *Los Angeles Times*, 8 April.

1987

a *Culture as Explanation*, Charles Carter lecture, University of Lancaster. (24 pp.) (See 1989c)

b (ed.) *Constructive Drinking: Perspectives from Anthropology*, Cambridge: University Press; and (1991) Paris: Maison des Sciences de l'Homme. (304 pp., pbk 1991)

c 'Les études de perception du risque: un état de l'art', in J.L. Fabiani and J. Theys (eds) *La société vulnérable*, Paris: Presse de l'Ecole Normale Supérieure.

d 'Wants', in John Eatwell, Murray Milgate and Peter Newman (eds) *The New Palgrave: A Dictionary of Economics*, vol. 4, Q–Z, Basingstoke/London: Macmillan. (RAB)

e 'The woman–priest problem: a cultural analysis', in Kristofer Schipper and Anne Marie Blondeau (eds) *Essais sur le rituel* I, Colloque du centenaire de la section des sciences religieuses de l'Ecole Pratique des Hautes Etudes, Bibiliothèque de l'Ecole des Hautes Etudes, Section des Sciences Religieuses, vol. xcii: 173–94, Louvain/Paris: Peeters. (RAB as 'The debate on women priests')

f 'Woman the measure of all things. Yvonne Verdier's *Façons de dire, façons de faire*', *Anthropology Today* 3(5): 2–4.

g 'The hardware store', in *Catalogue of the Hardware Exhibition* at Minneapolis College of Art and Design. (OAO)

h 'A ritual in time', review of Maurice Bloch *From Blessing to Violence*, *Times Literary Supplement*, 4402, 14 August: 870a.

i Review of L.S. Dubin *The History of Beads, from 30,000 BC to the Present*, *New York Times Book Review*, 29 November: 12.

1988

a 'Complexité culturelle: cuisine et société', *Sociétés*, September 19: 6–10.

b 'Les utilitzacions del perill en el procés de la identificació simbólica', in *Curs 18 Construint identitats: mites i símbols*, Barcelona: Fundació Caixo de Pensions (in Catalan).

c 'Taste', *Faces* (Children's Journal of Metropolitan Museum).

d 'The liturgical veto to assert women's views', *Catholic Herald*, Friday 22 July: 8.

e 'The whites and the yoke', review of Keith Griffin *World Hunger and the World Economy*, *Times Literary Supplement*, 4423, 8 January: 35a.

f   'Where there's muck: hazardous wastes', review of Brian Wynne (ed.) *Risk Management and Hazardous Waste: Implementation and the Dialectics of Credibility*, *Times Literary Supplement*, 4463, 14 October: 1143a–44.

g   Review of R.W. Lovin and F.E. Reynolds *Cosmogony and Ethical Order: New Studies in Comparative Ethics*, *Ethics* 98(2): 407–409.

1989

a   'The Hotel Kwilu – a model of models' (87th Distinguished Lecture, Annual Meeting of American Anthropological Association, 20 November 1988, Phoenix, Arizona), *American Anthropologist* 91(4): 855–65. (RAB)

b   'The background of the grid dimension: comment on James Spickard's guide to grid/group theory', *Sociological Analysis* 50(1): 171–76.

c   'Institutions of the third kind', *Journal of General Management* 14(4): 34–52. (Version of 1987a) (RAB)

d   'A typology of cultures: the example of the biosphere' (address to congress of German-speaking sociologists, Zurich, October 1988), *Kultur und Gesellschaft*, Frankfurt/New York: Campus Verlag. (RAB 'A credible biosphere')

e   'Correttezza delle categorie', *Rassegna Italiana di Sociologia* XXX(2): 207–38.

English: 'Rightness of categories', in Mary Douglas and David Hull (eds) 1992c.

f   'Culture and collective action', in Morris Freilich (ed.) *The Relevance of Culture*, New York: Bergin and Garvey. (RAB 'The normative debate and the origins of culture')

g   'The hungry generations', review of D. Arnold *Social Crisis and Historical Change*, V. George *Wealth, Poverty and Starvation*, P. Raikes *Modernising Hunger*, *Times Literary Supplement*, 4488, 7 April: 355a–56.

h   'A gentle deconstruction', review of Marilyn Strathern *The Gender of the Gift*, *London Review of Books*, 4 May, 11(9): 17–18.

1990

a   'Risk as a forensic resource', *Daedalus*, special issue on 'Risk', Fall, 119(4): 1–16. (RAB 'Risk and justice')

b   'The body of the world', International Social Science Journal, issue: 'Tales of cities: the culture and political economy of urban spaces', XLII(3): 395–99. (OAO)

French: 'Le corps cosmique', *Histoire des villes, Revue internationale des sciences sociales* 125: 439–42.

c   'La connaissance de soi', *La revue du MAUSS* 8: 125–36.

d   (and Marcel Calvez) 'The self as a risk taker: a cultural theory of contagion in relation to AIDS', *Sociological Review* 38(3): 445–64. (RAB)

e   'Die Idee des Selbst: ein Beispiel von Denkstil', *German Yearbook of Comparative Social Research*, Berlin: Berliner Institut für Vergleichende Sozialforschung. (English: 1992f)

f   'No free gifts', foreword to Marcel Mauss (1950) W.D. Halls (trans.) *Essay on the Gift. The Form and Reason for Exchange in Archaic Societies*, London: Routledge. (RAB)

     French: (1989) 'Il n'y a pas de don gratuit', *La revue du MAUSS* 4: 99–115.

g   'The pangolin revisited: a new approach to animal symbolism', in Roy Willis (ed.) *Signifying Animals: Human Meaning in the Natural World*, One World Archaeology, vol. 16, London: Unwin Hyman; reprint: (1993 hbk/pbk) London: Routledge. (TS 'Anomalous animals and animal metaphors')

h   'Converging on autonomy: anthropology and institutional economics', in Oliver E. Williamson (ed.) *Organization Theory, from Chester Barnard to the Present and Beyond*, Oxford: Oxford University Press. (RAB 'Autonomy and opportunism')

i   'The devil vanishes', *Tablet*, 28 April: 513–14.

j   'How to be green', *London Review of Books*, 13 September, 12(17): 8–9

k   Review of V.W. Turner and E.M. Bruner (eds) *The Anthropology of Experience*, *American Anthropologist* 92(1): 252–54.

1991

a   'Witchcraft and leprosy: two strategies of exclusion', *Man* NS 26(4): 723–36. (Originally for MIT conference on 'Epidemics: peoples in cultural studies', October 1990.) (RAB 'Witchcraft and leprosy: two strategies for rejection') (Also to be published in German.)

b   'The idea of a home: a kind of space', *Social Research* 58(1): 287–307. (OAO 'The idea of home')

c   'My circus fieldwork', *Semiotica* 85(3/4): 201–204.

d   'Ralph Bulmer among the master detectives', in Andrew Pawley (ed.) *Man and a Half: Essays in Pacific Anthropology and Ethnobiology in Honour of Ralph Bulmer*, Auckland: Polynesian Society Memoir no.48 (OAO 'Unnatural kinds'; TS 'Classified as edible')

e   'Foreword' to Robert A. Atkins, Jr *Egalitarian Community: Ethnography and Exegesis*, Tuscaloosa/London: University of Alabama Press.

f   'Faith, hope and probability', review of Ian Hacking *The Taming of Chance*, *London Review of Books*, 23 May, 13(10): 6–8.

g   'The spatial projection of social relations', review of Christina Toren *Making Sense of Hierarchy: Cognition as a Social Process in Fiji*, *Current Anthropology* 32(4): 500–501.

h   Note 'From Mauss to MAUSS', *Stanford French Review* 15(3): 412. (Excerpts from 1990f.)

i   Comment on W.E.A. van Beek 'The Dogon restudied: a field evaluation of the work of Marcel Griaule', *Current Anthropology* 32(2): 161–62 (of 139–67).

1992

a   *Risk and Blame: Essays in Cultural Theory*, London/New York: Routledge. (xii + 323pp.) (1994 pbk)

Italian (2 vols): (1994) Giovana Bettini (trans.) *Credere e pensare*, Introduction by Luisa Leonini, Bologna: il Mulino; (1996) Giovanna Bettini (trans.) *Rischio e colpa* with Introduction by Alessandro Dal Lago, Bologna: il Mulino.

b   *Objects and Objections*, Monograph Series of Toronto Semiotic Circle no.9, Toronto: Victoria College, University of Toronto. (v + 98 pp.)

c   (and David Hull) (eds) *How Classification Works: Nelson Goodman among the Social Sciences*, Edinburgh: Edinburgh University Press. (vi + 281 pp.)

d   'El nuevo ascetismo: cultura y medio ambiente', *Revista d'Occidente* October, 137: 29–54. (Spanish: 'The new asceticism: culture and environment')

e   'Risk and blame' (English version of 'Introduction' to Spanish, French and Italian editions of *Purity and Danger* pp. 3–14 with slight revision, see 1966a) in 1992a RAB, pp. 3–21.

f   'The person in an enterprise culture', in Shaun Hargreaves Heap and Angus Ross (eds) *The Enterprise Culture: Themes in the Work of Mary Douglas*, Edinburgh: Edinburgh University Press. (RAB 'Thought style exemplified: the idea of the self' with slight modifications)

g   'An institutional ecology of values', in Shaun Hargreaves Heap and Angus Ross (eds) *The Enterprise Culture: Themes in the Work of Mary Douglas*, Edinburgh: Edinburgh University Press.

h   'The consumer's conscience'. (OAO; TS 'The consumer's revolt')

i   'In defence of shopping', in Reinhard Eisendle and Elfie Miklautz (eds) *Produktkulturen: Dynamik und Bedeutungswandel des Konsums*, Frankfurt/New York: Campus Verlag. (OAO; TS 'On not being seen dead: shopping as protest')

j   'Hierarchie et voix de femmes (Angleterre–Afrique)', in Christian Descamps (ed.) *Philosophie et anthropologie*, Paris, Les séminaires du Centre Georges Pompidou: Espace International, Philosophie.

1993

a   *In the Wilderness: the Doctrine of Defilement in the Book of Numbers*, Sheffield: Journal for the Study of the Old Testament, Supplement Series no. 158, Sheffield Academic Press. (260 pp.)

Italian translation by Damanti forthcoming.

b   'Balaam's place in the Book of Numbers' (Huxley Memorial Lecture 1992), *Man* NS 28(3): 411–30.

c   'Emotion and culture in theories of justice', *Economy and Society* 22(4): 501–15. (Revised version of 'Justice sociale et sentiment de justice' in Joëlle Affichard and Jean-Baptiste de Foucauld (eds) 1995 *Pluralisme et équalité. La justice sociale dans les démocraties*, Paris: Editions Esprit.)

Italian: 1994 'Sentimento e cultura nelle teorie della giustizia', *il Mulino*, March/April, 352: 201–15.

d   'Governability – a question of culture', *Millennium (Journal of International Studies)*, issue dedicated to Aaron Wildavsky, 22(3): 463–81. (TS 'Prospects for asceticism')

e   'The forbidden animals in Leviticus', *Journal for the Study of the Old Testament* 59: 3–23.

f   'Atonement in Leviticus', *Jewish Studies Quarterly* 1(2): 109–30.

g   'Un point de vue anthropologique', *Dossier et forum, les conventions: réseaux* 62: 117–19.

h   'A quelles conditions un ascétisme environnementaliste peut-il réussir?', in Dominique Bourg (ed.) *La nature en politique, ou l'enjeu philosophique de l'écologie*, Paris: Association Descartes, L'Harmattan.

i   'Aaron Wildavsky – obituary', *The Times*, 24 September: 21.

j   'The idea of a good pot', Tate Gallery Conference on *Values in Art*, 22 October. (TS 'Bad taste in furnishing')

k   'Eschewing the fat. Food fadism in the light of global famine', *Times Literary Supplement*, 30 July, 4713: 3a–4.

l   Review of Jan Vansina *Paths in the Rainforest*, *Anthropos* 88(4/6): 625–27.

m   Review of K.S. Shrader-Frechette *Risk and Rationality*, *American Political Science Review* 87(2): 485.

n   Review of Yves Bonnefoy *Mythologies*, *History of Religions* 32(4): 374–76.

o   'Hunting the pangolin', comment on I.M. Lewis 'The spider and the pangolin', *Man* NS 28(1): 161–65.

1994

a   'The glorious Book of Numbers', *Jewish Studies Quarterly* 1(3): 193–216.

b   'Holy joy: rereading Leviticus; the anthropologist and the believer', *Conservative Judaism*, Spring XLVI (3): 3–14. (TS 'The cosmic joke')

c   'The stranger in the Bible', *Archives européennes de sociologie* 35(2): 283–98.

Italian: (1995) 'Di fronte allo straniero: una critica antropologica delle scienze sociali', annual lecture of *il Mulino Association*, 5 November, *il Mulino* XLIV(357): 5–24.

d   'Godfrey Lienhardt – obituary', *Anthropology Today* 10(1): 15–17.

e 'The depoliticization of risk' (English and Italian versions), *Teoria Sociologica* II(4): 13–31 & 32–48. English version reprinted in Richard J. Ellis and Michael Thompson (eds) (1997) *Culture Matters: Essays in Honor of Aaron Wildavsky*: Boulder CO/Oxford: Westview Press.

f 'The language of emotions in the social sciences', Paul Anand (ed.) special issue *The Foundations of Economics*, *Greek Economic Review* 17(2): 167–76.

g 'The genuine object', in Stephen Harold Riggins (ed.) *The Socialness of Things*, The Hague: Mouton de Gruyer. (OAO 'The genuine article: the socio-semiotics of things')

h 'The construction of the physician: a cultural approach to medical healing', in S. Budd and U. Sharma (eds) *The Healing Bond: the Patient–Practitioner Relationship and Therapeutic Responsibility*, London: Routledge. (TS 'The choice between gross and spiritual: some medical preferences')

i Review of H. Eilbergschwartz *The Savage in Judaism: an Anthropology of Israelite Religion and Ancient Judaism*, *Religion* 24(4): 384–86.

j 'Hunting the pangolin', reply to R.F. Ellen, *Man* NS 29(1): 182.

k ' "But why do we have to use this American Language?" An interview with Mary Douglas', *European Association of Social Anthropologists Newsletter* 13: 4–5.

l 'Conversazione con Mary Douglas tra antropologia sociale, filosofia e studi biblici', with Andrea Borsari, *Ossimori* 7: 124–33.

1995

a 'Red Riding Hood: an interpretation from anthropology' (13th Katherine Briggs Memorial Lecture, November 1994), *Folklore* 106: 1–7. (TS 'The uses of vulgarity: a French reading of Little Red Riding Hood')

b 'The cloud God, and the shadow self ', *Social Anthropology* 3(2): 83–94.

c 'Acceptance' (Bernal Prize), *Science, Technology and Human Values* 20(2): 262–66.

d 'The gender of the beloved', *Heythrop Journal* (special issue for Robert Murray on his 70th birthday), Thomas Deidun (ed.) 36(4): 397–408.

e 'Réflexions sur *Le Renard Pâle* et deux anthropologies: à propos du surréalisme et de l'anthropologie française', in C.W. Thompson (ed.) *L'autre et le sacré: surréalisme, cinéma, ethnologie*, Paris: L'Harmattan.

f 'Poetic structure of Leviticus', in David P. Wright, David Noel Freedman and Avi Hurvitz (eds) *Pomegranates and Golden Bells: Studies in Biblical, Jewish, and Near Eastern Ritual, Law, and Literature in Honor of Jacob Milgrom*, Winona Lake IN: Eisenbrauns.

g 'Demonology in William Robertson Smith's theory of religious belief', in William Johnstone (ed.) *Robertson Smith: Essays in Reassessment*, Sheffield: Journal for the Study of the Old Testament, Supplement Series no. 189, Sheffield Academic Press.

h   'Forgotten knowledge', in Marilyn Strathern (ed.) *Shifting Contexts* (ASA Decennial Conference Series, *The Uses of Knowledge: Local and Global Contexts*), London: Routledge.

i   'To honour the dead', in Geoff Dench, Tony Flower and Kate Gavron (eds) *Young at Eighty: the Prolific Public Life of Michael Young*, London: Carcanet.

j   'Table matters', review of Leon R. Kass *The Hungry Soul: Eating and the Perfection of Our Nature*, *Commonweal*, 10 March: 22–23.

1996

a   *Thought Styles, Critical Essays on Good Taste*, London/New York: Sage. (222 pp.)

b   'Introduction' to new edition of *Natural Symbols*, see 1970a.

c   'Introduction' to new edition of *The World of Goods*, see 1978b.

d   'Introduction' and 'A response from Mary Douglas', Review Colloquium on Mary Douglas (1993) *In the Wilderness*, *Religion* 26(1): 69–71, 81–89.

e   'Sacraments and society: an anthropologist asks, what women could be doing in the church', Proc. 1995 Catholic Theological Association, Leeds, *New Blackfriars*, January 77(899): 28–39.

f   'Sacred contagion', in John F.A. Sawyer (ed.) *Reading Leviticus: A Conversation with Mary Douglas*, Sheffield: Journal for the Study of the Old Testament, Supplement Series no. 227, Sheffield Academic Press: 86–106.

g   'Children consumed and child cannibalism: Robertson Smith's attack on the science of mythology', in Laurie L. Patton and Wendy Doniger (eds) *Myth and Method*, Charlottesville/London: University Press of Virginia.

h   'Losses and gains', in J.B. Schneewind (ed.) *Giving: Western Ideas of Philanthropy*, Bloomington/Indianapolis: Indiana University Press.

i   'Istituzioni: 2. Problemi teorici', in *Enciclopedia delle Scienze Sociali*, vol. 5, Istituto della Enciclopedia Italiana, Fondata da Giovanni Treccani.

j   Review of Emile Durkheim *The Elementary Forms of Religious Life*, Hans. Karen Fields *Contemporary Sociology* 25(4): 467–69.

k   Review of Howard Margolis *Dealing with Risk: Why the Public and the Experts Disagree on Environmental Issues*, *Journal of Public Policy* 16(4): 355–57.

1997

a   'A course off the menu', *Times Higher Education Supplement*, 22 August, 1294: 18–19.

b   'Taboo and sin', in John Middleton (ed.) *Encyclopedia of Africa South of the Sahara*, vol. 4, New York: Charles Scribner.

c   (with Des Gasper, Steven Ney and Michael Thompson) (eds) 'Human needs and wants', in Steve Rayner and Elizabeth L. Malone (eds) *Human Choice and Climate Change. Vol. I: The Societal Framework*, Columbus OH: Battelle Press.

d   Review of Caroline Walker Bynum *Resurrection of the Body in Western Christendom, 200–1336, Commonweal,* 14 February: 23–25.

1998

a   (with Steven Ney) *Missing Persons, a Critique of Personhood in the Social Sciences,* Berkeley: University of California Press (forthcoming November).
b   'Two books on God', reviews of Jack Miles *GOD: a Biography* and Richard E. Friedman *Disappearance of God: a Divine Mystery, Religion* 28: 65–69.

In press

(provisional title) *The Inner Room: Leviticus as Literature,* Oxford: Oxford University Press.

'A mouse, a bird, and some fish: for a new reading of Leviticus 11', in *Festschrift for David Grene,* Chicago: Chicago University Press.

'Why I have to learn Hebrew: the doctrine of sanctification', in George Bond (ed.) *Festschrift for Edmund Perry.*

'Religious taboo', *Encyclopedia of Language and Linguistics*

APPENDIX 2

Reviews of books written by Mary Douglas

Reviews of Mary Douglas's edited books, other than *Essays in the Sociology of Perception* (ESP), have been excluded, as have brief notes in *Bookworld*, *Choice*, *Contemporary Psychology*, *Library Journal*, and *Religious Studies Review*. A very few reviews to which I have seen references have also been excluded because I was unable to trace copies of them.

JOURNALS IN WHICH REVIEWS APPEARED:

AA	American Anthropologist
AAPSS	American Academy of Political and Social Science Annals
ABFRJ	American Bar Foundation Research Journal
AE	American Ethnologist
AfA	African Affairs
Afr	Africa
AJS	American Journal of Sociology
Am	America
Anth	Anthropos
ANZJS	Australian and New Zealand Journal of Sociology
APAJ	American Planning Association Journal
APSR	American Political Science Review
AQ	Anthropological Quarterly
AR	Africa Report
AS	African Studies
ASR	Archives de sociologie des religions
AT	Anthropology Today
AU	Afrika und Übersee
BAS	Bulletin of the Atomic Scientists
BJHS	British Journal for the History of Science
BJS	British Journal of Sociology
BR	Bible Review
BSOAS	Bulletin of the School of Oriental and African Studies

BTTLV	Bijdragen Tot de Taal-, Land- en Volkenkunde
CA	Current Anthropology
Cah	Cahiers d'outre mer
CBQ	Catholic Biblical Quarterly
CC	Christian Century
CD	Culture et développement
CH	Catholic Herald
CHS	Community Health Studies
Civ	Civilisations
Com	Commonweal
CRL	College and Research Libraries
Crux	Crux
CS	Contemporary Sociology
Des	Design
DS	Discourse and Society
Econ	Economist
ELQ	Ecology Law Quarterly
Enc	Encounter
EPA	Environment and Planning A
ET	Expository Times
Eth	Ethics
ETR	Etudes théologiques et religieuses
FAZ	Frankfurter Allgemeine Zeitung
GO	Government and Opposition
HJ	Heythrop Journal
HSM	Human Systems Management
IJAHS	International Journal of African Historical Studies
Int	Interpretation
Isis	Isis
ISSR	International Social Science Review
JAAR	Journal of the American Academy of Religion
JAH	Journal of African History
JAS	Journal of American Studies
JASO	Journal of the Anthropological Society of Oxford
JCA	Journal of Consumer Affairs
JEBO	Journal of Economic Behaviour and Organization
JGM	Journal of General Management
JHBS	Journal of the History of the Behavioral Sciences
JHPPL	Journal of Health Politics, Policy and Law
JJS	Jewish Journal of Sociology
JP	Journal of Politics
JR	Journal of Religion
JRAI	Journal of the Royal Anthropological Institute
JSS	Journal of Semitic Studies

JSSR	Journal for the Scientific Study of Religion
JTS	Journal of Theological Studies
Know	Knowledge
Lis	Listener
LRB	London Review of Books
LSR	Law and Society Review
Man	Man (later JRAI)
Mank	Mankind
Min	Minerva
Nat	Nature
NB	New Blackfriars
NEJM	New England Journal of Medicine
NR	New Republic
NS	New Society
NSt	New Statesman
NTT	Nederlands Theologisch Tijdschrift
NYRB	New York Review of Books
NYTBR	New York Times Book Review Magazine
OS	Organization Studies
PA	Psychopathologie africaine
PSS	Philosophy of the Social Sciences
PT	Poetics Today
QJS	Quarterly Journal of Speech
RA	Risk Analysis
Rar	Raritan
Rel	Religion
RFS	Revue française de sociologie
RP	Review of Politics
RRR	Review of Religious Research
RSR	Religious Studies Review
SBF	Science Books and Films
Sci	Science
Sem	Semiotica
Soc	Sociology
Socy	Society
SQ	Sociological Quarterly
SR	Sociological Review
SSJ	Social Science Journal
ST	Sunday Times
Tab	The Tablet
TES	Times Education Supplement
Theo	Theology
THES	Times Higher Education Supplement
TJT	Toronto Journal of Theology

TLS	Times Literary Supplement
TR	Times Review
Trib	Tribus
UQ	Universities Quarterly: Culture, Education and Society
USQR	Union Seminary Quarterly Review
Wor	Worship
WQR	Wilson Quarterly Review
YLJ	Yale Law Journal
Zyg	Zygon

REVIEWS

Congo Tribes and Parties (1961)

| AA | Alan P. Merriam, 1962, 64(3): 861–62. |
| Civ | E. Bustin, 1962, 12(2): 289–90. |

The Lele of Kasai (1963)

AfA	G. Lienhardt, 1964, 63: 298–99.
Anth	A. Vorbichler, 1964, 59(1–2): 322–23.
AR	Robert A. Lystad, 1963, 8(11): 27.
AS	Adam Kuper, 1963, 22: 134–35.
AU	A. Vorbichler, 1964, 47(3–4): 299–301.
Cah	J. Cabot, 1964, 17(66): 242.
JAH	Jan Vansina, 1964, 5(1): 141–42.
Trib	H. van Geluwe, 1964, 13: 193–94.

Purity and Danger (1966)

AA	Melford E. Spiro, 1968, 70(2): 391–93.
Anth	T.O. Beidelman, 1966, 61(3–6): 907–908.
Com	Peter Steinfels, 9 October 1970: 49–51.
JJS	Morris Ginsberg, 1966, 8(2): 270–74.
JSSR	W. McCormack, Fall 1967, 6(2): 313–14.
Man	Edwin Ardener, 1967, NS 2(2): 139.
NS	Alasdair MacIntyre, 23 June 1966: 26–27.
NTT	T.P. van Baaren, Fall 1967, 21: 241.
RRR	P.R. Kunz, Winter 1969, 10: 114–15.
Soc	Charles Madge, 1967, 1: 209–10.

TLS   'Dirt is disorder', anon. (Rodney Needham), 16 February 1967: 131.

French translation: *De la souillure*

ASR   R. Courtas, 1972, 17(33): 230–31.
CD   L. de Sousberghe, 1971, 3(2): 325–29.

Natural Symbols: Explorations in Cosmology (1970)

AJS   Shlomo Deshen, 1971–72, 77: 163–66.
BJS   David Martin, 1970, 21: 343–44.
CC   1 July 1970, 87: 824n.
Com   Peter Steinfels, 9 October 1970: 49–51. (with PD)
JASO   S. Milburn, 1970, 1(2): 101.
Lis   'Humanising, not symbolising', Alan Ryan, 3 September 1970: 314–15.
Man   K.O.L. Burridge, 1970, NS 5(3): 53–31.
NB   'The earthbound pangolin', Adrian Edwards, September 1970: 424–32.
NS   'Group and grid', James Littlejohn, 23 April 1970: 697.
NSt   'Conservative cosmologies', Jonathan Raban, 5 June 1970: 812–13.
NYRB   'Mythical inequalities', E.R. Leach, 28 January 1971, XVI(i): 44–45.
Rel   'The two bodies: social structure and natural symbolism', E.H. Pyle, Spring 1971, 1(1): 72–77.
Theo   J.G. Bishop, September 1970, 73: 422–23.
TLS   'Grids and groups', anon., 14 May 1970: 535.
Wor   'Magic and sacrament', M. Catherine Bateson, 1972, 46(1): 98–104.

Natural Symbols (1973) (revised edition)

ET   E.H. Lurkings, November 1973, 85: 61.
JTS   F.W. Dillistone, October 1974, 25: 548–50.
Soc   M. Marwick, January 1975, 9: 132–34.
ST   Paperback Short List, 1 April 1973: 40b.
Tab   'Ritual and romance', Terry Eagleton, 21–28 April 1973, 227 No. 6929/30: 391–92.

TLS	Anonymous review note of Pelican 1973 second edition, 28 September 1973: 1137.
TLS	Letter from publisher, Christopher MacLehose of Barrie and Jenkins, advising Pelican identical to 1973 hardcover second edition, 26 October 1973: 1314.
TR	Paperbacks, 26 April 1973: 10c.

German translation:
Ritual, Tabu und Körpersymbolik

| Anth | Justin Stagl, 1978, 73: 279–81. |

Implicit Meanings (1975)

AA	'Context, meaning and the Chomskyian notion of creativity', Beatriz Lavandera, 1977, 79(3): 638–41.
AJS	R. Rosaldo, March 1977, 82: 1152–56.
BJHS	'Where is the edge of objectivity?', B. Barnes and S. Shapin, March 1977, 10: 61–66.
Econ	N 8, 1975, 257: 125.
JASO	Keith Patching, 1975, 6(3): 218–19.
Man	Rodney Needham, 1976, NS 11(1): 127–28.
NB	'Life as fashion parade: the anthropology of Mary Douglas', Adrian Edwards, March 1977, 58: 131–39.
NSt	'Pangolin power', Alan Ryan, 21 November 1975, 90: 646–47.
SQ	Feature review, D. Silverman, E.G. Tiryakian, N.J. Davis, B. Schwartz, Spring 1978, 19: 355–68.
SR	J. Law and U. Sharma, May 1977, NS 25: 463–69.
ST	Booknote, 11 January 1976: 37h.
THES	'On cultural categories', Peter Winch, 16 January 1976: 16c.
TLS	'Dirt, danger and pangolins', Dan Sperber, 30 April 1976: 502–503.

Cultural Bias (1978)

| AA | Bradd Shore, 1979, 81(2): 434–35. |

The World of Goods (1978)

| AA | Abraham Rosman, 1982, 84(1): 211–12. |

AAPSS	L. Ferleger, March 1981, 454: 248–49.
APAJ	M.H. Krieger, July 1980, 46: 351–53.
CS	A. Bergesen, 1981, 10(3): 481–82.
Des	S. Hoar, 1981, 386: 18.
JCA	Kaja Finkler, 1980, 14(2): 493–95.
LRB	'Daughters, dress shirts, and spotted dicks', Geoffrey Hawthorn, 3 April 1980, 2(6): 1–3.
Sem	'Converging paths in semiotics and anthropology', M. Herzfeld, 1985, 56(1–2): 153–77.
Soc	L. Gofton, November 1981, 15: 626–27.
SR	I. Jamieson, February 1981, NS 29: 164–65.
SSJ	David Hamilton, January 1981, 18(1): 141–43.
TES	'Making sense of the world', Richard North, 9 January 1981: 22a.
TLS	'Naming, branding and marking', David Martin, 20 June 1980: 711.

Evans-Pritchard (1980)

AA	David M. Schneider, 1981, 83(3): 719–21.
Anth	J.W. Burton, 1982, 77: 284–88.
IJAHS	D. McCall, 1982, 15(3): 467–74.
JAAR	R.A. Segal, March 1982, 50: 164–65.
JHBS	Simon Ottenberg, July 1983, 19: 256–59.
LRB	'Cairo essays', E.R. Leach, 4–17 December 1980, 2(23): 24–25.
NS	'When is a master not a master?', Adam Kuper, 17 April 1980: 117–18.
PA	M. Singleton, 1982, 18(3): 400–401.
SBF	Frank Lagana, September/October 1981, 17: 11.
TES	'Stendhal of anthropology', Mary Jane Drummond, 18 July 1980: 20a.
THES	'A modern master of anthropology', J.H. Beattie, 4 July 1980: 12.
TLS	'The ethnographer as translator', T.O. Beidelman, 12 December 1980: 1420.

In the Active Voice (1982)

AA	Eugenia Shanklin, 1985, 87(1): 165–66.
AE	Stephen F. Gudeman, 1984, 11(1): 193–94.
BJS	Eileen Barker, 1984, 35: 139–40. (with ESP)

BTTLV   A. Deruijter, 1984, 140(1): 171–72.
CC   Booknote, 8 December 1982, 99: 1264.
Eth   R.E. Goodin, January 1984, 94: 346–47.
HJ   M.F.C. Bourdillon, 1984, 25(4): 523.
Know   A.A. Yengoyan, 1984, 6(2): 187–92.
Mank   J. Urry, December 1983, 14: 132–33. (with ESP)
NS   'Taking the biscuit', Christopher Driver, 13 May 1982, 60, 1017: 268–69.
SR   S. Rayner, August 1983, N.S.31: 568–72.
ST   'Cash and carry on', Alan Ryan, 30 May 1982: 42c.
TLS   'Interactive intentions', Stuart Sutherland, 13 August: 889.
UQ   K. Kumar, 1983, 37(1): 203–204.

Essays in the Sociology of Perception (1982) (ed.)

AE   Geoffrey M. White, 1984, 11(1): 194–95.
AJS   Rick E. Robinson, 1985, 91(3): 705–706.
BJS   Eileen Barker, 1984, 35:139–140. (with ITAV)
CS   R.P. Weber, 1983, 12(6): 730–31.
Crux   Irving Hexham, June 1984, 20(2): 28–29.
Eth   K.E.S., October 1983, 94: 166.
Isis   'Is there too much sociology of science?', David Edge, June 1983, 74: 250–56.
ISSR   D.E. Taub, 1983, 58(4): 240.
JSSR   J.V. Spickard, September 1984, 23: 318–19.
Mank   James Urry, 1983, 14(2): 132–33. (with ITAV)
PSS   D.M. Lowe, 1986, 16(2): 281–82.

Risk and Culture (1982)

AA   'Manufacturing danger: fear and pollution in industrial society', M.L. Kaprow, 1985, 87(2): 342–56.
AAPSS   G.H. Daniels, May 1983, 467: 237–38.
ABFRJ   'Blaming victims', R.L. Abel, 1985, 2: 401–17.
Am   Daniel J. Sullivan, 10 March 1984, 150: 176.
APSR   G. Weinstein, March 1983, 77(1): 203–204.
AQ   M. Agar, April 1983, 56: 102–104.
BAS   'The risk assessors', John P. Holdren, 1983, 39(6): 33–38.
CHS   B. Hocking, 1984, 8(1): 86–87.
CS   Paul W. Kingston, 1983, 12: 414.
ELQ   R.E. Cheit, 1983, 11(2): 241–63.
HSM   J.P. van Gigch, 1983, 4(1): 54–56.

ISSR	W. Gray, 1983, 58(2): 118–20.
JAS	Gerald Steinberg, April 1984, 18: 145–46.
JHPPL	'Living in a world of risk', Daniel Metlay, 1984, 9(2): 325–32.
JP	Gerald Steinberg, February 1984, 46: 313–16 (identical to his review in JAS).
JSSR	T. Robbins, June 1983, 22: 188–89.
Min	'The Manichaean conception of technological risk', A. Weinberg, 1982, 20(1/2): 246–50.
Nat	'Blunders in the business of risk', Dorothy Nelkin, 19 August 1982, 298: 775–76.
NEJM	Dale A. Rublee, 14 October 1982, 307(16): 1035.
NS	'Survival stakes', A. Ryan, 7 October 1982, 62, 1038: 47–48.
NYRB	'Why are you so scared?', Ian Hacking, 23 September 1982, XXIV(14): 30–32 & 41.
NYTBR	'Pollution as delusion', Langdon Winner, 8 August 1982: 8 & 18.
Rar	'America: fringe benefits', James A. Boon, 1983, 2: 97–121.
RFS	D. Dulcos, 1987, 28(1): 178–81.
RP	'Choice and risk in environmental control', P.D. Gaffney, October 1984, 46: 613–16.
SBF	Martin Thomas, March/April 1983, 18: 182.
Sci	'Explaining our fears', Mayer N. Zald, 1983, 219: 1211–12.
TLS	'Pollution and a sense of proportion', David Martin, 18 March 1983: 270.
USQR	M.A. Shields, 1983, 38(1): 114–18.
WQR	anon., Spring 1984, 8: 154–55.
YLJ	'Anthropologizing environmentalism', E.D. Elliott, 1983, 92(5): 888–99.
YLJ	'Culture and conflicting rationalities', D. MacLean, 1983, 92(5): 900–12.

Risk Acceptability According to the Social Sciences (1985)

CS	'Risk, uncertainty, and social organization', S. Rayner, 1989, 18(1): 6–9.
EPA	S.M. Macgill, October 1987, 19(2): 1411–13.
Eth	Carole A. Heimer, April 1988, 99: 630.
LSR	'Hazards, risks, and enterprise: approaches to science, law and social policy', J.F. Short, 1990, 24(1): 179–98.
Nat	'Culture in danger', Terence R. Lee, 15 January 1987, 325, 6101: 205.

NS	'Risk and uncertainty', Colin Ward, 6 February 1987, 79, 1258: 29.
RA	R.R. Killman, 1987, 7(1): 123.
SR	Peter Glasner, August 1987, 35: 624–26.
TLS	'Safety factors', Paul Seabright, 20 March 1987: 290.

How Institutions Think (1986)

AA	F.G. Bailey, 1987, 89(3): 759–60.
AJS	M.C. Kearl, July 1988, 94: 206–208.
ANZJS	H.K. Colebatch, 1988, 24(3): 513–15.
AT	'The faithful disciple: on Mary Douglas and Durkheim', R. Fardon, 1987, 3(5): 4–6.
CRL	Paul Metz, 1987, 48(4): 372 & 374.
CS	Bruno Latour, 1988, 17: 383–85.
Enc	Booknote, July 1987, 69: 53.
Eth	Mary Jane Osa, April 1987, 97: 88–89.
Isis	Trevor Pinch, 1988, 79(2), 297: 314–15.
JEBO	R.R. Nelson, 1988, 10(1): 134–36.
JGM	M. Warner, 1987, 13(1): 111–13.
JR	R. Segal, April 1988, 68: 350–51.
LRB	'Knowledge', Ian Hacking, 18 December 1986, VII(22): 17–18.
NR	'The anthropologist at large', Clifford Geertz, 25 May 1987, 196: 34 & 36–37.
NS	'Bower bird's nest', Alan Ryan, 12 June 1982, 80, 1276: 30.
OS	G. Hofstede, 1988, 9(1): 122–24.
PT	'Towards a cognitive anthropology', Rakefet Sheffy, 1989, 10(4): 847–50.
QJS	P.K. Tompkins, August 1988, 74: 354–56.
RSR	'Ethics and institutions: a review essay', James A. Donohue, January 1991, 17(1): 24–32.
Socy	L.A. Coser, March/April 1988, 25(3): 86–88.

Risk and Blame (1992)

AA	T.O. Beidelman, 1993, 95(4): 1065–66.
Anth	Dorothy Hammond, 1993, 88(4–6): 578.
BJS	Z. Bauman, 1994, 45(1): 143–44.
CA	'The cultural logic of perception', R. Paine, 1996, 37(4): 721–22.
Com	Paul Baumann, 1 December 1995, 122: 29–30.

CS	'Risk, society, and social theory', E. Draper, 1993, 22(5): 641–44.
Zyg	R. Launay, 1996, 31(2): 349–52.

In the Wilderness (1993)

BR	Ronald S. Hendel, June 1995, 11(3): 14, 51.
BSOAS	S. Weightman, 1995, LVIII(2): 353–55.
CBQ	R. Gnuse, 1995, 57(1): 124–25.
CH	'Un-jumbling Numbers', H.G.M. Williamson, 15 April 1994: 6.
ETR	T. Römer, 1996, 71(1): 104–5.
Int	J. Neusner, 1995, 49(3): 305–6.
JRAI	L. Werth, 1996, 2(2): 365–66.
JSS	G. Auld, 1995, 40(2): 326–27.
Rel	N. Smart, 1996, 26(1): 71–73.
Rel	J.L. Crenshaw, 1996, 26(1): 73–77.
Rel	K. Gutzwiller, 1996, 26(1): 77–81.
TJT	Tyler F. Williams, Fall 1995, 11(2): 230–311.
TLS	'Enclave in Judah', J.W. Rogerson, 12 August 1994, 4767: 28b.

Thought Styles (1996)

DS	Richard Henry, 1997, 8(3): 431–32.
FAZ	'Kultur im Sechserpack', Dirk Kaesler, 24 October 1996, 248: 15–16.
GO	'Developing the cultural analysis of Mary Douglas', Marco Verweij, 1997, 32(3): 421–30.
Soc	'More and more – academic books on consumer culture', Rachel Bowlby, 1997, 31(1): 153–61.
TLS	'The anthropologist at the checkout', Mary Margaret McCabe, 29 August 1997, 4926: 13.

APPENDIX 3

Concordance of the two editions of *Natural Symbols*

Mary Douglas's account of grid and group changed between the first hardback edition of *Natural Symbols* (1970, xvii + 177 pp.) and its second edition (Barrie and Jenkins, hbk, Penguin, pbk, 1973, 219 pp.). The 1973 hardback and paperback versions of the second edition are identical (a confusion clarified in an exchange of letters, see Appendix 2, 1973 *Natural Symbols*). The differing page lengths of these two editions owes more to format than text length. The text changed less than casual comparison has suggested (NS2/Soc). In a pre-word-processing age it seems that Douglas's revision was largely a scissors and paste job: swapping around passages within the book. Passages deleted from or added to the text are, therefore, potentially significant. While I doubt whether my parallel reading of the two editions has spotted every change, it seems worthwhile sparing any future critical reader some of the task of comparison. I take the most recently revised edition (1996 Routledge, xxxvii + 183 pp., hereafter NS2) as point of reference and note additions to it as well as deletions from the first edition, referred to as NS1.

Acknowledgements (NS2: vi–x):   (NS2: vii–viii) consists of (NS1: xvi–xvii) from the original 'Preface', which has otherwise been deleted or shifted elsewhere in the text. (NS2: vii–x) is clearly indicated as fresh acknowledgements due for the Pelican edition and dated December 1971. (NS2: xi–xx) is the 1996 'Introduction'.

Introduction (NS2: xxxi–xxxvii):   (NS2: xxxi–xxxiv) is new; (NS2: xxxiv, para 2 –xxxvii) aside from the last five lines of the chapter, is taken from (NS1: 62–64).

Chapter 1 Away from ritual (NS2: 1–19):   (NS2: 1–17) correspond to NS1; the final five lines of that chapter have been deleted and (NS1: ix–xii) of the original 'Preface' instated as (NS2: 17–19).

Chapter 2 To inner experience (NS2: 20–36):   identical to NS1 other than in suppression of the original diagram 4 (NS1: 35) and deletion of textual reference to it (NS1: 36, lines 4–6).

Chapter 3 The Bog Irish (*NS2: 37–53*):   is unrevised.

Chapter 4 Grid and group (*NS2: 54–68*):   is titled 'A rule of method' in NS1; (NS1: 56, lines 27–28) deleted; (NS1: 57–64) from line 12 the text is heavily revised (NS2: 57, para 2–68). Two pages (NS1: 62–64) have been moved to the Introduction of NS2.

Chapter 5 The two bodies (*NS2: 69–87*):   (NS2: 76, para 2–77, para 1) added; (NS2: 84, lines 6–9) added; (NS2: 86, para 2–87) added.

Chapter 6 Test cases (*NS2: 88–104*):   composed from two chapters in NS1–6 'A test case', and 7 'Sin and society'. (NS2: 89–90) instates reference to Robin Horton on spirit possession in Kalabari religion; (NS2: 93, lines 1–12) revised; (NS2: 94, para 3) revised; (NS1: 87) diagram 7 'The periphery' deleted; (NS2: 96, para 4, line 2) 'social control' substituted for 'social grid'; (NS2: 102, line 6) 'towards zero' inserted, lines 17–18 rephrased; (NS2: 103) caption to diagram 5 and reference to Jean Buxton amended. (NS2: 105, para 3) takes up Chapter 7 in NS1. (NS1: 103–106) deleted and new final paragraph added (NS2: 108–109).

Chapter 7 The problem of evil (*NS2: 110–25*):   although similar to the chapter of the same title in NS1, this chapter has been completely reordered. (NS2: 110) is new apart from its last four lines which together with (NS2: 111, lines 1–3) are from (NS1: 111, lines 1–7). (NS2: 111, lines 4–8) are new and followed by (NS1: 112, para 2–22, para 2), modified slightly following the publication of Douglas 1970b. (NS1: 107, para 2–110) then follows as (NS2: 120–124); (NS1: 122, para 3) is largely deleted, but the remainder of the original chapter then follows, aside from its last two sentences.

Chapter 8 Impersonal rules (*NS2: 126–44*):   while basically similar to NS1, this chapter has a number of minor amendments (some too minor to note), and incorporates material from the original 'Preface'. (NS2: 127, para 2) revised; (NS1: 129, para 1) slight revision and last sentence deleted; (NS2: 138–39, para 4, lines 8–11) inserted, 'social grid' replaced by 'strong grid'. (NS2: 140, para 3) is taken from the original Preface (NS1: xv, para 3), followed by (NS1: xv, para 2). (NS2: 143, para 3–144) is a new conclusion to the chapter.

Chapter 9 Control of symbols (*NS2: 145–59*):   this chapter is heavily amended. (NS2: 144–45, para 3) is new. (NS1: 142, para 3) deleted. (NS1: 144, para 2) replaced by (NS2: 149, para 3–150). (NS1: 146, lines 12–39) deleted. (NS2: 152, para 3 and 152–53, para 4) rephrased. (NS2: 153, para 2, lines 1–17) inserted. (NS1: 148, para 2, lines 1–14) deleted. (NS1: 149, para 2) deleted. (NS2: 154, para 5, line 1) rephrased. (NS2: 155, para 5) 'weakness of classification' replaces 'weakness of grid and group'. (NS1: 152, line 25–153, line 8) deleted; (NS1: 153, lines 15–24) deleted; (NS1: 154, lines 2–10) deleted. (NS2: 159) final two sentences of chapter added.

Chapter 10 Out of the cave (*NS2: 160–70*):   (NS2: 164, para 1) revised. (NS2: 169, final 5 lines–170, first 5 lines) inserted.

NAME INDEX

SUBJECT INDEX